STEPPE AND
CULTURES

BIBLIOTH
O.F.M

D1097961

KUBAN AND TEREK CULTURES
(CAUCASUS)

(CASPIAN SEA)

(Lake Van)

(Lake Urmiah)

Haran
PADAN-ARAM
Nineveh
Tepe Gawra
ASSYRIA
Asshur
Arrapkha

LAND OF THE AMORITES

Hamath
Tirqa
Euphrates River
Tigris River
Tepe Giyan
Tepe

Tadmar
Mari
River
Tuttul
Eshnunna
Der
BABYLONIA
Babylon
Kish
Susa
Shushan
ELAM
Nippur
Erech
Larsa
Ur
Eridu

Damascus

Record of the Promise: The Old Testament

Record of the Promise

THE OLD TESTAMENT

WILFRID J. HARRINGTON, O.P.

THE PRIORY PRESS • CHICAGO, ILLINOIS

NIHIL OBSTAT: *Very Rev. Gilbert J. Graham, O.P.*
Censor Librorum

IMPRIMATUR: ✝ *Most Rev. Cletus F. O'Donnell, J.C.D.*
Administrator, Archdiocese of Chicago
May 8, 1965

Library of Congress Catalogue Number 65-19357
© *Copyright 1965 by* THE PRIORY PRESS
2005 South Ashland Avenue, Chicago, Illinois 60608
Manufactured in the United States of America

Preface

In the Preface to Record of Revelation: The Bible *I indi-*
cated the scope of this work: it is planned as a textbook for the student
of Sacred Scripture, but it is also aimed at the interested layman. I
feel that the student will not regret the prospect of a wider audience,
for it has led me to avoid technicalities that might have awaited
the elucidation of his professor. As it is, my care has been to make
the book as self-explanatory as possible. This, in turn, accounts for
its length; an overbrief exposition would have left too many questions
unanswered.

Not that I imagine that all the problems of the Old Testament
have been faced. Indeed, it is best not to speak of "problems." What
I have tried to do is to approach the Old Testament in a positive
fashion and to present it illuminated by modern biblical scholarship.
I have (with rare exceptions) refrained from giving a series of more
or less conflicting views; rather, I have chosen, in each case, the
position that seems to me the most satisfactory. This is not to say
that I put forward merely personal views; the choice is personal,
but the position I adopt is always solidly supported by outstanding
scholars. I believe that this procedure is justified. The important
thing is to lead the student to an appreciation of the Bible, an object
that is not achieved by a medley of opinions—some of them dated
and ill-founded. The student, guided by his professor and helped
by his reading, will gradually become aware of other views; then

he will make his own informed choice and find that his knowledge of Scripture has grown and deepened.

In practice, I have leaned heavily on two works: the *Bible de Jérusalem*[1] and the *Introduction à la Bible*.[2] There seems little doubt that the forthcoming English translation of the *Bible de Jérusalem*, with its introductions to the different books, an elaborate system of notes, and perhaps best of all, a format which clearly indicates the literary units within a writing, will speedily become the students' Bible. There is no doubt that the *Introduction à la Bible* is far and away the best introduction by Catholic scholars. This is not to say, however, that I have blindly followed their lead; indeed, I have turned aside on occasion. A glance at the footnotes will make clear that I am deeply indebted to many other studies and to many scholars of all denominations. One of the deep joys of biblical studies is, in fact, the realization that Christian scholars, though differing in confession, can draw very close together in their exposition of the word of God. The acknowledgment of my debt will, I hope, inspire confidence in the reader: in a true sense this introduction is a collective effort.

I have consistently sought to bring out the religious significance of each biblical writing—after all, this is the ultimate purpose of our study of Scripture. It will be seen, however, that the religious message can be grasped only when the book is properly understood; this is why literary analysis looms so large throughout. And though I have developed some theological ideas at greater length, the work does not cease to be an *introduction* to the Bible, and makes no claim to be also a manual of biblical theology. It is meant to introduce the student to the Old Testament and to help him to read it intelligently. I am convinced that modern scholarship has indeed opened the Bible to us in a marvelous manner and my sole desire is to place that key in the hands of those who seek it. If they find that

---

[1] *La Sainte Bible,* traduite en français sous la direction de l'Ecole Biblique de Jérusalem (Paris: Cerf, 1957). See also the second revised edition in fascicle form. Henceforth, reference to this Bible will be abbreviated BJ; references to the fascicles will be abbreviated (BJ).

[2] A. Robert and A. Feuillet, *Introduction à la Bible* (Tournai: Desclée, 1957; second edition 1959), I. Henceforth references to this work will be abbreviated IB.

the key does turn in the lock they will soon learn to appreciate the Old Testament as a literary achievement of God's people and to savor it as God's own word; and they will find themselves not only witnesses of the unfolding stages of God's saving history but also, by faith, participants in that history.

Once again my sincere thanks are due to my colleagues, Father Liam G. Walsh, O.P. and Father Thomas P. McInerney, O.P., who have so patiently read through my typescript. I have profited from their shrewd observations and helpful criticism and I have been greatly encouraged by their fraternal interest in the progress of the work.

W.J.H.

Table of Contents

ix

xiii

Father Wilfrid Harrington, O.P. was born March 18, 1927 in the parish of Eyeries (near Castletownbere), County Cork, Ireland. After completing his secondary education at Dominican College, Newbridge, County Kildare, he entered the Dominican Order at St. Mary's, Cork, in 1947. His philosophical studies were taken in Ireland and his theological studies at the Angelicum University, Rome (1951-1954), where after his ordination he received the S.T.L. et Lic. Continuing his study of Scripture, Father Harrington earned the Baccalaureate in this field in 1955. Then he entered the École Biblique, Jerusalem, obtaining the degree Licentiate in Scripture in 1957.

Since returning to Ireland, he has been professor of Scripture at the Dominican House of Studies, Tallaght. Concurrently he is lecturer in Scripture at St. Patrick's College, Maynooth.

Father Harrington's published works include *Explaining the Gospels; A Key to the Parables; What is the Bible?; Genesis and Evolution; The Bible and Marriage.*

Record of Revelation: The Bible; Record of the Promise: The Old Testament; and *Record of the Fulfillment: The New Testament* are a fitting tribute to his keen scholarship and ability to communicate.

THE BOOKS OF THE BIBLE

Gn.: Genesis
Ex.: Exodus
Lv.: Leviticus
Nm.: Numbers
Dt.: Deuteronomy
Jos.: Joshua
Jgs.: Judges
Ru.: Ruth
1,2 Sm.: 1,2 Samuel
1,2 Kgs.: 1,2 Kings
1,2 Chr.: 1,2
   Chronicles
Ez.: Ezra
Neh.: Nehemiah
Tb.: Tobit
Jdt.: Judith
Est.: Esther
Jb.: Job
Ps.: Psalms
Prv.: Proverbs
Qoh.: Qoheleth
   (Ecclesiastes)
Ct.: Canticle of
   Canticles

Wis.: Wisdom
Sir.: Sirach
   (Ecclesiasticus)
Is.: Isaiah
Jer.: Jeremiah
Lam.: Lamentations
Bar.: Baruch
Ezek.: Ezekiel
Dn.: Daniel
Hos.: Hosea
Jl.: Joel
Am.: Amos
Obad.: Obadiah
Jon.: Jonah
Mi.: Micah
Na.: Nahum
Hb.: Habakkuk
Zeph.: Zephaniah
Hag.: Haggai
Zech.: Zechariah
Mal.: Malachi
1,2 Mc.: 1,2
   Maccabees
Mt.: Matthew

Mk.: Mark
Lk.: Luke
Jn.: John
Acts: Acts
Rm.: Romans
1,2 Cor.: 1,2
   Corinthians
Gal.: Galatians
Eph.: Ephesians
Phil.: Philippians
Col.: Colossians
1,2 Thes.: 1,2
   Thessalonians
1,2 Tm.: 1,2
   Timothy
Ti.: Titus
Phm.: Philemon
Heb.: Hebrews
Jas.: James
1,2 Pt.: 1,2 Peter
1,2,3 Jn.: 1,2,3 John
Jude: Jude
Ap.: Apocalypse
   (Revelation)

WORKS OF REFERENCE

ANEP: *The Ancient Near East in Pictures*
ANET: *Ancient Near Eastern Texts*
Atlante Biblico: Atlante Storico della Bibbia
BJ: *Bible de Jérusalem*
(BJ): A separate fascicle of the *Bible de Jérusalem*
BW: *Bibeltheologisches Wörterbuch*
DBS: *Dictionnaire de la Bible* (Supplement)
EB: *Enchiridion Biblicum*
IB: *Introduction à la Bible*
PCB: *Peake's Commentary on the Bible*
RB: *Revue Biblique*
VTB: *Vocabulaire de Théologie Biblique*

Record of the Promise: The Old Testament

| ONE | *An Outline History of Israel* |

Israel came face to face with her God at the moment of her emergence as a nation. Henceforth she was aware that God would constantly intervene in her history, and she came to know that he, the Creator, was active in all the events of history. Under his hand, nations came into being and passed away, and some of them, obeying his bidding though they did not know him, were instruments of punishment for his people or were its providential deliverers. The Bible, a faithful reflection of the life and faith of Israel, cannot be divorced from the history of Israel; indeed, it can be understood only in this context. To begin this study of the Old Testament, we shall set down, in sequence and as a whole, an outline of Israel's history. This provides the necessary setting and, as a conveniently built-in work of reference, will help our presentation of the wide and involved field of the Old Testament.

1. THE WORLD OF ISRAEL'S ORIGINS

Biblical history, in a strict sense, began with Abraham. He is a historical figure, a man of flesh and blood, even though we cannot

3

establish when he was born or when he died; the best we can say is that he probably lived in the nineteenth or eighteenth century B.C. This means that Israel appeared late on the world stage, for great civilizations had already passed away. It will be helpful to sketch in lightly the distant and the immediate background of the patriarchal age.

1) The Ancient World in the Third Millennium B.C.

History, properly speaking, demands documentation by contemporary inscriptions that can be read by us. This condition is verified for the first time in the early third millennium B.C.

MESOPOTAMIA   The creators of civilization in Lower Mesopotamia in the fourth millennium were the Sumerians, a people whose origin is still unknown. They invented cuneiform writing, made great progress in commerce, and developed a remarkably high culture. In the third millennium (c. 2800-2360 B.C.) we find them established in a system of city-states. Religion was highly organized and the temple scribes produced a vast body of literature; most of the epics and myths that are known to us in Assyrian and Babylonian versions were first given written form by the Sumerians.[1]

The Akkadians, a Semitic people, inhabited Mesopotamia at the same time as the Sumerians. They took over and adapted Sumerian culture and religion and, though their own language was entirely different, they borrowed the Sumerian cuneiform syllabic script. Eventually an Akkadian, Sargon, seized power and founded an empire which lasted for over a hundred years (c. 2360-2180 B.C.). The considerable literature of this period is in Akkadian.[2]

EGYPT   In the early third millennium Egypt emerged into history as a unified nation; the kings of Upper Egypt had gained ascendancy over the whole land and the Old Kingdom (twenty-ninth to the twenty-third century B.C.) was founded. Egypt's classical age began with the rise of the Third Dynasty (c. 2600 B.C.). This was the period of the earliest pyramids, though the great pyramids were built in the Fourth Dynasty (twenty-sixth to the twenty-fifth century B.C.). Egyptian religion, like that of Mesopotamia, was a highly-de-

---

[1]For a selection of Sumerian texts see J. B. Pritchard, *Ancient Near Eastern Texts* (Relating to the Old Testament) (Princeton University Press, 1955[2]). Henceforth this book will be abbreviated ANET.

[2]See *ibid.*, passim.

veloped polytheism; the texts of this period are almost entirely religious.

PALESTINE   The early third millennium in Palestine was a time of great urban development and the towns, though small, were well built and strongly fortified, as excavations at Jericho, Megiddo, and elsewhere show. The population was predominantly Canaanite (a Semitic people). It is likely that Canaanite religion was already established as we know it from the Bible and from the fourteenth-century Ras Shamra texts. There are no Palestinian inscriptions from this millennium.

2) The Eve of the Patriarchal Age

MESOPOTAMIA   The Akkadian Empire was brought to an end about 2180 B.C. by a barbarian people called the Guti. About a hundred years later the power of these invaders was broken by the Sumerians; here we witness a rebirth of Sumerian culture under the kings of the Third Dynasty of Ur (c. 2060-1950 B.C.). The founder of the dynasty, Ur-nammu, is known especially for his law code, the oldest we possess. However, the Akkadian language had entrenched itself during the ascendancy of Akkad, and by the eighteenth century Sumerian was no longer spoken, though it continued as a written language for centuries.

EGYPT   The Old Empire came to an end in the twenty-third century B.C. and was followed by a period of disorder known as the First Intermediate (twenty-second to the twenty-first century B.C.). Internal disunity, with rival pharaohs claiming the throne, produced social chaos and economic depression. The literature of the period[3] reflects the prevalent spirit of dejection. About the middle of the twenty-first century—roughly contemporaneous with the Sumerian renaissance—the land was reunited by the first kings of the Eleventh Dynasty. The beginning of the second millennium marked the start of another period of stability, the Middle Kingdom.

PALESTINE   Late in the third millennium Palestine suffered the shock of invasion by seminomadic peoples, during which most of the Canaanite towns were destroyed; the twentieth century was the period of greatest disruption. Though the newcomers settled in Pal-

---

[3]See *ibid.,* pp. 405-10, 441-44.

estine, the country was not fully occupied, while in southern Trans-jordan sedentary occupation ceased altogether. These newcomers were part of a Semitic people called the Amorites.

We have seen that, long before Abraham was born, great civiliza-tions had not only existed but had waxed strong and then waned, sometimes to waken again to a fresh flowering. World history did not begin with Israel. And yet, when the Lord called Abraham from his country and his kindred and his father's house (Gn. 12:1) a history did begin—the *Heilsgeschichte*, God's saving history. And though Israel, as a nation, emerged in the thirteenth century, her roots are firmly fixed in the earlier centuries; Abraham is indeed the father of this nation. Once again we shall look at the contemporary scene in order to see more clearly, silhouetted against that backdrop, the ancestors of the Chosen People.

3) The Patriarchal Age

MESOPOTAMIA   The Third Dynasty of Ur came to an end about 1950 B.C. A contributory factor in its fall was the incursion of the Amorites; by the eighteenth century almost every state in Mesopota-mia was ruled by Amorite kings. They had adopted Sumerian and Akkadian culture and wrote in Akkadian. Until the middle of that century there was rivalry between the city-states of Lower Mesopota-mia: Isin, Larsa, Mari, Babylon, and Elam. Two newly-discovered law codes come from this period (both nineteenth century B.C.): one, in Akkadian, from Eshnunna; the other, in Sumerian, promulgated by Lipit-Ishtar of Isin.[4] Both show striking similarities with the Covenant Code (Ex. 21-23).

Mari and Assyria were the rival contenders in Upper Mesopotamia. Eventually Mari emerged as the dominant city-state in that region, and for half a century (c. 1750-1700 B.C.) it stood as one of the major powers of the day. Excavations have brought to light a city of great size and wealth, and an abundance of tablets and fragments (over 20,000) in old Akkadian (official correspondence and business documents). Its people were Northwest Semites who had adopted Akkadian culture and who spoke a language akin to that of Israel's ancestors.

---

[4]See *ibid.*, pp. 161-63, 159-61.

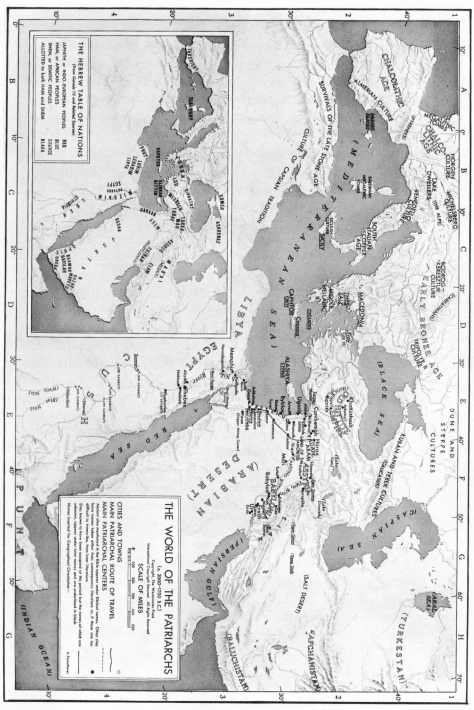

THE HEBREW TABLE OF NATIONS
(From Genesis 10 and Related Sources)

JAPHETH or INDO-EUROPEAN PEOPLES   RED
HAM or AFRICAN PEOPLES   BLUE
SHEM or SEMITIC PEOPLES   ORANGE
ALLOTTED to both HAM and SHEM   BLACK

THE WORLD OF THE PATRIARCHS
(c. 2000–1700 B.C.)
Copyright, The Westminster Press
International Copyright Secured. All Rights Reserved

SCALE OF MILES
0   100   200   300   400   500

CITIES AND TOWNS
MAIN PATRIARCHAL ROUTE OF TRAVEL
MAIN PATRIARCHAL CENTERS

Ancient sites mentioned in the Bible appear under Biblical names. Other cities
have names taken either from contemporary literature or, if these are too
difficult to transcribe, from later literature.

Sites known to have been occupied at the period but the names of which are
unknown, appear under later names, and are underlined in black.

Names inserted for Geographical Orientation—

o In Parentheses

In the keen Mesopotamian rivalry one power eventually emerged triumphant: Babylon; and the man who engineered the triumph was Hammurabi (1728-1686 B.C.). He had control of most of the great valley of the Tigris and Euphrates. The cultural flowering of Babylon at this time has left us a wealth of texts. Most remarkable for our purpose are the Babylonian accounts of the Creation and the Flood, which are copies of ancient Sumerian epics.[5] Hammurabi is best known for his famous law code, based on a long legal tradition already represented by the codes of Ur-nammu, Lipit-Ishtar, and Eshnunna.[6] It has numerous and striking parallels with the laws of the Pentateuch.

The empire of Hammurabi practically ended with him. In the seventeenth and sixteenth centuries B.C. a new people, the Hurrians, pressed down from the north; by the middle of the second millennium they had won control of Upper Mesopotamia and Northern Syria, while Babylon itself was split internally. One of the cities with a predominantly Hurrian population was Nuzi, and the fifteenth-century Nuzi texts, which reflect Hurrian laws, are important for an understanding of patriarchal customs.[7] It was not the Hurrians, however, but a Hittite king, in a bold expedition from Asia Minor, who (c. 1530 B.C.) sacked Babylon and brought the First Dynasty to a close. For some time to come the kingdom of Mitanni, with a predominantly Hurrian population, maintained the leading position in Upper Mesopotamia. It survived a collision with Egypt in the early fifteenth century, but was finally overcome by the Hittites in the fourteenth century. Assyria, which had been a vassal of Mitanni, now, under Ashur-uballit I, became the dominant power in Upper Mesopotamia.

EGYPT   In contrast to the confusion in Mesopotamia, Egypt, in the early patriarchal age, was remarkably stable: the First Intermediate was over and the Middle Kingdom had been founded. The Twelfth Dynasty, with its capital at Memphis, maintained itself in power for over two hundred years (1991-1786 B.C.). This was a period of great prosperity and a golden age of Egyptian culture. Wisdom literature abounded; from this time, too, comes the delightful *Tale*

---

[5]See *ibid.*, pp. 60-72.
[6]See *ibid.*, pp. 163-80.
[7]See *ibid.*, pp. 219-20.

of Sinuhe.[8] A loose Egyptian control extended over most of Palestine and Phoenicia, while Byblos was an Egyptian colony. The Execration Texts give us an impression of the extent of Egyptian control in Asia.

> These consist of two series of inscriptions from the twentieth and nineteenth centuries which illustrate how Pharaoh sought to bring magical powers to bear on his enemies, actual or potential. In the first series, imprecations against various foes were inscribed on jars or bowls, which were then smashed—thus making the imprecation effective. In the other, the imprecations were written on clay figures representing bound captives. The places mentioned indicate that the Egyptian sphere included western Palestine, Phoenicia to a point north of Byblos, and southern Syria.[9]

In the eighteenth century the power of the Middle Kingdom declined; before the end of the century rival dynasties (the Thirteenth and Fourteenth) contended for power, thus leaving the way open to an invasion of a foreign people called the Hyksos. The name means "rulers of foreign peoples" or "foreign chiefs." It seems probable that most of the Hyksos rulers were Canaanite or Amorite princes from Palestine and southern Syria; they were certainly Semites. The Hyksos won control of the whole of Egypt and placed their capital at Avaris (Tanis); they ruled Egypt from about 1700 B.C. to 1560 B.C. It is not unlikely that the ancestors of Israel entered Egypt during this time.

A movement against the conquerors began in Upper Egypt. Amosis, the founder of the Eighteenth Dynasty, took Avaris and expelled the Hyksos from Egypt (c. 1560 B.C.); he even pursued them into Palestine. This marked the beginning of the New Empire (1560-715 B.C.) and the hour of Egypt's greatest glory. For the moment, however, we are concerned only with the Eighteenth Dynasty (1560-1345 B.C.). Under Thutmosis III (c. 1500-1450 B.C.), Egypt reached the zenith of its power: the empire extended to the Euphrates. This expansion brought Egypt into conflict with the kingdom of Mitanni in Upper Mesopotamia, a conflict which ended in a treaty; relations between the countries remained peaceful.

In the fourteenth century the young Pharaoh Amenophis IV (1377-1358 B.C.) brought about a strange revolution. A devotee of Aten (the Solar Disk), he promoted the cult of this, the sole god (for it

---

[8]See *ibid.*, pp. 414-19, 18-22.
[9]J. Bright, *A History of Israel* (Philadelphia: Westminster Press, 1959), pp. 47 f.

does seem that the Aten cult, if not a strict monotheism, was something approaching it), and changed his own name to Akhenaten (the Splendor of Aten). This brought him into conflict with the priests of Amun; hence he left Thebes and built his new capital, named Akhetaten, at modern Tell el-Amarna. This period, then, is known as the Amarna Age.

Due to the internal dissension, Egyptian power waned, a fact that is illustrated by the Amarna letters: clay tablets discovered in the excavation of Tell el-Amarna.[10] Written in Akkadian, the diplomatic language, they are, for the most part, frantic appeals for help by Pharaoh's vassals in Palestine and Phoenicia: many towns are in open rebellion against Egypt; trouble is everywhere fomented by an element called the Habiru. To make matters worse, this eclipse of Egypt coincided with the rise of the Hittite Empire under Shuppiluliuma (c. 1370-1345 B.C.). Most of Syria and northern Phoenicia came under Hittite control and the kingdom of Mitanni was conquered. In Egypt the situation was saved by Horemheb (c. 1350-1315 B.C.). He managed to put the country back on a sound footing and ruthlessly removed all vestiges of the Aten cult. With him the Eighteenth Dynasty came to an end.

The real founder of the Nineteenth Dynasty was Seti I (1315-1301 B.C.), who soon regained possession of Palestine, thus coming into direct conflict with the Hittites. Under his successor Rameses II (1301-1234 B.C.) there was full-scale war, which dragged on until about 1271 B.C. when a treaty was signed by the two countries; copies of this treaty have been found in Egypt and in the Hittite capital.[11] Henceforth the long reign of Rameses II was peaceful and marked a period of prosperity for Egypt. But this brings us to the time of the Exodus and is best considered in the context of that event.

THE HITTITES   The Hittites were an Indo-European people who, by the mid-sixteenth century, had established a strong kingdom in eastern and central Asia Minor, with its capital at Hattusas (Bogazköy). We have noted that a Hittite king, Mursilis I, brought the First Babylonian Dynasty to an end about 1530 B.C. The expedition had no lasting effect; it was more than a century before Hittite influence was again felt outside Asia Minor.

---

[10]See ANET, pp. 483-90.
[11]See *ibid.*, pp. 199-203.

Under Shuppiluliuma (c. 1370-1345 B.C.) the Hittite kingdom became an empire extending over Syria and Phoenicia, with Mitanni as a vassal state. Soon the Hittites clashed with a renascent Egypt, but under Hattusilis III (c. 1270-1250 B.C.) hostilities came to an end. (A copy of the treaty with Rameses II has been found at Bogazköy.) But if there was peace in the west, the Hittites were being harassed in the east by the Assyrians under the energetic successors of Ashur-uballit I—Adad-nirari I (c. 1298-1266 B.C.) and Shalmaneser I (1266-1236 B.C.)—and the Assyrians gained control of Mitanni. Indeed, the Hittite Empire was doomed, but at the hands of another enemy; its fall may be mentioned here though it forms part of the background to the Exodus and Conquest. By the middle of the thirteenth century the Hittites had increasing difficulty in maintaining their position against coalitions of Aegean peoples in western Asia Minor. Finally the empire was engulfed by these groups whom the Egyptians named the Peoples of the Sea.

THE HABIRU   Groups known as Habiru were found over all western Asia from the third millennium to about the eleventh century B.C. The name does not have an ethnic connotation; it is a social designation (or so it would appear).

> The term apparently denoted a class of people without citizenship, without fixed place in the existing social structure. At times pursuing a seminomadic existence, living either peacefully or by raiding, as occasion offered they settled in the towns. They might, in disturbed times, hire themselves (so in the Amarna letters) as irregular troops for whatever advantage they could gain. Or they might, when driven by need, dispose of themselves as clients to men of station, or even sell themselves as slaves (as at Nuzi); in Egypt, numbers of them were impressed as labourers on various royal projects. On occasion, however, some of them—like Joseph—rose to high position.[12]

For, as we shall see, it is reasonable to suppose that the Hebrew ancestors belonged to this class.

PALESTINE   In the period from 2000 B.C. to 1750 B.C. Palestine was infiltrated by seminomadic groups, who began to settle down in western Palestine and in northern Transjordan; the Execration Texts and archaeological data are proof of this. However, the central mountain range was thinly populated. It seems certain that the newcomers were Amorites, of the same Northwest-Semitic stock as

---

[12]Bright, *op. cit.*, p. 85.

the Canaanites; hence the two peoples speedily merged. It appears, too, that some of the Hurrians (in the Bible called Horites) had spilled into the land from northern Mesopotamia. In the seventeenth and sixteenth centuries B.C. Palestine was part of the Hyksos Empire and the city-state system developed—the same political system that obtained at the time of the Israelite conquest.

2. THE PATRIARCHS

Our sketch of the world of Israel's origins has had the purpose not only of underlining the comparative modernity of biblical history but also, and more immediately, of setting the biblical story in its proper framework right from the beginning. Besides, our knowledge of that other world has wonderfully illuminated the world of the Bible. At the same time, it has assured us that the traditions which have preserved the memory of the patriarchs must indeed stem from patriarchal times. For, when the traditions are examined in the light of the evidence, the stories of the patriarchs fit authentically into the milieu of the early second millennium.

It must be noted, however, that the narrative of the patriarchal age is at once historical and popular. Passed on for centuries by oral tradition, it accurately describes the essentials but freely develops and amplifies the story according to the character of the various personages. It is a family history which takes no account of general history or of political events. (Gn. 14 is an exception.) It is religious history since it not only sees the divine Providence in everything but also presents and explains events in a religious light in order to demonstrate a definite thesis: the one, only God has chosen one people to dwell in one land: Canaan. Hence the promises of God and the relations of the patriarchs with the land of Canaan.

Contemporary evidence shows that the traditions relating to Abraham, Isaac, and Jacob are not only probable but well-grounded. In a popular, distinctive form they preserve the memory of the origin of the people of Israel. Thus, what is said of the patriarchs regarding their seminomadic way of life agrees with the history of Palestine and adjacent countries in the nineteenth and eighteenth centuries as we know it from archaeology.[13] They are portrayed as semi-

---

[13]See Roland de Vaux, "The Hebrew Patriarchs and History," *Theology Digest,* 12 (1964), 227-40.

nomads living in tents; partly nomad, going from place to place in search of pasture, even as far as Egypt in times of drought; partly sedentary since they remained for long periods at Shechem, Hebron-Mambre, Beer-sheba, and Bethel. Their wanderings in Palestine fit perfectly into the situation of the Execration Texts. As nomads they had a profound sense of family or clan and hence of collective responsibility and of the necessity for preserving purity of blood. Then, too, their juridical and social customs agree with the juridical and social customs of the same period throughout the East. Thus the rite of making a treaty (Gn. 15:7-11), the contract for the purchase of the cave of Machpelah (Gn. 23:17 f.), the adoption of a servant in lieu of a son (Gn. 15:1-3), the custom by which a sterile wife permits her husband to have intercourse with her hand-maid, with the child born of the union not being the heir without special adoption (Gn. 16:1 f.; 30:1-6, 39-13), the right of the first born (Gn. 25:29-34), the practice of levirate (Gn. 38)—and many others—are paralleled in the Nuzi texts, the Hittite laws, and later Assyrian laws (which reflect earlier legislation). But this is a general background and all we can say with confidence is that the customs and laws—and the events—reflected in Gn. 12-50 fit best between the twentieth and seventeenth centuries B.C.

We can be a little more precise about the geographical background of the patriarchal narratives. The biblical tradition mentions Haran as the starting-point of Abraham's journey (Gn. 11:32; 12:5; cf. Jos. 24:2 f.); and a further tradition (Gn. 11:28,31; 15:7) specifies that Abraham's father, Terah, had earlier migrated to Haran from Ur. The home of Laban, Abraham's kinsman, is placed in Paddan-Aram (Gn. 27:43; 28:10; 29:4) and, more precisely, in the city of Nahor in Aram-naharaim (Mesopotamia) (Gn. 24:10); and Laban is repeatedly called an Aramean (Gn. 25:20; 28:1-7; 31:20,24). An early cultic credo began: "A wandering Aramean was my father" (Dt. 26:5). It seems that the name, originally designating the Aramaic-speaking people of Upper Mesopotamia, was gradually extended to neighboring seminomadic peoples who adopted the same language.

There appears to be a relationship, too, between the patriarchs and the Habiru mentioned above. Undoubtedly, there is a similarity between the name "Hebrew" (*'ibri*) and *Habiru*. It is surely significant that the name "Hebrew," in the Old Testament, is practically confined to narratives of the earliest period and occurs chiefly in the mouth of a foreigner speaking to the Israelites (e.g., Gn. 39:14,17; Ex. 2:6; 1 Sm. 4:6,9) or of an Israelite identifying himself to foreigners (e.g., Gn. 40:15; Ex. 3:18; 5:3). It is reasonable to think that the patriarchs would have belonged, or were regarded as belonging, to the social class of Habiru.

Finally, the Hyksos must be considered. These Semitic princes ruled Egypt for almost a century and a half (c. 1700-1560 B.C.). It is entirely credible that this period is the setting of Joseph's career and marks the beginning of the Hebrew sojourn in Egypt. The Hyksos would have welcomed fellow Semites and would have permitted one of them to attain high office.

It appears, then, that the patriarchs were a part of that migration of seminomadic groups which brought a new population into Palestine in the early centuries of the second millennium B.C.

> We may assume that among these migrating clansmen, though no contemporary text observed them, there moved an Abraham, an Isaac, and a Jacob, chieftains of sizable clans, who remembered their origins in "the plains of Aram" near Haran. The nucleus of the later Israel was to come from their number. Normally peaceful herdsmen, they roamed unsettled areas chiefly in the southern and central mountain range and the Negeb, in search of seasonal pasture for their flocks. But like the land-hungry, statusless Habiru that they were, they would fight if sufficiently provoked or if the occasion seemed propitious. Whether from necessity or choice, they continued this mode of life for generations, long after others of their kind had settled down. Probably as early as the Hyksos period some of their number (e.g., Joseph) found their way to Egypt, to be followed subsequently, under pressure of hard times, by others. And there they ultimately found themselves state slaves.[14]

We may tentatively suggest the following dates:

c. 1850 B.C.: Arrival of Abraham in Canaan.

c. 1850-1700 B.C.: The patriarchs in Palestine.

c. 1700-1250 B.C.: The Hebrews in Egypt.

3. EXODUS AND CONQUEST
1) *The Background*

EGYPT The long reign of Rameses II (1301-1234 B.C.), especially after the treaty with the Hittites (c. 1271 B.C.), was one of prosperity and of great building activity. The rebuilding of the capital

---

[14]Bright, *op. cit.*, p. 86.

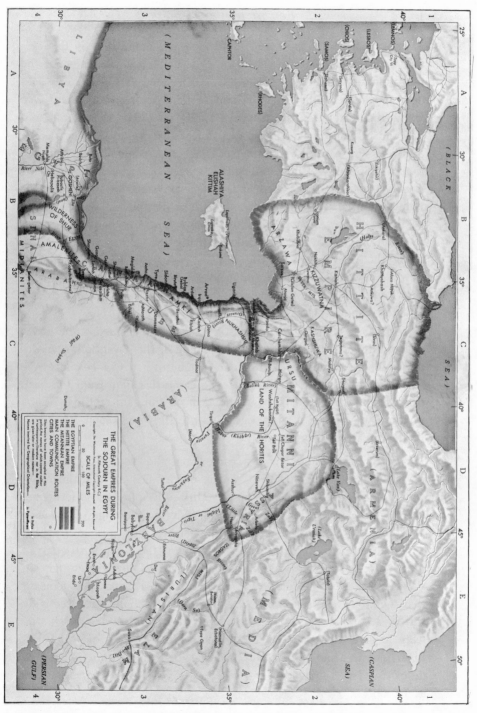

THE GREAT EMPIRES DURING
THE SOJOURN IN EGYPT
In Fifteenth Century B.C.

SCALE OF MILES

THE EGYPTIAN EMPIRE
THE HITTITE EMPIRE
THE MITANNIAN EMPIRE
MAIN COMMUNICATION ROUTES
CITIES AND TOWNS

Avaris, started by Sethi I (1317-1301 B.C.) was completed by Rameses and the new city named "The House of Rameses." The reign of the next pharaoh, Merneptah (1234-1225 B.C.) ended in a period of weakness and anarchy that saw the end of the Nineteenth Dynasty. We know from a stele of his fifth year (c. 1230 B.C.) that Merneptah campaigned in Palestine.[15] Among foes defeated there he lists the people of Israel—the earliest reference to Israel in a contemporary inscription. Significantly, Israel is listed as a people, not a territory, so it is not yet sedentary. Indeed, it is not clear what the stele reference implies, perhaps no more than a clash with some of the Israelites of the Exodus. About this same time Merneptah had to face an invasion of Libyans and the Peoples of the Sea who moved on Egypt along the African coast. The raiders were repelled but Egyptian power was weakened; during the subsequent period of anarchy Egyptian control of Palestine ceased—a circumstance favorable to the Israelite conquest and consolidation.

With Rameses III (1197-1165 B.C.) a new era seemed to be about to dawn for Egypt: this was the beginning of the Twentieth Dynasty (1200-1085 B.C.). But almost at once, Rameses had to face successive waves of the Peoples of the Sea, who came this time from the east, along the Mediterranean coast, and beat on the gate of Egypt. Each invasion was staved off but Egypt was terribly weakened. The days of her greatness were over.

THE PEOPLES   These peoples came from the Aegeo-Cretan world
OF THE SEA   and had been on the move since the mid-thirteenth century. They had overthrown the Hittite Empire and Merneptah had to repel an invasion from the west. Later, in the reign of Rameses III, from the Asia Minor they had overrun, they pushed by land and sea, in wave after wave, against Egypt; the Egyptian fleet and army just managed to keep them at bay. The change wrought in Palestine by their appearance is important. In the first place it meant that the attempt to re-establish Egyptian control there was effectively stifled; secondly, some of these people, notably the Philistines—who were to give their name to the whole country—settled on the Palestinian coast. Thus the nation that was to come within an ace of destroying Israel arrived in Palestine at approximately the same time as Israel.

---

[15]See ANET, pp. 376-78.

CANAAN   In the thirteenth century the two chief ethnic groups in Palestine were the Canaanites, a Northwest Semitic people, already in Palestine and Syria in the third millennium, and the Amorites, also Northwest Semites who had come into the land in the early second millennium; among them were the ancestors of Israel. For the most part the Bible does not distinguish sharply between these peoples for, by the time of the conquest, the Amorites had adopted the language and culture of Canaan. Other elements were Hurrians (Horites) from the Hyksos period. By "Hittites" are meant elements who had come from the parts of northern Syria once under Hittite control (most likely they were Hurrians). Other inhabitants of the land (Hivites, Jebusites, Girgashites, Perizzites) are of unknown origin. But all had become essentially Canaanite in culture.

Politically, Canaan was a patchwork of small city-states without a central authority. During the period of Egyptian dominance these cities were vassals of Egypt; when Egyptian control declined they were at the mercy of invaders. Culturally, the Canaanites were advanced; more remarkable is the development of writing among them. By the end of the third millennium a syllabic script had been developed at Byblos, and it was the Canaanites, too, who invented the linear alphabet that is the ancestor of our own. The fourteenth-century Ras Shamra (Ugarit) texts, which preserve, in a poetic style akin to early Hebrew verse, the myth and epic of Canaan, are of great value and interest.[16] "It must be stressed, and stressed again, that the age of Israel's origins was one of widespread literacy."[17]

Canaanite religion was essentially a fertility cult. Head of the Canaanite pantheon was El, but the chief active deity was Ba'al (Lord). Female deities, variously named Asherah, Astarte, Anat, represented the female principle in the fertility cult. A central element of Canaanite myth was the death and resurrection of Ba'al, corresponding to the annual death and resurrection of nature. In this context such rites as sacred prostitution become understandable: by sexual union at the shrine, the union of god and goddess was reenacted, and by a sort of sympathetic magic the desired fertility in soil, beast, and man was secured. Though the Bible vehemently condemns it, the Canaanite religion continued to have a powerful

---

[16]See *ibid.*, pp. 129-55.
[17]Bright, *op. cit.*, p. 108.

fascination for the Hebrews, especially when they had settled down to agricultural life.

2) The Exodus

It may seem strange that, after a relatively full presentation of the historical background, we shall go on to treat of the Exodus itself in a few lines. The truth is that, when we get down to details, the situation is seen to be extremely complicated; and this outline is obviously not the place for a thorough review of all the evidence.

We have suggested that the Hebrews settled in Egypt during the Hyksos period. It is understandable that, after the expulsion of the hated invaders, the Egyptians should have looked with no friendly eye on the Semitic elements in their midst: "There arose a new king over Egypt, who did not know Joseph" (Ex. 1:8). In any case we know that the Hebrews had become slaves, forced to labor at the building of Pithom and Raamses (Ex. 1:11). The latter is the ancient Hyksos capital of Avaris, rebuilt by Pharaohs Sethi I and Rameses II and named by the latter "House of Rameses"; the reference seems to demand the presence of the Hebrews in Egypt during at least part of the reign of Rameses II. On the other hand, the stele of Merneptah seems to demand the presence of Israel in Palestine by 1230 B.C. (or, perhaps, 1220). At any rate, a thirteenth-century date for the Exodus seems assured.

If we wish to be more precise, we must consider two alternatives:
1. Pharaoh of the oppression: Sethi I (1317-1301 B.C.)
   Pharaoh of the Exodus: Rameses II (1301-1234 B.C.)
2. Pharaoh of the oppression: Rameses II
   Pharaoh of the Exodus: Merneptah (1234-1225 B.C.)

In conclusion the best we can say is that the Exodus is most likely to have taken place between 1250 B.C. and 1230 B.C. To this uncertainty of date we might add that the exact route of the Israelites is uncertain. The truth is that the relevant Pentateuch passages are liturgical texts which celebrate the saving event, the mighty intervention of Yahweh; in the liturgy the event of the past became a saving event of the present. But this could be only because God really had intervened to save his people. So, if we are sure neither of exact date nor of exact location, we are certain that the Exodus itself was, and remained, the central *fact* in Israel's history.

The traditional site of Sinai is not unchallenged, though a reasonable case can be made for it. But, again, it is what happened at

Sinai that is important: there Israel received the Law and Covenant which made her a people. Nor are we very clear about Israel's subsequent wanderings. All we can say is that the headquarters of the desert sojourn was Kadesh, an oasis fifty miles south of Beer-sheba.

A final point concerns the number of the Israelites who took part in the Exodus. Here the biblical numbers cannot be taken at their face value: over 600,000 fighting men (Ex. 12:37; 38:26; Nm. 1:46; 2:32; etc.)—which would give a total population of two to three millions. Such a throng would require a month to cross the Red Sea and, stretched out in a column, would reach over one hundred miles! Besides, the Sinai peninsula today supports at most 10,000 inhabitants, and at a low living standard. If we are to avoid geographical and historical absurdities we must say that the total population, including the elements that had joined after the liberation, was not likely to be more than 20,000 people or, at the most, 30,000.[18]

3) The Conquest

Chapters ten and eleven of Joshua link the conquest of the whole of the south and the conquest of the whole of the north of Palestine with two expeditions of Canaanite kings and with two battles, at Gibeon and "by the waters of Merom." The countercampaigns against these kings are depicted as having been carried out with the participation of all the tribes and under the leadership of Joshua. But it is clear from several references in Jos. and from the first chapter of Jgs. that this is an idealized picture: to Joshua, the conqueror, are attributed the successes won by others in later times; for the essential fact is that these successes were due ultimately to God —"The Lord God of Israel fought for Israel" (Jos. 10:42).

But if we are certain that the Conquest was a more complicated and a far slower affair than Jos. 10-11 would suggest, we may not deny the essential historical fact of a conquest under Joshua. The archaeological evidence, while providing some major problems, on the whole confirms the biblical presentation. It is true that Jericho, long thought to offer the decisive proof, is now seen to be no help in this matter. It is true that Ai, said to have been captured by Joshua (Jos. 8:1-23) is now known to have been destroyed about 2200 B.C. and to have remained unoccupied until the twelfth century

---

[18]See P. Lemaire and D. Baldi, *Atlante Storico della Bibbia* (Rome: Marietti, 1955), p. 85. Henceforth this book will be abbreviated *Atlante Biblico* (Biblical Atlas).

B.C. (It may be that the story of Jos. 8 originally referred to the taking of Bethel, little more than a mile away, which was violently destroyed in the second half of the thirteenth century B.C.) But it is also true that, on the positive side, a number of places in Southern Palestine, said to have been taken by Israel, appear to have been destroyed in the latter half of the thirteenth century—for example, Debir (Jos. 10:38 f.), Lachish (10:31 f.), Eglon (10:34 f.), and, in the north, Hazor (11:10).

We may conclude, with J. Bright:

> The evidence is really very impressive, and it is not sound method to brush it aside. It does not, to be sure, substantiate the biblical narrative in detail; nor does it allow us to suppress evidence that the conquest was also an involved process. We have two pictures of the conquest to keep in mind. If they are not to be artificially harmonized, neither is one or the other to be ruled out. However complicated the Israelite occupation of Palestine may have been, and however schematized the narrative of Joshua, it may be regarded as certain that a violent irruption into the land took place late in the thirteenth century.[19]

The precise date of the conquest depends, of course, on the date adopted for the Exodus—here, about 1250-1230 B.C. We may take it that the "forty years" of wandering need not be interpreted too literally; it was probably much shorter. Thus the conquest would have taken place between 1220 B.C. and 1200 B.C.

Without going into detail we might add that there is evidence to suggest that components of Israel had been in Palestine before the conquest under Joshua. A large element of the Palestinian population was of the same Amorite stock as Israel and would have joined forces with the incoming Israelites. In support of this view we have the impression that much of the land, especially in central Palestine, did not have to be conquered. And the Covenant ceremony (Jos. 24) could well mark the formal incorporation of these other elements into the tribal structure of Israel.

4. THE PERIOD OF JUDGES
1) *The Background*

The world situation favored the invasion of the Israelites and their settlement in Canaan. Though Egypt still maintained her claims on

---

[19]Bright, *op. cit.*, p. 120.

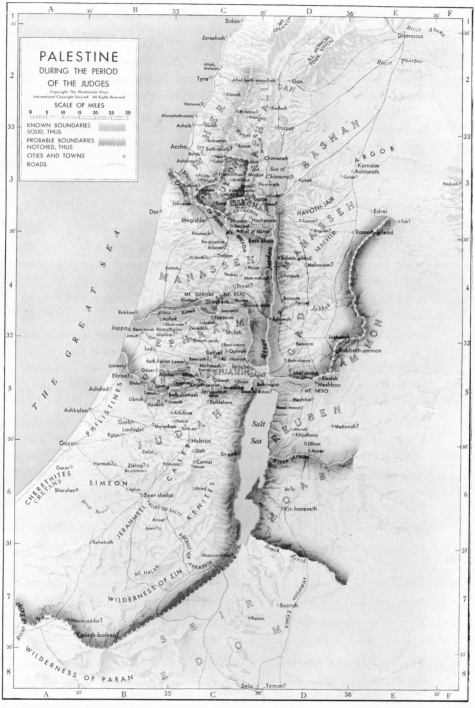

PALESTINE
DURING THE PERIOD
OF THE JUDGES

Copyright, The Westminster Press
International Copyright Secured   All Rights Reserved

SCALE OF MILES
0   5   10   15   20   25   30

KNOWN BOUNDARIES
SOLID, THUS
PROBABLE BOUNDARIES
NOTCHED, THUS
CITIES AND TOWNS   o
ROADS

Sidon

Zarephath

MT. LEBANON

River Abana

Damascus

River Pharpar

MT. HERMON
SENIR, SIRION

Ahlab,
Mahalab?

Tyre

Abel-beth-maachah

Dan

Kanah

Hammon?

Misrephoth-maim?

Ahazor?

Iron?

Kedesh

Achzib

Abdon

Beth-emek

Hazor

Accho

Beth-anath?

Waters of Merom

Achshaph?

Neiel

Rehob?

Cabul

Ramah

Chinnereth

BASHAN

ARGOB

Karnaim
Ashtaroth

Golan?

Nobah?

Dor

Jokneam

Megiddo

Taanach

En-gannim

Ibleam

Aruboth?

Sochoh

MT. CARMEL

VALLEY OF JEZREEL
JIPHTAH-EL

ZEBULUN

ISSACHAR

Rimmon

Madon

Hannathon

Japhia

Chisulloth

Shimron

Sea of
Chinnereth

Hammath

Aphek

HAVOTH-JAIR

Edrei

Tob?

Camon?

MANASSEH

MACHIR

Ramoth-gilead

Jabesh-gilead

Mahanaim?

Succoth
Penuel

River Jabbok

GAD

AMMON

Beth-shan

Bezek

Abel-meholah?

Tirzah?

MT. GERIZIM

MT. EBAL

Shechem

Pirathon?

Kanah

Janoah?

Tappuah

Shiloh

Ophrah

Gilgal?

Jericho

Zeredah

Lebonah

EPHRAIM

Timnath-serah?

Baal-hazor

Bethel

Ai

Naarath?

Rakkon?

Aphek

Eben-ezer?

Ramathaim-
zophim?

Joppa

Jehud?

Bene-berak

Lod

Beth-haran Lower?

Gezer

Beeroth?

Michmash

Ramah

Jabneel?

Ekron

Ajalon?

Mizpah?

Gibeah

BENJAMIN

Kirjath-jearim?

Ashdod

Chephirah?

Debir?

Bethel-hoglah?

Zorah?

Beth-shemesh?

Stone of Bohan?

Timnah?

Abel-shittim?

Elealeh?

Heshbon

MT. NEBO

Medeba?

Baal-meon?

Ashkelon

Gath?

Mareshah

Keilah

Adullam

Bethlehem

Lachish

Beth-zur?

Libnah

Azekah

Jarmuth?

Hebron

PHILISTINES

Eglon?

Gaza

Gerar

Mattanah?

Salt
Sea

REUBEN

Ataroth?

Kirjathaim?

Dibon?

Aroer?

MOAB

Adamah

Zaphon?

Betonim?

Jogbehah?

Rabbath-ammon

Beth-nimrah?

Jabbok

Jazer?

Ziklag?

En-rimmon?

Hormah?

Ehtomah?

Carmel

Maon

En-gedi?

Ziph

CALEB

JUDAH

KENITES

Arad

Beer-sheba

SIMEON

CHERETHITES
CRETANS

Sharuhen?

Ashan?

Brook Besor?

Rehoboth?

Azem?

Aroer?

JERAHMEEL

VALLEY OF SALT?

ASCENT OF AKRABBIM

Hazezon-tamar?

Arnon?

Kir-hareseth

River Arnon

Brook Zered

KING'S HIGHWAY

MT. HALAK

WILDERNESS OF ZIN

SEIR

EDOM

Bozrah

Punon

Sela

Teman?

MT. SEIR

Azmon?

Hazar-addar?

Kadesh-barnea?

WILDERNESS OF PARAN

River of Egypt

THE GREAT SEA

DAN

NAPHTALI

ASHER

ZEBULUN

MT. OF MOREH

Shunem

Hapharaim

MT. GILBOA

Well of Harod

Jezreel

Dothan

Thebez

Abel-meholah?

Tabbath?

Jabneel?

Gibbethon?

Ekron

Jabesh

Beth-anoth?

Ophrah

Jericho

the Syrian coast, she was unable to do anything at all to implement them; eventually even the claims ceased. In Asia Minor the Hittite Empire had disappeared. Assyria had been a force in the thirteenth century, but her power had waned. Under Tiglath-pileser I (c. 1114-1076 B.C.), she knew a brief resurgence, but soon sank into a slumber that lasted for two centuries. In Upper Mesopotamia and Syria small Aramean states sprang up. Until the middle of the ninth century Israel could be free of serious interference on the part of great powers. The first threat came from a people no greater than herself and, like herself, a recent invader: the Philistines.

2) The Amphictyony

Early Israel was a confederation of twelve tribes united in Covenant with Yahweh. There was no central government and the various tribes enjoyed complete independence, while tribal society was on a patriarchal basis. The rallying point of the confederation was the shrine which housed the Ark of the Covenant; during most of the early period it was located at Shiloh. This system resembles the religious league of a somewhat later period in Greece, which was called an "amphictyony." The Delphic League, for instance, had twelve members; the number probably points to a monthly mainte-nance of the central shrine.

The Covenant assembly at Shechem (Jos. 24) suggests that the amphictyony was already in existence. It seems that a league of clans must have existed before the conquest—a campaign that de-manded concerted action. It is reasonable to look for the origin of the amphictyonic system at Sinai (though we may not doubt that it took on its final and classical form only after the settlement) and to see it as a concrete expression of the Covenant of Yahweh with his people. Indeed, the tent that housed the Ark was "the Tent of Meeting"—the place of tribal assembly presided over by Yahweh. Later on, in Palestine, the shrine of the Ark still remained the meet-ing-point and the heart of the confederacy; Shiloh quickly became the center of assembly (Jos. 18:1; Jgs. 18:31).

3) The Period of Judges[20]

The Judges (*shophetim*), like the *suffetes* of Tyre and Carthage, were "tyrants" who led the people in war and who saved them

---

[20]See *Atlante Biblico*, pp. 103-12.

from danger. The "Judge" essentially was a man chosen by God to free the oppressed people; his mission was therefore charismatic. He was not a saint, but a hero in the service of the community, and was invested with moral and physical strength sufficient to assert his authority over his fellow citizens and to bring about the downfall of his enemies. The mission of the Judge varied according to the circumstances, and, generally, he acted on behalf of a particular tribe. There is no question of a "government" of Judges, nor is it possible to establish their chronological order with exactitude, since some may have been contemporaries.

The chronology of Jgs., which appears to give 410 years for the period of Judges, is evidently artificial; this is indicated by the recurrence of 40 years (= a generation) and of 80 and 20. The total is arrived at by adding the years of the Judges, but some may have overlapped. From extrabiblical data we know that the conquest took place at the end of the thirteenth century and that the reign of David began before 1000 B.C. The period of Judges, then, is not more than one and one-half centuries (the middle of it is marked by the victory of Taanach under Deborah and Barak [c. 1125 B.C.]). This victory was earlier than the Midianite invasion (Gideon) and the Philistine expansion (Samson).

POLITICAL SITUATION AT THE BEGINNING OF THE PERIOD OF JUDGES   1. *The Israelites.* At the death of Joshua the Promised Land was far from being conquered. The elders, who succeeded Joshua, were unable to maintain the unity of the people and there was a manifest lack of central authority: "In those days there was no king in Israel; every man did what was right in his own eyes" (Jgs. 17:6). The Canaanites still held out at important points, while the constant contact with this people had grave effects on the religion of Yahweh. The Israelites, in fact, held only the mountain regions; the Canaanites and Philistines, with their chariot forces, held the plains. Judah and Simeon, aided by the Calebites, gained the territory of Hebron and the Negeb. The "House of Joseph" (Ephraim and Manasseh) got control of the central region north of Jerusalem; the Ark of the Covenant was established in the sanctuary of Shiloh in Ephraim. None of the tribes won all of the territory allotted to them by Joshua; hence there was rivalry among the tribes and migration of discontented clans. Ephraim gained territory at the expense of Manasseh—which in its turn pushed north into Issachar and Asher—while Dan emigrated to the sources of the Jordan, under pressure of Amorites who took Aijalon and Bethshemesh. Judah and Simeon alone attained a measure of stability, though they soon became isolated from the northern tribes; this is the germ of the future political schism. It is remarkable, for instance, that they are not mentioned in the canticle of Deborah (Jgs. 5).

2. *The Canaanites* and the division of Israel. The Canaanites were established in Accho, Harosheth, Megiddo, Taanach, and Bethshan, thus separating Ephraim from the northern tribes. The southern tribes, Judah and Simeon, were cut off from Benjamin and the "House of Joseph" by Jerusalem and Gezer and the cities of the Gibeonite confederacy: Gibeon, Chephirah, Beeroth, and Kiriathjearim. The tribes of Transjordan were cut off from the rest by the Jordan valley, and they had to be on the defensive against Ammon and Moab.

3. *The Philistines.* One of the most important changes wrought in Palestine by the invasion of the "Peoples of the Sea" was the installation along the littoral south of Carmel of peoples from the Aegeo-Cretan world, notably the Philistines. They established themselves in the Shephelah (the hill country west of the mountain region of Judah) and the corresponding coast, southward from Jaffa. Their allies, the Tsikal pirates, had their center further north at Dor and had control of the plain of Sharon. The Philistines had a colony at Aphek which controlled the route to Jezreel (Esdraelon). Politically they formed five toparchies with capitals at Gaza, Ashkelon, Ashdod, Ekron, and Gath. Each toparchy was ruled by a *seren,* the five forming a Supreme Council of the nation. They had a well-equipped army and a strong force of chariotry, and with their unity and military strength the Philistines were a great danger to the Israelites during the period of Judges (and after). At first, however, it was the unconquered cities in their midst that caused trouble.

4. *Transjordan.* From about the twentieth century B.C. until the thirteenth, central and southern Transjordan had remained without settled population. In the thirteenth century, however, new Semitic peoples settled there: the Edomites and the Moabites. The former settled in the highlands east of the Arabah (continuation of the

Jordan valley) between the southern end of the Dead Sea and the Gulf of Aqabah, while the latter established themselves north of Edom, east of the Dead Sea. When we first come to know of them they were already set up as kingdoms (Gn. 36:31-39; Nm. 20:14; 22:4). A third people, the Ammonites, settled northeast of Moab. Farther north were the Amorite states of Heshbon and Bashan which were conquered by the Israelites.

THE JUDGES   1. *Othniel.* Judah and Simeon were menaced by Edomite incursions (Edom, not *Aram* [= Mesopotamia]) (Jgs. 3:8, 10). Yahweh raised up Othniel, the Calebite who defeated the Edomites. He was the only Judge of Judah.

2. *Ehud.* The Moabites subdued Reuben and, crossing the Jordan, established themselves in the plain of Jericho. They compelled the Benjaminites to pay tribute. Ehud brought the tribute to Eglon, the king, in his dwelling beyond the Jordan, and assassinated him. He then declared a "holy war" and drove the Moabites across the river.

3. *The Canaanite reaction.* The Canaanites, with fortresses from Accho to Bethshan, held the valley of Jezreel, and began to molest the northern tribes. The prophetess Deborah, in her contact with the tribes, stirred them to revolt. When she thought they were emotionally prepared, she declared the "holy war" and set up as leader *Barak* of Naphtali. Issachar, Ephraim, Benjamin, Zebulun, and Naphtali answered the call. Barak took counsel with Zebulun and Naphtali at Kedesh of Galilee and led 10,000 men to Tabor, the place indicated by Deborah.

The Canaanites assembled a large force, with 900 chariots, under Sisera of Harosheth, and camped south of Megiddo; the battle was fought between Megiddo and Taanach. Heavy rain had made the Kishon overflow and the chariots were bogged down. Barak attacked the Canaanites in front, while others, coming from the south by Taanach, took them on the flank. The Canaanites fled and Sisera was killed by the woman Jael. In the canticle of Deborah, Reuben, Gad, Dan, and Asher were blamed for failing to join Barak. The victory of Taanach, "by the waters of Megiddo," had lasting effects. The Canaanites, deprived of their chariots, never recovered. They still held the cities, but excavations at Megiddo point to a decline which set in at this time.

4. *The Midianites.* After the victory of Taanach the Israelites had possession of the fertile plain of Jezreel and were engaged in agriculture. The way was open to two quite different dangers: the temptation of the fertility cult and nomad incursions. The Midianites came from the south along the confines of Moab and Ammon, then up the Jordan valley nd into the plain of Jezreel at Bethshan. The domestic camel was now extensively used and they were able to carry out lightning raids. Eventually a savior appeared: Yahweh raised up *Gideon,* a young man of Ophrah. He destroyed the altar of Baal on the high place of Ophrah and built one to Yahweh in its place. For this he was named Jerubbaal—"that Baal may defend himself (from him)." His war against the Midianites had, probably, different phases which are difficult to distinguish.

He assembled the people of Manasseh and neighboring tribes. With a chosen band (300) he surprised the Midianites camped at the foot of Moreh and put them to flight. Gideon pursued them beyond Bethshan and across the Jordan, because the law of blood compelled him to avenge his two brothers slain at Tabor by the Midianite chiefs Zebah and Zalmunna. At a place called Karkor, deep in Transjordan, he caught up with the Midianites and seized their chiefs, who were later put to death. But the Midianites would have raided again the following year. This time Gideon had the fords of the Jordan watched. When the raiders went to flee across the river as before they were intercepted by the Ephraimites; their leaders, Oreb and Zeeb, were captured and killed. The Ephraimites, who arrogated to themselves a certain hegemony among the tribes, tried to pick a quarrel with Gideon, but he spoke diplomatically and was able to pacify them. The grateful people offered Gideon a hereditary princedom; he refused the title but accepted the substance.

Gideon was succeeded by his son Abimelech whose mother was a woman of Shechem. Supported by the Canaanite clan of Shechem he massacred his brothers and declared himself king. He reigned for three years, and not peacefully. In striving to put down a revolt he destroyed Shechem. Finally he was killed at the siege of Thebez —by a millstone thrown from a tower by a woman.

5. *Transjordan.* In Transjordan, Gad, Reuben, and the half-tribe of Manasseh were in difficulties. The Ammonites were established at the upper courses of the Jabbok and wanted to push into the

THE JUDGES		
GREATER JUDGES	TRIBE	OPPRESSOR
Othniel	Judah	Edomites
Ehud	Benjamin	Moabites
Barak (Deborah)	Naphtali	Canaanites
Gideon	Manasseh	Midianites
Jephthah	Gad	Ammonites
Samson	Dan	Philistines
LESSER JUDGES		
Shamgar	Simeon?	Philistines
Tola	Issachar	
Jair	Manasseh (territory of Gilead)	
Ibzan	Asher?	
Elon	Zebulun	
Abdon	Ephraim?	

CHRONOLOGICAL SEQUENCE OF JUDGES
1. Oppression of Cushan-rishathaim and the Edomites: *Othniel.*
2. Oppression of Eglon, king of Moab: *Ehud.*
3. Oppression of the Canaanites—Sisera: *Deborah* and *Barak* (c. 1130 B.C.).
4. Midianite oppression: *Gideon;* kingship of Abimelech; Tola; Jair.
5. Ammonite (and Philistine) oppression: *Jephthah;* Ibzan; Elon; Abdon.
6. Philistine oppression (c. 1100 B.C.): Shamgar; *Samson;* Eli;
7. Samuel (c. 1050 B.C.).

fertile lower reaches and to get as far as the Jordan. The Palestinian tribes, owing to pressure from the Philistines, were unable to help. This was towards the close of the period of Judges (c. 1050 B.C.).

The chieftains of Gilead gathered at Mizpah could find no military leader. Finally they appealed to an outlaw who had been driven from his clan and was now a highwayman in the region of Tob (north Transjordan). *Jephthah* agreed to lead them, on condition of receiving the title of prince (*rosh*). In order to gain time he entered into negotiations with the Ammonites, and all the while was building up an army. Eventually, he turned on the Ammonites and defeated them; in fulfillment of his rash vow, he sacrificed his only daughter (Jgs. 11:31-39). The Ephraimites, who had turned against Jephthah, were driven back across the Jordan.

6. *The Philistine peril.* The Philistines, already strongly established in the Shephelah, had been slowly and methodically expanding. From Ekron and Gath they were spreading into Dan and Judah, while the weakening of Canaanite power had opened up the coastal plains to them. It appears that this expansion did not alarm Judah, Simeon, and Dan at first, and there were only a few isolated instances of resistance. One such who resisted was Shamgar. Another was the last of the "great Judges," *Samson,* the very type of the popular hero.

From Aphek the Philistines began to molest Ephraim and Benjamin. Eli, the priest, exercised a sort of judgeship at Shiloh. The Philistines wanted to get control of Shiloh and Bethel—the religious and political centers—and defeated the Israelites at Ebenezer. Now they had control of the whole mountain region. *Samuel* organized a national resistance, but not with any great measure of success.

5. THE RISE OF THE MONARCHY

1) *The Institution of the Monarchy*

The authority of Samuel was more religious than political. Besides, his sons were unworthy to succeed him and the people did not want them. The Philistine danger was pressing; they were established in the mountains of Ephraim, while the Ammonites had resumed their raids on Gilead. It was felt that a king was needed to unite the people against their enemies. 1 Sm., however, gives two very different traditions of the institution of the monarchy.

THE   1. *The antimonarchist tradition* (1 Sm. 8; 10:17-24;
TRADITIONS   12). Samuel was old and his sons did not walk in his
footsteps; the people demanded a king so that they could be like
other nations. Yahweh assured Samuel that the people rejected not
him but Yahweh. In the name of Yahweh Samuel warned the people
of the price they would have to pay for a king. The people still
persisted, so Yahweh told Samuel to accede to their request. He
assembled the people at Mizpah and proceeded to choose a king
by lot. The lot fell on Saul, son of Kish, of the tribe of Benjamin.
Samuel then made profession of his fidelity as Judge. He showed
how God had always taken care of his people. The demand of the
monarchy was a grave fault; as a sign, Yahweh sent thunder and
heavy rain—in the harvest time! However, Yahweh would not reject
his people despite their fault, if they remained faithful. Samuel
retired from public life after the election of Saul.

2. *The monarchist tradition* (1 Sm. 9; 10:1-16; 11). This time
the narrative is centered on Saul. Samuel is presented as a prophet
(seer) rather than as a Judge, and Saul meets him by chance.
Saul sets out in search of the asses of his father Kish. His servant
advises him to consult the "seer" at Ramah. On the previous day
Yahweh had warned Samuel of Saul's imminent arrival and had
designated him as king. Saul was anointed secretly by Samuel.

The antimonarchist narrative is late; it presupposes sad experience of the failure of the monarchy. The monarchist tradition, on
the other hand, is near the events; its popular style is a gauge of
authenticity. In fact, the monarchy is the natural fruit of the unity
that was being achieved towards the close of the period of Judges,
for unity was imperative in face of the growing Philistine peril.

The last Judge anointed the first king, and this first king has
many of the traits of a Judge. The charismatic nature of this kingship is marked: the king is chosen by God, possessed by his Spirit;
it is this Spirit that moves him to great exploits. A new element is
the recognition by all the tribes of a permanent authority conferred
on the chosen king. Thus appears for the first time the concept of
a national monarchy. This notion was not borrowed from the Canaanites—a multitude of city-states; nor from the Philistines—a league
of "tyrannies." The kingship of Israel was modeled on those of

Ammon, Moab, and Edom, set up shortly before the conquest, and on those of the Aramean kingdoms of Syria. Rather than imitation, it is parallel development among peoples akin in race and but recently sedentarized.

THE REIGN   Saul was proclaimed king by the people of Gilgal about
OF SAUL   1030 B.C. and made his headquarters at Gibeah, four miles north of Jerusalem, where he built a fortress. The Philistines had, apparently, not given much weight to the institution of the monarchy and Saul did not provoke them. Eventually Jonathan, as a token of revolt, overturned a Philistine stele at Gibeah (LXX). The Philistine reaction was immediate: they invaded Benjamin and set up their camp at Michmash. The Israelites hid or fled to Transjordan, while, in Gilgal, Saul tried to collect an army around him. With his troops he went up and camped at Geba, opposite Michmash. After a sortie by Jonathan, panic was sown in the Philistine ranks and they gave way before an Israelite attack.

After the victory of Michmash, Saul took action against the peoples along his frontiers: the Ammonites, Moabites, Edomites, and the Arameans of the north, and built up a standing army. A special action was his campaign against the Amalekites in order to preserve the southern tribes from the raids of these nomads of the Negeb. Saul disobeyed the command of Yahweh conveyed to him by Samuel and was rejected for his disobedience. Separate traditions (1 Sm. 13:8-15; 15:1-31) of Saul's rejection reflect speculation on the problem of how and why the Lord's anointed could be set aside. The tragedy of Saul is that he was unable to choose between obedience to Yahweh, who had chosen him, and the wishes of the people, who had acclaimed him. He sought a compromise. The Prophet intervened to protect the absolute rights of Yahweh against the people and the king. The opposition, inherent in the monarchy, between profane policy and the interests of Yahweh, is already stressed. This strife of king and prophet will occur over and over in the history of the monarchy.

For the appearance of David at the court of Saul we again have two traditions:

1. David is called as a minstrel to the court of Saul and becomes his armor-bearer. As such he accompanies the king to the war

against the Philistines and thus is able to meet the challenge of the Philistine champion (1 Sm. 16:14-23; 17:1-11; 17:32-53).

2. David is a young shepherd unknown to Saul. He comes to visit his brothers in the army just as Goliath is making his challenge (1 Sm. 17:12-30; 17:32-53; 17:55—18:2).

Both traditions merge in the narrative of the single combat; this victory was the beginning of David's rise to fame.

After his rejection Saul was seized by an "evil spirit" (it is obvious, from now on, that Saul is neurotic) and David became his minstrel and *aide-de-camp*. David's successes convinced Saul that this was his rival, and he was moved by an insane desire to destroy him. David was hounded through the wilderness of Judah, until, in desperation, he placed himself beyond Saul's clutches by becoming a vassal of a Philistine prince, Akish, *seren* of Gath, who ceded to him the territory of Ziklag. This gave him the opportunity, by a dangerous double game, of ingratiating himself both with his overlord and the princes of Judah.

Meanwhile, the Philistines decided to move against Saul. They mustered their troops at Aphek. David had deceived Akish so effectively that the suspicions alone of the other Philistine leaders saved him from the decidedly awkward situation of having to take the field against his own people. The Israelites were disastrously defeated at Mt. Gilboa and Saul and his sons were killed. We should not think of Saul as a bad man—rather, he was a sick man, and unfortunate; he is a tragic figure, not without considerable nobility.

Despite the failure of Saul and his defeat it was felt that a king was still the only hope. The men of Judah anointed David king of Hebron (c. 1010 B.C.). The northerners went their own way. Abner, general of Saul, collected the remnants of the broken army in Transjordan and proclaimed Ishbaal (Ishbosheth), son of Saul, king in Mahanaim. There was civil war. Eventually Abner, breaking with Ishbaal, came over to David, but was murdered by Joab, David's right-hand man, who saw that his own position was threatened. Soon Ishbaal too was assassinated and David was left with no rival. He had already been king of Judah for seven years when, at Hebron, he was anointed king of Israel by the elders of Israel. Thus, about the year 1000 B.C., David became king of Judah *and* Israel.

2) *The Reign of David* (*c. 1010-970* B.C.)

By the anointing at Hebron, David became king of Judah and Israel, that is, king of a united kingdom. We do not know very much about his reign even though 2 Sm. is entirely dedicated to it. But this history is more concerned with showing the fate of Jerusalem, which was to become the sanctuary of the Ark of the Covenant, and to fix the succession to the throne of David. (It is really a family history.) Still, we can distinguish the salient points of his reign.

WAR OF INDEPENDENCE   Apparently the Philistines had ignored the king of Judah; but when David was proclaimed king of Judah and Israel they realized the danger and reacted at once. Taking the offensive they occupied Bethlehem and camped in the valley of Rephaim, west of Jerusalem. David organized the resistance from the fortress of Adullam. The war was long, but David eventually drove the invaders back and, pursuing them into their own country, captured Gath. The Philistine power was broken forever, and Philistine mercenaries served in David's royal bodyguard.

Next it was necessary to absorb the foreign islands within the national territory. From the situation under Solomon we gather that David had won possession of Megiddo, Taanach, Bethshan, and the other Canaanite towns. He won over the Gibeonites by delivering up to them the descendants of Saul (the latter had treated them harshly). Then he turned to the Jebusite stronghold of Jerusalem. The capture of Jerusalem was of considerable historical importance: David had won a residence, situated more or less in the center of his kingdom, which was his own personal property; this freed him from the undue influence of any tribe. It was his royal residence and became the religious capital too by the transference of the Ark there.

THE EMPIRE OF DAVID   Once the Philistines had been defeated and the Canaanite cities occupied, the power and importance of David's kingdom had already outstripped that of neighboring states; it became a danger to them. The Ammonites were the first to react, and they found ready allies in the small Aramean states to the north. War was declared. In the first campaign, David's general, Joab, was able to prevent the joining of the Ammonites with

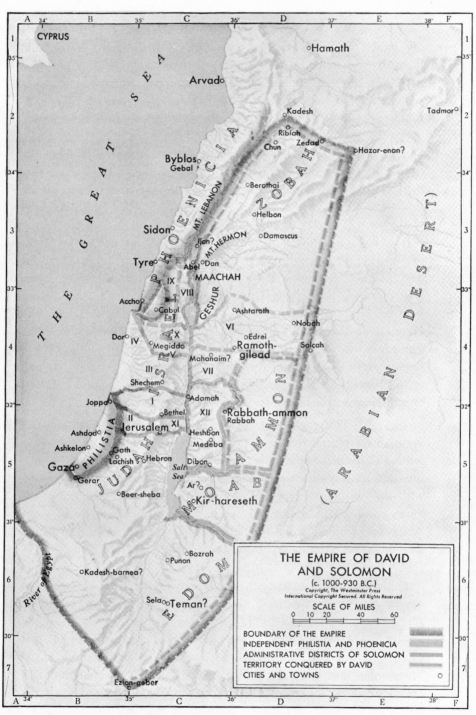

THE EMPIRE OF DAVID
AND SOLOMON
(c. 1000-930 B.C.)
Copyright, The Westminster Press
International Copyright Secured. All Rights Reserved

SCALE OF MILES

0 10 20   40   60

BOUNDARY OF THE EMPIRE
INDEPENDENT PHILISTIA AND PHOENICIA
ADMINISTRATIVE DISTRICTS OF SOLOMON
TERRITORY CONQUERED BY DAVID
CITIES AND TOWNS

the forces of their allies, the Arameans of Beth-rehob, Zobah, and Maacah. The latter retreated at the first onset, and the Ammonites withdrew to their capital of Rabbath-ammon; Joab, who was not prepared for a siege, retired to Jerusalem. Next year the war was resumed. Hadadezer of Zobah had formed an Aramean league which, under the general Shobach, invaded Transjordan. David went against him in person and inflicted a severe defeat on him at Helam; the Ammonites were now isolated. In the third campaign, commanded by Joab, Rabbath-ammon was besieged and taken. (It was during this siege that David was guilty of adultery with Bathsheba and of the murder of her husband.)

It is very difficult to fix the chronology of the other campaigns of David. Edom was annexed to the kingdom, giving Israel access to the Gulf of Aqabah and control of the great caravan route. Moab was subdued, as well as Damascus, and David made an alliance with the king of Hamath. He entered into commercial relations with Hiram I of Tyre. The empire of David included all Palestine (the Philistines, as vassals, held a narrow coastal strip); and in Transjordan: Edom, Moab, and Ammon, and northwards as far as Kadesh on the Orontes, that is, including Damascus and Aram Zobah and terminating on the confines of the allied kingdom of Hamath.

DOMESTIC   The realization of national unity, the creation of a
TROUBLES   centralized and personal power, the considerable extension of his possessions, the introduction of new customs into public life—and all this in a few decades—could not but come into conflict with the old spirit of liberty of the tribes. The national unity was based solely on the personality of the king. And David could never really free himself from the influence of the tribes of the south, and especially from that of the great families of Hebron.

But there was tension within the royal family, now grown large through diplomatic marriages. David's own crime of adultery and murder was the beginning of ills, as foretold by the Prophet Nathan. Amnon's rape of his half-sister Tamar was avenged, in blood, by her full-brother Absalom. Some years later Absalom staged a revolt that came within an ace of overthrowing David. The king had to flee to Transjordan, but there the well-tried and faithful personal troops of David defeated the rebel army. Joab killed Absalom, despite the orders of the king, and then succeeded in stopping the conflict.

David, in coming to terms with the rebels, had appointed Amasa, Absalom's commander, as his own commander-in-chief, entrusting him with the subduing of another, and less serious, revolt that broke out among the Northerners. Again Joab assassinated his rival, and then went on to crush the revolt himself; David accepted the *fait accompli* and Joab remained as general.

THE   At the death of Absalom, Adonijah became heir ap-
SUCCESSION   parent. He was supported by the representatives of the Hebron tradition: Joab, Abiathar, and the princes of Judah. An opposing party led by Nathan, Zadok (the new priest of Jerusalem), and the royal guard supported Solomon, son of Bathsheba. Adonijah gathered his supporters for a banquet at En-rogel; this was interpreted by the others as a token of revolt. Through the intervention of Bathsheba, David was induced to designate Solomon as his successor. Solomon was taken, with royal pomp, to the spring of Gihon and there anointed and proclaimed king. Adonijah and his party submitted.

3) *The Reign of Solomon (c. 970-931* B.C.)

Solomon soon got an opportunity of getting rid of his rival Adonijah and quickly disposed of Joab too; the priest Abiathar was banished. He organized a great religious festival at the old sanctuary of Gibeon, in the midst of which he had a prophetic dream and received magnificent promises; the ceremony ended in Jerusalem.

THE EMPIRE   The death of David had awakened hopes of in-
OF SOLOMON[21]   dependence in some of the conquered territory. The Edomite prince Hadad, who had found refuge in Egypt, returned to Edom where he established an independent principality. Solomon still retained control of the mines and of the caravan route. Among the Arameans a certain Rezon won possession of Damascus and founded a dynasty that was to become the great enemy of Israel. Apart from these losses, however, the empire of David was maintained. The territory properly Israelite was protected by a series of fortresses provided with garrisons, including the new chariot divisions.

ADMINISTRATION   For internal administration Solomon divided the
OF THE KINGDOM   kingdom into twelve prefectures (plus Judah

----

[21]See *ibid.*, pp. 120-23.

which had a special administration). The districts did not correspond to the area of the twelve tribes, but to the months of the year: each had to supply all that was necessary to support the royal household for one month. Labor was also recruited according to the districts. The army was reorganized and modernized and Jerusalem was refortified. The fortresses of Hazor, Megiddo, Beth-horon, and Gezer dominated the traditional route between Syria and Egypt. Baalath and Tamar, southwest of the Dead Sea, guarded the "copper route." We have a good idea of these Solomonic constructions from the walls and the remains of the great stables uncovered at Megiddo.

Solomon did not use his military force to make war; rather, he used it to bolster up his diplomacy. Egypt's support of Hadad was disturbing, so the king sought an alliance with Egypt and married the daughter of Pharaoh (commonly believed to be Psusennes II). Solomon entered into commercial relations with Hiram of Tyre, who had already established friendly relations with David. Solomon imported horses from Cilicia and sold them in Egypt and in return traded Egyptian chariots with Syria. The mineral resources of the Arabah were exploited and a great foundry has been excavated at Ezion-geber on the Gulf of Aqabah. Here, too, with Hiram, he had built a trading fleet; perhaps it was the appearance of these ships along the Arabian coasts that moved the queen of Saba (Sheba), on the southwest of the Arabian peninsula, to visit Solomon. All this trade provided riches that were to become proverbial in the country and also won Solomon renown among the neighboring princes.

THE GREAT   David had hoped to build a temple to Yahweh;
CONSTRUCTIONS   now Solomon was ready to do so. His difficulty was lack of architects and skilled workmen, which were supplied by Hiram. He also provided the timber from the forests of Lebanon (cut by Solomon's men). The logs were floated along the coast, probably to Tell Qasileh on the right bank of the Yarkon (near modern Tel Aviv). The foundation of the Temple was laid in 969 B.C. and the building was completed seven years later. South of the sacred enclosure Solomon built the royal palace, which included the "house of the forest of Lebanon," the throne room, and a special apartment for the daughter of Pharaoh. These great constructions at Jerusalem gave to the kingdom of Solomon a splendor never

before achieved in Israel, but the exactions they entailed in taxes and labor weighed heavily on his subjects and boded ill for the stability and permanence of his kingdom.

THE REVERSE   Solomon's constructions and his love of ostentation
OF THE COIN   were a heavy burden on the kingdom; he was even obliged to cede part of his territory in payment to Hiram. For a king of the Chosen People, Solomon was too immersed in worldly affairs. His vaunted wisdom was mainly profane and his religious sentiment went much less deeply than that of David. The popular prophets who had at first acclaimed him now turned against him, and he was condemned by the Prophet Ahijah of Shiloh.

In internal policy Solomon made no advance in the unification of the kingdom. In fact his favoritism, shown in the special administration of Judah, fomented the existing tension and sowed the seeds of the schism. It is not surprising that there should have been a movement of revolt during his lifetime, nor that it should have come from the house of Ephraim, nor that its leader should be involved in the forced-labor policy, nor that it should have the support of a prophet. The leader of the revolt was the Ephraimite Jeroboam, an organizer of labor, and he was supported by Ahijah. The rebellion was premature; Jeroboam, forced to flee, found refuge with Shishak (Shoshenq) of Egypt, founder of the Twenty-second Dynasty. This reception of the rebel was a bad augury for the kingdom of Israel. Solomon died about 931 B.C.

6. THE DIVIDED MONARCHY

1) The Schism (1 Kgs. 12; 2 Chr. 10)

Rehoboam, son of Solomon, was at once accepted as king by the Judeans. It was necessary, because of the dual monarchy, that he should be accepted by the Israelites too. These held for the primitive concept of royalty: the king, chosen by Yahweh, is acknowledged by his subjects and enters into a pact with them. That is why Rehoboam went to Shechem, the meeting-place of the tribes of the north. These had no objection, in principle, to the king, but they asked that he should lighten the burden of taxes and of work levies imposed by his father. The intransigent arrogance of Rehoboam provoked the rupture and the situation worsened when he got

Adoram, the hated master of works, to intervene; the latter was promptly lynched and the king had to flee to Jerusalem. Rehoboam, with his well-organized army, might yet have put down the revolt, but the Prophet Shemaiah dissuaded him from civil war. The schism was a *fait accompli*.

But it is not altogether correct to term the disintegration of the dual monarchy a "schism." Such a separation is rather a return to the situation that had prevailed since the conquest and it is the union, incomplete and unsteady, achieved under David and Solomon, that is revealed as the exceptional situation in the history of the Chosen People. But there followed a religious schism in the strict sense, and this was the graver aspect. Jerusalem had become the religious capital—with its Temple enshrining the Ark of the Covenant —of the kingdom of David and Solomon, and this religious center insured a certain political unity.

Jeroboam knew this and saw that his people must be won away from allegiance to Jerusalem. This was all the more necessary since the Temple cult was a constant reminder of Yahweh's eternal Covenant with David—and the North had broken with the house of David. Hence Jeroboam set up two official shrines, with an organized cult and priesthood, at opposite ends of his kingdom: Bethel and Dan. Bethel had been a holy place in the time of the patriarchs and Dan was a shrine in the period of Judges. The golden bulls (in 2 Kgs. 12:28 contemptuously called "calves") set in these shrines were not idols; we know from Semitic iconography that these were pedestals upon which the invisible Yahweh was conceived as standing or enthroned—in much the same way that Yahweh was enthroned upon the cherubim in the Temple. Certainly Jeroboam did not wish to change the essential nature of Yahwism, but the bull symbol was too evocative of the fertility cult to be safe, and a breach was open to the infiltration of Canaanite religious practices. This religious schism was the sin of Jeroboam so stigmatized by the orthodox tradition, the "original sin" of Israel.[22]

The period of the divided monarchy is covered by the Books of Kings (from 1 Kgs. 12 onwards) and also, for Judah, by Chronicles (from 2 Chr. 10 onwards). In Kgs. the presentation of the history

---

[22]See Roland de Vaux, *Les Livres des Rois* (BJ) (Paris, 1958[2]), p. 14.

of the kingdoms is synchronized: a king of Israel is dated in terms of the contemporary king of Judah, and the next Judean king is dated by cross reference to the reigning king of Israel. This can be confusing and it has seemed better, in this outline, to take the kingdoms separately. It should also be noted that Kgs. reflects the outlook of the deuteronomical editors of the book,[23] especially with regard to the centralization of the worship in Jerusalem and the removal of local shrines (the "high places"). Hence all the kings of Israel are condemned because of the "original sin" of Jeroboam I; while the religious conduct of the kings of Judah is either condemned outright or praised, with the qualification that "the high places were not removed." Hezekiah and Josiah alone merit unreserved approval. But before going on to treat of the two kingdoms it will be helpful to sketch in the historical background of the divided monarchy.

2) *The Background of the Divided Monarchy*

ASSYRIA   Just at the turn of the eleventh century, under Tiglath-pileser I (c. 1114-1076 B.C.), Assyria was on the verge of becoming a dominant force in Mesopotamia, but circumstances checked her rise to power. The Assyrian resurgence began under Ashur-dan II (934-912 B.C.) and his successors. Ashur-nasir-pal II (883-859 B.C.) overran Upper Mesopotamia and campaigned in northern Syria. He was succeeded by Shalmaneser III (859-824 B.C.) who undertook to complete the work of his father by opening up the commercial routes to the west. In 858 B.C. northern Syria was invaded and devastated and the Phoenicians sent gifts to the conqueror. The states of central Syria were fully alive to the danger that threatened. Hamath and Damascus united and persuaded the neighboring states to join an anti-Assyrian league. Ahab made an important contribution: 2,000 chariots and 10,000 infantry.[24] When Shalmaneser returned in 853 B.C. he was met at Qarqar on the Orontes by a confederacy of eleven kings. The Assyrian king claimed a great victory but, significantly, he did not advance on Hamath and Damascus and it was several years before he was ready to try again. In 841 B.C. Shalmaneser invaded Aramean territory and laid siege to Damascus. Failing to capture the city, he devastated the country and took

[23]See p. 165.
[24]See ANET, pp. 277-79.

tribute from Tyre, Sidon, and Jehu of Israel; the latter is depicted on the black stele of Shalmaneser.[25] Internal troubles, coupled with the pressure of neighboring states, prevented the Assyrians from maintaining control of the west; this situation persisted under the next king, Shamshi-adad V (824-811 B.C.) and under Queen Semiramis who was regent during the minority of Adad-nirari III (811-783 B.C.). The latter resumed the campaigns against the Aramean states and about the year 802 B.C. Benhadad II of Damascus and Jehoahaz of Israel had to pay tribute. Once again, however, the Assyrians were unable to consolidate their gains. The kings Shalmaneser IV (783-773 B.C.), Ashur-dan III (773-754 B.C.), and Ashur-nirari V (754-745 B.C.) were scarcely able to maintain a foothold west of the Euphrates, for Assyria was not only weakened by internal dissensions but also was menaced by the kingdom of Urartu, in the Armenian mountains, which was expanding to the west and east.

Succeeding to the weak kings who had been unable to prevent the expansion of Urartu, and who had lost control of Syria, Tiglath-pileser III (745-727 B.C.) is the real founder of the Assyrian empire. He defeated the Chaldeans (Babylonians) in the south and broke the power of Urartu in the north. In a series of campaigns, begun in 738 B.C., he gained dominion over Syria: "Menahem of Samaria" paid tribute. Later, Rezin of Damascus and Pekah of Israel joined in a league against Assyria; in 734 B.C. Tiglath-pileser attacked. First he moved along the coast and subdued the Philistine cities; then turning against Israel he devastated Galilee and Gilead and deported their inhabitants. This deportation of peoples was calculated policy: patriotic sentiment and a spirit of rebellion would be dulled in a population that had been uprooted from its homeland. In 732 B.C. Damascus fell; Rezin was executed and many of his people were deported. Israel too would have been destroyed altogether had not the pro-Assyrian party got rid of Pekah and put Hoshea on the throne. Judah became a vassal of Assyria.

Shortly after Shalmaneser V (727-722 B.C.) had succeeded to the throne, Hoshea got involved in another intrigue against Assyria;

---

[25]See J. B. Pritchard, *The Ancient Near East in Pictures* (Princeton University Press, 1954), plate 355. Henceforth this book will be abbreviated ANEP. See ANET, pp. 280 f.

the Assyrian king acted at once. In 724 B.C. Hoshea was arrested and Samaria was besieged; it held out for three years, but fell to Sargon II (722-705 B.C.) in 721 B.C. After this Sargon was fully occupied in the east, particularly against Marduk-apal-iddina (Merodach-baladan) who had won control of Babylon in 721 B.C. and was not finally driven out of it by Sargon until 710 B.C. In the previous year (711 B.C.) the Assyrian king had put down a revolt in the west and had taken Ashdod.

Sargon was succeeded by his son Sennacherib (705-681 B.C.) who was at once faced with rebellion at both extremities of his empire. Marduk-apal-iddina had again taken possession of Babylon and had set himself up as king (703 B.C.). While Sennacherib was trying to dislodge him, the western provinces, supported by Egypt, rose in revolt—Hezekiah of Judah played a prominent part. Sennacherib defeated Marduk-apal-iddina in 703 B.C. and devastated the Chaldean region. Then, in 701 B.C., he was free to move into Syria. His own account of the campaign[26] tells how he was called into Palestine by a revolt. The ringleaders were the king of Sidon, the king of Ashkelon, the inhabitants of Ekron, and Hezekiah of Judah. In four operations Sennacherib proceeded first against the cities of the North and subdued Tyre; then he moved against Ashkelon; next he dealt with Ekron whose king Padi had been handed over by his subjects to Hezekiah and was kept prisoner in Jerusalem; lastly came the turn of the king of Judah. The country was overrun, forty-six fortified towns were taken and Hezekiah was shut up in Jerusalem "like a bird in a cage." Sennacherib did not take the city but imposed a heavy tribute and had the king of Ekron restored to his throne.

After this Sennacherib was fully occupied for some time in the east where Babylon was in open rebellion; the rebellion was put down in 689 B.C. It seems that about this time Hezekiah, with promise of support from Egypt, had again rebelled. The Assyrian king moved to the west about 688 B.C.; at this time Lachish was taken and Jerusalem was besieged.[27] Tirhakah of Egypt came to Hezekiah's aid and Sennacherib intercepted him. The outcome of the encounter is unknown. But Jerusalem was not taken because

---

[26]See ANET, pp. 287 f.
[27]The two-campaign theory has been adopted. See p. 62.

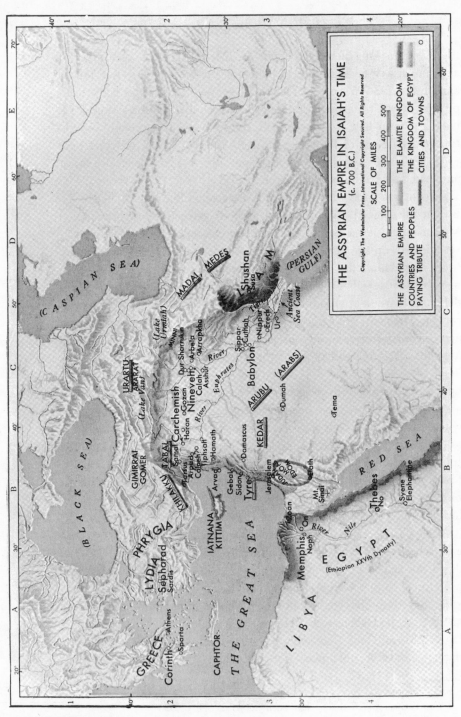

THE ASSYRIAN EMPIRE IN ISAIAH'S TIME
(c. 700 B.C.)

Copyright, The Westminster Press, International Copyright Secured. All Rights Reserved

SCALE OF MILES

0   100 200 300 400 500

THE ASSYRIAN EMPIRE   THE ELAMITE KINGDOM
COUNTRIES AND PEOPLES   THE KINGDOM OF EGYPT
PAYING TRIBUTE   CITIES AND TOWNS

the Assyrian army was decimated by an epidemic (2 Kgs. 19:35), and also because Sennacherib's presence was required in Assyria (2 Kgs. 19:7).

Sennacherib was assassinated in 681 B.C. and was succeeded by his son Esarhaddon (681-669 B.C.). He campaigned in Egypt where he defeated Tirhakah and captured Memphis (671 B.C.). Soon Tirhakah rebelled and Esarhaddon's son and successor, Ashurbanipal (669-632 B.C.), crushed the rebellion (c. 667 B.C.). In 663 B.C. the Assyrians came again and destroyed the ancient capital of Thebes.

The Assyrian Empire had reached its apogee under Ashurbanipal, but its decline was extremely rapid. Egypt was too far away to be effectively controlled and in 650 B.C. the Assyrian garrisons were evacuated. The reason is that Assyria herself was menaced by a formidable invasion of Indo-European peoples: Medes, Cimmerians, and Scythians. There was internal strife also. In 652 B.C. the king's brother, Shamash-shum-ukin, led a revolt in Babylon and won the support of the Elamites; Babylon was taken in 648 B.C. by Ashurbanipal who then turned on Elam. The date of Ashurbanipal's death is uncertain, but 632 B.C. is probable. The greatest of the Assyrian kings, and almost the last of them, he is particularly remembered for his great library, discovered in excavations at Nineveh, which sheltered, among other copies of ancient Babylonian myths and epics, the famous creation and flood stories.[28]

Ashur-etil-ilani (632-629 B.C.) had a short reign and was succeeded by Sin-shar-ishkun (629-612 B.C.). In 626 B.C. the Chaldean prince Nabopolassar took possession of Babylon. This was the beginning of the Neo-Babylonian Empire. Soon Assyria was fighting for her life against the Babylonians and Medes. Until 614 B.C. the struggle was indecisive, but in that year the Medes took Ashur, the ancient Assyrian capital. In 612 B.C. Nineveh itself fell to Nabopolassar and the Medes and Sin-shar-ishkun perished in the utter destruction of his city. This was the decisive stroke. The Assyrians, under Ashur-uballit II (612-606 B.C.) made a last stand at Haran, but in 610 B.C. they were driven out and the king fled, with the remnant of his forces, west of the Euphrates.

---

[28]See ANET, pp. 60-99.

Meanwhile, Egypt had taken a hand. Psammetichus I thought it politic to maintain two rival powers in Mesopotamia, and intervened on the side of Assyria; some Egyptian forces were dispatched in 616 B.C. In 609 B.C. the next pharaoh, Neco II, arrived at Carchemish with a large force. He and Ashur-uballit attempted to retake Haran, but failed. Neco retired west of the Euphrates and set up his headquarters at Riblah. By 606 B.C. the Assyrian Empire was definitely at an end, and in 605 B.C. Nebuchadnezzar crossed the river and crushingly defeated the Egyptians at Carchemish; news of the death of his father prevented him from exploiting his success to the full.

EGYPT   In Egypt the Twenty-first Dynasty was overthrown (c. 945 B.C.) by a Libyan named Shishak (Shoshenq) who founded the Twenty-second Dynasty (945-725 B.C.) and made Bubastis his capital. Shishak (945-925 B.C.) had granted Jeroboam political asylum; but then, after the political schisms, he had invaded and devastated Palestine. He had hopes of re-establishing the Egyptian Empire in Asia, but internal weakness prevented him even from maintaining control in Palestine. It was centuries before Egypt would again intervene.

The Twenty-fifth Dynasty was founded (c. 715 B.C.) by Piankhi, an Ethiopian king. Egypt was keenly aware of the strength and threat of Assyria and was anxious that the Assyrian advance should not reach her own borders. Consequently it became deliberate Egyptian policy to undermine Assyrian authority in Palestine; and Egyptian help, or promise of help, stands behind the anti-Assyrian leagues of the future. But Egypt was never again more than a broken reed.

The Pharaoh Shabako (710-696 B.C.) supported the revolt that led to the Assyrian invasion of 701 B.C.; an Egyptian army went to the relief of Ekron but was defeated. The next king was Shebteko (696-695 B.C.), but his brother Tirhakah became coregent and effective ruler in 690 B.C.; the latter fomented another rebellion in Palestine, but when he marched to Hezekiah's aid (c. 688 B.C.) he was checked, and probably defeated, by Sennacherib. In 671 B.C. Esarhaddon invaded Egypt and occupied Memphis. Tirhakah escaped and began an attempt to regain his throne. He was once more defeated in another Assyrian campaign under Ashurbanipal (c. 667 B.C.). This time a prince called Neco was set in his place by the Assyrians. But Tirhakah's successor, Tanutamun, continued the resistance, and in a third Assyrian campaign (663 B.C.) Thebes, the ancient capital, was destroyed. This was the end of the Twenty-fifth Dynasty.

Neco was succeeded by his son Psammetichus I (663-609 B.C.) who, during the period of Assyria's final decline, became independent and founded the Twenty-sixth Dynasty. When he realized that the Medes and Babylonians were threatening to destroy Assyria, he decided to intervene on the side of the latter; his policy was the shrewd one of maintaining rival powers in Mesopotamia. He sent troops to the east in 616 B.C., but it was too late to save Assyria. His son Neco II (609-593 B.C.) marched with a large army to Carchemish on the Euphrates in 609 B.C. and supported Ashuruballit in an attempt to retake Haran. (At Megiddo, Josiah, who had intercepted Neco, was defeated and killed.) The assault on Haran failed and Neco set up his headquarters at Riblah in Syria; the Egyptian army remained stationed west of the Euphrates. In 605 B.C. Nebuchadnezzar, prince-royal, defeated the Egyptians at Carchemish and then, following their retreat, struck again at Hamath. In 601 B.C. Nebuchadnezzar (now king) moved on Egypt and was met at the frontier by Neco; a fierce pitched battle was fought and the Babylonians, if not defeated, at least were forced to retire.

The next pharaohs, Psammetichus II (593-588 B.C.) and his son Apries (Hophra) (588-566 B.C.), resumed the policy of stirring up and supporting revolt in Palestine. In 690 B.C. Psammetichus appeared in Palestine and, later, Apries prevailed on Tyre and Sidon to join a league against Babylon. During the siege of Jerusalem in 587 B.C., Pharaoh appeared in the Shephelah with an Egyptian army, but was quickly forced to retire. All that the Egyptians could now do was to grant shelter to refugees from a devastated Judah. In 569 B.C. Amasis succeeded Apries, and in 568 B.C. Nebuchadnezzar invaded Egypt. The details of this campaign are obscure, but it marked the end of conflict between Babylon and Egypt.

DAMASCUS Already during the reign of Solomon an Aramean named Rezon seized Damascus and made himself king. With the breakup of the empire of Solomon, the position of Damascus became much stronger. Soon we find Baasha of Israel making a treaty with Ben-hadad I of Damascus; then we see the same Ben-hadad harass northern Galilee at the request of Asa of Judah. During the reign of Ahab, Ben-hadad II first invaded Israel and then suffered a shattering defeat. Thereupon the two erstwhile foes became allies against a common Assyrian peril. They formed part of a coalition which met, and checked, Shalmaneser III at Qarqar on the Orontes in 853 B.C. But once the immediate danger was over, war between Damascus and Israel was resumed and dragged on.

Ben-hadad II was assassinated (c. 842 B.C.) by Hazael. In 841 B.C. Shalmaneser III laid siege to Damascus, but when the Assyrian army had retired Hazael turned on Jehu who had paid tribute to Shalmaneser. Jehu lost the whole of Transjordan, and his son Jehoahaz became a vassal of Hazael's successor, Ben-hadad III. Aramean forces pushed along the coast as far as Philistia. However, Damascus was crushed by Adad-nirari III (c. 802 B.C.); its grip on Israel was broken, and Jeroboam turned the tables by annexing some Aramean territory.

The last king of Damascus was Rezin (c. 740-732 B.C.). He and Pekah of Israel became leaders of a coalition against Assyria. In an attempt to force the hand of Ahaz they invaded Judah; their intention was to place an Aramean, the "son of Tabeel" (Is. 7:6) on the throne of Judah. Tiglath-pileser moved quickly against the coalition. In 732 B.C. Damascus was taken and destroyed, Rezin was executed, and a large part of the population was deported. It was the end—as it soon would be the end for Israel.

BABYLON   During the reign of Sin-shar-ishkun, the Chaldean prince Nabopolassar defeated the Assyrians at Babylon and made himself king there in 626 B.C.; this was the foundation of the Neo-Babylonian Empire. Nabopolassar (626-605 B.C.), with Cyaxares, king of the Medes, utterly destroyed the Assyrian Empire. He was succeeded by his capable son Nebuchadnezzar (605-562 B.C.) who had already defeated Assyria's Egyptian allies. In 604 B.C. Nebuchadnezzar was in the Philistine plain and destroyed Ashkelon. It was probably at this time that Jehoiakim became a vassal of the Babylonian king (2 Kgs. 24:1). In 601 B.C. Nebuchadnezzar moved on Egypt and was met by Neco in a pitched battle; the Babylonians were obliged to retire. Jehoiakim promptly rebelled, but Nebuchadnezzar was not ready to take decisive action until 598 B.C. Jehoiakim had been succeeded by his son Jehoiachin, who surrendered after a siege of three months. The king and the leading citizens were deported to Babylon, and the king's uncle, Mattaniah (Zedekiah), was installed in his place. The Babylonians were back again in 588 B.C. to quell a revolt in which Zedekiah was implicated. Jerusalem was besieged—a siege that was momentarily raised when the Babylonians went to intercept the Egyptian army of Apries—and fell in 587 B.C. The city was destroyed and a group of the population was deported to Babylon; this was the end of the Davidic monarchy. The assassination of Gedaliah, the governor appointed by the Babylonians, seems to have been the occasion of another deportation in 582 B.C.

Nebuchadnezzar was able to maintain his position of successor to Assyria despite the challenge of his former ally, the Median King Cyaxares, who built up a powerful state with its capital at Ecbatana. Nebuchadnezzar campaigned in the west in 585 B.C. when he laid siege to Tyre (which did not fall); in 582 B.C., when he deported some of the inhabitants of Judah; and in 568 B.C. when he invaded Egypt. With his death, Babylonian power declined rapidly. This later phase of Babylonian history forms the background of the Exile.

Throughout the whole of the monarchy, the history, first of the united kingdom, and then of Israel and of Judah, reflects the decline and rise of the great powers. David achieved his remarkable success and Solomon was able to maintain his position because no foreign influence bore on Palestine. This situation came to an end soon after the death of Solomon and aggravated the weakness of the divided monarchy. Assyria began to harass and hamper the two small kingdoms, and destroyed Israel at last. Assyria and Babylon dominated the last century of Judah and the latter brought it, too, to an end. Any measure of prosperity or success in Israel and Judah was gleaned during brief moments of decline in the East, and the great armies were back again, without fail, to snatch away whatever little had been gained. Assyria and Babylon were the scourges of God, to punish his ungrateful and stubborn people; but God would also raise up another nation to be the instrument of his mercy.

7. THE KINGDOM OF ISRAEL

A feature of the monarchy in Israel is lack of stability: no royal family remains in power for long, and a change of ruler usually comes as a result of an army revolt. To indicate this lack of continuity we speak of different "dynasties."

1) Dynasty of Jeroboam I

JEROBOAM I (931-910 B.C.): The Northern tribes gathered at She-
1 KGS. 12:20—14:20;   chem proclaimed Jeroboam, who had
CF. 2 CHR. 13   returned from his refuge in Egypt,
king of Israel. He set up his capital at Tirzah (Tell el-Far'ah, northeast of Shechem). To counteract the unifying influence of Jerusalem he set up national shrines at Bethel and Dan and organized his own cult and priesthood. Israel comprised, in principle, the ten Northern tribes but, in fact, Benjamin was divided between the two kingdoms. We know scarcely anything of the reign of Jeroboam except that there was continual friction between himself and Rehoboam of Judah and that Abijah inflicted a heavy defeat on Jeroboam near Bethel.

NADAB (910-909 B.C.): Son of Jeroboam, Nadab was the victim
1 KGS. 15:25-32   of a conspiracy. Thus ended the First
Dynasty.

2) Dynasty of Baasha

BAASHA (909-886 B.C.): Baasha, head of the conspiracy against
1 KGS. 15:33—16:7   Nadab, became king, and, to remove pos-
sible rivals, exterminated the family of Jeroboam. He was an energetic leader who drove Asa of Judah back within the limits of his own kingdom, and took and fortified Ramah, six miles north of Jerusalem. Asa appealed to Ben-hadad I of Damascus who attacked northern Israel and won some territory there. This led to the downfall of the Dynasty of Baasha.

ELAH (886-885 B.C.): Elah, son of Baasha, reigned for less than
1 KGS. 16:8-14   two years; he was assassinated by Zimri,
officer of a chariot division.

ZIMRI (885 B.C.—SEVEN DAYS): This was a period of anarchy.
1 KGS. 16:15-22   Zimri exterminated the family of
Baasha. The army did not accept the *coup d'état,* and Omri, commander of the army, was declared king and besieged Zimri in Tirzah; Zimri died in the royal palace which he had set on fire. Omri was opposed by another competitor, Tibni, and there was civil war for four years. Omri triumphed in the end.

3) Dynasty of Omri

OMRI (885-874 B.C.): The reign of Omri includes the four years
1 KGS. 16:23-28 of struggle with Tibni. After this he set
about repairing the damage caused by the civil war. He changed
his capital from Tirzah to Samaria, which remained the capital of
Israel until the destruction of the kingdom. The change was a significant one, comparable to the selection of Jerusalem by David.
Though the Bible tells us little about him, Omri was regarded by
the Assyrians as the founder of the Northern Kingdom which they
continued to name *bit Humri*, the "house of Omri." We learn, inci-
dentally, of an unfortunate war with Damascus in which Omri lost
some territory; apart from this his reign was crowned with success.
He put an end to strife with Judah, where Asa was reigning, and
was able to re-establish his dominion over Moab. He entered into
a commercial alliance with the Phoenicians, and his son Ahab married
Jezebel, daughter of Ethbaal, king of Tyre.

An important factor of this period is the rebirth of Assyrian power
under Ashur-nasir-pal II.

AHAB (874-853 B.C.): Ahab succeeded his father and had a bril-
1 KGS. 16:29—22:40 liant reign. His alliance with Tyre proved
advantageous, and the wealth of his kingdom is manifested by the
great constructions at Samaria, Megiddo, and Jericho. The army
was reorganized and a powerful chariot division was stationed at
Megiddo. Unfortunately, this material prosperity was accompanied
by religious decadence, chiefly due to the influence of Jezebel who
was fanatically attached to the Phoenician cult. The worship of Baal
was introduced into Samaria and the faithful of Yahweh were persecuted. The Yahwistic reaction was represented by the extraordinary
figure of Elijah the Tishbite (from Tishbe in Gilead).

Ahab concluded a treaty with Jehoshaphat of Judah, which was
sealed by the marriage of Athaliah (daughter or sister of Ahab)
with Jehoram, son of Jehoshaphat. The alliance of Israel with Phoenicia
affected the commercial interests of the Arameans, and the king of
Damascus, Ben-hadad II, tried to destroy the growing power of
Israel. He invaded Israel and besieged Samaria, but was driven back
with losses. The following year he tried again and this time was
disastrously defeated at Aphek, east of Lake Tiberias. Ben-hadad
was captured and Ahab concluded a treaty with him.

This accord between the two states was dictated by a common danger: Assyrian expansion under Shalmaneser III. An anti-Assyrian league was formed to which Ahab made an important contribution: 2,000 chariots and 10,000 infantry. Shalmaneser was met in 853 B.C. at Qarqar on the Orontes by the confederacy of eleven kings, and though he claimed a great victory he did not press his alleged advantage. Once the immediate danger was past the league broke up. Ben-hadad infringed the treaty of Aphek, and Ahab declared war; with Jehoshaphat of Judah he moved against the frontier town of Ramoth-gilead. Ahab was mortally wounded in the engagement. Despite this reverse the reign of Ahab had been very successful, at least materially. The old religion was saved only by the efforts of Elijah and Elisha.

AHAZIAH (853-852 B.C.):   Ahab was succeeded by his son Ahazi-
1 KGS. 22:52—2 KGS. 1:18   ah who reigned one year only. Mesha of Moab rebelled during this reign. (The mission of Elijah was undertaken under Ahab and Ahaziah.)

JEHORAM (852-841 B.C.):   Ahaziah was succeeded by his brother
2 KGS. 3:1—10:17   Jehoram. He attacked Moab from the south with the aid of the king of Judah (probably Jehoram) and the king of Edom. The expedition was at first successful, but was later checked at Kir-hareseth, the Moabite capital. Mesha, in his stele, claims a victory.[29] This reverse led to the defection of Edom; and, in Judah, Libnah was lost to the Philistines. In Damascus Ben-hadad II was assassinated by Hazael who seized power. Jehoram profited from the disturbances at Damascus to take Ramoth-gilead and war broke out between himself and Hazael. In an encounter at Ramoth-gilead, Jehoram was wounded and retired to Jezreel where his cousin Ahaziah of Judah came to visit him. This was the moment that Elisha chose to bring the dynasty of Omri to an end.

Jehu was commander of the army at Ramoth-gilead; there he was anointed by a disciple of Elisha and was proclaimed king by the army. He set out in haste for Jezreel and killed Jehoram, who had come out to meet him; Ahaziah fled, but was overtaken and wounded at Ibleam and died at Megiddo. Jehu entered Jezreel and had Jezebel, the queen-mother, thrown from a window. He

---

[29]See *ibid.*, pp. 320 f.

THE KINGDOMS OF ISRAEL AND
JUDAH IN ELIJAH'S TIME
(c. 860 B.C.)

Copyright, The Westminster Press
International Copyright Secured. All Rights Reserved.

SCALE OF MILES

0 10 20   40   60

KINGDOM OF ISRAEL
KINGDOM OF JUDAH
KINGDOM OF AMMON
KINGDOM OF ARAM (SYRIA)
PHILISTINE AND
PHOENICIAN TERRITORY
CITIES AND TOWNS   o

seemed mad with blood and massacred all about him: many func-
tionaries of the king of Judah, who were in Jezreel, were killed;
the family of Omri was wiped out; the prophets and worshipers of
Baal were massacred and the temple of Baal at Samaria was destroyed. Thus Jehu exterminated the dynasty of Omri and destroyed
too the religion of Baal that was the sad fruit of that dynasty.

4) Dynasty of Jehu

JEHU (841-814 B.C.): We know that Jehu was king in or before
2 KGS. 10:28-36   841 B.C., because he figures on the black
stele of Shalmaneser III, dated 841 B.C. When in that year Damascus
was attacked by Shalmaneser III, Jehu inaugurated his new policy
by not only not helping Hazael but by sending tribute to the invader.
In 839 B.C. Shalmaneser returned, but Damascus still held out; the
Assyrian king retired and domestic troubles held his attention. Hazael
then turned on Israel. He won possession of Transjordan as far as
the Arnon. Phoenicia and Judah had already broken with Jehu. At
his death the kingdom of Israel had dwindled to a third of its size.

JEHOAHAZ (814-798 B.C.): Son of Jehu, Jehoahaz found himself
2 KGS. 13:1-9   in difficulties with Hazael. Elisha remained faithful to the Dynasty of Jehu and his influence at court
was great; he foresaw the difficulties and encouraged king and people.
About the year 802 B.C. Adad-nirari III intervened in Syria; Damascus
was devastated and Israel had to pay tribute. But the Assyrians had
to retire owing to troubles in the east.

JEHOASH (798-783 B.C.): Jehoash was the son of Jehoahaz. Da-
2 KGS. 13:10-13   mascus had been weakened by the Assyrian invasion. Jehoash defeated the Arameans in three battles and
won back the lost territory. Under his reign Israel slowly returned
to its old prosperity, and there was a parallel renaissance in Judah.
Jehoash had a clash with Amaziah of Judah at Bethshemesh and
went on to take Jerusalem. (The mission of Elisha was undertaken
under Jehoram and Jehoash.)

JEROBOAM II (783-743 B.C.): The long reign of this able prince
2 KGS. 14:23-29   gave Israel the illusion of a return
to Solomonic times. The Bible has not much to say of him; it is
certain, however, that his reign marked the apogee of Israel. Ex-

cavations at Samaria and Megiddo, as well as the Books of Amos and Hosea, illustrate the prosperity of the kingdom. All the territory of Israel was free from foreign influence and Judah was an ally, if not indeed a tributary state; trade and commerce flourished in both kingdoms. For the first time, however, the "social question" emerged: the wealth was in the hands of a few and the mass of the people lived in misery. Amos paints a vivid picture of the state of affairs. (The Prophets Amos and Hosea; the latter continued his mission under the successors of Jeroboam.)

ZECHARIAH (743 B.C.):   The reign of Jeroboam II was followed
2 KGS. 15:8-12   by a period of anarchy. His son Zechariah
remained on the throne for six months only; he was assassinated by Shallum. This is the end of the Dynasty of Jehu. A period of anarchy followed.

SHALLUM (743 B.C.):   Shallum reigned for one month only. His
2 KGS. 15:13-16   rival, Menahem of Tirzah—a representative
of the pro-Assyrian party—disposed of him and seized power.

5) Dynasty of Menahem

MENAHEM (743-738 B.C.):   Menahem displayed all the cruelty of
2 KGS. 15:17-22   the Assyrians towards his rivals. He
submitted to Tiglath-pileser III, paying him a rich tribute, and was recognized by him.

The development of history is now dominated by the reawakening of Assyria: Tiglath-pileser III (745-727 B.C.) is the real founder of the Assyrian Empire. In the Bible he is called Pul; from Assyro-Babylonian documents we know that he took the Babylonian throne and ruled there under the name Pulu. In 738 B.C. he gained control over Syria; in that year "Menahem of Samaria," with a number of other kings, paid tribute. In order to pay this tribute Menahem had heavily taxed his nobles and as a pro-Assyrian he had lost the support of the people. On the testimony of the Prophet Hosea it seems that his reign was marked by the strife of pro-Assyrian and pro-Egyptian parties.

PEKAHIAH (738-737 B.C.):   Menahem was succeeded by his son
2 KGS. 15:23-26   Pekahiah who reigned only two years.
He was assassinated by Pekah. This ended the Dynasty of Menahem.

PEKAH (737-732 B.C.):   Pekah was the son of Remaliah, general
2 KGS. 15:27-31   of Pekahiah; he was an anti-Assyrian. His
first act was to enter into alliance with Damascus, for Rezin of
Damascus had seen the need for an anti-Assyrian league. The two
kings tried to win over Jotham of Judah, but without success. Alliance
with Judah was important because it would place the league in
immediate contact with Egypt. Thus Rezin and Pekah decided to
attack Judah; they would overthrow the reigning dynasty and put
on the throne a certain "son of Tabeel," an Aramean. Jotham died
and his son, Ahaz, had to bear the brunt of this, the Syro-Ephraimite
war. Meanwhile, support for the league had been growing. It now
included Tyre, Sidon, Gaza, Philistia, Edom, and the queen of the
Arabs. Ahaz was defeated by the Syro-Ephraimites and was besieged
in Jerusalem; he appealed to Tiglath-pileser III. The year was 734 B.C.
and the Assyrian king was probably already on the march against
the league. Aram and Israel formed the heart of the league, and
so the Assyrian king decided to isolate them from actual and potential
supporters. To prevent any interference from Egypt he subdued
Philistia; he took Gaza, whose king, Hanun, fled to Egypt. Tiglath-
pileser then turned on Israel; he devastated Galilee and Gilead
and deported the inhabitants. In 733 B.C. he campaigned against
Rezin who put up a fierce resistance; but in 732 B.C. Damascus fell:
Rezin was executed and his people deported. Israel too would have
been destroyed altogether, but the pro-Assyrian party overthrew Pekah
and placed Hoshea on the throne.

HOSHEA (732-724 B.C.):   Israel was now reduced to Samaria. The
2 KGS. 17:1-4   conquered territory, whose inhabitants
had been deported, was divided into three Assyrian provinces: Megiddo, Dor, and Gilead.

In 727 B.C. Tiglath-pileser III died; when his son Shalmaneser,
governor of Phoenicia, went to take possession of the throne, the
anti-Assyrian party was given a new lease of life. But Shalmaneser V
(726-722 B.C.) was recognized as king throughout the empire. The
Phoenician cities, however, had rebelled. Shalmaneser besieged Tyre
but could not take it; during the siege (c. 725 B.C.), Hoshea of
Samaria paid the annual tribute. Soon, however, the king came to
hear that Hoshea was conspiring with Egypt; he acted at once.

In 724 B.C. Hoshea was arrested and Samaria was besieged; Samaria held out for nearly three years. In 722 B.C. Shalmaneser V died and was succeeded by Sargon II (722-705 B.C.). In 721 B.C. Samaria fell to Sargon. The population was deported, in stages, beginning with the ruling class. The mass of the people, some 27,290 according to Sargon,[30] was deported to Upper Mesopotamia and there lost their identity. Peoples from other regions were brought in and settled in their place and the colonization of Samaria continued during the reign of Sargon and his successors. These colonists brought their own religions, but accepted Yahweh as a local deity; the Israelites who were left became lost in the midst of this pagan syncretism. After the fall of Samaria the destiny of Yahwism was centered on Judah alone.

8. THE KINGDOM OF JUDAH

In sharp contrast to Israel, the principle of Davidic succession was rigidly adhered to in Judah. While kings of Judah were sometimes assassinated, the rightful heir automatically came to the throne; there was no question of overthrowing the line of David.

REHOBOAM (931-913 B.C.):   On the death of Solomon, his son
1 KGS. 14:21-31; 2 CHR. 10-12   Rehoboam was at once recognized as king of Judah. He failed to be proclaimed king of Israel; in fact he precipitated the schism. Just at this time Palestine became a target for Egyptian expansion. Shishak (Shoshenq), founder of the Twenty-second Dynasty—who had granted asylum to Jeroboam—invaded Judah; Rehoboam had to surrender the treasure of his capital. It appears that the Egyptian expedition traversed the whole country, because a stele with the name of this Pharaoh was found in Megiddo. The Egyptians did not retain control over Palestine. Rehoboam built a line of fortresses along his frontiers. Apart from the Egyptian exaction his reign seems to have been prosperous. His religious conduct is condemned.

ABIJAM (913-911 B.C.):   Abijam succeeded his father. The enmity
1 KGS. 15:1-8; 2 CHR. 13   between the two kingdoms broke out in open hostility. Abijam inflicted a crushing defeat on Jeroboam I

---

[30]See *ibid.*, pp. 284 f.

at Zemaraim near Bethel and Judah won control of all the territory of Benjamin. His religious conduct is condemned.

ASA (911-870 B.C.): Asa lost to Baasha the territory
1 KGS. 15:9-24; 2 CHR. 14-16 that Abijam had won. He had to face a serious incursion of nomads from the Negeb, but he defeated them. When Baasha had taken and fortified Ramah, six miles north of Jerusalem, Asa appealed to Ben-hadad I of Damascus and persuaded him to break his alliance with Baasha. The latter had to abandon his conflict with Asa who promptly took Ramah and fortified Geba and Mizpah. This recourse to foreigners was a grave error; yet the religious conduct of Asa is praised—though he did not remove the "high places." He became ill towards the end of his reign.

JEHOSHAPHAT (870-848 B.C.): Jehoshaphat was already coregent
1 KGS. 22:41-51; 2 CHR. 17-20 during the illness of his father. He had friendly relations with Ahab of Israel, and his son, Jehoram, married Athaliah, the daughter (or sister) of Ahab. Kgs. and Chr. each shows the reign of Jehoshaphat in a different light, though both present him as a sincere Yahwist who continued the tradition of Asa; but the "high places" were not removed.

1. Kgs. presents his reign as unfortunate. He took part in the expedition against Ramoth-gilead in which Ahab was killed. Even before this he may have been one of the league of kings which met the Assyrians at Qarqar. He had control of Edom and Eziongeber, but his fleet, which he had built for trade with Ophir, was destroyed in port. If the "king of Judah" who took part in the expedition against Mesha is Jehoshaphat, and not his son Jehoram, we have another unfortunate episode.

2. Chr. on the other hand, gives more space to the Yahwism of the king and also paints his reign as prosperous and fortunate. He won control over Edom and victoriously countered an invasion of Maonites supported by Moabites and Edomites; he won tribute from the Philistines and the Arabs. In internal administration he organized the kingdom militarily and established a judiciary. He set up a commission, composed of officials and Levites, to instruct the people in the Torah.

It seems we can reconcile these accounts by supposing that, if Jehoshaphat shared in the misfortune of Israel in joint ventures, he met with success when acting on his own. His gravest error was the introduction of an Omrite princess into the dynasty of David; this was to have serious consequences in the dynastic, religious, and political fields.

JEHORAM (848-841 B.C.): The son of Jehoshaphat, who had mar-
2 KGS. 8:16-24; 2 CHR. 21   ried Athaliah, Jehoram was an anti-
Yahwist and permitted the cult of Baal. He took part with Joram of Israel in an unsuccessful expedition against Mesha of Moab. As a result Edom became independent and Libnah was lost to the Philistines. His religious conduct is condemned.

AHAZIAH (841 B.C.): Ahaziah was the son of Jehoram. He joined
2 KGS. 8:25—9:29;   Joram of Israel in an expedition against
2 CHR. 22:1-9   Ramoth-gilead and was killed by order of
Jehu. His religious conduct is condemned.

ATHALIAH (841-835 B.C.): On the death of Ahaziah, his mother
2 KGS. 11;   Athaliah seized power. She was able
2 CHR. 22:10—23:21   to do this in virtue of her official posi-
tion as *gebirah* or "Grand Lady"—a position held by the queen-mother. She began her reign by massacring all the royal family, a necessary measure if she was to keep the throne. Fortunately for Judah, the sister of Ahaziah, wife of the high priest Jehoiada, was able to rescue her little nephew, Joash, the infant son of Ahaziah.

It was a disastrous reign for the religion of Yahweh. The worshipers of Baal who had escaped the suppression of Jehu found refuge at the court of Judah, and Baal had his temple in Jerusalem, served by the priest Mattan. The Temple of Yahweh was allowed to stand, more or less without interference. Both religious and national sentiment was opposed to Athaliah but, in view of the principle of Davidic succession, there seemed to be no way out of the impasse—there was no heir of David. However, unknown to the people, the young Joash was growing up in the shelter of the Temple.

At last Jehoiada, the high priest, organized the revolt. He won over the Temple and palace guards, and on a sabbath, when the three corps of guards were on duty, he received their oath of allegiance and entrusted the young descendant of David to their protection. Joash, then seven years old, was proclaimed king in the

Temple. Athaliah, roused by the clamor, came to the Temple; she was dragged outside the sacred precincts and killed.

JOASH (835-796 B.C.): During his minority Joash was under the
2 KGS. 12; 2 CHR. 24   guardianship of Jehoiada who brought him
up a sincere Yahwist. He restored the cult and repaired the Temple. At this time Hazael of Damascus, who was harassing Israel, made his presence felt even in Judah, and Joash was constrained to pay a heavy tribute. Perhaps it was as a result of this indignity that he fell victim to a palace plot. His religious conduct is praised; but the "high places" were not removed.

AMAZIAH (796-781 B.C.):   Damascus had been weakened by the
2 KGS. 14:1-22; 2 CHR. 25   Assyrians, and Jehoash of Israel had
brought back prosperity to his kingdom; there was a parallel improvement in Judah. Amaziah avenged the death of his father. He moved against the Edomites and took their stronghold, Sela (Petra), and he rebuilt Elath on the Gulf of Aqabah. Carried away by these successes, he challenged Jehoash of Israel. He was defeated at Bethshemesh and Jehoash went on to take Jerusalem. At the occasion of this national disaster, Amaziah had to flee from Jerusalem; he sought refuge at Lachish, but was put to death. His religious conduct is praised—except for the "high places."

UZZIAH (AZARIAH) (781-740 B.C.): The reign of Uzziah, son of
2 KGS. 15:1-6; 2 CHR. 26   Amaziah, contemporary with
that of Jeroboam II, marks a period of stability, with both kingdoms availing of the weakness of Damascus and the eclipse of Assyrian power. It was a period of expansion, with increase in trade and material prosperity.

Uzziah exploited the success of Amaziah against the Edomites and developed Elath. In an expedition against the Arabs he insured the passage to the south; he also gained advantages over the Philistines and Ammonites. Internally, his reign was marked by the strengthening of the defenses of Jerusalem, by a reorganization of the army, and by the development of agriculture. He became leprous towards the end of his life and handed over the administration to his son Jotham. According to Chr. the leprosy was a punishment for his usurpation of certain priestly prerogatives; this would appear to hint at a tension between the priesthood, grown strong under Jehoiada, and the monarchy.

JOTHAM (740-736 B.C.):   Uzziah was succeeded by his son
2 KGS. 15:32-38; 2 CHR. 27   Jotham who had already been co-regent. We know nothing of his short reign except that he continued the policy of his father and saw the beginning of the Syro-Ephraimite war. His religious conduct is praised—with the usual reservation.

AHAZ (736-716 B.C.):   Pekah of Israel and Rezin of Damascus,
2 KGS. 16; 2 CHR. 28   who had formed a league against Assyria, invited Jotham to join them, but he refused to be drawn into the league. The allies declared war, meaning to overthrow the dynasty and place on the throne a creature of their own, a certain "son of Tabeel." This was the situation Ahaz inherited from his father. Meanwhile, many other states had joined the league, and these took action. Edom gained possession of the port of Elath, the Ammonites freed themselves from the tribute imposed by Jotham, the Philistines attacked the towns of the Shephelah, and the Syro-Ephraimites invaded Judah. Ahaz moved against them, but was defeated; he retired to Jerusalem where he was besieged. Isaiah tried to persuade the king that he needed only to have trust in Yahweh and all would be well: this is the purpose of the Immanuel prophecy and its background. But Ahaz rejected the counsel of Isaiah and turned for help to the king of Assyria, and despoiled the Temple treasury in order to send rich gifts. Thus Ahaz freed himself from a difficult situation by taking upon himself the yoke of Ashur. It was 734 B.C. when Tiglath-pileser III moved against the league,[31] and in 732 B.C., with all resistance broken, in the Damascus that had fallen to him, the Assyrian king held a great assembly to receive the homage and tribute of his vassals.

Ahaz had chosen to become the vassal of Assyria, while Isaiah had strenuously counseled strict neutrality. At first sight it would seem that the king was right. Submission to the might of Assyria was inevitable and it was politically a shrewd move to anticipate it. But it was not the appeal of Ahaz that had moved Tiglath-pileser

---

[31]See *ibid.*, p. 283.

to take action against the league—he would certainly have done so in any case. The kingdom of Judah was of no importance to Assyria since it lay beyond the great roads of Syria and Egypt. The king would have been satisfied with a strict neutrality on Judah's part, and neutrality would have safeguarded the national and religious independence of the country. But by declaring himself a vassal, Ahaz had invited Assyrian interference in Judah, with all its political and religious consequences. In the political field it entailed absolute submission;[32] any gesture of independent action would be regarded as an act of rebellion. The way was open to cultic and religious influences. Thus when Ahaz was in Damascus in 732 B.C. he sent back to Jerusalem the model of an altar he had seen there and ordered the immediate construction of a similar altar. On his return he inaugurated it himself and installed it in place of the bronze altar which Solomon had set before the entrance to the Temple. These and other cultic changes are modifications, inspired by Assyrian cult, and partly by Syrian cult, introduced into the cult of Yahweh; they were bound to have repercussions on the religion of Yahweh.

During the reign of Ahaz the kingdom of Israel fell (721 B.C.). The king was dissuaded by Isaiah from joining another anti-Assyrian league; Sargon II easily crushed this revolt in 720 B.C. The Assyrian danger was more and more pressing: the Assyrian province of Samaria ran along the northern frontier of Judah and the provinces of Gaza and Ascalon lay to the west. Judah was in a sad state: the country was a vassal of Assyria, foreign influence had weakened national sentiment and religious syncretism had weakened Yahwistic sentiment. The religious conduct of Ahaz is roundly condemned.

HEZEKIAH (716-687 B.C.):   The great glory of the son of Ahaz is
2 KGS. 18-20; 2 CHR. 29-32   the restoration of pure Yahwism. This was due to the personal activity of the young and energetic king, but it was also due in great measure to the support of the Prophets, Micah, who exercised his ministry during this reign, and Isaiah, whose mission, held in check by Ahaz, developed effectively under Hezekiah.

Religious reform, even from a political point of view, was the first essential task. The chief aims of the reform were: the extirpation

---

[32]See *ibid.*, p. 501 (inscription of Barrakab).

of idolatrous practices; the re-establishment of pure Yahwism (involving the purification of the Temple); and the centralization of the cult, that is, the suppression of the "high places." The role of the Prophets in these reforms is obscure; they were, it seems, not particularly interested in the cultic reforms, but demanded interior, spiritual reform. The preaching of these Prophets, however, must have aided a reform that was, at least in part, the practical realization of that return to Yahweh which was the burden of their preaching. Jeremiah testifies that the preaching of Micah was efficacious (Jer. 26:18 f.).

The religious reform was accompanied by a national restoration. Judah seems to have been left unmolested by the Assyrians until 701 B.C.; the expedition of 711 B.C. was not aimed at Hezekiah, who had remained neutral. Besides, during this time Sargon and Sennacherib were fully occupied in the east. There was a return of prosperity to the kingdom. It must have been during this period that the great tunneled canal from Gihon to Siloam was cut; it was too difficult a job to have been carried through in the stress of a siege.

In 703 B.C. Marduk-apal-iddina (Merodach-baladan) had taken Babylon for the second time and had installed himself as king. From there he sent an embassy to Hezekiah during the latter's illness; undoubtedly his real motive was to stir up a diversion in the west while he sought to consolidate his position. Sennacherib defeated Marduk-apal-iddina in 703 B.C. and devastated the region around Babylon. During this campaign Phoenicia and the Palestinian states as well as Edom and Moab had rebelled (with Egyptian encouragement and support). Sennacherib moved into Syria in 701 B.C.; we have two accounts of this campaign:

1. *Assyrian account.*[33] The Assyrian king was called into Palestine by a revolt. The principal leaders were: the king of Sidon; the king of Ashkelon; the inhabitants of Ekron; and Hezekiah of Judah. There were four operations: against the Phoenician cities, Sidon and Accho; against Ashkelon; against Ekron; and against Jerusalem. Sennacherib did not take Jerusalem, but accepted tribute.

2. *Biblical account.* Hezekiah rebelled by refusing to pay tribute. Sennacherib suddenly appeared against him. All the fortified cities

---

[33]See *ibid.*, pp. 287 f.

of Judah were taken; Hezekiah submitted and paid tribute. Sennacherib, from Lachish, sent an army against Jerusalem and demanded the surrender of the city; this force retired to meet the Egyptian army of Tirhakah. From Libnah another demand for surrender was sent to Hezekiah. The Assyrian army was decimated by "the angel of the Lord."

While it is not surprising that the Assyrian Annals say nothing of the disaster which befell the king's army in Palestine, it is surprising that the capture of Lachish is not mentioned, especially since this event was depicted in bas-relief in Nineveh.[34] The most satisfactory explanation is to suppose that the biblical account has conflated two campaigns. The first, in 701 B.C., ended with the payment of tribute by Hezekiah. Then, in 690 B.C., Tirhakah became coregent in Egypt and fomented rebellion in Palestine (Hezekiah was implicated). Sennacherib was engaged in the east where Babylon was in open rebellion but, in 688 B.C., he moved to the west. Lachish was taken and Jerusalem was besieged; Tirhakah's relief army was driven back. Nevertheless the city was not taken because the Assyrian army was struck by an epidemic (2 Kgs. 19:35) and also because Sennacherib's presence was required at home (2 Kgs. 19:7).

The rebellion of Hezekiah ended in the reduction of Judah to the mountain district around Jerusalem. The king dedicated the last years of his life to the restoration of the public life of his gravely-stricken people. His religious conduct is praised without reserve. (The mission of Isaiah and Micah was undertaken under Jotham, Ahaz, and Hezekiah.)

MANASSEH (687-642 B.C.): 2 KGS. 21:1-18; 2 CHR. 33:1-20   The long reign of Manasseh was disastrous for the religion of Yahweh. The reforms of Hezekiah had not been popular because they had been aimed at inveterate habits; now there was a strong reaction. Besides, under Ashurbanipal, Assyria was at the height of its power and its influence was felt in the cultic and religious field; as a faithful vassal, Manasseh sought to please his masters by yielding to this influence. However, there was resistance, particularly in the circle of those who were faithful to the teaching of Isaiah; the suppression of this resistance was cruel and effective.

---

[34]See ANEP, plates 371-74.

Nevertheless, Manasseh's loyalty seemed suspect and he was sent in chains to Babylon; this probably happened after 648 B.C. when Ashurbanipal, having taken Babylon, reasserted his authority in Palestine. The king was released after a few years. On his return he tried to do something about restoring the religion of Yahweh. He also set about strengthening the defenses of his capital and kingdom, but death cut short his work. His religious conduct is condemned.

AMON (642-640 B.C.): Manasseh was succeeded by his 2 KGS. 21:19-26; 2 CHR. 21-25 son Amon who belonged to the antireform, pro-Assyrian party. He reigned only two years before being assassinated by a palace conspiracy. His religious conduct is condemned.

JOSIAH (640-609 B.C.): The assassination of Amon displeased the 2 KGS. 22:1—23:30; "people of the land" (that is, the citizens 2 CHR. 34-35 who enjoyed full civil rights), who were faithful to the Davidic line; they rose against the conspirators and placed on the throne the son of Amon, Josiah, a child of eight.

The reign of Josiah coincided with the sudden collapse and fall of Assyria; it is this factor that enabled the young king to push through his reform and permitted him to reorganize his kingdom. Though the Bible is silent about the internal profane policy of Josiah, it is certain that there must have been a national renaissance which went hand-in-hand with the religious reform and policy of independence. There were territorial gains, too, but we cannot determine them. The Megiddo incident points to a reorganization of the army.

Josiah began his reform in his twelfth year (628 B.C.). This reform attacked primarily the Assyrian cult, and was therefore also a rejection of foreign domination. In his eighteenth year, when the secretary Shaphan was sent to see about the collection for the restoration of the Temple, the priest Hilkiah gave him "the book of the law" which had been found in the Temple; this providential discovery gave a fresh impetus to the reform. It is generally agreed that the "book of the law" is the deuteronomical code (Dt. 12-26), the legal tradition of the Northern Kingdom, which was brought to Jerusalem by Levite refugees about the time of the fall of Samaria in 721 B.C.; it was deposited in the Temple to be neglected and, eventually, forgotten.

The hopes raised by the national restoration under Josiah were rudely dashed. In 609 B.C. Neco, seeking to maintain the balance of power in Mesopotamia, went to the aid of the stricken Assyrians. He followed the normal route of Egyptian armies going into Syria—along the coast road towards Carmel, then inland at Megiddo. Josiah intercepted him at Megiddo and was defeated and killed. It seems that Josiah was striving to uphold his policy of independence. The Egyptians were a threat whether they were to re-establish Assyria or to profit from the situation by seizing Palestine. The tragic death of the king meant the end of the reform and the beginning of the end of Judah. The reform had come too late; the Exile was needed for a thorough purification of Yahwism. The religious conduct of Josiah is praised without reserve. (Zephaniah and Nahum undertook their mission during the reign of Josiah.)

JEHOAHAZ (609 B.C.): After the death of Josiah the "people of
2 KGS. 23:31-35; the land" proclaimed Jehoahaz, his son,
2 CHR. 36:1-4 king. Three months later Neco summoned
Jehoahaz to his headquarters in Riblah, deposed him, and deported him to Egypt. He placed his brother Eliakim on the throne, changing his name to Jehoiakim.

JEHOIAKIM (609-587 B.C.): Jehoiakim was a vassal of Neco and
2 KGS. 23:36—24:6; paid tribute to Egypt; to do this he
2 CHR. 36:5-8 oppressed the people. The tragic
death of Josiah had been a scandal for Judah; Yahweh had not saved the pious king and the promises of the prophets were misleading. There was a violent anti-Assyrian reaction, headed by the king and court, and all the old syncretism invaded the Temple.

Meanwhile, Nebuchadnezzar, as general of his father Nabopolassar, had defeated Neco at Carchemish and had driven him back to Egypt. In 604 B.C., now king, he was in Palestine and destroyed Ashkelon; it was probably at this time that Jehoiakim changed allegiance and became a vassal of Babylon. In 601 B.C. Nebuchadnezzar moved on Egypt, but had to retire without gaining his objective. At this time Judah was split by factions; the pro-Egyptian party gained the upper hand and Jehoiakim rebelled. Nebuchadnezzar was not free to take personal action immediately, but he dispatched local Babylonian forces, together with bands of Edomites, Ammonites, and Moabites to harass the country. In 598 B.C. the Babylonian king moved. Before he arrived in Palestine Jehoiakim had died, under obscure circumstances, and had been replaced by his son Jehoiachin. The religious conduct of the last four kings of Judah is condemned.

JEHOIACHIN (597 B.C.): Jerusalem was besieged and Jehoiachin 2 KGS. 24:8-17; surrendered after three months. The king 2 CHR. 36:9-10 and the queen-mother, together with the leading citizens, were taken to Babylon. This is the first deportation.

ZEDEKIAH (597-587 B.C.): Nebuchadnezzar installed as king the 2 KGS. 24:18—25:7; uncle of Jehoiachin, the twenty-one year 2 CHR. 36:11-13 old Mattaniah, to whom he gave the name of Zedekiah. (As in the case of Jehoiakim, this is a Yahwistic name, and would scarcely have been imposed by a Babylonian; perhaps, in both cases, it is a question of a coronation name.) Due to the deportation of the leading citizens the kingdom was almost in a state of anarchy. Zedekiah was weak and quite unable to control the rival parties: one, represented by Jeremiah, counseled submission to the Babylonians; the other and stronger party sought the support of Egypt and had the favor of the people. In 590 B.C. Psammetichus II appeared in Palestine; after this, Zedekiah, whose conduct was suspect, went to Babylon to clear himself. All this time Jeremiah preached against alliance with Egypt and had to contend with false prophets; and Ezekiel, who had been deported with Jehoiachin, foretold the fall of Jerusalem.

Zedekiah finally yielded to the Egyptian party. A league was formed with Ammon; and Apries (who had succeeded Psammetichus) persuaded Tyre and Sidon to join. Nebuchadnezzar acted at once: he subdued Phoenicia and blockaded Tyre and then sent his main force against Judah. In 588 B.C. Jerusalem was besieged. All the fortresses of the kingdom were taken; only Lachish and Azekah held out for some time.[35] The siege was lifted when Apries appeared in the Shephelah with an Egyptian army, but he was quickly driven back and the siege was resumed. The city held out stubbornly

---

[35]The fall of Azekah is poignantly illustrated by one of the Lachish Letters (ostraca discovered at Lachish): an officer in charge of an observation post writes to the commander in Lachish that the fire signals of Azekah can no longer be seen (see ANET, p. 322).

THE KINGS OF JUDAH AND ISRAEL

| David | c. 1010-970 |
| Solomon | c. 970-931 |

JUDAH		ISRAEL		ASSYRIA	
Rehoboam	931-913	Jeroboam I	931-910	Ashur-dan II	934-912
Abijah	913-911			Adad-nirari II	912-890
		Nadab	910-909		
Asa	911-870	Baasha	909-886		
		Elah	886-885		
		Zimri	885		
		Omri	885-874	Ashur-nasir-pal II	883-859
Jehoshaphat	870-848	Ahab	874-853		
		Ahaziah	853-852	Shalmaneser III	859-824
Jehoram	848-841	Jehoram	853-841		
Ahaziah	841				
Athaliah	841-835	Jehu	841-814		
Joash	835-796				
		Jehoahaz	814-798	Shamshi-adad V	824-811
Amaziah	796-781	Jehoash	798-783	Adad-nirari III	811-783
Uzziah	781-740	Jeroboam II	783-743	Shalmaneser IV	783-773
				Ashur-dan III	773-754
				Ashur-nirari V	754-745
				Tiglath-pileser III	745-727
		Zechariah	743		
		Shallum	743		
Jotham	740-736	Menahem	743-738		
		Pekahiah	738-737		
Ahaz	736-716	Pekah	737-732		
		Hoshea	732-724	Shalmaneser V	727-722
				Sargon II	722-705
		721—Fall of Samaria			

		EGYPT			
Hezekiah	716-687	Piankhi	c. 715		
		Shabako	710-696	Sennacherib	705-681
		Shebteko	696-685		
Manasseh	687-642	Tirhakah	690-667	Esarhaddon	681-669
		Neco I	667-663	Ashurbanipal	669-632
Amon	642-640	Psammetichus I	663-609		
Josiah	640-609				
				Ashur-etil-ilani	632-629
				Sinsariskun	629-612
		Neco II	609-593	Ashur-uballit II	612-606

				NEO-BABYLONIAN EMPIRE	
				Nabopolassar	626-605
Jehoahaz	609				
Jehoiakim	609-597			Nebuchadnezzar	605-562
Jehoiachin	697				
Zedekiah	597-587	Psammetichus II	593-588		
		Apries	588-566		
587—Fall of Jerusalem					

despite terrible famine conditions. In July, 587 B.C., the wall was breached. Zedekiah, with some of his officers, escaped by night and fled towards Jericho, but they were captured and taken before Nebuchadnezzar at his headquarters in Riblah. The sons of Zedekiah were executed in his presence, then he was blinded and sent to die in a Babylonian prison. The walls of the city were levelled, the Temple and buildings were burned, and the sacred vessels were carried off. Part of the population was deported to Babylon. The kingdom of Judah had come to an end.

After the fall of Jerusalem. Judah had become a Babylonian province. Before he left Syria, Nebuchadnezzar appointed as governor a certain Gedaliah, a man of noble family who, as a seal found at Lachish bearing his name indicates, had been a chief minister of Zedekiah. He settled at Mizpah, apparently because Jerusalem was uninhabitable, was supported by a small Babylonian garrison, and had the moral support of Jeremiah. Gedaliah sought to conciliate the people, but he fell victim to a plot hatched by one Ishmael, a member of the royal house; the Babylonian garrison and some Jews faithful to Gedaliah were massacred. Ishmael escaped to Ammon, while many Jews, fearing Babylonian vengeance, fled to Egypt, taking with them an unwilling Jeremiah. In fact, Nebuchadnezzar did not at once chastise the Jews. Jer. 52:30 speaks of a third deportation in 582 B.C.; this would have been about five years after the murder of Gedaliah. (Jeremiah carried on his mission from the reign of Josiah until after the fall of Jerusalem.)

There were three deportations (in 597 B.C., 587 B.C., and 582 B.C.), but it is difficult to arrive at a definite figure. In Jer. 52:28-30 precise totals for the three deportations are given and the sum for all is only 4,600. This seems a reasonable figure for, though it probably counts only adult males, the grand total would probably not be more than four times that many—perhaps, at most, 20,000 people.

9. EXILE AND RESTORATION

1) The Background

LAST YEARS OF THE   With the death of Nebuchadnezzar in 562 B.C.
BABYLONIAN EMPIRE   Babylonian power declined rapidly; the situation was aggravated by lack of internal stability. The son of Nebu-

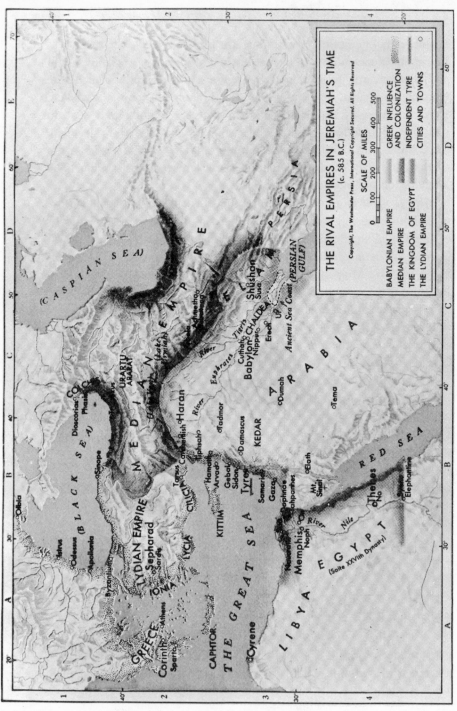

THE RIVAL EMPIRES IN JEREMIAH'S TIME
(c. 585 B.C.)

Copyright, The Westminster Press, International Copyright Secured. All Rights Reserved

SCALE OF MILES

0   100 200 300 400 500

BABYLONIAN EMPIRE
MEDIAN EMPIRE
THE KINGDOM OF EGYPT
THE LYDIAN EMPIRE

GREEK INFLUENCE
AND COLONIZATION
INDEPENDENT TYRE
CITIES AND TOWNS

chadnezzar, Avil-marduk (562-560 B.C.)—the Evil-merodach who released Jehoiachin (2 Kgs. 25:27-30)—reigned only two years; it is likely that his brother-in-law, Neriglissar (560-556 B.C.), came to the throne as a usurper. His son and successor, Labashi-marduk (556 B.C.), was a minor and was soon removed by Nabonidus (556-539 B.C.) who seized the throne. This king seems to have been more of an archaeologist than a ruler: he excavated temple sites in Babylonia and had ancient inscriptions deciphered. For reasons that are not clear he resided for eight years (c. 552-545 B.C.) at the oasis of Teima in the Arabian desert[36] and left the affairs of the empire in the hands of his son Belshazzar.

The Medes, under Cyaxares, had been a potential danger to Babylon and the same threat persisted under Astyages (585-550 B.C.). Thus when Cyrus, a Persian prince, rebelled against his Median overlord, he was supported by Nabonidus. But Cyrus soon proved a greater menace than Media had ever been and Nabonidus quickly entered into a defensive alliance with Amasis of Egypt (569-525 B.C.) and Croesus of Lydia (c. 560-546 B.C.). In 546 B.C. Lydia was defeated; though Cyrus did not move at once, his rapidly-growing power made the fate of Babylon inevitable. In 539 B.C. Cyrus attacked and Nabonidus was defeated at Opis on the Tigris and subsequently taken prisoner. Cyrus' general, Gobryas, took Babylon without striking a blow; Belshazzar was killed, apparently assassinated. The short-lived Neo-Babylonian Empire was at an end.

THE RISE Cyrus, a Persian, was ruler of the small kingdom of OF PERSIA Anshan in southern Iran and was a vassal of Astyages, king of the Medes. In 555 B.C. he rebelled; by 550 B.C. he had seized Ecbatana, the capital of Astyages, and had taken over the Median Empire. In 546 B.C. he invaded Lydia (in western Asia Minor), now allied with Babylon and Egypt, and took the capital Sardis. Lydia was incorporated into his realm and, apparently, he had control of Upper Mesopotamia. The Egyptian alliance was now of no avail and Babylonia was isolated. But Cyrus was in no hurry; he campaigned in the East and extended his dominion almost as far as India. Then in 539 B.C. he won Babylon at the price of a

---

[36]See Wilfrid J. Harrington, *Record of Revelation: The Bible* (Chicago: The Priory Press, 1965), p. 76, for the text of the "Prayer of Nabonidus" found in Qumran (4Q).

single battle.[37] Cyrus was master of the greatest empire the world had known.

Cyrus was an enlightened ruler who sought to win the respect and loyalty of his subject peoples. It is clear that the Babylonians themselves, aware of his magnanimous character, had gladly changed masters; no doubt this helps to explain the astounding ease of his conquest. He was particularly careful to respect the religious susceptibilities of his subjects and he allowed them cultic autonomy; he even permitted peoples who had been deported by the Babylonians to return to their homelands. All this meant no weakening of political power. The Persian army was maintained at full strength and a complex governmental system was set up to control the vast empire, which was divided into provinces and satrapies. But Cyrus' general policy sets his benevolent treatment of the Jews in a clearer light. For in 538 B.C., the first year of his reign in Babylon, Cyrus published an edict authorizing the return of the Jewish captives to Judah and providing funds for the rebuilding of the Temple (Ez. 1:2-4; 6:3-5). It is no wonder that Second Isaiah (the unknown author of Is. 40-55) has painted, in glowing colors, the career of this liberator, the Lord's Anointed (Is. 45:1; cf. 44:28—45:13; 41:2 f., 25).

There was peace throughout the Persian Empire, but Cyrus was killed in a campaign against nomadic peoples beyond his eastern frontier. He was succeeded by his son Cambyses (530-522 B.C.), who conquered Egypt—which remained under Persian control until 401 B.C. In 522 B.C., while Cambyses was absent, Gaumata usurped the throne. Cambyses died—apparently he committed suicide—and an officer, Darius, accepted and supported by the army, overthrew Gaumata. Darius I (522-486 B.C.), during his first two years, had to cope with rebellion on all sides; the Persian Empire seemed about to break in pieces. But when he had passed through the crisis, Darius not only consolidated his position but further extended the boundaries of his realm so that, under him, Persia reached her zenith. His one failure was in Greece where the battle of Marathon (490 B.C.) checked his bid to take that country.

Darius was succeeded by his son Xerxes I (486-465 B.C.). Babylon rebelled and was destroyed. In 480 B.C. Xerxes invaded Greece, over-

---

[37]Cyrus' account of his Babylonian triumph is recorded on the Cyrus Cylinder; see ANET, pp. 315 f.

whelmed the Spartans at Thermopylae, and captured Athens. However, the decisive naval battle of Salamis, and subsequent military reverses, forced the Persians from Europe. Xerxes was ultimately assassinated and replaced by a younger son, Artaxerxes I Longimanus (465-424 B.C.). This takes us to the age of Nehemiah, the subject of the following section.

2) Judah after 587 B.C.

In the campaign of 588-587 B.C. Judah was utterly devastated; not only Jerusalem but all the towns of the Shephelah and mountain country were razed. Apart from the deportees, thousands must have died by the sword or of starvation and disease, and thousands must have fled the country, finding refuge especially in Egypt. The political situation is difficult to ascertain. However, the country was not re-populated with other peoples as had happened in Samaria; though the neighboring Edomites, Ammonites, and Arabs did settle in parts of it. The remainder of the land, where a very poor people dwelt (considerably less than 20,000), was annexed to the administration of Samaria. It was a limited territory; for one thing, the Edomites had advanced half-way between Hebron and Bethlehem. Yet, despite its complete destruction, Jerusalem still attracted spirits attached to Yahwism and in the ruins of the Temple people came to pray (see Lam.). But hope for the future rested, not on this pitiful debris, but, as Jeremiah and Ezekiel had promised, with the exiles in Babylon.

3) The Exiles in Babylon

It should be kept in mind that the Jews exiled in Babylon were the cream of the country: its political, ecclesiastical, and intellectual leaders. This explains why the total (4,600 adult males) given by Jeremiah is so restricted. They lived in special settlements near Babylon and their lot was not unduly hard. Indeed there was the opportunity of economic advancement and many of them did so well that they elected to remain on in Babylon after Cyrus had opened the way for a return to Palestine.

It was inevitable that many Jews, their faith shaken by the terrible disaster that had befallen their nation, were won over by Babylonian culture. But others only clung more closely to their past. In God's inscrutable plan, the Exile was one of the most fruitful moments in the history of Israel. The people learned to know their God as never before, and, encouraged first by Ezekiel and then by the great Second Isaiah, they were buoyed up by a new and unquenchable hope. Most important of all, from our point of view, the Bible as we know it began to take definite shape. The Temple was gone with its elaborate cult; hence the faithful of Yahweh fell back on their traditions. This was the time when the Deuteronomic history was given its final form, when the sayings of the prophets were compiled, and when the priestly tradition was fixed. A new community was being forged for the final stage of God's preparatory plan.

4) The Restoration

In the first year of his reign in Babylon (538 B.C.) Cyrus issued a decree which authorized the restoration of the Jewish community and the cult of Yahweh in Palestine (Ez. 1:1-4; 6:25). The decree covered not only the return of the sacred vessels which Nebuchadnezzar had carried off, it also directed that the cost of rebuilding the Temple should be met out of imperial funds. The Jews in Babylon were encouraged to support the whole venture financially and all who wished to do so were free to return to Judah. Shesh-bazzar, "prince of Judah," that is, a member of the royal family and, seemingly, a son of Jehoiachin, was put in charge of the project. A small group set out under his leadership. One of the first tasks of the returned exiles was to restore the altar of holocausts. In the midst of the Temple ruins a regular cult was re-established—the first, essential thread of the past had been picked up again. In the spring of 537 B.C. the foundation of the Second Temple was laid.

But this seems to have been the extent of the first attempt at restoration. Only a handful had returned: Jews who had done well in Babylon were content to remain there, while a whole generation had grown up to whom Palestine was a foreign land. The Jews who had been left in Judah, and those who had taken over Jewish lands, were not pleased to see the exiles coming back. Furthermore the returned Jews themselves refused proffered Samaritan help in rebuilding the Temple. Because of this the first friendly advances hardened into opposition and the work had to cease altogether. The people grew despondent and the venture was in imminent danger of fading out. But a further group of exiles returned, sometime between 538 B.C. and 522 B.C., under the leadership of Zerubbabel and the high priest Joshua. Zerubbabel, a descendant of Jehoiachin, succeeded his uncle Shesh-bazzar as *pekah* (governor). Yet, by the end of the reign of Cambyses, the total population (including both returned exiles and Jews already in the land) of the tiny territory of Judah cannot have been much more than 20,000.

Discouragement was aggravated by tensions within the community. Not all who had returned, and still fewer of those who had never left, were imbued with the highest motives. Some were quick to profit from the misfortunes of others (Is. 58:1-12; 59:1-8) and certain syncretistic religious practices still prevailed—apparently among the people who had remained in the land (Is. 57:3-10; 65:1-7,11; 66:3 f., 7). The bitter reality seemed to mock the words of Second Isaiah. But the Prophets Haggai and Zechariah countered the despondency and in 520 B.C. Zerubbabel began, in earnest, the rebuilding of the Second Temple. There was an anxious moment when Tattanai, satrap of Abar-nahara ("Beyond the River"—the trans-Euphrates satrapy, which included Syria and Palestine), questioned Zerubbabel's authorization. He decided to inquire into the authenticity of the decree of Cyrus; in the meantime, he did not hold up the work. The decree of Cyrus was found in the royal archives of Ecbatana, the summer capital. Darius I published a new decree in favor of the construction of the Temple, with precise indications of cult provision and expenses and with sanctions against any who might oppose the decree (Ez. 6:1-12). During the Pasch of 515 B.C. the Second Temple was dedicated.

We know nothing of the situation in Judah during the next half-century and more. Zerubbabel is not mentioned again. It is possible that, as a descendant of David and the center of messianic hope (see Hag. 2:23; Zech. 6:9-14), he was removed by the Persian authorities.[38] Some time during this period the province of *Yehud* (Judah) was set up; in extent it was roughly the same as the territory entrusted to Gedaliah in 587 B.C. Its northern limit was Bethel; to the south it reached a little beyond Bethlehem; in the west it was limited by the province of Ashdod. Though the Temple had been restored, all attempts to rebuild the walls of Jerusalem were opposed by the Samaritans. It was left to Nehemiah and Ezra to bring about the full restoration of the Jewish community.

---

[38]See Bright, *op. cit.*, p. 355.

10. THE WORK OF NEHEMIAH AND EZRA

1) The Background

Judah had become a Persian province and, until the rise of Alexander the Great, the fortunes of the Jewish community were inseparable from the history of the Persian Empire. The long reign of Artaxerxes I Longimanus (465-424 B.C.) was beset with difficulties. In 460 B.C. the king faced a rebellion in Egypt, which had been stirred up by a Libyan named Inaros. Megabyzus, satrap of Abar-nahara, led the campaign against Egypt; it dragged on until 454 B.C. when Inaros was taken prisoner. Subsequently (449-448 B.C.) Megabyzus himself rebelled, but ended by being confirmed in his office. After this it was in the king's interest to look to the stability of Abar-nahara, and he showed a concern for Palestinian affairs. In 449 B.C. Artaxerxes agreed to the peace of Callias whose terms required that the Greek cities of Asia Minor be granted independence and that the Persian fleet be excluded from the Aegean. However, the Peloponnesian War (431-403 B.C.) enabled Persia to regain control of the Greek cities.

Xerxes II, who succeeded his father, was assassinated after little more than a month on the throne. Following further disorders, another son of Artaxerxes, Darius II Nothus (423-404 B.C.), became king. He was succeeded by Artaxerxes II Mnemon (404-358 B.C.). In 401 B.C. Egypt became independent; in the same year Artaxerxes had to face a revolt led by his brother, Cyrus the Younger. At Cumaxa in Babylonia, Cyrus was defeated and killed; the campaign, and especially the subsequent retreat of 10,000 Greek survivors of Cyrus' army, has been immortalized by Xenophon in his *Anabasis*. Shortly after this the Western satraps rebelled and won Egyptian support, but about the year 360 B.C. the revolt collapsed.

2) Chronology of Ezra-Nehemiah

We have no direct evidence of the situation in Judah between 515 and 445 B.C., but it is clear enough from the following period that there was an air of disillusionment in the tiny province. The Davidic monarchy had not been restored and the drab reality reflected nothing of the glowing colors of Second Isaiah. A political reorganization and spiritual renewal of the community were urgently needed and, happily, the men who would accomplish both were soon to appear.

Yet surprisingly enough, since they are the architects of Judaism, the relationship of the careers of Ezra and Nehemiah remains a perplexing problem.

The real difficulty is to determine the date of Ezra's arrival in Jerusalem; the date of Nehemiah's career is certain, being independently confirmed by evidence from the Elephantine texts.[39] There are three main positions: some accept the order apparently adopted in Ezra-Nehemiah; others argue that the solution lies in taking Artaxerxes II into consideration; still others claim that the "seventh year" (Ez. 7:7) is a scribal error for the thirty-seventh year of Artaxerxes I. We shall set these positions out more clearly as follows:

1. According to the order of Ezra-Nehemiah:[40]

a) Ezra arrived in Jerusalem in 459 B.C.: the seventh year of Artaxerxes I (Ez. 7:8).

b) Nehemiah arrived in Jerusalem in 445 B.C.: the twentieth year of Artaxerxes I (Neh. 2:1).

c) Nehemiah remained twelve years (Neh. 13:6), that is, until 433 B.C.

d) He came to Jerusalem a second time, still under Artaxerxes I (465-424 B.C.).

2. Many authors invert the order of the texts—the object of the Chronicler (the author of 1,2 Chr.-Ez.-Neh.) was to place the *religious* work of Ezra before the political restoration of Nehemiah.[41]

a) Nehemiah arrived in 445 B.C.: the twentieth year of Artaxerxes I.

b) He remained twelve years—until 433 B.C.

c) He made a brief return to Jerusalem after 433 B.C.

d) Ezra came to Jerusalem in 398 B.C.: the seventh year of Artaxerxes II (404-358 B.C.).

3. The visit of Ezra may be placed between the two missions of Nehemiah.[42] This is achieved by a textual correction of Ez. 7:8.

---

[39]See *ibid.*, p. 363. For a note on the Elephantine texts see p. 79.

[40]This chronology is followed, for example, by Heinisch-Heidt, *History of the Old Testament* (Collegeville, Minn.: The Liturgical Press, 1952), pp. 330-40; L. H. Grollenberg, *Atlas of the Bible,* trans. Joyce M. H. Reid and H. H. Rowley (Camden, N.J.: Nelson, 1959), p. 100.

[41]This order is followed, for example, by the following (though the probability of the other positions is always acknowledged): G. Ricciotti, *History of Israel,* trans. C. della Penta and R. Murphy (Milwaukee: Bruce, 1955), II, nn. 108-20. *Atlante Biblico,* p. 164; BJ, p. 405.

[42]See Bright, *op. cit.,* pp. 275-386; see IB, I, pp. 713 f.

Ezra arrived not in the seventh but in the thirty-seventh year of Artaxerxes I: in 428 B.C.

   a) Nehemiah arrived in 445 B.C.: the twentieth year of Artaxerxes I.
   b) He remained from 445 B.C. to 433 B.C.
   c) Ezra arrived in 428 B.C.: the thirty-seventh year of Artaxerxes I.
   d) Nehemiah returned between 433 B.C. and 424 B.C.

Therefore Ezra and Nehemiah were contemporaries.

None of these views can claim to solve all the problems. Since the third seems the most satisfactory, however, it is followed in our presentation of the work of Nehemiah and Ezra.

> Though it may seem to contradict the plain sense of the biblical account, which puts Ezra first, a comparison of Ezra-Nehemiah with the Greek version of I Esdras [an apocryphal book] (and with Josephus, who follows it) may suggest that the Chronicler's work has suffered serious dislocation, in all likelihood after leaving his hands. The order of events in our Bibles is probably the result of this secondary disarrangement. At any rate it is believed that the reconstruction offered below is true to the biblical evidence, while affording an intelligent picture of the events.[43]

3) Nehemiah

After the disappearance of Zerubbabel the district of Judah seems to have been administered from Samaria. There was constant friction with the Samaritan officials; attempts to build the walls of Jerusalem were frustrated. In 445 B.C. a delegation from Jerusalem, led by Hanani (brother of Nehemiah) came to Susa, the Persian capital. Nehemiah, cupbearer (a position of high rank) to Artaxerxes I, was informed of the deplorable conditions in Judah. Taking advantage of his access to the king he had himself invested with full powers to restore the fortifications of Jerusalem; he may have been immediately appointed governor of Judah. Although armed with letters to the officials of Abar-nahara, he met with opposition from Sanballat (governor of Samaria), Tobiah (governor of Ammon in Transjordan), and Geshem "the Arab" (a sheik of northwestern Arabia). Yet despite all opposition, Nehemiah built the walls of Jerusalem in fifty-two days, and he arranged for the repopulation of the city. The whole province could have numbered no more than 50,000 inhabitants.

Though Nehemiah was governor of Judah until 433 B.C. we know little of his administration; what evidence there is, however, supports

---

[43]Bright, op. cit., p. 363.

the view that he was a just and able ruler. Nevertheless, the opposition against him continued and he was also aware that a religious reform was called for. He returned to Susa in 433 B.C., and though his absence was a short one, many abuses arose while he was away. Through the complacency of the high priest Eliashib, Tobiah, the Ammonite governor and enemy of Nehemiah, obtained quarters in the Temple itself; and a grandson of Eliashib married the daughter of Sanballat, another bitter opponent of Nehemiah.

Nehemiah returned to Judah, certainly before the death of Artaxerxes I, and, most probably, within a year or two of his return to Susa. At once and with energy he attacked the abuses: he took over the quarters that had been allotted to Tobiah and expelled the grandson of Eliashib. According to Josephus this marked a definite break with the Samaritans and the beginning of a religious schism: Sanballat built a temple on Mt. Gerizim after his son-in-law had been banished from Jerusalem. However, it seems more probable that the temple came later. In general, Nehemiah attacked mixed marriages, the violation of the sabbath observance, and the rapacity of the upper classes. We do not know how long this second term of office lasted; all we can say is that by 410 B.C. a Persian named Bagoas was governor.[44]

4) Ezra

During Nehemiah's second term as governor the man who was to push through the much-needed religious reform arrived on the scene. The measures taken by Nehemiah in this field had been *ad hoc* solutions; there was need for something more radical and better organized. Ezra was of a priestly family and was learned in the Law; he was a "scribe." His commission (see Ez. 7:12-26) was quite different from that of Nehemiah, and concerned religious matters only. He carried with him a copy of the Law of Moses together with a rescript from the king which, in effect, made that Law the state law of the Jewish community. His authority extended over all Jews living in Afar-nahara.

> Ezra's status is concealed in the title "scribe of the law of the God of heaven" (Ez. 7:12). This does not denote a doctor of the law in the later sense—though tradition with some justice (see v. 6) came to consider Ezra as such—but was Ezra's official title as a

---

[44]See p. 80.

commissioner of the government. He was "Royal Secretary of the Law of the God of Heaven" (that is, the God of Israel) or, to modernize somewhat, "Minister of State for Jewish Affairs," with specific authority in the territory of Afar-nahara.[45]

In 428 B.C. Ezra came to Jerusalem from Babylon at the head of a large company. Two months after his arrival, on the Feast of Tabernacles, he initiated his reform, which had the support of the high priest Johanan. He read the Law to the people, and the people swore to uphold it. On the whole the demands of the Law, especially in the matter of cult, caused no difficulty, but the question of mixed marriages did prove to be a real crux. Some two months later, at an extraordinary assembly of the people, Ezra set up a commission to deal with the problem. Early in the following year the matter was radically dealt with: foreign wives and their children were sent away. However, we are not sure that these sweeping measures were conscientiously implemented, because the memoirs of Ezra finish abruptly at this point. At any rate such legislation did assure the separate identity of the Jewish people and, inevitably, did bring about their isolation.

The religious reform of Ezra certainly presupposed the political stability achieved by Nehemiah, but the latter was a reformer also. Though the canonical books of Ezra-Nehemiah give no clear-cut evidence that Nehemiah and Ezra were contemporaries, that assumption is not unreasonable. We depend almost exclusively on the memoirs of Ezra and Nehemiah and on the Chronicler's presentation of them; hence we have to take different viewpoints into account. The Chronicler himself, whose interests were primarily ecclesiastical, is understandably more interested in Ezra; while Nehemiah's memoirs are largely a personal apologia. Nehemiah is content to describe the part he played in the religious reform, while the Chronicler gives all the credit to Ezra.

At any rate, Nehemiah and Ezra, between them, had established a theocracy and founded Judaism. The Jews were politically subject to Persia, but they formed a recognized community and were authorized to regulate internal affairs in accordance with the Law of their God. And the Law which Ezra had brought with him, and around

[45]Bright, *op. cit.*, p. 370.

which he had reorganized the Jewish community, is, plausibly, the complete Torah, the *Pentateuch*. What is certain is that henceforth the distinguishing mark of a Jew would be adherence to the Law of Moses.

5) *The Elephantine Colony*

We learn from documents[46] (papyri and *ostraca* dated 498-399 B.C.) found on the island of Elephantine, just north of the first cataract of the Nile and opposite Aswan, that a Jewish military colony was established on the island, with a temple to Yahweh. It was there when the Persians conquered Egypt in 525 B.C. It was probably set up by Apries (588-569 B.C.) and was composed largely of refugees from Judah after 587 B.C. A study of the names shows that there were Arameans among the Jews; the nature of the syncretistic cult suggests that the colonists had originated among the mixed population around Bethel.[47] Besides Yahweh other divinities were worshiped: Eshem-bethel, Herem-bethel, Anath-bethel. It may be, however, that these names represent hypostatizations (personifications) of certain aspects of Yahweh (thus, for example, Eshem-bethel = "Name of the House of God"). While their Yahwism was obviously far from orthodox, these Jews of Elephantine still looked to Jerusalem as spiritual center.

The Jewish colony was favorably regarded by the Persians, since it was in the interest of the colonists to uphold Persian authority. But when the power of the Great King waned, the Jews became the object of national resentment. Aswan was the sacred city of the ram-headed god Khnum; a temple dedicated to him stood on the island of Elephantine. The Jewish animal sacrifices, and especially the immolation of a great number of lambs at the Pasch, were offensive to the worshipers of Khnum. When in 410 B.C. the satrap of Egypt, Arsames, was absent, the temple of Yahweh was destroyed in the course of a riot. Yadoniah, priest of the Elephantine community, wrote to Johanan, the high priest at Jerusalem, requesting him to use his good offices on their behalf to enable them to rebuild their temple. He received no reply, which is not surprising since

---

[46]See ANET, pp. 491 f.
[47]See Bright, *op. cit.*, p. 327; *Atlante Biblico*, p. 166.

the Jerusalem religious authorities must have been scandalized at the very idea of a temple of Yahweh anywhere else except in the holy city. Three years later (407 B.C.) the Elephantine Jews wrote again, but this time to Bagoas, governor of Judah, and also to Delaiah and Shelemiah, sons of Sanballat, governor of Samaria. Bagoas and Delaiah did intervene on their behalf and the temple was rebuilt; animal sacrifices, however, were henceforth excluded. This temple did not stand for long. Egypt became independent of Persian rule in 401 B.C. and the last document from Elephantine is dated 399 B.C.—the colony must have disappeared about this time. Apart from their intrinsic interest, the Elephantine papyri assure us that Nehemiah was no longer governor of Judah in 407 B.C.; most probably he had been succeeded by Bagoas some years previously.

11. FROM EZRA TO ANTIOCHUS IV

We have almost no direct information covering the period between 427 B.C. and 167 B.C.; in other words, between the memoirs of Ezra and 1 Maccabees there is a lacuna of two and one-half centuries. All we know is that Jewish life continued along the pattern set by Ezra and Nehemiah and that during these centuries much of the Old Testament, as we know it, took final shape. (The last of the prophets appeared in this period: Joel and the author of Zechariah 9-14.)

1) The Background

Since we know so little of the Jewish history of this period it will not be possible to link up wider issues with conditions in Judah. However, a general grasp of the events of world history is necessary for the understanding of such books as Daniel.

THE END OF THE PERSIAN EMPIRE   Artaxerxes II had lost Egypt and had nearly lost his throne to his younger brother Cyrus; but his successor, Artaxerxes III Ochus (358-338 B.C.), vigorous and cruel, reconquered Egypt in 342 B.C. Yet despite appearances, the Persian Empire was finished. Artaxerxes III died by poison and was succeeded by his son Arses (338-336 B.C.), a minor, who was poisoned in his turn. The next king, Darius III Codomanus (336-331 B.C.), came to the throne in the same year that Alexander became king of Macedonia; in five short years the immense Persian

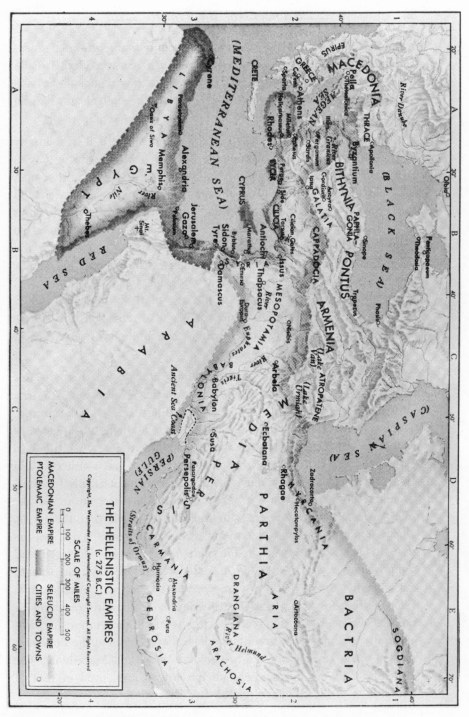

THE HELLENISTIC EMPIRES
(c. 275 B.C.)

Copyright, The Westminster Press, International Copyright Secured. All Rights Reserved.

SCALE OF MILES

0   100   200   300   400   500

| MACEDONIAN EMPIRE | SELEUCID EMPIRE |
| PTOLEMAIC EMPIRE | CITIES AND TOWNS o |

Empire was to fall to the Macedonian conqueror. In 333 B.C. Alexander defeated the Persian army at Issus. In 331 B.C. Darius made his last stand at Gaugamela in Iran. Defeated once again, he was assassinated by one of his satraps. This was the end of the Persian Empire.

ALEXANDER THE GREAT   It is no part of our purpose to treat in any
(336-323 B.C.)   detail the career of Alexander the Great.
He succeeded his father Philip in 336 B.C. In 334 B.C. he began his campaign and won control of Asia Minor. In 333 B.C. he defeated the Persians at Issus and advanced along the Mediterranean coast towards Egypt where he was welcomed as a liberator. Palestine was now under his control. In 331 B.C. Alexander moved into the heart of the Persian Empire and brought it to an end. In 326 B.C. he had advanced into India, beyond the Indus, but his troops refused to go any farther. In 323 B.C., at the age of thirty-three, he fell ill and died in Babylon. His brief career had changed the whole pattern and life of the East, a change that ultimately was to affect the history of the Jews.

THE SUCCESSORS   When Alexander died in 323 B.C. his generals
OF ALEXANDER   disputed possession of the empire. In 315 B.C., after seven years of struggle, four outstanding leaders had appeared. These were: Antigonus, the most prominent, who held all the territory from the Mediterranean to Central Asia; Cassander, who ruled in Macedonia; Ptolemy Lagi, who possessed Egypt and southern Syria (in connection with him must be mentioned Seleucus, his foremost general); and Lysimachus in Thrace. Antigonus aspired to be the sole successor of Alexander, with the natural result that the others allied against him; in the ensuing struggle Seleucus came to the fore. In 302 B.C., at Ipsus in Phrygia, Antigonus was defeated and slain. Seleucus won possession of Babylonia and Syria, and though assassinated in 280 B.C., was succeeded by his son, Antiochus I. Ptolemy remained in possession of Egypt, his empire reaching as far as Damascus. By the year 281 B.C. we find the empire of Alexander divided into three great kingdoms: the kingdom of the Ptolemies (Egypt); the kingdom of the Seleucids (Asia); and Macedonia. The Ptolemies and the Seleucids alone interest us and, even at that, it will suffice to list the kings of the two dynasties.

THE PTOLEMIES		THE SELEUCIDS	
Ptolemy I Soter	323-285	Seleucus I Nicator	312-280
Ptolemy II Philadelphus	285-246	Antiochus I Soter	280-261
		Antiochus II Theos	261-246
Ptolemy III Euergetes	246-221	Seleucus II Kallinikos	246-226
		Seleucus III Keraunos	226-223
Ptolemy IV Philopator	221-203	Antiochus III (the Great)	223-187
Ptolemy V Epiphanes	203-181	Seleucus IV Philopator	187-175
Ptolemy VI Philometor	181-146	Antiochus IV Epiphanes	175-163

2) *The Jews under the Ptolemies*

It seems that Palestine had quietly accepted Alexander's control and the political and religious constitution of Judah was not changed in any respect. When the political situation had at last been stabilized after the death of Alexander, Palestine was ruled by the Ptolemies until 198 B.C. The position of Judah seems to have remained just the same as it had been under Persia. The high priest was regarded as head of the community and increasingly took on the character of a secular prince. It was a period of peace and relative prosperity. Inevitably, Greek cultural influences made inroads into the Jewish society and the seeds of a future violent conflict were sown.

At this time the Jewish population of Egypt grew rapidly. The greatest concentration of Jews was in the new city of Alexandria which soon became a center of Jewish life. Early in the third century the Greek-speaking Jews of Alexandria translated the Torah into Greek, and the rest of the Bible followed in due course; this was the Septuagint Version (LXX).

3) *The Jews under the Seleucids*

There were frequent wars between the Ptolemies and the Seleucids, but the former were able to retain their hold on Palestine and Phoenicia for a long time. The situation changed when Antiochus III (the Great) (223-187 B.C.) came to the throne of Antioch. He extended his kingdom to the frontiers of India and then turned to the West. His first campaign (217 B.C.) began successfully, but he was seriously defeated by Ptolemy IV at Raphia near the Egyptian border. Several years passed before he moved again. Finally in 198 B.C., at Panium near the source of the Jordan, he routed the Egyptian army. Palestine was annexed to the Seleucid Empire. According to the Jewish historian Josephus, the Jews welcomed the change and Antiochus treated them with great consideration, guaranteeing them the right to live in accordance with their own law.

Meanwhile, the Carthaginian general, Hannibal, who had been defeated by the Romans at Zama in 202 B.C., fled to the Seleucid court. Antiochus advanced into Greece and Rome declared war. Antiochus was driven back and in 190 B.C., at Magnesia in western Asia Minor, he was disastrously defeated. He had to hand over hostages and pay a huge indemnity; desperate for money, he was killed in 187 B.C. while attempting to rob a temple in Elam. His successor, Seleucus IV (187-175 B.C.) tried—through his minister Heliodorus and with the connivance of certain Jews—to get possession of funds deposited in the Temple of Jerusalem, but the attempt was thwarted (2 Mc. 3). The high priest Onias III was obliged to journey to the court in order to clear himself of slanders brought against him by a certain Simon (2 Mc. 4:1-6).

Seleucus IV was assassinated by Heliodorus who planned to place on the throne Seleucus' minor son Antiochus, ignoring the claims of an older son Demetrius, who was a hostage in Rome. But a third pretender appeared, Antiochus, brother of Seleucus IV, who had formerly been a hostage. Antiochus landed in Syria with an army and expelled Heliodorus. He acted as regent for his young nephew Antiochus, but with the title of king. The latter was assassinated in 169 B.C. and the uncle ruled alone. With the arrival on the scene of Antiochus IV Epiphanes (175-163 B.C.) the very existence of Judaism was threatened. The danger that his policy was to offer to the Jewish way of life was augmented by a tragic split within the community.

During the later Persian period the impact of Hellenistic culture was being felt in Western Asia. As a result of the conquest and of the deliberate policy of Alexander the Great, the spread of the Greek language and Greek ideas proceeded at an amazing rate; Greek soon became the *lingua franca* of the civilized world. Jews of the Diaspora absorbed the Greek language and culture; the Jews of Palestine could not escape the influence since the land was dotted with Greek colonies. In the main, this influence was not direct; Greek thought was in the air and it was inevitable that something of it should have been absorbed. Some Jews, however, were swept off their feet and, faced with Greek culture, grew ashamed of their own way of life, to the point of repudiating it. As so often happens, they proved more zealous for things Greek than the Greeks themselves. The Syrian king, in his attempt, first to Hellenize Judah and then to destroy the Jewish religion, found enthusiastic allies within the Jewish community, especially among the priestly classes.

4) *The Jewish Diaspora*[48]

The term *Diaspora* (Dispersion) is frequent in Judaism of the Hellenistic period and is used to designate the totality of Jews who lived outside of Palestine. There was nationalistic sentiment in the term: the Jews who had to live outside the holy land were "disseminated" among the Gentiles. But not all the Jews of the Diaspora were involuntary exiles.

Many of the Jews of the Exile had elected to stay on in Babylon; hence Babylon remained an important center of Judaism. With the spread of Hellenism new important centers appeared, notably Alexandria. The Jews had a privileged place there and their colony grew quickly. Alexandria was the chief port of the Mediterranean; from it the way opened to the Greek and Roman world and to Asia Minor. The Seleucid capital, Antioch, which came close after Alexandria in importance, was another center of Judaism; it commanded the eastern Mediterranean and was open to Syria.

A characteristic of the Diaspora was the close contact between the various cells. This contact was maintained despite the different characteristics of the communities; Jerusalem was always the center of the whole vast network. The constitution of the single communities varied according to place and according to the juridical position of each in a particular city or state. Everywhere, however, synagogues sprang up and the offices of *archōn* and *archisynagōgos* were constant elements. The *archōn* was a collective office, which

---

[48]See Ricciotti, *op. cit.*, nn. 180-200.

varied as to number and also as to duration and range of power; it handled the administrative and juridical affairs of the community. The *archisynagōgos* was an official who presided over the cult.

In the third century B.C. the Hebrew Bible was translated into Greek at Alexandria. This version, the Septuagint (LXX), was the Bible of the Jews of the Diaspora. It was a development of capital importance not only for Judaism but for Christianity, since the Septuagint became the Bible of the early Church. But the providential role of the Diaspora is not limited to this: the active proselytism of many Jews prepared the way for the spread of Christianity. Gentiles who had been attracted by the monotheism and the high moral code of Judaism found in the new religion all that they had sought.

12. THE MACCABAEAN REVOLT AND THE HASMONAEAN DYNASTY

1) *The Background: Antiochus IV to Antiochus VII* (175-129 B.C.)

Antiochus IV Epiphanes (175-163 B.C.) was anxious to unify his realm. This is the chief reason why he pushed forward so vigorously a policy of Hellenization. In 170 B.C. he invaded Egypt. He captured the young Ptolemy VI at Memphis and then moved on Alexandria where Ptolemy VII (brother of the other) had been declared king; Antiochus declared himself regent of his prisoner. He eventually agreed to retire, laden with immense booty, and left both Ptolemies reigning—in Memphis and Alexandria respectively. In 168 B.C. Antiochus was back in Egypt, but this time the Romans intervened— as protectors of Egypt. Antiochus was met by the legate, Popilius Laenas, who bluntly presented him with an ultimatum from the Roman senate; Antiochus retired. When the Maccabaean revolt had taken a serious turn in 165 B.C., Antiochus was committed to a campaign against the Parthians, leaving his regent, Lysias, to take care of the Palestinian situation. Early in 163 B.C. he died at Tabae in Persia. The subsequent history of the Seleucids is very involved.

Antiochus IV had designated his young son Antiochus V Eupator (163-161 B.C.) as his successor and had appointed his friend Philip as regent. Lysias, however, declared himself regent and took the young king into his charge; together they moved against Judas Mac-

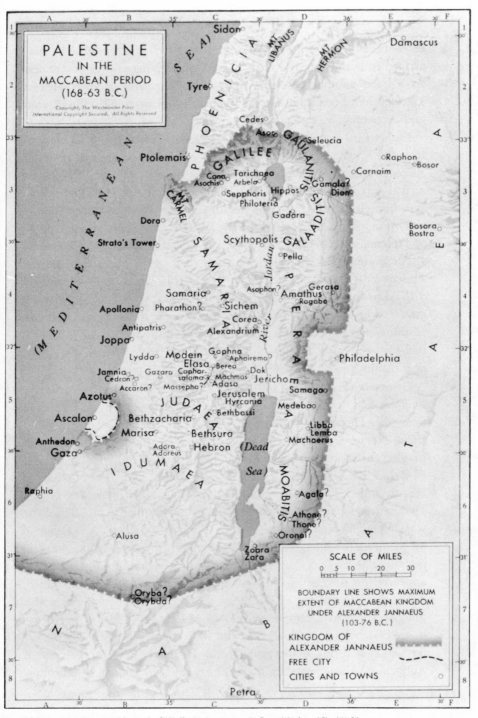

PALESTINE
IN THE
MACCABEAN PERIOD
(168-63 B.C.)

Copyright, The Westminster Press
International Copyright Secured. All Rights Reserved.

SIDON
SEA) Sidon
Damascus
MT LIBANUS
MT HERMON
Tyre
PHOENICIA
Cedes
Asor
Seleucia
Raphon
Bosor
GALILEE
GAULANITIS
Carnaim
Ptolemais
Cana
Tarichaea
Gamala?
Dion
Asochis
Arbela
Sepphoris
Hippos
Philoteria
MT CARMEL
Gadara
Bosora
Bostra
Dora
SAMARIA
Scythopolis
GALAADITIS
Strato's Tower
Jordan
Pella
Samaria
Asophon
Amathus
Gerasa
Apollonia
Pharathon?
Sichem
Ragabe
Antipatris
Corea
Joppa
Alexandrium
River
Philadelphia
Lydda
Modein
Gophna
Aphairema
Berea
Elasa
Jamnia
Gazara
Caphar-
Dok
Jericho
Cedron
salama
Machmas
Samaga
Accaron?
Massepha?
Adasa
Jerusalem
Azotus
Hyrcania
JUDAEA
Medeba
Ascalon
Bethzacharia
Bethbassi
Libba
Marisa
Bethsura
Lemba
Anthedon
Adora
Hebron
(Dead
Machaerus
Gaza
Adoreus
MOABITIS
Raphia
IDUMAEA
Sea)
Agata?
Athone?
Thone?
Alusa
Oronai?
Zoara
Zara
Oryba?
Orybda?
N
A
Petra

MEDITERRANEAN

(M

SCALE OF MILES
0 5 10   20   30

BOUNDARY LINE SHOWS MAXIMUM
EXTENT OF MACCABEAN KINGDOM
UNDER ALEXANDER JANNAEUS
(103-76 B.C.)

KINGDOM OF
ALEXANDER JANNAEUS
FREE CITY
CITIES AND TOWNS

cabaeus. But soon they had to advance against Philip who had arrived in Syria from the East; he was quickly driven out of Antioch. In 161 B.C. another pretender appeared: Demetrius, son of Seleucus IV, who had been a hostage of Rome. He captured and killed Lysias and Antiochus V and assumed power.

Demetrius I Soter (161-150 B.C.) was an ambitious king who planned to restore Seleucid power. He failed to win the full support of his subjects and was regarded suspiciously by the Romans. Eventually a rival appeared: Alexander Balas, backed by Attalus II of Pergamum, put himself forward as an illegitimate son of Antiochus IV and was promptly recognized by the Romans. In 152 B.C. he landed at Ptolemais (Acre) and in 150 B.C. he defeated and killed Demetrius I. Alexander Balas (150-145 B.C.) married Cleopatra, a daughter of Ptolemy VI of Egypt. In 147 B.C. Demetrius (son of Demetrius I) arrived in Cilicia and was supported by his father's friend, Apollonius, governor of Coelesyria (the territory between the Lebanon and Mt. Hermon). In 145 B.C. he won an unexpected ally in Ptolemy VI (who had turned against his son-in-law); together they defeated Alexander near Antioch.

Demetrius II Nicator (145-138 B.C.) was now king of Syria. Before long he had to deal with a revolt in Antioch; and then Trypho, a general of Demetrius, supported the claim of a young son of Alexander Balas, whom he named Antiochus VI. The kingdom of Syria was divided between the rival kings, Demetrius II and Antiochus VI (145-142 B.C.). Trypho (142-138 B.C.), who had been acting as regent, killed his young charge in 142 B.C. and took the crown. Demetrius II had to campaign against the Parthians; in 140 B.C. he was taken prisoner by the Parthian king Mithradates I. (Released by Mithradate's successor, Arsaces, Demetrius reigned for a second period: 129-125 B.C.) In 138 B.C. Antiochus, brother of Demetrius, appeared on the scene and Trypho was at last defeated and killed. Antiochus VII Sidetes (138-129 B.C.) brought the short-lived Jewish independence to a temporary end in 134 B.C. In 130 B.C. he reconquered Babylonia and Media, but the following year (129 B.C.) he was killed in battle against the Parthians. The successors of Antiochus VII, occupied in domestic rivalry, lost control of Palestine.

2) The Maccabaean Revolt[49] (1,2 Mc.; Dn.)

THE PERSECUTION   The determined policy of Antiochus IV (175-
OF ANTIOCHUS IV   163 B.C.), the Hellenization of his kingdom,
sooner or later was bound to drive the Jews into rebellion. At
first, however, the king got all the support he could have wished
for from Hellenized Jews.

Jason, brother of Onias III the high priest, went to Antiochus
and, in return for the high-priestly office, offered a large sum of
money and undertook to carry through the Hellenization of Jerusalem;
he was promptly confirmed as high priest. His work of Hellenization
was supported by many elements in the city and by the powerful
Tobiad family of Ammon. In 172 B.C. Antiochus was approached
by a certain Menelaus (brother of Simon, an enemy of Onias III)
who offered him a huge bribe; again money spoke and Menelaus
obtained the high priesthood. He entered Jerusalem and Jason fled
to Ammon. Onias III, in Antioch, was assassinated by Andronicus,
minister of the king.

Antiochus IV entered Jerusalem in 169 B.C. on his return from
his first campaign in Egypt and, with the connivance of Menelaus,
plundered the Temple. Next year the king invaded Egypt again,
but he had to retire when faced with an ultimatum of the Roman
Senate. Meanwhile, at a rumor of the king's death, Jason attacked
Jerusalem; Menelaus was able to hold out in the citadel north of
the Temple. At the approach of Antiochus, Jason fled; his subsequent
fugitive course ended with his death in Sparta. Antiochus interpreted
the action of Jason as a revolt and decided to deal with it as such.

In 167 B.C. he sent his commander, Apollonius, against Jerusalem
with a large force. Many of the people were massacred, the city
was partly destroyed, and its walls were razed. A fortress, called
the Acra, was built; it dominated the Tyropoeon valley and the
Temple and was manned by a strong Syrian garrison. The Acra
was, in fact, a colony of Hellenized pagans and renegade Jews, with
the constitution of a Greek *polis*. The decree of Antiochus III, which
guaranteed the free observance of Jewish law, was abrogated; instead,
Jewish religion was proscribed. The Temple was dedicated to Olympian Zeus (Antiochus presented himself as a visible manifestation

---

[49]See *Atlante Biblico*, pp. 176-88.

of Zeus; he is so depicted on coins and his name Epiphanes means "[the god] manifest"), and a pagan altar (the "abomination of desolation" [Dn. 9:27; 11:31; 12:11]) was erected over the altar of holocausts. On 25 Chislev (December 8), 167 B.C., pagan sacrifices were offered in the Temple. About the same time the Samaritan temple on Mt. Gerizim was dedicated to Zeus Xenios. Antiochus' actions stiffened Jewish resistance and drove the hesitant into rebellion. A veritable reign of terror launched against the Jews only meant that the explosion came more speedily than it might have.

THE HOLY WAR   Mattathias, a priest of Modein, west of Jerusalem, (167-164 B.C.)   gave the signal for revolt. With his five sons he fled to the mountains of Judaea and was soon joined by other rebels. Particularly valuable support was provided by the Hasidim (Hasidaeans), a group entirely dedicated to the Law. The elderly Mattathias died in 166 B.C., but not before he had entrusted the leadership of the rising to his son Judas Maccabaeus (166-160 B.C.).

Judas organized "flying columns" and harassed the enemy by successful guerilla tactics. Philip, the Phrygian commander of the Acra garrison, had to seek reinforcements from Apollonius, governor of Samaria. In the mountains of Ephraim, Judas intercepted these reinforcements and killed Apollonius. Next, Seron, military commander of Coelesyria, moved against Judas—only to be disastrously defeated at Beth-horon. At this time Antiochus IV was obliged to take action against the Parthians, but he instructed his deputy Lysias to crush the rebellion in Judah. Large forces, under the generals Nicanor and Gorgias, were sent against Judas (165 B.C.); in a night attack on their camp near Emmaus he put the Syrians to flight. In 164 B.C. Lysias himself moved into Palestine, but he was defeated at Bath-zur. As a result an agreement was reached with Antiochus IV on 15 Xanthicus (April 15), 164 B.C. (see 2 Mc. 11:27-33): a general amnesty was declared and the ordinances that had caused the revolt were abolished. On 25 Chislev (December 8), 164 B.C.—three years to the day after the pagan profanation—Judas had the Temple purified and sacrifice offered.

PUNITIVE EXPEDITIONS   The concessions of the king gave rise to (164-163 B.C.)   a wave of anti-Jewish feeling among the Hellenists, and orthodox Jews suffered. Judas decided to undertake punitive expeditions. He and Jonathan went to the aid of Jews who were besieged in Dathema and then subdued several other towns in Gilead while they were about it. Simeon was equally successful in Galilee. In a foolhardy move, a contingent which Judas had left in Jerusalem attacked Jamnia and was defeated.

REVERSES AND RESPITE (162 B.C.) Antiochus IV died in 163 B.C. and was succeeded by his young son Antiochus V Eupator (163-161 B.C.), though the real ruler was Lysias. Judas attacked the Acra—an action contrary to the accord of 15 Xanthicus—and Lysias and the young king moved against him. Judas met them at Bethzechariah; he was defeated and his brother Eleazar fell in the battle. Lysias advanced on Jerusalem, where Judas had retired, and besieged it. The fall of the city was imminent when Lysias heard that Philip (the regent designated by Antiochus IV) had arrived in Syria, and he made a hasty peace with Judas. The Jews were granted full religious freedom; in return they recognized the king. Lysias had executed Menelaus and had appointed as high priest Alcimus, a Hellenized Jew who was not accepted by the Maccabees.

THE WAR OF ALCIMUS (161-159 B.C.) In 161 B.C. Demetrius I Soter (161-150 B.C.) came to power in Syria. He recognized Alcimus as high priest and sent Bacchides, governor of the province Beyond the River (the Afar-nahara of the Persians) to insure that he took office. Judas, fearing treachery, refused to be drawn into a meeting with Bacchides. The Hasidim accepted Alcimus, though some of them were massacred for their pains. When Bacchides retired, Judas commenced to harass the Hellenists; Alcimus went to Antioch and appealed to the king. Nicanor (who had earlier been defeated at Emmaus) was entrusted with the task of subduing Judas, but after some skirmishing a truce was arranged. Alcimus denounced the truce and Nicanor was forced to act. On 13 Adar (March), 160 B.C., Nicanor was defeated and killed at Adasa, five miles north of Jerusalem; the "Day of Nicanor" was celebrated thenceforth as an annual feast. Judas entered into an alliance (couched in very vague terms) with the Romans.

The war was not over, however. Bacchides advanced into Palestine and in April, 160 B.C., Judas was defeated and killed at Beerzeth, about twelve miles north of Jerusalem. The triumphant Hellenists carried out savage reprisals and the spirit of resistance was fanned to flame again. Jonathan (160-143 B.C.) proved a worthy successor

to Judas and began a guerilla war. In May, 159 B.C., Alcimus died
and Bacchides returned to Antioch.

A BREATHING-SPACE   Jonathan and his followers had retreated to
(159-152 B.C.)   the desert of Judah and studiously avoided
open conflict. The Hellenists appealed to Bacchides, but his attempts
to take Jonathan failed. Eventually the peace proposals of Jonathan
were accepted by Bacchides who thereupon returned to Antioch.
Jonathan established himself at Michmash and gradually consolidated
his position. He was accepted as the political and religious head
of the people.

THE BALANCE OF   In 152 B.C. Alexander Balas landed at
POWER (152-143 B.C.)   Ptolemais. Demetrius I hurriedly offered
Jonathan the right to raise troops and declared him his ally, ordering
the Jewish hostages held in the Acra to be released. Jonathan at
once occupied and fortified Mt. Sion, while the Syrian garrisons set
up by Bacchides, except those at Beth-zur and in the Acra, were
withdrawn. Alexander Balas now approached Jonathan and offered
him the high priesthood, the title "Friend of the King," and the
right to wear a purple cloak and a golden crown; Jonathan promptly
changed allegiance. For the rest of his career he was to keep up
this shrewd, and often dangerous, double game between the rival
claimants to the Syrian throne. On the Feast of Tabernacles 152 B.C.
Jonathan officiated as high priest for the first time.

In 150 B.C. Alexander Balas (150-145 B.C.) defeated Demetrius.
Jonathan was appointed general (*stratēgos*) and governor (*meridarchēs*) of Judaea. When Demetrius II appeared on the scene, Apollonius, the governor of Coelesyria who supported him, moved on
Jonathan, but he was defeated at Azotus (146 B.C.). Jonathan was
further honored and was given the territory of Ekron. In 145 B.C.
Demetrius, in alliance with Ptolemy VI of Egypt, defeated Alexander
Balas. Demetrius II Nicator (145-138 B.C.) decided that Jonathan
would make a valuable ally. He summoned Jonathan to a conference
at Ptolemais and confirmed the titles he had received from Alexander;
he also ceded to him the districts of Lydda and Rathamin (west
of Jerusalem) and Aphairema (north of the city). Some time later
Jonathan helped Demetrius to put down a revolt in Antioch, following an assurance that the garrison of the Acra would be evacuated.
The king did not keep his promise.

Meanwhile, Trypho, a general of Alexander Balas, supported the claim of a young son of Alexander, Antiochus VI (145-142 B.C.). Jonathan switched his allegiance to Antiochus VI and found himself appointed the supreme military commander in Syria; his brother Simon was general of the whole Palestinian coast. Jonathan held the generals of Demetrius in check in northern Syria and, at home, fortified Jerusalem. He sent letters to Rome and Sparta. Trypho, who had designs on the throne, was alarmed by the growing power of Jonathan; in 143 B.C. he had the Jewish leader treacherously arrested in Ptolemais.

Simon (143-134 B.C.) now became high priest and governor. Trypho invaded Palestine and made a pact with Simon who had intercepted him. This pact was conveniently forgotten when Trypho was urgently pressed to come to the relief of the Acra. Heavy snow prevented this move and he was forced to retire; but he killed Jonathan before he left the country. Next year (142 B.C.) Trypho assassinated Antiochus VI and reigned in his stead (142-138 B.C.).

INDEPENDENCE   Simon now turned to Demetrius II (who still held part of the kingdom) and was confirmed as high priest and governor. The year was 142 B.C., henceforth regarded as the year of Jewish independence: "The yoke of the Gentiles was removed from Israel, and the people began to write in their documents and contracts, 'In the first year of Simon the great high priest and commander and leader of the Jews'" (1 Mc. 13:41 f.). That same year the Acra fell. The hated symbol of foreign domination was gone at last.

In 140 B.C. Demetrius II was taken prisoner by the Parthians and two years later he was succeeded by his brother, Antiochus VII Sidetes (138-129 B.C.), who disposed of Trypho. The new king demanded of Simon that he should relinquish Joppa, Gazara, and the Acra, all of which he had taken beyond the terms of agreement with Demetrius. When Simon refused to yield, Antiochus sent his general Cendebeus against him; Cendebeus was defeated by John and Judas, the sons of Simon.

Then tragedy befell the Jews: Simon was treacherously murdered by his son-in-law Ptolemy. With his sons, Mattathias and Judas, the high priest had gone to inspect the fortress of Dok near Jericho, and there, at a banquet, he fell victim of a plot, while his two sons and their mother were held as hostages. Ptolemy then appealed to

Antiochus VII for troops and asked to be appointed governor. An attempt to assassinate John, the remaining son of Simon, failed; instead, John was acclaimed in Jerusalem and accepted by the people as high priest and governor.

3) The Hasmonaean Dynasty[50]

From John Hyrcanus onwards the Maccabaean princes are known as the Hasmonaeans (after Hashmon, an ancestor of the family); though it might be said that the dynasty had really begun with Simon Maccabaeus who had achieved independence.

JOHN HYRCANUS I, HIGH PRIEST (134-104 B.C.)   With the survival of John and his acclamation by the people, the plans of Ptolemy were set at nought. Very soon the latter found himself besieged in the same fortress of Dok. However, he managed to escape to Transjordan, though not before killing his hostages. Jewish troubles were only beginning. In 134 B.C. Antiochus VII, whose attempt to cow Simon had failed, advanced into Palestine; he took Joppa and Gazara and besieged Jerusalem. John was obliged to surrender, and though he still remained high priest and governor, he had to pay tribute. As a vassal of Antiochus he took part in a campaign against the Parthians. The short-lived days of independence seemed at an end.

Nevertheless circumstances favored the Jews. In 129 B.C. Antiochus VII was killed in action against the Parthians, and the Seleucids lost control of Palestine. John Hyrcanus was free to act. He conquered Moab (from the Nabataeans), won control of Samaria—promptly destroying the temple on Mt. Gerizim—and campaigned in Idumaea. He was warmly supported by the Hasidim, now beginning to be known as Pharisees. John Hyrcanus died in 104 B.C. The subsequent history of the Hasmonaeans is a sorry page of Jewish history. Fortunately, for our purpose, since it falls outside the canonical histories, it can be treated even more briefly than the preceding stages.

ARISTOBULUS I, HIGH PRIEST AND KING (104-103 B.C.)   John Hyrcanus had arranged that his son Aristobulus should be high priest and that the civil power should be shared by all five sons under

---

[50]See *ibid.*, pp. 188-97.

the authority of their mother. Aristobulus, however, seized power: he threw his mother into prison, where she died, killed Antigonus, and imprisoned the other three brothers. He claimed the title of king and annexed Galilee and Ituraea. When Aristobulus died in 103 B.C. his wife Alexandra (Salome) released the three brothers; the eldest, Alexander Jannaeus, became king and her husband.

ALEXANDER JANNAEUS, HIGH PRIEST AND KING (103-76 B.C.) Determined to extend his territory, Alexander attacked Ptolemais, with the support of Cleopatra of Egypt. He captured Gaza and became master of the whole littoral, except Ashkelon. On the other hand, Alexander broke with the Pharisees and estranged the people. When officiating at the Feast of Tabernacles he was insulted by the people; he retaliated by turning his mercenaries on them and 6,000 of his people perished. Later, a defeat in Transjordan at the hands of the Nabataeans was the signal for revolt, and civil war dragged on for six years. Alexander at last put down the revolt with great cruelty. After this he conquered the Hellenistic cities of Pella, Gerasa, etc. (later known as the district of Decapolis). Alexander Jannaeus died in 76 B.C. and was succeeded by his wife Alexandra.

ALEXANDRA, QUEEN (76-67 B.C.) Alexandra's son, John Hyrcanus II, was high priest (76-67 B.C.; 63-40 B.C.). Her second son, Aristobulus II, received the military command. The queen placated the Pharisees and won their support. Hyrcanus II became king on the death of his mother, but was at once opposed by his brother Aristobulus who defeated him near Jericho. Hyrcanus fled to Jerusalem and was there besieged and forced to surrender.

ARISTOBULUS II, HIGH PRIEST AND KING (67-63 B.C.) Hyrcanus still had much support; the most effective was that of the governor of Idumaea, Antipater. In 65 B.C. John Hyrcanus II (supported by Antipater) and Aretas II, king of the Nabataeans, besieged Aristobulus in Jerusalem. Meanwhile, Pompey, who had conquered Asia Minor, had sent his legate Scaurus to Syria. Both parties appealed to him, but Scaurus ordered Hyrcanus and Aretas to raise the siege. Aristobulus inflicted a heavy defeat on the retreating force. Pompey entered Palestine in 63 B.C. Aristobulus surrendered personally, but Jerusalem resisted and was taken after a siege of three months. This marked the end of Jewish independence. Hyrcanus was established as high priest and received the title of ethnarch. Pompey carried Aristobulus and his son Antigonus off to Rome; Alexander, a second son, escaped on the way.

JOHN HYRCANUS II, HIGH PRIEST   The territory of the ethnarch had
AND ETHNARCH (63-40 B.C.)   been reduced by Pompey and now comprised: Judaea, part of Idumaea, Galilee, and Peraea. The presence of Rome assured internal and external peace, while Antipater, minister of Hyrcanus, was the real ruler. In 57 B.C. Alexander, son of Aristobulus II, appeared and rallied the partisans of his father. Gabinius, procurator of Syria, moved against him; he was besieged in the Alexandreion (a fortress over the Jordan valley) and surrendered. Gabinius divided the territory of the ethnarch into five toparchies which were answerable to the procurator; Hyrcanus retained only the administration of the Temple and an empty title. Aristobulus II, with his sons Alexander and Antigonus, escaped from Rome in 56 B.C. and arrived in Palestine. Gabinius quelled the attempted revolt; Aristobulus was captured and sent back to Rome. In 55 B.C. Alexander attempted another revolt but was defeated near Tabor.

The civil war between Caesar and Pompey began in 49 B.C. Caesar freed Aristobulus, planning to send him to Palestine to stir up trouble there; Aristobulus, however, was poisoned. Antipater persuaded Pompey to execute Alexander, who was being held prisoner at Antioch. Pompey was defeated in 48 B.C. at the battle of Pharsalus. Antipater went to the aid of Caesar in Egypt, and in 47 B.C. Julius Caesar was in Palestine. Hyrcanus was confirmed as ethnarch and Antipater was made procurator of Judaea; the sons of Antipater were governors: Phasael in Jerusalem and Herod in Galilee. In 44 B.C. Caesar was assassinated and Antipater supported Crassus, who had come to Syria. Antipater was poisoned and was succeeded by Herod (43 B.C.). The battle of Philippi took place in 42 B.C. and next year Mark Anthony was in the East. Herod and Phasael, who supported him, were named tetrarchs and Hyrcanus remained high priest.

The Parthians invaded Syria in 40 B.C. and Antigonus (son of Aristobulus II) seized his chance. With the help of the invaders he besieged Herod and Phasael in Jerusalem. Herod managed to escape, but Phasael committed suicide; Hyrcanus had his ears cut off, a mutilation which barred him from the office of high priest.

FROM THE EXILE TO THE END OF THE HASMONAEAN DYNASTY

JUDAH	NEO-BABYLONIAN EMPIRE	
	Nabopolassar	626-605
587—Fall of Jerusalem	Nebuchadnezzar	605-562
	Avil-marduk	562-560
	Neriglissar	560-556
Exile	Labashi-marduk	556
	Nabonidus	556-539
	Cyrus took Babylon	539

JUDAH	PERSIAN EMPIRE	
538—Edict of Cyrus	Cyrus	550-530
Return under Shesh-bazzar		
Return under Zerubbabel	Cambyses	530-522
515—Temple dedicated	Darius I	522-486
	Xerxes I	486-465
445-433—Nehemiah governor	Artaxerxes I	465-424
Second term between 433 and 424		
428—Arrival of Ezra	Xerxes II	424
Bagoas governor	Darius II	423-404
	Artaxerxes II	404-358
	Artaxerxes III	358-338
	Arses	338-336
	Darius III	336-331
	Battle of Gaugamela	331
	End of Persian Empire	

ALEXANDER THE GREAT 336-323

THE PTOLEMIES			THE SELEUCIDS	
Ptolemy I	323-285	The Jews under the Ptolemies	Seleucus I	312-280
Ptolemy II	285-246		Antiochus I	280-261
Ptolemy III	246-221		Seleucus II	246-226
			Seleucus III	226-223
Ptolemy IV	221-203	198—Seleucid conquest of Palestine	Antiocus III	223-187
		The Jews under the Seleucids		
Ptolemy V	203-181		Seleucus IV	187-175
Ptolemy VI	181-145		Antiochus IV	175-163
		167—Religious persecution		
		Maccabaean revolt		
		Judas 166-160		
		164—Temple purified		
			Antiochus V	163-161
		Jonathan 160-143	Demetrius I	161-150
			Alexander Balas	150-145
			Demetrius II	145-138
Ptolemy VII	145-116	Simon 143-134	Antiochus VI	145-142
			Trypho	142-138
		142—Independence		
			Antiochus VII	138-129
		134—Simon assassinated		

THE HASMONAEAN DYNASTY

Ptolemy VIII	116-108	John Hyrcanus I	134-104	Demetrius II		129-125
Ptolemy IX	108-88	Aristobulus I	104-103	Antiochus VIII		125-96
				Antiochus IX		115-95
Ptolemy VIII	88-80	Alexander Jannaeus	103-76	Anarchy		
				Tigranes, king of Armenia,		
Ptolemy X	80			occupied Syria, 63-69		
Ptolemy XI	80-51	Alexandra	76-67	Aretas III		85-60
		Aristobulus II	67-63	63—Roman province of Syria		
		End of Jewish independence				
Cleopatra	51-30	John Hyrcanus II	63-40			
		Antigonus	40-37			
		End of the Hasmonaean Dynasty				
		Herod the Great 37 B.C.-4 A.D.				

ANTIGONUS, HIGH PRIEST   The Roman reaction to the Parthian in-
AND KING (40-37 B.C.)   vasion was rapid: by 39 B.C. Asia Minor
and Syria had been recovered. Herod had made his way to Rome
where he was recognized as "King of the Jews" by Octavian and
Anthony—and given the task of winning his kingdom. In 39 B.C.
Herod, at the head of Roman legions, landed at Ptolemais. The war
against Antigonus went on for three years; Herod laid siege to
Jerusalem in 37 B.C. (and married Mariamme, a Hasmonaean princess,
during the siege). Antigonus was captured and sent to Antioch where
he was executed. The Hasmonaean dynasty was at an end. The
subsequent history of Herod and his successors forms the background
of the New Testament and is treated in Volume Three of this series.

13. THE PHYSICAL GEOGRAPHY OF PALESTINE

Palestine is the coastal belt which links the valley and delta of the
Nile with the valley of the Tigris and Euphrates to form the "Fertile
Crescent." In comparison with the two great arms of this crescent,
Palestine is small indeed. The area west of the Jordan is only 6,000
square miles; the addition of the Transjordan region brings the total
area to no more than 10,000 square miles. The traditional limits of
the country, Dan in the north and Beer-sheba in the south (see 1
Kgs. 4:25) are only 150 miles apart. From east to west the distances
are much less: from Accho to the Sea of Galilee is 28 miles, widening
to about 60 miles between the Mediterranean and the Dead Sea.

1) Physical Structure

The physical structure of Palestine is relatively simple and the land
may be divided into four main sections: (1) the Coastal Plain; (2)
the Central Hill Country; (3) the Jordan Valley; (4) the Plateau
of Transjordan.

1. *The Coastal Plain.* The Palestinian coastline is almost unbroken.
The bay of Accho, north of Mt. Carmel, is too open to be really
safe. In former times Accho (Ptolemais, Acre) was the port; today
the modern port of Haifa is on the south of the bay. The only other
seaport is Jaffa (Joppa), midway along the coast—again offering
very little protection. It is not surprising, then, that the Israelites
never became a seafaring people. The coastal plain may be divided
into three parts: the plain of Accho (or Acre) north of Mt. Carmel;

the plain of Sharon from Carmel to Jaffa—only twelve miles at its widest—the more extensive Philistine plain south of Jaffa.

2. *The Hill Country* forms the backbone of the land and again may be taken in three parts: Galilee, Samaria, and Judah. The hills of Galilee rise to 4,000 feet in the north (Upper Galilee) and slope towards the south (Lower Galilee). Galilee, particularly Lower Galilee —the region of Nazareth—is relatively fertile. Between Galilee and Samaria lies the wide and very rich valley of Jezreel (Esdraelon), running from the bay of Accho to Mt. Gilboa and giving easy access to the Jordan valley. The pass of Megiddo links Jezreel to the plain of Sharon; while to the north of the valley of Jezreel rises the isolated Tabor, 1850 feet above sea level. The mountains of Samaria extend from Gilboa (1737 ft.) to Baal-hazor (3333 ft.). In the center of the territory are the twin mountains of Ebal (3085 ft.) and Gerizim (2890 ft.), with the little plain of Shechem at their foot. There is no clear-cut division between Samaria and Judah. Jerusalem stands at 2593 feet and the land rises towards Hebron (3346 ft.). Between the mountain country of Judah and the Philistine plain lies a series of gently sloping hills, the Shephelah; this is the only really fertile part of Judah. To the east, running towards the Jordan valley and the Dead Sea, is the arid "Wilderness of Judah." South of Hebron, between Beer-sheba and the Gulf of Aqabah, is the Negeb, a dry limestone plateau. In former times the northern part of this region was populous and today the Israelis are restoring something of its fertility.

3. *The Jordan Valley* is part of a great rift or geological fault running from Syria to Africa. The Jordan rises on the eastern slopes of Mt. Hermon. At Lake Huleh (now almost entirely drained) the river is only six feet above sea level. Between Huleh and the Sea of Galilee (a distance of ten miles) it drops almost 700 feet. The Sea of Galilee, a large fresh-water lake abounding in fish, is 685 feet below sea level. From the Sea of Galilee to the Dead Sea the Jordan winds a tortuous course, and empties into the Dead Sea at 1275 feet below sea level. Having no outlet, the water of the Dead Sea contains about 25 per cent salt deposits and tolerates no life. The continuation of the Jordan Valley, from the Dead Sea to the Gulf of Aqabah, is called the Arabah.

4. *The Plateau of Transjordan* is divided into five sections by four rivers: the Yarmuk, just south of the Sea of Galilee; the Jabbok, halfway towards the Dead Sea; and the Arnon and Zered which flow into the Dead Sea. North of the Yarmuk was the biblical Bashan; Gilead stretched on both sides of the Jabbok with Ammon to the east. South of the Arnon lay Moab, and further south, Edom.

2) Climate

Small as Palestine is, its climatic conditions are varied. Along the coastal plain the average annual temperature is about 67 degrees Fahrenheit. Inland, Jerusalem, at its altitude of 2600 feet, has an average temperature of 63 degrees Fahrenheit. At Jericho (700 feet below sea level) the winter is pleasant, but the summer heat is almost unbearable. The average temperature of the Transjordan Plateau is roughly the same as in Jerusalem.

Strictly speaking Palestine has two seasons. From October to mid-May is the wet season, which reaches its climax in the months of January and February; in these months there are violent storms of wind, thunder, and torrential downpours. This winter rainfall is necessary for life because much of Palestine is without springs or running streams and the rain water has to be carefully collected in cisterns hewn out of the rock. Besides, the early (October) and late (April-May) rains are vital for agriculture. The prevailing wind is west (or southwest); this wind is cooling and there is a considerable drop in temperature at sunset. The occasional east wind brings the oppressive *khamseen,* the sirocco.

| *The Pentateuch*

1. THE PENTATEUCH

1) The Title

The first five books of the Bible make up an ensemble which the Jews call the *Torah*—the Law. The first certain testimony to this usage appears in the prologue of Sir., and the appellation was current at the beginning of our era. In Greek it became *hē pentateuchos (biblos)*—"the book in five volumes," which became in Latin, *Pentateuchus (liber)*. This division into five books was attested by the LXX. It named the books according to their content. Thus:

Genesis—begins with the *origin* of the world.
Exodus—deals with the *exodus* from Egypt.
Leviticus—contains the law of the priests of the tribe of *Levi*.
Numbers—because of the *census* of chapters 1-4.
Deuteronomy—the "*second Law*"; a Greek interpretation of Dt. 17:18.

In the Hebrew the Jews designated the books by the first word, or the first important word, of the text. (Cf. the titles of encyclicals.)

2) The Books

GENESIS *Bere'shîth*—"In the beginning": the history of the preparation of the Chosen People.

1. External form; Gn. is divided into ten "generations"—*tôledôth*.

   1) Toledoth of heaven and earth—1:1-2, 4a.

101

    2) Toledoth of Adam—5:1
    3) Toledoth of Noah—6:9
    4) Toledoth of Sons of Noah—10:1
    5) Toledoth of Shem—11:10
    6) Toledoth of Terah—11:27—Abraham
    7) Toledoth of Ishmael—25:12
    8) Toledoth of Isaac—25:19
    9) Toledoth of Esau—36:1
   10) Toledoth of Jacob—37:2
  2. According to subject matter.
    1) Primeval History: 1-11.
    2) History of the Patriarchs of the Chosen People: 12-50:
       Abraham—12:1—25:18.
       Isaac and Jacob—25:19—26:43.
       Joseph—27-50.

The primeval history is like an introduction to the Bible, an introduction to the history of salvation. It reaches back to the beginning of the world and includes all men in its perspective. It tells of the creation of the universe and of man; it tells of the Fall and of its consequence: the growing perversity that is punished by the Deluge. After Noah the earth is again repeopled. The genealogies, at first general, concentrate finally on one man, Abraham, the father of the Chosen People. The patriarchal history depicts the great ancestors:

1. *Abraham* is the man of faith whose obedience is rewarded by God; he will have a posterity and his descendants will possess the Promised Land.

2. *Jacob* is the man of guile who supplants his brother Esau, slyly wins the blessing of his father Isaac, and surpasses in trickery his uncle Laban. But all his ability would be to no purpose if God had not chosen him before his birth and had not renewed the promises and the Covenant which he had made with Abraham.

3. *Isaac* is a very pale figure beside Abraham and Jacob; he is mentioned only because of his father and of his son. The twelve sons of Jacob are the ancestors of the twelve tribes of Israel. The closing chapters of Gn. (37-50) are consecrated to one of them:

4. *Joseph*, the wise man. This narrative differs from what has gone before. There is no visible intervention of God and no new

revelation. The whole is a moral teaching: the virtue of a wise man is rewarded and Providence can draw good from the sins of men.

Genesis is complete in itself: it is the history of the ancestors of the Chosen People.

The next three books form a unit: the formation of the Chosen People and the establishment of its social and religious law are shown in the framework of the life of Moses.

EXODUS   *We'elleh shemôth*—"These are the names": the history of the exodus of Israel from Egypt and the journey to Mt. Sinai; the Covenant with God and the earliest legislation.

1. Deliverance from Egypt—1:1—15:21.
2. The Desert Journey—15:22—18:27.
3. The Covenant at Sinai—19-40.

Moses had had a revelation on Mt. Sinai and there had heard the ineffable name of God. To this holy place he led the people now free from their bondage. In a striking theophany God made a Covenant with his people and gave them his laws. The Covenant was immediately broken by the adoration of the golden calf, but God pardoned his people and renewed the Covenant. The cult was organized by means of special prescriptions and ordinances.

LEVITICUS   *Wayyiqra'*—"(Yahweh) called": legislation regarding the cult and priestly ministry; it contains primitive laws with many later additions.

1. Sacrificial ritual—*torah sacrificiorum*—1-7.
2. The inauguration of priests—Aaron and his sons—8-10.
3. Laws on legal purity—*torah munditiae*—11-15.
Appendix: ritual of the day of Expiation (*Yôm kippur*)—16.
4. Law of sanctity—*torah sanctitatis*—17-26.

Appendix: redeeming of persons, animals, and goods consecrated to Yahweh.

Leviticus, almost entirely legislative, interrupts the narrative.

NUMBERS   *Bammidbar*—"in the desert": the name derives from the census of the people in chapters 1-4; but this preoccupation of numbering, ordering, repeating, pervades the whole book. The book is partly historical, partly legislative. The laws are frequently laid down in the light of a particular event. It both supplements the preceding legislation and adapts it to other and later circumstances.

1. Preparations for the departure from Sinai—1:1—10:10.

2. The desert Journey—10:11—21:35.
3. The land of Moab—22-36.

Numbers treats of the desert journey from Sinai. The departure from Sinai was preceded by a census of the people (1-4) and the great offerings were made for the dedication of the Tabernacle (7). After the celebration of the second Pasch the Israelites left the holy mountain (9-10) and, journeying by stages, arrived at Kadesh where an unsuccessful attempt was made to penetrate into Canaan from the south (11-14). After a long sojourn in Kadesh they set out again and came to the plateau of Moab, opposite Jericho (20-25). The Midianites were conquered and the tribes of Gad and Reuben settled in Transjordan (31-32). Around the narrative of these events are grouped the ordinances and prescriptions which complete the legislation of Sinai or prepare the way for the settlement in Canaan.

DEUTERONOMY 'Elleh haddebarim—"These are the words": the repetition (transcription, Dt. 17:18 [LXX]) of the preceding laws; or rather a *recapitulation* of the religious history of the people of Israel from Sinai onwards; and from this history the following moral lesson is drawn: Yahweh the one true God is to be served faithfully. The recapitulation is given in three sermons of Moses spoken at the close of his life. These discourses are full of grave admonitions and exhortations; hence the special oratorical, "deuteronomical" style. A code of laws has been incorporated into the second discourse. These laws are contained elsewhere in the Pentateuch; here they are somewhat changed and perfected.

1. First discourse of Moses—1:1—4:40.
2. Second discourse of Moses—4:41—48:64.
   a) Introduction—4:41-49.
   b) Decalogue as foundation of the Covenant—5-11.
   c) Code of Deuteronomy (12-26) and conclusion—12-28.
3. Third discourse of Moses—29-30.
Appendix—31-34.

The appendix covers the last days of Moses: the mission of Joshua; the canticle and blessing of Moses; and his death.

3) *The Pentateuch as a Whole*

In form the Pentateuch appears as a series of legal texts in a historical framework. It is primarily as the Law of the Chosen People that the book was accepted and recognized as obligatory; it was *Torah*, "Law," not only for Jews but for Samaritans. This Torah makes known to us the constitution of the people of God and the conditions of the divine choice. The different elements of narrative and laws are unified by the theme of the divine plan whose object is the setting up of the people of Israel as a theocratic nation, with Palestine as fatherland and the Mosaic Law as charter.

The central plan and unifying idea of the Pentateuch is summed up in a little credo which the Israelite recited at the offering of the first fruits in the sanctuary:

> A wandering Aramean was my father; and he went down into Egypt and sojourned there, few in number; and there he became a nation, great, mighty and populous. And the Egyptians treated us harshly, and afflicted us, and laid upon us hard bondage. Then we cried to the Lord the God of our fathers, and the Lord heard our voice, and saw our affliction, our toil and our oppression; and the Lord brought us out of Egypt with a mighty hand and an outstretched arm, with great terror, with signs and wonders; and he brought us into this place and gave us this land, a land flowing with milk and honey (Dt. 26:5-9; cf. 6:20-24; Jos. 24:2-13).

Here we learn that God had chosen Abraham and his descendants and had promised them the land of Canaan. Then, when the whole plan seemed to have come to naught in Egyptian bondage, Yahweh intervened again and delivered his people; he made a Covenant with them and brought them into the Promised Land. These facts underlie the different traditions; the ultimate structuring of the material into a great synthesis was guided by the very same facts. Hence the Pentateuch, in its basic facts, in the units which variously reflect these facts, and in its final shape is built around the ideas of election and efficacious intervention and covenant.

2. LITERARY CRITICISM OF THE PENTATEUCH

1) Analysis of the Pentateuch

CERTAIN LITERARY CHARACTERISTICS[1] Despite its unity of plan, of spirit, and of doctrine the Pentateuch shows the marks of real complexity.

---

[1]See A. Robert, *Initiation Biblique* (Tournai: Desclée, 1954), pp. 112 f.; English edition, *Guide to the Bible*, trans. E. P. Arbez and M. R. P. McGuire (New York: Desclee, 1960[2]), pp. 160-62.

1. With regard to the substance, there is, both in the narratives and in the legislation, discontinuity and disorder. Thus Gn. 4:26 and 5:1; 19:38 and 20:1 do not follow in order. The passage 2:4b–4:26 is a unit which interrupts the narrative of 2:4a–5:1 f. The laws of Ex., Lv., and Nm. are not in any discernible historical context, and within the codes the logical sequence is not determined.

2. With regard to the form, there are differences in the vocabulary, syntax, and especially the style and general procedure of composition.

3. The variable use of the divine names Yahweh and Elohim is a singular phenomenon. The problem is this: if it is true that frequently the divine names alternate without apparent reason, how is it that in many other cases they vary in accordance with the theological conceptions and literary character of different sections? So understood, the problem of the divine names is only a particular aspect, though very striking, of 1. and 2. (above) and requires the same principle of solution.

4. Finally, if one concedes the reality of the foregoing problems, one cannot refuse to admit the existence of doublets (for example, Gn. 1:1–2:4a and 2:4b-25; 12:10-20; 20:1-18 and 26:1-11; etc.). By doublets we mean, not the mere repetition of identical data, but the repetition of one same identical fact with differences that are more or less marked. So defined, the fact of doublets does not constitute a new problem distinct from the above-mentioned phenomena, it is simply a crucial case where all the foregoing observations converge. Consequently the problem of doublets cannot receive any other solution than that adopted for the other factors.

THE CRITICAL HYPOTHESES   Especially from the seventeenth century onwards, exegetes began to treat of the problem of the Pentateuch. The foundation of this scientific literary criticism was laid by Richard Simon (1678) and Jean Astruc (1753). Here is a summary of the scientific criticism of the Pentateuch according to its principal systems.

1. *The Earlier Documentary Hypothesis*: theory of different sources. Astruc distinguished two principal sources in Gn.: A document—Elohistic; B document—Yahwistic (afterwards = E and J), plus ten other minor sources. Eichhorn (1780-83) and Ilgen (1798) extended this division to the whole Pentateuch. The Pentateuch was a compilation made by an unknown author, sometime between

Joshua and Samuel, of documents written by Moses and his contemporaries. They named Lv. the *Priester-kodex* (P).

2. *Hypothesis of Fragments.* This is a development of the preceding theory. The sources indicated above are declared to be made
up of various fragments of earlier documents; but these are, in part,
later than Moses. Geddes (1792, 1800), Vater (1802-1805), and De
Wette (1805) supported this theory.

3. *Supplementary Hypothesis.* This is a reaction against such a dis-
section of the Pentateuch. There is one original source (*Grundschrift*)
= ±E, which contains the history of the world to Moses—written
at the time of the Judges or Samuel. Because of many lacunae in E
a later author (or authors), J, from the time of Saul (or Solomon;
Hezekiah) made many borrowings from another early tradition to
fill the gaps in E and to supplement it. Dt. was added in the seventh
century. This is the theory of Ewald (1843-55), Knobel (1857, 1861),
and Schrader (1869).

4. *The Later Documentary Hypothesis.* This was directed against
the foregoing theory. J does not supplement the Elohistic source
but is an independent document which treats of the same history
under a different aspect. In this Elohistic source we may distinguish
the protohistorical source E and the legal source P. The source J
may be divided into J and D (Dt.). Thus we have the "four-document theory" in the order JEDP. This theory was supported by
Reuss (1833), Graf (1866), and Kuenen (1869).

Julius Wellhausen gave this theory a foundation on the Hegelian
philosophy of religion and cult: Since "sense religion" (*Gefühlsre-
ligion*) is always taken to precede "rational religion" (*Vernunftre-
ligion*), Wellhausen, in looking for traces of this evolution in the
Old Testament, distinguished the "religion of the desert" (*Wüstenre-
ligion*)—a mixture of animism, totemism, fetishism, polydemonism, and
polytheism (especially in J, also in E)—from monolatry[2] (Yahweh the

---

[2]Animism: the belief that certain material objects are possessed by spirits;
totemism: worship of an animal which is regarded as the ancestor of a clan,
or as a particular god; fetishism: the superstitious veneration of an inanimate
object; polydemonism: a belief in many supernatural powers, especially evil
spirits; monolatry: restriction of worship to one god while other gods may be
held to exist; monism: the philosophical doctrine which explains all that is in
terms of a single reality; it can also stand for the doctrine of one supreme being
as opposed to a belief in a good and an evil principle.

God of Mt. Sinai—in J and E). The prophets introduced monotheism (D), which the priests reduced to monism (P). According to this theory the Pentateuch would have arisen in the following fashion:

The oldest traditions are contained in the Yahwistic document (J) which came from the kingdom of Judah (because of the prominence given in it to the tribe of Judah and because the narrative centers around Hebron, a Davidic town); it dates from the tenth century, the peaceful time of Solomon. Next comes the Elohistic document (E) from the kingdom of Israel (the emphasis is on the northern tribes); it is somewhat later than the other—perhaps ninth century. After the destruction of the Northern Kingdom in 721 B.C. these two sources were united in one document (JE). Dt. (D) was written in the reign of Josiah and was soon added to the others; hence we get: JED. Finally, the priestly document (P) was written during the Exile, or perhaps soon afterwards (sixth to the fifth centuries B.C.). This is because it contains laws that were unknown in the monarchic age and because it presupposes the centralization of the cult which is inculcated in Dt., and because it distinguishes between priests and levites as Ezekiel had begun to do (Ezek. 43:10-16). It is the law promulgated by Ezra (Neh. 8) and it was joined to the others to form JEDP.

The four-document hypothesis is still accepted—though always in a less rigid form, and often in a much modified form—by the majority of scholars. Within the general framework of the hypothesis, a new critical method was introduced by H. Gunkel (1888-1913): *Formgeschichte* (History of Literary Forms) or *Gattungsgeschichte* (History of Literary Genres). The purpose of the method is to identify and isolate the smaller units that make up the large literary entities and to set these units in their original historical milieux; in other words, to establish their *Sitz im Leben*, their "setting in life." While this approach, in the hands of certain critics, has led to markedly radical positions, it has, when judiciously used, helped our understanding of the Pentateuch. The same method has been applied, with conspicuous success, to the Psalms and the Gospels.

The more recent development of Pentateuchal higher criticism is to be found in the Scandinavian school (Nyberg, Birkeland, Pedersen, Engnell). These see in the Pentateuch not so much various documents as very old *traditions*. Recollections of olden times were

passed on orally for centuries; the essentials were faithfully transmitted, but the accidentals varied according to differences in circumstances, culture, and the like. They may have been written down, in
part, at an early date; as such they may have been incorporated into
the Pentateuch. But it makes little difference if these traditions, or
some of them, were still in oral form when they took their place
in the Pentateuch.

2) *The Origin of the Pentateuch*[3]

THE COMPOSITION OF   The classic documentary theory is no longer
THE PENTATEUCH   accepted without question. The efforts to
make it more precise have led to arbitrary and subjective divisions of
the text. The literary problem of the date and edition of the text in
its final form is taking second place to the *historical* question of the
origin of the "documents"; and these latter are being considered in a
less rigid fashion, in a way more consistent with real life.

It is clear that the origin of the "documents" must be put at a
very early date. Archaeology and the history of Near-Eastern peoples
have shown that many of the laws and institutions of the Pentateuch
have extrabiblical parallels that are much earlier than the date attributed to the "documents." Furthermore many narratives in the Pentateuch presuppose a milieu that is not that of the "documents," but
is very much older. The problem of the Pentateuch, however, remains
and must be faced. There must be some explanation of the doublets,
the repetitions, the disagreements that abound in the Pentateuch,
and which strike the reader from the first page of Gn. We cannot
really explain these facts by a compilation of "documents" which
had been largely fixed in writing, and which were dismembered
and regrouped by a mechanical procedure of literary composition.
On the other hand, these facts denote at the very least certain
"traditions" which were originally connected with the sanctuaries
and recited there. They were formed into cycles in a given atmosphere
and under the influence of a dominant personality. Eventually they
were incorporated into the Pentateuch. Thus, instead of "documents"
JEDP, we should speak of *traditions*: the yahwistic, elohistic, and
priestly traditions of the first four books of the Pentateuch. Dt.
and the "deuteronomical tradition" form a distinct problem.

---

[3]See Roland de Vaux, *La Genèse* (BJ), pp. 13-17.

THE FOUR   1. *The Yahwistic Tradition.* It is called "Yahwistic"
TRADITIONS   because it employs the name Yahweh right from the
creation narrative. It has a special vocabulary, a vivid and colorful
style, and a delicate psychological perception. In a simple and figurative form it gives a profound solution to the grave problems that
torment every man. The history of the Fall and of human depravity
is transformed into the history of salvation—both by striking interventions of God and by the hidden workings of divine Providence (for
example, in saving Noah, leading Abraham to Canaan, bringing back
Jacob, exalting Joseph, freeing Israel from Egypt, and guiding the
people in the desert). The only legislative material belonging to this
tradition is the so-called "Yahwistic" code of Ex. 34.

2. *The Elohistic Tradition.* It uses the name Elohim, for, according to this tradition, the name Yahweh was first revealed to Moses
on Sinai. It has a distinctive vocabulary and sober style. The relations
of God with men are less intimate. The divine manifestations are
on a less material plane and anthropomorphism is avoided. God
remains invisible; he speaks from the midst of fire or cloud; frequently
he speaks in dreams; more often still he acts through the medium
of angels. The "elohistic" Covenant code (Ex. 21-23) is attributed
to this tradition.

3. *The Priestly Tradition.* This tradition is especially interested
in the organization of the sanctuary, in the sacrifices and feasts, and
in the persons and religious functions of Aaron and his sons. All the
legislation in Exodus (except the two Covenant codes), in Leviticus,
and in Numbers is to be attributed to this tradition. But even the
narrative has a legalistic and liturgical bias. It is not easy to fit
the various "priestly" narrative sections into a single continuous narrative. Yet it is the priestly tradition that gave its definitive form
to the Pentateuch.

4. *The Deuteronomical Tradition.* This tradition is limited to the
last book of the Pentateuch. Deuteronomy is largely a recapitulation
of the foregoing history from Horeb onwards; it also repeats the
laws in part. The recapitulation is prompted and marked by a distinctive idea: History reflects the love of Yahweh for his Chosen
People. Yahweh freely chose Israel for his own people, and the
people must acknowledge him as its only God and offer him cult in
his one sanctuary. This doctrine is put forward in a special oratorical,

exhortatory style that is recognizable even in the legislation. The deuteronomical tradition does not affect the other traditions, which in turn have no influence on Dt. (It is perhaps true to say that Dt. *may*, here and there, have slightly changed the first two traditions in a deuteronomical sense.) The same doctrine and style are to be found in Joshua, Judges, Samuel, and Kings, which with Dt. make up a homogeneous literary corpus.

SUMMARY   The *yahwistic* tradition is found especially in Gn. (from chapter 2 onwards), and in Ex. and Nm.

The *elohistic* tradition is found in the same three books, beginning at Gn. 20. (According to some Gn. 15:1-5 is also elohistic.)

The *priestly* tradition begins in Gn. 1 and runs right through the book; it continues through Ex. and Nm. and entirely accounts for Lv. Briefly, then:

Gn., Ex., Nm.: Mixture of yahwistic, elohistic, and priestly traditions.

Leviticus: priestly tradition only.

Deuteronomy: deuteronomical tradition only.

THE APPROXIMATE DISTRIBUTION OF

J, E, AND P TRADITIONS IN GN., EX., AND NM.

YAHWISTIC TRADITION (J)

Gn. 2:4b—4:26; 5:29; 6:1-4; 6-8 (with P—Flood); 9:18-27; 10:8-19; 21:24-30; 11:1-9; 12—13; 15; 16 (with P); 18—19; 21:1-2a,6b-7; 21:22-34 (with E); 22:11,14-15,18; 24—27 (with other elements in 25); 28:13-16,19a; 29—30; 31:1,3,21, (27,31,38-40 ?); 31:43—32:3 (with E); 46:1-6 (with E); 47:1-6,13-31; 48:1-2,7-22 (with E); 50 (with E).
Ex. 1:6-14; 2:11-22; 3—4 (with E); 5:5—6:1; 7—11 (with E and P); 12:29-34,38-39; 13:17—14:31 (with E and P); 15:22-27; 16:15-20; 17:1-7 (with E); 19 (with E); 24:1-2,9-11; 34:1-28 (Yahwistic Code).
Nm. 10:29-32; 11:4-34 (with E); 14 (with E and P); 16 (J or E with P); 20:1—22:21 (with E); 22:22-35; 24.

ELOHISTIC TRADITION (E)

Gn. 20; 21:8-21,22-34 (with J); 22 (with J elements); 28:10-12, 17-18, 20-22; 29:15-30 (?); 31 (with J elements); 32:13b-22; 34 (with J); 35:1-20 (?); 37 (with J); 40—42 (J elements in 41); 45 (with J); 46:1-7 (with J); 48:1-2,7-22 (with J); 50 (with J).
Ex. 1:15-22; 2:1-10; 3—4 (with J); 5:1-4; 7—11 (with J and P); 13:17—14:31 (with J and P); 17:1-7 (with J), 8-16; 18; 19 (with J); 20:1-21; 20:22—23:19 (Elohistic Code); 23:20-33; 24:3-8,12-15,18b.
Nm. 10:33a; 11:4-34 (with J); 12:1-3; 14 (with J and P); 16:1b-2, 12-15, 25-34(?); 20—22 (with J); 23; 32.

PRIESTLY TRADITION (P)

Gn. 1:1–2:4a; 5:1-28,30-32; 6–8 (with J—the Flood: 6:9-22; 7:6-11, 13-16a,18-21,24; 8:1-2a,3b-5,13a,14-19); 9:1-17,28; 10:1-7,20,22-23,31-32; 11:10-32; 16:3,15-16; 17; 21:2b-6a; 23; 25:7-17 (with E) (?); 25:19-21,26b; 27:46–28:5; 28:6-9; 35:22b-29; 36:6-14; 46:8-27; 47:7-12,27-28; 48:3-6; 49:29-33; 50:12-13.

Ex. 1:1-5; 2:23-25; 6:2–7:7; 7–11 (with J and E); 12:1-20,43-50; 13:17–14:31 (with J and E); 16 (with J); 25–31; 34:29-33; 35–40.

Lv. The whole book.

Nm. 1:1–10:28; 12:1-20,43-50; 13:1-17a; 14 (with J and E); 15; 16 (with J and E); 17–19; 25:1-18; 26–31; 33–36.

Dt. 32:48-52 (?); 34:1a,7-9 (?).

DEUTERONOMICAL TRADITION (D)

All Deuteronomy.

D-style passages: Ex. 12:24-27; 13:3-16.

Special sources: Gn. 14; 49:1-28; also elsewhere.

3) *The Formation of the Traditions*

If we regard the Pentateuch as being formed of various parallel "traditions" which had evolved in the course of time, then we cannot hope to fix with any exactitude the date at which any of the traditions was formed. But we may venture an approximation. We must begin with Deuteronomy which, undoubtedly, was connected with the reform of Josiah towards the close of the seventh century B.C. The kernel of our Dt., especially the deuteronomical code, represents the customs of the North brought to Jerusalem by the Levites after the fall of the kingdom of Israel (721 B.C.). This law, found in the Temple in the time of Josiah, was promulgated in the framework of a discourse of Moses. A new edition, with additions in the same spirit, was made at the beginning of the Exile.

The *priestly* tradition is later than Dt. It was formed during the Exile and afterwards joined to the two traditions that are older than Dt.: the *yahwistic,* which had taken shape about the reign of Solomon; and the *elohistic,* which is a little later.

It is more important to know *where* these traditions were formed. It seems natural to think of the sanctuaries which were the meeting places of the Israelites. There were related the wonders wrought by God, his benevolence towards the people he had chosen; there too, the great deeds of the ancestors were extolled. These epic narratives formed the commentary at the feasts which commemorated the interventions of God in the history of the people. It is still more natural to imagine that the codes of laws took shape at the sanctuaries. First of all there were the liturgical laws and cult prescriptions governing the priestly offices. Then, too, the people must have turned to the priests for juridical decisions and moral directives.

The *yahwistic* tradition is undoubtedly of Judaean origin: much of the narrative centers around Hebron; and in the story of Joseph, Judah is shown in a favorable light.

The *elohistic* tradition is generally held to be of Northern origin: it speaks of the activities of the patriarchs in Bethel and Shechem; in the story of Joseph, Reuben and Ephraim figure largely.

The *priestly* tradition is that of the priests of the Temple.

The *deuteronomical* code appears to represent the traditions of the Northern Kingdom brought to Jerusalem by the Levites after the fall of Israel.

Briefly, then:

Yahwistic tradition: Reign of Solomon—10th cent. B.C. (Judah).

Elohistic tradition: Somewhat later—9th cent. B.C. (Israel).

Deuteronomical tradition: Code formed before 721 B.C.; promulgated during reign of Josiah (640-609 B.C.); enlarged edition at the beginning of the Exile (587-538 B.C.). (Israel.)

Priestly tradition: Formed during the Exile; took its final shape most likely after the Exile. (Jerusalem.)

4) The Formation of the Pentateuch

The Yahwistic and Elohistic traditions had taken final shape and had been combined in a single narrative (JE) shortly after 721 B.C. Deuteronomy (built around the earlier code) began to take shape in the time of Josiah and received its final form during the Exile. The priestly tradition grew up contemporaneously with Deuteronomy. Eventually, a priestly writer edited the whole corpus. He took the JE epic as his basis and built into it, at various points, the material, mostly legislative, of the Temple tradition. He detached Dt. from the deuteronomical history[4] and inserted it as a fitting epilogue to the story of Moses. Most of this editing was done during the Exile, but the work was not finished before 538 B.C. Since it seems very likely that the "book of the Law of Moses" brought to Jerusalem by Ezra in 428 B.C. (Neh. 8:1) was the Torah, it may be assumed

---

[4]See p. 153.

that the Pentateuch had taken final shape in the fifth century B.C.; the ultimate work marked the close of a long and involved process that had begun in the Mosaic age. This process may be represented graphically:

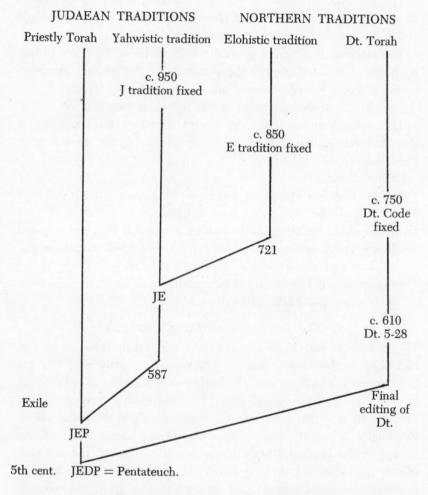

JUDAEAN TRADITIONS   NORTHERN TRADITIONS

Priestly Torah   Yahwistic tradition   Elohistic tradition   Dt. Torah

c. 950
J tradition fixed

c. 850
E tradition fixed

c. 750
Dt. Code
fixed

721

JE

c. 610
Dt. 5-28

587

Exile

Final
editing of
Dt.

JEP

5th cent.   JEDP = Pentateuch.

5) *The Tradition of Mosaic Authorship*

The Pentateuch carries neither name nor signature. Except in Dt., Moses does not speak in the first person and his literary activity is mentioned only in passing. Yet the Torah, when it finally took shape, was attributed to him. We find that our Lord and the Apostles, like their contemporaries, invoked the authority of Moses.

Sometimes they speak, without further precision, of the "Law of Moses" or of the "Book of Moses" and sometimes they mention facts narrated in the Pentateuch. Twice only (Acts 3:22; Rom. 10:19) are determined passages attributed to Moses. The Jews of the Christian era maintained the traditional belief in the Mosaic origin of the Pentateuch, while the Fathers echoed the testimony of Scripture and of Jewish tradition.

Modern literary analysis of the Pentateuch has proved that the work took final shape many centuries later than Moses;[5] it is clear that the traditional conception of Mosaic authorship has to be understood in a broad sense. We have identified the four main strands that together form our Pentateuch, and we have noted the approximate date of each of them. At the same time we should note carefully that the date and place of *formation* of these traditions are not the time and place of their *origin;* they began at a much earlier date.

> The basis of the Pentateuch, the substance of the traditions which it incorporates and the kernel of its legislation go back to the time when Israel became a people. Now, this epoch is dominated by the figure of Moses: he was the organizer of the people, the originator of its cult, its first lawgiver. The earlier traditions which had been preserved up to his time and the meaning of the events which were linked with his name, were forged into a national epic. The religion of Moses has marked for all time the faith and practice of the people; the Law of Moses has remained its rule of life.[6]

We may thus affirm the Mosaic origin of the traditions which make up the Pentateuch. These bear the stamp of the milieux in which they were formed and treasured but, as living traditions, they live by the life and vigor which Moses had imparted to them. This realistic view does, moreover, "establish the large share and the profound influence of Moses as author and legislator."[7]

6) Appendix: The Historical Character of Gn. 1-11

With regard to the first eleven chapters of Genesis, two main factors have to be taken into account. In the first place, these narratives

---

[5]This is admitted in the letter of the Secretary of the Biblical Commission to Cardinal Suhard (1948); see *Enchiridion Biblicum*, n. 580 (henceforth, references to this work will be abbreviated EB); Robert, *op. cit.*, I, p. 774.

[6]Roland de Vaux, *op. cit.*, p. 20.

[7]Cf. Letter to Cardinal Suhard; EB, n. 580; Robert, *op. cit.*, I, p. 774.

do not contain history in the modern sense of the word.[8] Secondly, the authors (though this applies to the Yahwist in a particular way) are not only using pre-existing material, but the narrative moves in the circle of ideas of Semitic mythology.[9] This is not to say that the Paradise story, for instance, is derived from *Enuma Elish* or the Flood story from the Babylonian account of the Flood;[10] it does mean that the Yahwist, and the priestly writer, were familiar not only with the Mesopotamian cosmogony (notion of the universe), but inevitably shared the common ideas of ancient Semitic peoples.

The following assessment of the Paradise story (Gn. 2-3) may be extended, more or less directly, to the whole narrative of primeval history.

> The author has, by skillful creative imagination, woven into a unified whole popular traditions and background elements drawn from highly-diversified sources. Paradise is, geographically speaking, nowhere. Man is described as a primitive agriculturist; this is not only historically impossible, but was known to be impossible by the ancient Semitic peoples. The biblical conception of the pre-Canaanite inhabitants of Canaan, fragmentary as are our notions, did not regard them as urban-agricultural. The formation of man from clay is not only imaginative, but is paralleled in Mesopotamian literature. The order of creation—man, beasts, woman—is evidently an imaginative arrangement, invented for the purposes of the narrative. The serpent is symbolic on the basis of allusions alone. The trees are symbolic, as is their eating; and the curses reflect a social and cultural milieu which is not that of primitive man, but of Mesopotamian and Palestinian civilization in the first or second millennium B.C.[11]

If all this is so, how may we speak of history in any sense? Obviously we may only do so if we give the term a very wide connotation. Our concern is to guard against the mistaken view that the figures and symbols of these narratives have no objective basis, and perhaps we may eventually find a more satisfactory way of describing this strange literary form. As it is we realize that these chapters describe, in a popular way, the origin of the world and of the human race. They relate, in a simple and figurative style,

---

[8]See EB, n. 581; Robert, *ibid.*, p. 775.

[9]See J. L. McKenzie, *Myths and Realities* (Milwaukee: Bruce, 1963), pp. 182-200.

[10]See ANET, pp. 60-72; 93-95. The Akkadian Creation Epic is named *Enuma Elish* ("when on high"), after its opening words.

[11]McKenzie, *op. cit.*, pp. 169 f.

fundamental truths such as the creation of all things by God, the special divine intervention in the production of the first man and woman, the unity of the human race, the sin of the first parents, the depravity and hereditary sufferings which followed the Fall. "But these truths are, at the same time, facts, and if the truths are certain the facts are therefore real. It is in this sense that the first eleven chapters of Genesis have a historical character."[12] God really did make the world "in the beginning." God really intervened in a special way and in a given moment of time—and the human race appeared on this earth. The first parents of the race did sin and evil made its entry into the world. All these are objective facts, historical events, even if they belong to *primeval* history. We cannot date them, we have no other record of them, we do not know how they came to pass—all we do know is that they did really happen.

3. THE CHARACTERISTICS OF THE TRADITIONS

1) *The Yahwist*

The work of the Yahwist is a synthesis, both in form and in substance; yet this writer is one of the most creative literary artists of Israel. He gathered together the traditions of the tribes and of the sanctuaries and reworked them in order to make the old relevant to the new. Many of these old narratives are aetiologies, that is, their purpose was to explain, in a popular way, some facts in tribal history, or the names of places, or certain aspects of the cult. The Yahwist combined these different materials in a new literary structure, a great epic extending from the creation of the world to the conquest of Transjordan. Some of the individual stories, taken by themselves (for example, the angel marriages [Gn. 6:1-4] and the Tower of Babel [Gn. 11:1-9]), betray a primitive theological outlook; but, used by the Yahwist, they play their part in the presentation of his elevated theology.[13] The fact that he did not write as an independent author, but limited his scope to the reworking of older traditions, should be kept in mind—together with the fact that we no longer possess the whole of his epic. These facts explain a certain unevenness and certain inconsistencies in his work.

---

[12]De Vaux, *op. cit.*, p. 35.
[13]See pp. 130-35.

The style of the Yahwist is distinctive. He loves concrete and striking expressions and excels in describing character, for he is a penetrating psychologist. He writes with liveliness, clarity, and polish and is able to sketch a scene with a few bold strokes. He wears his theological proficiency so lightly that his purpose can be misunderstood. Thus, in images, with apparent naïveté, he gives a profound answer to the grave problems which are raised by the presence of evil in the good world created by God: Why death, the pains of woman, the sweat of man (Gn. 3)? Why the dispersion of peoples and their mutual lack of understanding (Gn. 11)? Can the just intercede for the guilty (Gn. 18)? The moral development (or rather retrogression) of humanity is traced in gloomy colors, but the story of repeated falls is transformed into a history of salvation by striking divine interventions, or by the hidden providence of God who saves Noah, leads out Abraham, brings back Jacob, raises Joseph, delivers the people from Egypt, and guides them in the desert. Intimate, concrete relations unite man to God who appears in human form, acts in a human manner, and feels human sentiments: Yahweh shapes man as a potter would; he walks in the garden during the cool of the evening; he accepts the hospitality of Abraham and converses with him; he is sorry and he is angry. But these anthropomorphisms[14] clothe a very elevated idea of God, who always remains the master of his creature, who does not lower himself by his care for that creature, who maintains, unimpaired, his essential holiness.

The Yahwist is keenly aware of the forces of evil at work in the world; he has no illusions about humanity and he unpityingly exposes human weakness, but he is an optimist at heart. He has confidence in nature and her laws, which will not be disrupted by another deluge. He shows the persistence and expansion of life, the good fortune of the sons of Jacob, Israel delivered from slavery, the twelve tribes on their way to a land flowing with milk and honey. This

---

[14]An anthropomorphism (or "manlikeness") is a manner of describing God or of speaking of him in human terms. It is something we cannot avoid altogether if we are to speak of him at all. Thus, though we know that he is a Spirit, we can speak of the "hand of God" and of God "hearing" our prayers. If the Yahwist makes very free use of anthropomorphisms this does not indicate a primitive notion of God, but is the expression of faith in a personal God, a God who really takes an interest in human affairs; a God, we might say, who is taken for granted.

optimism is based on a knowledge of Yahweh, on confidence in his plan and in his power. Yahweh is transcendent, but draws near to men; and this nearness is expressed in bold anthropomorphisms. He demands of men faith, courage, and confidence in the traditions and in the life of the nation.[15]

The Yahwist regards Yahweh as the national God. By revealing himself to Abraham, by delivering the heirs of Abraham from slavery, and by giving them his law he has become *their* God. He does not cease to be the God of all peoples, for his choice of this people is universalist in its ultimate scope: all the nations of the earth will bless themselves by Abraham. But the future belongs to Israel, for Yahweh, her God, alone has power on earth. God gives a share in this power, a part in his plan, to whom he wills; the author emphasizes the absolute freedom of God's choice by contesting the automatic right of the first born. Thus the prayer of Abel is heard in preference to that of Cain, Isaac is chosen instead of Ishmael, Jacob instead of Esau, Judah instead of his three older brothers. In this context it may be noted that the messianic prophecies of the Pentateuch occur in the Yahwist's epic: Gn. 3:15, which promises salvation by the seed of the woman; the prophecy of Jacob regarding Judah (Gn. 49:10); Balaam's prophecy of the star coming forth from Jacob (Nm. 24:17).

The Yahwist's epic falls into three parts: primeval history; the patriarchal tradition; the Mosaic tradition.

PRIMEVAL   The primeval history, constructed from elements of very
HISTORY   different kinds, proclaims that all evil comes from sin
and testifies to a growth in evil. Yet the widening chasm between God and man remains spanned by a bridge of mercy and is matched by an increasing power of grace. In the call of Abraham (Gn. 12:1-3) primeval history is linked with sacred history and finds its meaning in this link.[16]

THE PATRIARCHAL   The Yahwist continues his theological synthesis
TRADITION   by utilizing the patriarchal traditions. In his
eyes, Abraham is the model patriarch. Yet the promises of God are destined not for him but for his posterity. By linking the cycle of

---

[15]See H. Cazelles, IB, I, pp. 348-80. This study has influenced our treatment of the traditions.
[16]See p. 135.

Abraham to the cycle of Isaac the author intended to mark the unity of the cult of the *Elohim* of Abraham, honored at Hebron, and of the *El 'Olam* ("God anciently honored") worshiped at Beersheba and in the Negeb. The further joining of the cycle of Jacob extends the cultic unity to Bethel and to the shrines of the North. Right through the patriarchal epoch runs the cult of the same God (the "God of the fathers") and the participation of successive generations in the same divine promises. Important sections of the cycle of Joseph are due to the Yahwist. Joseph is a providential instrument and the hero of this story, but he is not the heir of the promises. Thus the Yahwist closes with Jacob and his blessing and the assurance that the monarchy will be the inheritance of Judah.

THE MOSAIC For the Yahwist, Moses is the last of the patriarchs,
TRADITION and again the cultic identity is stressed. The God who revealed himself to Moses in the burning bush is the "God of the fathers" (Ex. 3:16). Yahweh is the God who has delivered Israel, his first-born son, at the cost of the first born of Egypt (Ex. 4:22 f.). This God set his people free and established the Pasch as the national feast of liberation. He wills that pilgrimage should be made to his holy mountain (Ex. 24:1 f., 9-11) and there Israel receives from him the commandments in the form of a ritual decalogue (Ex. 34). The union between the Israelite and his God will be maintained by the rite of national pilgrimage to the seasonal feasts (Ex. 34:18,22 f.).

> In the eyes of the Yahwist the central figure and the creator of the religion of Israel is neither patriarch nor king nor wise administrator: it is Moses who communicates to the people the will of God, his words. But Moses does not deliver the people by his own powers, or in virtue of his birth or of his wisdom; he saves them by the divine Revelation which he passes on to the people when they come in pilgrimage into the presence of Yahweh.[17]

2) *The Elohist*

The Elohist begins with the call of Abraham and therefore does not have a primeval history; in this he lacks the universal scope of the Yahwist. Similarly the Elohist does not show the theological depth, much less the literary artistry, of the Yahwist. However, in

---

[17]Cazelles, *op. cit.*, p. 360.

comparing the work of both authors, it is well to keep in mind that circumstances have been unkind to the Elohist. Both J and E (from Abraham onwards) cover much the same ground, and the Judaean editors who combined the Northern and Southern traditions after the fall of Samaria in 721 B.C. understandably gave preference to the Yahwist's epic. It is not possible to reconstruct the E narrative as a continuous account and its impact suffers as a result.

Yet what the Elohist loses in vividness and brilliance he gains somewhat in moral sensibility. His sense of sin is more refined than that of the Yahwist. For instance, he avoids the impression that Abraham had lied to Abimelech by stating explicitly that Sarah was the patriarch's half-sister (Gn. 20:12). Jacob's flock increased not by trickery on his part but because God did not permit Laban to harm him (Gn. 31:3-13, 36-42). For him the law is more moral than cultic. The basis of it, as it finds expression in the Decalogue, concerns man's duties towards God and towards his neighbor. These duties are made more explicit in the Covenant Code (Gn. 20:22–23:19) where the respect of one's neighbor and of his goods is regulated by customs and precepts that have been sanctioned by God.

The Elohist tends to emphasize the distance of God from men, at least in comparison with the Yahwist's approach. Anthropomorphism is restricted: God does not come to walk among men (cf. Gn. 3:8; 18:1 ff.), but speaks from heaven (Gn. 21:17) or in dreams (Gn. 15:1; 20:3, 6; 28:12). Indeed, it is stated explicitly: "Let not God speak to us, lest we die" (Ex. 20:19). Dreams figure largely in the story of Joseph and, as one would expect, the narrative which treats of this ancestor of the Northern tribes of Ephraim and Manasseh is more developed than in the Yahwist tradition. Here, too, the moral perception of the Elohist brings out the religious significance of the events: "As for you, you meant evil against me; but God meant it for good, to bring it about that many people should be kept alive, as they are today" (Gn. 50:20).

Perhaps, after all, the loss of immediacy with God and with his revealed word in E does not have the force it seems to have at first sight. It certainly serves to throw into prominence the special status of Moses, and it was calculated to produce this effect. To Moses the name of God, *Yahweh,* was revealed. He alone could speak to Yahweh "mouth to mouth" and could "behold the form of the Lord" (Nm. 12:8). Even more strikingly it is said of him: "The Lord used to speak to Moses face to face, as a man speaks to his friend" (Ex. 33:11); and he reflected the radiance of the divine glory (Ex. 34:29-35). He is the Prophet *par excellence*, filled with the spirit of God which he communicates to the elders (Nm. 11:10-30). Hosea can comment: "By a prophet the Lord brought Israel up from Egypt and by a prophet it was preserved" (Hos. 12:13). Likewise, Abraham is called a prophet (Gn. 20:7) and Miriam a prophetess (Ex. 15:20). The significance given to the prophet and his office must mean that E has influenced the development of prophecy in Israel.

3) The Deuteronomist[18]

The kernel of Deuteronomy is the legal code (Dt. 12:1–26:15) of Northern origin, going back ultimately to the Mosaic age; the narrative part, the three discourses of Moses, are much later, from just before and after the Exile. The second discourse is especially fitting in the mouth of the great leader, because the essential purpose of Dt. is a revival of Mosaic teaching as it was understood in the seventh century B.C.; it is a reform program, not an innovation. Hence the appeal for Covenant renewal, made with urgency, the repetition of "this day," the here and now of the divine election, and the involvement of the present generation of Israel in the Covenant made at Horeb.[19] The law of the one sanctuary (Dt. 12:1-12) is inspired by the same reforming spirit: to preserve the purified cult of Yahweh from all contamination.

The style of the deuteronomist is distinctive. (We shall see that deuteronomical passages in the history Jos.-Kgs. are readily discernible.) In the discourses, characteristic turns of phrase keep cropping up. God is always "the Lord thy God" or "the Lord your God." Canaan is described as "a land flowing with milk and honey," and, in order that they might possess it, God had delivered his people from Egypt "with a mighty hand and an outstretched arm." This is why the people are admonished to "hear the voice of the Lord your God" and to "keep his statutes and his commandments and

---

[18]For a further treatment, see pp. 148-52.

[19]See B. W. Anderson, *Understanding the Old Testament* (Englewood Cliffs, N.J.: Prentice-Hall, 1957), p. 313.

ordinances" and to "fear the Lord your God." Above all, they are
exhorted: "You shall love the Lord your God with all your heart,
and with all your soul and with all your might." And throughout
there is the frequent reminder that faithful observance of the commandments of Yahweh will insure a blessing, and the warning that
neglect of the commandments will bring upon them the anger of a
loving but just God.

This warning should have been unnecessary, for these "statutes,
commandments, and ordinances" are not a heavy burden imposed
from without, but are intimate, interior: "For this commandment
which I command you this day is not too hard for you, neither is
it far off. . . . The word is very near you; it is in your mouth and
in your heart, so that you can do it" (Dt. 30:11,14). Yahweh is a
Father who gives his life-giving Word to Israel, the Word that
brings happiness and long life. It is the Word that reveals: "The
secret things belong to the Lord our God; but the things that are
revealed belong to us and to our children forever, that we may do
all the word of this law" (Dt. 29:29). A theology of the people of
God, and a theology of the life-giving Word, it is also a theology of
Revelation.[20]

Another characteristic of Dt., and one which witnesses to the
Northern origin of the tradition, is the influence of Hosea. That
Prophet, too, looked back to the Exodus as to the happy honeymoon
period of Israel's religion. None more fittingly than he has painted
the undying love of Yahweh for his faithless spouse, because he
drew his colors from life, from his own unhappy experience. It is
significant that "love" is a key word of Dt. (for example, Dt. 7:8;
10:15; 26:6; 30:6-20). Indeed, together with the whole deuteronomical
history, it becomes a commentary on chapter eleven of Hosea: "When
Israel was a child I loved him, and out of Egypt I called my son.
But the more I called them the further they departed from me. . . .
How can I give you up, O Ephraim" (11:1-2,8).

Hosea is not the only prophet whose influence is evident. Jeremiah
(chapter 31) had foreseen a deliverance, a return, a new Covenant;
it was in this spirit that Dt. was completed. And in its final chapters,
too, our book joins Second Isaiah, who described the new journey

---

[20]See Cazelles, *op. cit.*, 370.

across the desert and the victory over the nations now summoned to adore the God of Israel, the only true God. Other images are borrowed from Ezekiel who also described the return from the Exile and the new division of the holy land around the new sanctuary (Ezek. 37; 40-48; cf. Dt. 3:12-17). Thus inspired by the prophetical books, Deuteronomy, in its final edition, is a witness to a crucial stage in religious history when a Monarchy yielded place to a Church.[21]

4) The Priestly Tradition

The broad spirit of Deuteronomy did not appeal to the conservative-minded clergy of Jerusalem. These took their stand on the transcendence of Yahweh: instead of bringing God, and the word of God, near to men they sought rather to raise man to God by fidelity to the traditional laws and prescriptions. Their rule was the command: "You shall be holy; for I the Lord your God am holy" (Lv. 19:2).

At much the same time that the deuteronomical code took shape in the North, the traditions of the Jerusalem priests were compiled in the Holiness Code (Lv. 17-26). Like the deuteronomical code, it opens with the law of one sanctuary and then gives several series of prescriptions regarding morality, marriage, the priests, the sacrifices, and the feasts; it closes like Dt. with blessings and curses (Lv. 26). Israel is conceived as an 'edah, a worshiping community, ruled by the priests. The date of the Holiness Code is uncertain; it may well have been edited during the reign of Josiah, shortly before the fall of the nation, but it certainly contains many much older laws.

During the Exile the deported priests, cut off from the elaborate, ritual worship of Yahweh in his Temple, saw that their duty was to organize the religious life of the community in these different surroundings and circumstances. It seemed to them that the foundations on which this religious life might be built must be a common national origin, common traditions, and an authentic priesthood. Thus the priestly history took shape. The religious institutions of Israel were authorized and given greater force by being set in a historical framework; by projecting all these institutions back into the Mosaic

---

[21]See H. Cazelles, *Le Deutéronome* (BJ), p. 17.

age, it is dramatically emphasized that they had their beginning at Sinai. The whole presentation is pervaded by a theology of the divine presence and by the demands of a God of holiness.

It is relatively easy to isolate the P material of the Pentateuch. Since much of the priestly work is editorial, this material does not form a unified structure; but it is possible to discern, and present coherently, the priestly view of Israel's history. God's revelation is conceived as following a systematic plan which unfolds in four successive eras or dispensations: Creation; the Covenant with Noah; the Covenant with Abraham; the Sinai Covenant.[22] Each stage is marked by different privileges and duties and different divine names are employed: *'Elohim* in the first two stages; *'El Shaddai* for the patriarchs; and *Yahweh* for the time of Moses.

Though the dry, technical style of P is readily recognizable, the priestly writer can sometimes reach sublime heights; his masterpiece is the creation story (Gn. 1–2:4a). While its form and rhythm point to liturgical use, and while the rearrangement of eight works into a six-day week points to pre-existing traditional material, it was surely one author who gave final form to the story. The understanding, or misunderstanding, of this creation story depends on the answer to the question: What does the author of the story teach us? The plain answer is that he teaches two facts: 1) God made all things.[23] 2) The sabbath is of divine institution. These two things he wishes to drive home. He believed that God created the world, but he understood no more than we (much less indeed) how it was created. He might have stated his belief bluntly, but he judged it much more effective to parcel out the work and so emphasize the fact that God made *everything*. The result of it all is that the writer's assertion, "In the beginning God created heaven and earth," is true, divinely true, but that the description of the work of creation is a product of his imagination.

For the creation story is, from the literary viewpoint, patently an artificial composition. We find that the work of the six days is so distributed that there is a close correspondence between the first

---

[22]See pp. 137-39.

[23]This truth is, of course, complex, and includes a number of facts such as the special creation of man; still these can be fairly considered as the component parts of one inclusive fact.

day and the fourth, between the second and the fifth, between the third and the sixth. We also find that the author shares the ideas of his own time and not those of the scientific twentieth century. The people for whom he wrote—and he himself for that matter— were quite unable to grasp an abstract notion of creation (not because of lack of intelligence, but simply because of their Semitic mentality), but they did understand work; hence he presents the Creator as a Workman who completed his work in six days and then took a rest. The climax of this work is the creation of man and woman in the image and according to the resemblance of God, and their dominion over the whole material and animal world. The terms of this creation imply a state of friendship with God. It is taught that God instituted marriage and sanctified it. When all was finished, "God blessed the seventh day and sanctified it, because on it God rested from all his work of creation" (Gn. 2:3). Thus, very neatly, the story of creation is rounded off by the declaration that it was God himself who has begun the sabbath rest: the Chosen People can do no better than imitate their God.[24]

If we look again at the priestly history as a whole, we see it as the fruit of a theological reflection on the ancient liturgical tradition and customs preserved by the Jerusalem priests. Fidelity to these traditions is the only guarantee of a life in union with God, the only means of bringing about the fulfillment of God's purpose for Israel. This follows from a consideration of that plan as it gradually unfolded.

> There was a covenant of God with all humanity in the person of Noah—it assured earthly existence if men would respect the life of creatures. There was a covenant with Abraham—it guaranteed his descendants a future in the Promised Land if they would observe the sabbath and circumcision. There was a more personal covenant with the Aaronitic priesthood, which made of them the associates of God and the dispensers of the divine benefits: the cult is the sensible sign of divine grace. The monarchy had failed; in the mind of the priestly writer, Aaron must henceforth take its place—Israel in Exile is sustained by the priesthood in her fidelity to the national and religious traditions. For Israel is "a kingdom (ruled by) priests and a holy nation" (Ex. 19:6).[25]

---

[24]See W. Harrington, *Genesis and Evolution* (New York: Paulist Press, 1963), pp. 13-20; 24-26.
[25]Cazelles, IB, p. 376.

5) *The Message of the Pentateuch*[26]

The religion of the Old Testament, like that of the New, is a historical religion: it is based on the revelation made by God to certain men in given times and places and on the interventions of God at certain determined moments. The Pentateuch, which traces the history of these relations of God with the world, is the foundation of the Jewish religion, its sacred book *par excellence,* its Law. In it the Israelite found the explanation of his own destiny and a way of life.

The Pentateuch is drawn into a unity by the threads of promise and election, of covenant and law which run through it. To Adam and Eve, after the Fall, God gives the assurance of salvation in the distant future; after the Flood he reassures Noah that the earth will never again be so disastrously stricken. Abraham is the man of promises—for himself and for his posterity and through them for all mankind. In God's free choice of Abraham the election of Israel is foreseen and included. The Pentateuch is also the book of covenants: tacit with Adam; explicit with Noah, Abraham, and Moses. Each covenant is a free exercise of divine initiative, an act of benevolence; God demands in return fidelity and obedience. The Law which he gives will make explicit the divine demands and prepare the way for the fulfillment of the promises.

The unifying themes of the Pentateuch continue into the rest of the Old Testament, for the Pentateuch is not complete in itself. It tells of the promise but not of its fulfillment and it closes before the entry into the Promised Land. But even when the Conquest is achieved the fulfillment is not yet, for the promise looks ultimately to Christ, to the new Covenant and to his new Commandment.

A Christian reading of the Pentateuch should follow the sequence of events. Genesis first sets in opposition the goodness of God the Creator and the faithlessness of sinful man and then shows, in the patriarchs, the reward of faith. Exodus is a sketch of our redemption. Numbers represents the time of trial when God instructs and chastises his children and prepares his elect. Leviticus may be fruitfully read with the last chapters of Ezekiel or after the books of Ezra and Nehemiah. The unique Sacrifice of Christ has rendered obsolete the ceremonial of the Temple, but the demands of purity and sanctity in the service of God retain their force. Deuteronomy can be read with Jeremiah; for it is close to that Prophet in time and spirit.

---

[26]See Roland de Vaux, BJ, pp. 7 f.

4. DOCTRINAL ASPECTS OF THE PENTATEUCH

1) *The Theology of Primeval History*[27]

If we are to understand the first eleven chapters of Genesis we must be aware of two factors. First, these chapters combine two of the four distinct traditions that make up the Pentateuch—the earliest and the latest. A second factor, already suggested in the case of the Yahwistic tradition, is that we are dealing with theology—not in the scholastic sense of course—but theology nevertheless. The greater part of these chapters is due to the Yahwist; a study of his contribution and method is especially rewarding. We shall see how he and the priestly writer have quarried their material in varied quarters and how, from ancient and weathered stuff, they have built a fabric that was altogether new.

THE PRIESTLY PRIMEVAL HISTORY   Seeing that the priestly writer had the final say in the formation of the Pentateuch it is not unexpected that Genesis should open with a priestly passage. The characteristic style is in evidence from the first. Already in these early chapters we find the unfolding of a plan that stands out clearly in Genesis. From the priestly point of view God's revelation follows a prearranged design that manifests itself in four successive eras or dispensations: Creation; and the Covenants with Noah, with Abraham, and with Moses.[28]

The priestly creation story (Gn. 1:1–2:4a) is not, and is not meant to be, a scientific treatise on the origin of the world and man's beginning; rather it declares that the existence of all things and their meaning lie in God's hands. The world and everything in it has come from him, but the formation of man is his masterpiece, the pride of his creation. He is made "in the image of God" and set apart from the animals. Man was blessed, that he might increase and multiply, but with the blessing there went a prohibition: he may eat of fruit and vegetables only; he must be a vegetarian. The priestly narrative ends with the observance of the sabbath:

---

[27]See W. O hUrdail (Harrington), "Diagacht na Luath-Staire—Gn. 1-11," *Irisleabhar Muighe Nuadhat* (Maynooth, 1964), 52-59.

[28]In Gn. 1-11 the priestly material is distributed as follows: 1:1–2:4a; 5:1-32; 6:9-22; 7:6-11, 13-16a, 18-21, 24; 8:1-2a, 3b-5, 13a, 14-19; 9:1-17, 28; 10:1-32; 11:10-32.

God rested from his creative work. Straightway the interest is switched to Israel and her observance of the sabbath. This basic institution of Israel is given depth and meaning when it is thus brought into contact with God's creative work and attached to the Creator himself.

Mention of the sabbath observance is an anticipation of the call of Israel, and the priestly writer employs genealogies to demonstrate how, in fact, that choice was made. He uses the device to step quickly from creation to the second stage of the divine plan, the Covenant with Noah; thus we find that Gn. 5 takes us from Adam to Noah. An extraordinary longevity is attributed to the antediluvian patriarchs because it was imagined that the duration of human life had diminished from one world epoch to the next: it will be no more than 600-200 years in the period between Noah and Abraham and from 200 to 100 years from the time of the Hebrew patriarchs.[29]

We must remember that the priestly tradition has no story of the Fall, but here we have something more or less corresponding to that story. Hence we must understand man's diminishing life span as a steady deterioration seen in relation to the progress of evil, for a long life is a blessing from God (Prv. 10:27) and will be one of the blessings of the messianic age (Is. 65:20). In other words, the ages attributed to these patriarchs have a symbolic value only. Ancient Babylonian traditions knew a list of ten kings with fantastically long reigns, who lived before the deluge. The biblical writer uses a similar ancient tradition for his own purpose.

According to the priestly writer the Flood came as a result of the corruption of mankind: Noah alone was found righteous. The waters of God's judgment destroyed all living things, except those that had found shelter in the ark. Gn. 6-9 is a blend of priestly and Yahwistic narratives, but these can be isolated rather easily and then each story presents the characteristic style and outlook of its original setting. Here again an ancient and widespread tradition has been pressed into the service of religious teaching.

The climax of the story is God's Covenant with Noah, and the divine promise never again to devastate the earth. A new privilege was granted: animal flesh might be eaten provided the animal had been properly slaughtered. This involved a practical recognition of

---

[29]See Roland de Vaux, *La Genèse* (BJ), pp. 53 f.

God's absolute authority over life, symbolized by blood, and was seen as the origin of sacrifice, another basic religious institution (Gn. 9:1-5). Once again there was an accompanying prohibition: the blood of man—he who, despite his corruption, is still "in the image of God" (Gn. 9:6)—must not be shed. The delightful closing touch is that the "bow in the clouds," every shining rainbow after a storm, will stand as a reassuring pledge of the Covenant between God and man (Gn. 9:8-17). From this Covenant with all men, the priestly writer, by means of a genealogy (Gn. 11:10-32) moves to the man who is the center of the next stage. But this third dispensation, the Covenant with Abraham, and the later Covenant with Moses at Sinai, fall outside our present scope.

THE YAHWIST'S   The Yahwist was the first theologian and one
PRIMEVAL HISTORY   of the greatest writers of Israel. He wrote in
the tenth century B.C., during the peaceful reign of Solomon; thus, long before the priestly writer, and more strikingly, he presented the choice of Israel in the perspective of God's purpose for all mankind. With true theological insight he perceived that God's dealings with Israel must have a wider issue, and he linked that particular history to general human history and began at the beginning. He constructed his primeval history from elements of very different kinds, but its main lines were of stark simplicity. On the one hand he testified that all evil, a growing corruption, came from sin, and on the other hand that this growth was matched by the active presence of God's mercy.[30]

The opening verses (Gn. 2:4b-6) of the Yahwistic creation narrative serve as an introduction to the real purpose of the account, the formation of man; a setting has been provided but all the interest is centered on this one creature. Thus the plants and trees of Gn. 2:9-17 are those of the garden of Eden which is the home of man, and the formation of the animals (vv. 19 f.) is not related for its own sake but as an introduction to the formation of woman. The Yahwist has nothing to say about the creation of the world apart from the simple statement that Yahweh made the earth and the heavens.

---

[30]In Gn. 1-11 the Yahwistic material is distributed as follows: 2:4b—4:26; 6:1-8; 7:1-5, 7-10, 12, 16b, 17, 22b; 8:2b-3a, 6-12, 13b, 20-22; 9:18-27; 11:1-9.

In the formation of man, the Workman of the priestly narrative has given place to a Potter. The "dust from the ground" is fine potter's clay and God shaped it into a human form; then he breathed into that lifeless figure a breath of life and the figure became a man. But "it is not good for man to be alone": the writer has in mind something more specific than man's gregarious instinct; he is thinking, rather, of man's deep-felt need of another being like himself, one of the same nature as he, yet not quite himself. Then follows the charming description of the parade of animals before man. He imposes names on them; thus, at one and the same time, manifesting his knowledge of their nature and expressing his dominion over them. Though all these creatures have been formed, as he was, from clay, he is unable to find one among them that can share his life, that can hold converse with him—for he alone has been livened by the divine breath.

The seemingly artless description of the formation of woman presents a viewpoint that is nothing less than revolutionary. There was a universal tendency to regard woman as a chattel and to consider her as a being decidedly inferior to man. By describing her—in figurative terms—as made from man, the Yahwist presents her as a being of the same nature as man, his equal; a truth which man is made to acknowledge openly. She is, therefore, in the fullest sense, his helper, one entirely suited to him, particularly by her union with him in marriage.

Man, the creature, exists in dependence on God and in relation to another human being; but in this world the man finds temptation. The tempter, in the form of a serpent, prevails on him to rebel against his dependence. Therefore, immediately after his account of the creation of the first man and woman, the author describes the entry of sin into the world. The first sin is not a sin of mankind in the abstract, for mankind exists only in individual men and women; it is the common sin of the first human couple. Essentially it was the transgression of a divine command, figuratively described as the prohibition to eat a certain fruit. The tempter insinuates that they will become "like divine beings, knowing good and evil" (Gn. 3:5). The "knowledge of good and evil" which would be theirs means that they would have arrogated to themselves the right of deciding between good and evil, of being a law unto themselves in the

moral order. So, in effect, they would have become independent of
God. They were tempted to deny their creaturehood in the hope
of transcending that condition.

While the first sin was not sexual in nature it does follow that
man-woman relations were involved in the process of the sin and
suffered the consequences of the Fall. Woman was given to man
as "a helper fit for him" (Gn. 2:18), but she became his seductress
and led him into evil. Man, created before woman, was by nature
her leader; yet, yielding to her seduction, he weakly followed her.
In place of communion in one flesh (Gn. 2:24) they find complicity
in crime. And when the crime had been committed, that harmony
that had formerly marked their relations was shattered: Adam sought
to cast all the blame on Eve (Gn. 3:12). But even before this they
had already felt that something had gone wrong: "The eyes of
both were opened and they knew that they were naked" (Gn. 3:7).
This is obviously meant to be seen in sharp contrast to Gn. 2:25:
"Both were naked, the man and his wife, and they were not ashamed
the one before the other." A shadow had fallen on sex; though good
in itself, it can henceforth easily aggravate the relations between
man and woman. The sentence of God: "You shall crave to have
your husband and he shall lord it over you" (Gn. 3:16b) further
underlines the disharmony that had been introduced. The domination
of man and degradation of woman will replace the perfect union
in mutual love that would have marked their relations, while fruit-
fulness, a normal sequel to sexual union, is set in a context of
suffering: "I will greatly multiply your pain in childbearing, in
pain you shall bring forth children" (Gn. 3:16a). The misery of
woman's travail at birth is matched by man's travail on the soil.
Finally, both are banished from the happiness of the garden. All
this is nothing more than the actual condition of the human couple;
man and woman, essentially good, have been wounded by sin and
stand in need of redemption.

The present state of man, subject to suffering and death, is therefore the work not of God but of man himself, and follows on the
sin of the first man; all men are born into this state. But man has
not been definitively vanquished and is not hopelessly subjected
to the forces of evil. The Yahwist attaches to maternity a hope

based on God himself (Gn. 3:15). It is probable that he saw in the saving motherhood of Eve the prototype of the royal motherhood (cf. Is. 7:14; Mi. 5:2 [3] and the care taken in Kgs. to name the queen-mothers of Judah), and therefore of the messianic motherhood. In this sense, the text is not only messianic but takes its place in Marian theology. But even apart from this, the gesture of Yahweh in providing clothes for the unhappy couple (Gn. 3:21) is a touching indication of his care for them.

The following chapters are closely linked to the story of the Fall because they serve to illustrate the alarming proliferation of sin; we move quickly to the first murder. Cain is really the ancestor of the Kenites (Nm. 24:21 f.) and the Yahwist is obviously intrigued by the fate of that strange tribe.[31] Though they, like the Israelites, were worshipers of Yahweh (Nm. 10:29; Jgs. 1:16), they never really achieved a sedentary life, but wandered restlessly on the limits of the cultivated land (1 Chr. 2:55). However, Gn. 4:1-16 no longer relates the story of a tribe, nor does it any longer reflect the traditional animosity between farmer and nomad; now it belongs to primeval history, to the beginning of human history. We are shown what happened when mankind had fallen from obedience to God: the man who associates with sin has become its slave. Yet, despite his crime and his subsequent separation from God, Cain remains under God's protection (Gn. 4:15 f.). Again the mercy of Yahweh accompanies his just punishment.

The genealogy of the Kenites (Gn. 4:17-26) opens with the statement that Cain (a murderer) built the first city. This was an unpromising start to civilization and the song of Lamech shows that cultural advance was accompanied by violence. Originally a savage desert chant, it is used to mark a further progress in evil: the execution of vengeance which God had reserved to himself (Gn. 4:15) is claimed by man and exercised arbitrarily and without limit. In keeping with his universalist outlook the Yahwist notes briefly that from the time of Enosh, that is, almost from the beginning, "men

---

[31]See G. von Rad, *Genesis*, trans. J. Marks (Philadelphia: Westminster Press, 1961), p. 104. The presentation of the theology of these chapters owes much to Professor von Rad.

began to call upon the name of the Lord" (Gn. 4:26). He is not
seeking to deny the certain tradition that the divine name was first
revealed to Moses (Ex. 3:14); rather he wishes to show that the
worship of the true God was the primeval religion of mankind.

The inexorable growth of sin comes to a climax in the story of
the angel marriages (Gn. 6:1-4). This story was originally an aetiology
designed to explain the origin of the legendary Nephilim (cf. Nm.
13:33; Dt. 2:10), a race of giants: they were the children of a marriage of heavenly beings with human women. But under the Yahwist's
pen it has become a dramatic illustration not only of man's general
corruption but of a more widespread deterioration. And, at last,
God's patience is exhausted at this final proof that "every imagination
of the thoughts of man's heart was only evil continually" (Gn. 6:5).
Yahweh was "sorry," "grieved to the heart" that he had ever created
man: he will utterly destroy man and all living things. But at once
his mercy steps in: "Noah found favor in the eyes of the Lord"
(Gn. 6:8).

By means of the ancient popular tradition of the Flood the
Yahwist presents God's judgment on sin. In a true sense it is the
Last Judgment and hence, more emphatically than in the other
episodes, the saving will of God is manifest. The ark in which
Noah's family and the pairs of animals found refuge was a sign of
Yahweh's intention to deliver a remnant, and with it to make a new
beginning in history. But at this point too appears the naked mystery
of the contrast between God's punishing anger and his forbearing
grace. Yahweh had seen that man's inclinations were evil and had
decided on the Flood (Gn. 6:5); now he declares that, though
man is unchanged—"the imagination of man's heart is evil from his
youth" (Gn. 8:21; cf. 6:8)—he will never again destroy all living
creatures as he had done. The constant rhythm of seasons will be
a lasting sign of his promise (Gn. 8:22).

And, indeed, the course of evil, temporarily checked by the Flood,
soon gathers momentum again. The story of Noah's drunkenness
(Gn. 9:18-27) makes this point; but it also marks a polemic against
agricultural Canaan with its wine-drinking and sexual license. The
unsuspecting Noah, like the Israelites coming in from the desert
(cf. Nm. 25:1-3), was taken unawares by the potent taste of
Canaanite civilization; when he realized how he had been overcome

he pronounced a curse on Canaan.[32] No doubt the story of Noah's curse was seen as the explanation of the defeat of the Canaanites by the invading Israelites. As usual, the Yahwist has used the story for his own ends.

Another aetiology, typically divorced from its original purpose, rounds off the primeval history. For it is obvious that the story of the Tower of Babel was a popular answer to the problem of the origin of nations and languages, and a popular explanation of the name "Babel" (Babylon). But the Yahwist is not interested in these matters; in his eyes the story shows how men, in their striving for fame, unity, and political development, set themselves against God. And it illustrates how, once again, as at the beginning, the pride-inspired rebellion ended in hopeless confusion. This time the word of judgment seems to be the final word.

However, the Yahwist is still master of the situation, for at this point he knits together primeval history and sacred history. We were left with a welter of nations scattered over the face of the earth (Gn. 11:9); now Abraham is called from the multitude of nations "that in him all the families of the earth shall be blessed" (Gn. 12:1-3). The transition is dramatic. Hitherto the narrative concerned humanity as a whole; now God chooses one man and makes him the beginning of a new nation and the recipient of an unconditional promise of salvation. That promise goes beyond Abraham, beyond the nation which he fathers, to all generations. The primeval history has not ended in unrelieved gloom, but in the most impressive manifestation of God's saving grace. Already at the beginning of sacred history—the *Heilsgeschichte*—the end is vaguely seen; and this firm link between primeval and sacred history is the first link in the chain of messianic development. The promise of Gn. 12:1-3 finds its fulfillment in the Son of Abraham who crushed the head of the serpent and who draws all men to him (Jn. 12:32).

2) *The Exodus*

Biblical history—God's saving history (*Heilsgeschichte*)—begins with Abraham—more precisely with God's choice of Abraham. Yet the

---

[32]It is clear that originally the narrative spoke of Shem, Japheth, and Canaan. A redactor, wishing to restore the familiar triad, Shem, Ham, and Japheth, introduced Ham and described him as "the father of" Canaan. The inconsistency is evident in verse 24 where Canaan is Noah's "youngest son."

decisive event in Israel's history was several centuries later than the Patriarch: this was the Exodus. The term "Exodus" signifies the going out of the Hebrews from Egypt; or, in a wider and more usual sense, the whole complex of events between the deliverance from Egypt and the entry into the Promised Land (Ex. 3:7-10). This great event became, in Jewish and Christian thought, the type and the guarantee of all other interventions of God on behalf of his people.[33]

The Exodus marked the beginning of the people of God, for then it was that God brought forth Israel (Dt. 32:5-10) and established a father relationship, full of love and solicitude (Hos. 11:1; Jer. 31:9; Is. 63:16; 64:7). Since it is a sign of the divine love, the Exodus, by that very fact, is a gage of salvation: the God who had delivered his people from the bondage of Egypt will again save that people in the hour of danger, when it is threatened by Assyria (Is. 10:25 ff.; Mi. 7:14 f.) or by Babylonia (Jer. 16:14 f.; Is. 63–64). Alas, Israel responded with ingratitude to the divine care (Am. 2:10; Mi. 6:3 ff.; Jer. 2:1-8; Dt. 32), proving unfaithful to the love of the desert days (Hos. 2:16; Jer. 2:2 f.).

Throughout the Old Testament the Exodus remained the central moment in Israel's history and in her memory, and that saving event reverberates in the New Testament.

> In the Old Testament, prophet and priest, psalmist and historian alike look back to the Red Sea and Mt. Sinai, and when Jesus talked with Moses and Elijah on the mountain of Transfiguration, their subject was his *exodus*—the Greek for "departure" (Lk. 9:31)—which he had to accomplish at Jerusalem; so inwoven was that event into the texture of God's dealings with men. The Exodus is for the Old Testament and Judaism what the life, death, and resurrection of Christ are for the New Testament and Christianity. And for Christians, what Jesus brought to fulfillment was the purpose of the Exodus.[34]

3) *The Covenants*

To express the nature of the link which exists between God and his people the Old Testament uses the word *berith* (rendered in Greek

---

[33]See M.-E. Boismard, *Vocabulaire de Théologie Biblique* (Paris: Cerf, 1961), pp. 342 f. Henceforth references to this work will be abbreviated VTB.

[34]D.M.G. Stalker, *Peake's Commentary on the Bible*, M. Black and H. H. Rowley, editors (London: Nelson, 1962), n. 175 a. Henceforth references to this work will be abbreviated PCB.

by *diathēkē* and in Latin by *testamentum*). In English it is generally translated as "covenant." The term "covenant," which in its technical theological sense concerns the relations of men with God, was borrowed from the social experience of men, from the fact of treaties and alliances between peoples and individuals. In practice, the religious use of the term regards a special type of covenant, that in which one partner takes the initiative and imposes the conditions. Therefore God lays down the terms, demanding of his people that it should keep the Covenant (Gn. 17:9; 19:5)—while he binds himself by promise. The Pentateuch (P tradition) describes three Covenants made by God with men.

1. THE COVENANT WITH NOAH   Coming after the era of creation, the Covenant with Noah is, for the priestly writer, the second stage of the divine plan; following on the catastrophe of the Flood it was a new beginning, a Covenant with all mankind. In this immediate context of the Flood, too, the sign of this Covenant, the rainbow, is meaningful. "The Hebrew word that we translate 'rainbow' usually means in the Old Testament 'the bow of war.' The beauty of the ancient conception thus becomes apparent: God shows the world that he has put aside his bow."[35] God promised Noah that he would never again destroy the earth. A new privilege was introduced: animal meat might be eaten provided it was bloodless, for blood, symbolizing life, was sacred to God. There was an accompanying prohibition against the wanton shedding of blood.

2. THE COVENANT WITH ABRAHAM (GN. 17:1-14)   The third stage of the divine plan was a Covenant with Abraham. It involved the divine promise that Abraham would be the father of many nations. This Covenant, however, was made not only with Abraham, but with his descendants too: to him and to them the land of Canaan will be granted as an everlasting possession. This Covenant was unconditional and could not fail—unlike the Sinai Covenant which could and did fail. The sign of the Covenant was circumcision, and the individual Israelite who did not observe this rite did not belong to the Covenant community. The J version (Gn. 15:1-21) refers to an ancient covenant ceremony well known to many ancient peoples:

---

[35]Von Rad, *op. cit.*, p. 130.

certain animals and birds were halved and laid opposite each other and the partners to the treaty walked between the pieces, thus sealing the treaty and invoking a curse upon themselves if the treaty should be broken; hence the term used of covenant-making is *karath berith*, literally, "to cut a treaty." In this passage we are told that Yahweh, in the shape of a flaming torch, performed the rite and passed between the parts of the victims.

3. THE COVENANT AT SINAI   At Sinai the people, delivered from Egyptian bondage, entered into a Covenant with Yahweh, and the cult of Yahweh was established as the national religion. A study of Hittite treaties has shed light on the nature of this Covenant.[36] Two types of treaty may be distinguished: the parity pact and the suzerainty pact. In a parity covenant both parties, standing on equal terms, bound themselves by bilateral obligations. The suzerainty covenant, on the other hand, was made between a king and his vassal and was unilateral. The suzerain "gave" a covenant and the vassal was obliged to accept and obey the conditions of the suzerain. Yet such a covenant was not just an assertion of power and authority on the part of the suzerain: it was explicitly regarded and presented as an act of benevolence, and the vassal accepted the obligations in a sense of gratitude. In keeping with this conception the covenant was couched in an "I-Thou" dialogue form. The Sinai Covenant followed this pattern exactly.

At the vision of the burning bush Yahweh revealed to Moses both his name and his plan for Israel: he willed to deliver Israel from Egypt and to install his people in the land of Canaan (Ex. 3:7-10, 16 f.). This plan presupposed that Israel was the object of his choice and the recipient of a promise; the Exodus demonstrated that God was capable of imposing his will ("You have seen how I bore you on eagles' wings and brought you to myself" [Ex. 19:4]) and the people responded by faith (Ex. 14:31). Then God revealed the terms of the Covenant: "If you will obey my voice and keep my covenant, you shall be my own possession among all peoples; for all the earth is mine, and you shall be to me a kingdom of

---

[36]See G. E. Mendenhall, "Law and Covenant in Israel and the Ancient Near East," *The Biblical Archaeologist*, 17 (1954), 26-76.

priests and a holy nation" (Ex. 19:5 f.). Israel will henceforth be his kingdom, his people which will render him due cult.[37] In return, God will "tabernacle" in the midst of his people: "They shall know that I am the Lord their God, who brought them forth out of the land of Egypt that I might dwell among them" (Ex. 29:46). The Sinai Covenant, however, was conditional. In granting this Covenant to Israel and in making promises, God imposed conditions which Israel must observe. But these laws and institutions were laid down and established in order that Israel should be a holy people; they are an expression of divine benevolence, even though failure to observe them will entail a curse (Lv. 26:14-39).

The ceremony of the making of the Covenant is described in Ex. 24. Moses built an altar at the foot of Sinai and set up twelve pillars to represent the twelve tribes. Victims were sacrificed; half the blood was collected and kept in basins and half of it was thrown against the altar as a sign of Yahweh's participation in the rite. Moses read the "book of the Covenant" and the people pledged themselves to accept and obey Yahweh's ordinances. Then he cast the rest of the blood on the people, saying: "Behold the blood of the Covenant which the Lord has made with you in accordance with all these words" (v. 8).

The Covenant of Sinai revealed in a definitive manner an essential aspect of the plan of salvation: God had willed to join himself to men by establishing a cultic community dedicated to his service, ruled by his law, the recipient of his promises; the New Testament will fully realize this divine project. Though the Covenant was God's free gift to Israel it became enmeshed in the historical destiny of Israel to such an extent that salvation tended to be regarded as the reward of human fidelity to the law. Its limitation to one nation tended to obscure the universal scope of God's plan, while the promises of temporal rewards could cause men to lose sight of the religious object of the Covenant: the establishment of the kingship of God over Israel and through Israel over the whole world. Nonetheless the Covenant of Sinai dominated Israel's history and the development of revelation.[38]

---

[37]See J. Giblet and P. Grelot, VTB, p. 21.
[38]See *ibid.*, pp. 22 f.

4) The Law

The Hebrew term *tôrah* has a wider signification, one less strictly juridical, than the *nomos* of the Septuagint (LXX) or the English "law"; it is a "teaching" given by God to men in order to regulate their conduct. This is why the whole Pentateuch, and not only the legislation, is called the Torah. In fact, framed in a narrative setting, the Pentateuch contains the ensemble of prescriptions which ruled the moral, social, and religious life of the people. All of these prescriptions—moral, juridical, and cultic—have a religious character, and the whole corpus is presented as the charter of a Covenant with Yahweh and is linked with the narrative of happenings in the desert where the Covenant was made.

While it remains true that the basis of the legislation goes back to the time of Moses, the present form of the Pentateuch includes many laws of later ages. It is simply not conceivable that a legal code, drawn up for a small nomad people in the thirteenth century B.C., would have remained unchanged for over a thousand years while that people became successively an agricultural community, a monarchy, and a Church. Laws are made to be applied and must necessarily be adapted to changing conditions. For instance, much of the priestly legislation found in Ex. 25-31; 35-40, bears the stamp of later times. The Covenant Code (Ex. 20:22–23:19) is the law of a pastoral and agricultural society and met the conditions of an Israel already settled in Palestine. The ritual laws of Ex. 34:14-26 date from the same time but show some influence of Dt. Leviticus took its final shape after the Exile, in the Second Temple, but the basis of it goes back to the primitive ritual of the desert. The Law of Holiness (Lv. 17-26) seems to have been codified towards the end of the monarchy. The deuteronomical code (Dt. 12-26) is earlier than the fall of Samaria in 721 B.C., and though it shows a development that is influenced by an appreciation of the love of Yahweh for his people and of Israel's consequent obligation to act as he would act, it is basically a reinterpretation and a new presentation of earlier laws.

It seems possible to identify some of the earlier laws of the Pentateuch on the basis of form. Two general types are readily noted: casuistic (or hypothetical) law; and apodictic (or categorical) law.

Both types are well represented in Ex. 22: the hypothetical type in verses 1-17 ("If . . ." with the provision in the third person); and the apodictic form in verses 18, 21 f. ("Thou shalt not . . ." with the injunction in the second person). Hypothetical law was common throughout the ancient world, especially in Mesopotamia and among the Hittites, and is best represented by the Code of Hammurabi.[39] Apodictic law is peculiar to Israel. This fact powerfully strengthens the argument that the Decalogue (to take a striking example) goes back to Moses. The Ten Commandments (in Hebrew the "Ten Words") are given twice (Ex. 20:2-17; Dt. 5:6-18); both versions are in apodictic form—though several of the commandments have been expanded in later times—and both go back to a common primitive form set out in sharp, terse language. In general, it may be said that the apodictic laws are early and may very well represent a nucleus that originated with Moses.

Throughout the Old Testament the Law is everywhere present and it directly or indirectly influences the thought of the sacred writers.[40] The priests are *ex officio* guardians of the Torah and specialists in its interpretation (Hos. 5:1; Jer. 18:18; Ezek. 7:26) and it is their duty to teach the people (Dt. 33:10; Hos. 4:6; Jer. 5:4 f.). Under their authority the Torah developed and was compiled. The prophets recognized the authority of this Torah (Hos. 9:12; 4:1 f.; Jer. 11:1-12; Ezek. 22:1-16,26). Their high moral doctrine was nothing more than a profound understanding of the demands of the Mosaic Law. The historians of Israel clearly saw the birth of the nation in the Covenant of Sinai. Among them, the Deuteronomist judged events in the light of the deuteronomical code, while the Chronicler was guided in his work by a completed Pentateuch. The wisdom of the sages is enlightened by the Torah, and Sirach states explicitly that the true Wisdom is nothing other than the Law (Sir. 24:23 f.). The psalmists extol the Law (cf. Ps. 19 [18]:7-14; 119 [118]). Finally, Ezra set the Torah as the authoritative rule for the faith and practice of the postexilic community and as the center of its life. Attachment to the Law inspired the Maccabaean revolt and supported the martyrs and heroes of that rising.

---

[39]See ANET, pp. 163-80.
[40]See P. Grelot, VTB, pp. 544-46.

Yet this devotion to the Law had its dangers, and the tragedy of Judaism is that it succumbed to these dangers. The first mistake was to set all precepts, religious and moral, civil and cultic, on the same plane instead of ordering them, in correct hierarchy, around the one precept that would give meaning and life to all of them (Dt. 6:4). As a result, the Law became the preserve of casuists and became so overladen with minutiae that it turned into an insupportable burden (Mt. 23:4; Acts 15:10). The second danger, and a more insidious one, was to base man's justification on a meticulous observance of the Law rather than to visualize it as the work of divine grace, freely bestowed; it meant that man could justify himself. It needed the forceful teaching of St. Paul to make clear, once and for all, that man is not justified by the works of the Law—but by faith in Jesus Christ (Gal. 2:16; Rom. 3:28).

THREE	*The Deuteronomical History*

The reader who has, for the first time, patiently, or per- haps doggedly, worked through the Book of Kings will understandably feel more than a little confused by it all. He may have accepted the view that the religion of the Old Testament, just like that of the New Testament, is essentially historical. But surely *this* kind of history has no obvious religious bearing? If he has read further afield he may be excused for failing to find any real link between Joshua-Judges (with 1 Samuel thrown in for good measure) and Kings. Yet the link is there, and the whole has a religious significance; but one must be able to discern this.[1]

It is a vital matter for us to see the Bible through the eyes of the men who wrote it because, word of God though it is, it has come to us in human dress. This proper focusing is necessary, not only for the purpose of reading Scripture intelligently, but for the much more important reason—though it comes to the same thing in the end—that it is the only way in which we can understand the intentions of the divine Author. When we read biblical history in this light we quickly realize that it is not a hopeless muddle of unrelated events or a mere procession of petty kings and their tiresome squabbles. To the eyes of the biblical historian these details fit, each in its place, into the unified plan of a great mosaic.

---

[1] See W. Harrington, "A Biblical View of History," *The Irish Theological Quarterly*, 29 (1962), 207-22. The article in question forms the basis of this chapter.

143

Thus we find that the apparently isolated books of the Old Testament are in fact grouped to form larger units. The books Joshua-Kings are closely bound together and 1,2 Chronicles, Ezra, and Nehemiah are so many chapters of one work. Even 1 and 2 Maccabees are parallel accounts of the same events. Biblical history is not aimless and, despite the tragedies with which it deals, it is always ultimately hopeful. It could scarcely be otherwise since the biblical historian is at all times keenly aware that God holds the reins of history in a firm grasp. God is active in history, above all in the history of his own people.

In the present chapter we shall consider the first of these biblical histories, Joshua-Kings, together with the introduction which gives meaning to the work: Deuteronomy. When we have grasped the background of the deuteronomical history and have reflected on the epoch in which it took shape, we shall realize what a treasure has been bequeathed to us. These varied pages straightway take on a new significance as we see them now shot through with the unshakable faith of men who could look long and candidly on centuries of national infidelity and then turn to Yahweh their God with greater trust and confidence than ever. The sad story of failure is lighted up by hope, by the conviction that the Lord who once led his people out of Egypt, "with a mighty hand and an outstretched arm," can set them up once more on the ruins of the past, or can lead them back again from another captivity. Unfaithfulness was the cause of all the evils that had been showered upon them, whereas trust in Yahweh and fidelity to his Law are the gage of divine blessings, the blessings that can yet be theirs if they will but turn to their God in sincerity and truth. This confidence was the cornerstone of postexilic Judaism, that cradle of the New Testament and of a greater hope.

1. THE CONSCIENCE OF A NATION

The king of Assyria invaded all the land and came to Samaria, and for three years he besieged it. In the ninth year of Hoshea the king of Assyria took Samaria and deported the Israelites to Assyria. . . . And this happened because the Israelites had sinned against the Lord their God who had taken them up out of the land of Egypt, from the power of Pharaoh, king of Egypt, and had adored other gods. . . . They built for themselves high places wherever they dwelt . . . they did wicked things, provoking the Lord to anger, and they served idols. . . . They despised his laws and the Covenant which he had made with their fathers and the warnings which he gave them. . . . And they rejected all the commandments of the Lord their God. . . . Therefore the Lord was very angry with Israel, and removed them out of his sight. The tribe of Judah alone was left (2 Kgs. 17:5-7, 9-11, 15 f., 18).

The Lord did not turn from the fierceness of his great anger which was kindled against Judah. . . . And the Lord said: "I will remove Judah also out of my sight, as I have removed Israel, and the Temple of which I said: My Name shall be there" (2 Kgs. 23:26 f.).

Judgments such as these are understandable only when we see in proper perspective the events that evoked them; the main lines, at least, of Israel's history, up to the end of the monarchy, must be recalled.

When in chapter twelve of Genesis Abraham is introduced, we enter a new era; we stand at a decisive moment in religious history, and at the emergence of a Chosen People. Abraham received a divine command to leave his country and kindred and his father's house and to go into a land which the Lord would show him; and at the same time he was promised that he would be the ancestor of a great nation. He heard and obeyed and came into the land of Canaan. There he grew old with Sarah his wife; the promise had not yet been fulfilled and still he put his trust in Yahweh, the life-giver. He had faith in God and in the word of God and found salvation:

" 'Look at the heavens and, if you can, count the stars.' And he said to him: 'So shall your posterity be.' Abraham believed the Lord, who credited the act to him as justice" (Gn. 15:5 f.). Abraham remains for all future ages the man of faith, the father of a great nation, the friend of God, recipient of the promise of God.

The promise was renewed to his descendants, Isaac and Jacob, and the brilliant career of Joseph seemed to herald its fulfillment. Then followed the hopeless years of slavery in Egypt. Where now was the glorious future promised to the sons of Abraham? Then an event occurred, a tremendous event, that was to echo through all the extent of Israel's history: Yahweh himself intervened.

When the Egyptians maltreated us and oppressed us and imposed hard labors on us, we cried to the Lord the God of our fathers. The Lord heard our cry and saw our misery, our toil and our oppression, and the Lord brought us out of Egypt with a mighty hand and an outstretched arm, with great terror, with signs and wonders. He brought us into this place and gave us this land, a land flowing with milk and honey (Dt. 26:6-9).

Throughout the Old Testament we find that the Exodus is the central event in Israel's memory; the Exodus, though it is the work of Yahweh, immediately conjures up the dominant figure of Moses. He not only led the people from Egypt, but he it was who, afterwards, forged that motley crowd of refugees into a nation and set on foot a mighty religious movement and, further, gave the impetus to the great literary achievement that is the Pentateuch. "The religion of Moses has marked for all time the faith and practice of the people; the law of Moses has remained its rule of life."[2]

Moses indeed merited the glowing tribute paid to him in a later age: "Since then no prophet has arisen in Israel like Moses, whom the Lord knew face to face" (Dt. 34:10). Yet he had led the people only to the threshold of the Promised Land; it was for Joshua, his successor, to take the final step. But if Joshua was the man who led the people in to take possession of the land that Yahweh had given them, this was precisely because the mantle of Moses had fallen on him (cf. Dt. 34:9).

The Israelites were in the land, but they had not yet conquered the whole of it; the struggle went on for two centuries. Towards the close of that period the failure of Saul threatened the very existence of the nation, but David saved the situation and succeeded in establishing a kingdom and even a modest empire. By that fact, David took his place beside Abraham and Moses: these are the three great architects of the people of God. Once again there is a divine promise:

> The Lord declares to you that the Lord will make you a house. When your days are fulfilled and you lie down with your fathers, I will raise up your son after you, who shall come forth from your body, and I will establish his kingdom. . . . And your house and your kingdom shall be made sure forever in my presence; your throne shall be established forever (2 Kgs. 7:11 f., 16).

This is the first of a long series of prophecies which pointed to a Messiah from the line of David. Culmination and fulfillment, both,

---

[2]Roland de Vaux, BJ, p. 5.

are found in the opening words of St. Matthew: "The book of the genealogy of Jesus Christ, the son of David" (Mt. 1:1).

And yet the historical kingdom of David did not stand. Solomon was able to maintain, more or less intact, the conquests of his father, but on his death the kingdom, united by David, broke apart and Israel (or the Northern Kingdom) and Judah henceforth went their separate ways. A religious schism followed the political division and Judah alone remained true, not only to the Davidic dynasty, but also—in principle at least—to the orthodox faith. Israel fell to the Assyrians in 721 B.C. and disappeared from history. Judah alone was left. A century after the fall of Israel the Southern Kingdom seemed to be entering, with renewed vigor, into an era of promise; the young king, Josiah (640-609 B.C.), asserted his independence and set on foot a religious reform. The future was full of hope, but these hopes were rudely dashed when the king fell in a disastrous battle and the kingdom of Judah moved quickly to destruction. In 587 B.C. Jerusalem fell to Nebuchadnezzar and its inhabitants were deported to Babylon. This must have seemed the end. The house built by Abraham and Moses and David had crashed in ruins and, worse still, the promises of Yahweh had failed.

For men of faith this was unthinkable. There must be a solution to the formidable problem, a problem that had faced them even before the fall of Jerusalem; for Judah had barely survived the Assyrian flood in which Israel had been swept away. History provided the answer: Yahweh had not failed, it was the people who failed their God. Such, at least, was the verdict of Deuteronomy.

The deuteronomical outlook was profoundly religious and striking in its singlemindedness: the nation stood or fell by its fidelity or unfaithfulness to Yahweh and to his Law. This outlook inspired men of faith and vision, who not only measured their history by that yardstick, but set about editing their traditions, giving, in the process, to that history, their own distinctive theological slant. We owe, then, to the deuteronomists not only the present form of the books Joshua-Kings, but also our awareness of the significance of their content. For us, no less than for them, it is the meaning of history that matters.

At the head of this section we have set out, as an indication of the spirit which animated their work, the deuteronomists' verdict on the fall of Israel and Judah. This work may be fittingly described as a national examination of conscience and they faced up to the task with pitiless candor. Like the prophets, they are witnesses to what is unique about the religion of Israel, not monotheism only, but ethical monotheism: the one God of Israel is a *just* God. It is because he is just that he punishes the sins of his own people more severely than the sins of those he has not chosen (cf. Am. 3:2). But all who turn to him will find only love and mercy: this is the final word of the deuteronomical history.

2. THE BOOK OF DEUTERONOMY

The last of the five books of the Pentateuch is, in its Hebrew dress, known by its opening words: "These are the words." But in the Greek translation, coming as it did after the other books, and in view of the code of laws enshrined in it, it became the *deuteros nomos*, the "second law"—Deuteronomy (cf. Dt. 17:18). In reality, it is something far more than a code of laws and not at all a second law, in the sense of a repetition of an earlier code. Deuteronomy is one of the most important books of the Old Testament. A measure of that importance is the frequency with which it is cited in the New Testament; in many ways it is close to the spirit of the Gospel. But if we hope to grasp its full significance we must establish its *Sitz im Leben*, the time and circumstances in which it emerged.

Quite like the other books of the Pentateuch, Deuteronomy has its roots firmly struck in the Mosaic tradition. The Law that Moses had given his people was destined to grow and develop and to be adapted to the changing circumstances of the history of the people. This Law was essentially religious, a precious heritage which had to be preserved intact and which could bear additions only in an authentic line of development—a task which fell to the Levites. At the sanctuaries, when the people came on pilgrimage, practical solutions were given in difficult cases and new regulations were formulated —but always in the spirit of the Mosaic legislation. In other words, the Law of Moses continued to be applied in new social and economic conditions; and some, at least, of these new solutions became fixed and were set down in writing (cf. Hos. 8:12). It was in this way that the legal material now found, not only in Deuteronomy but throughout the Pentateuch, took shape.

Before the final catastrophe of 721 B.C., when the kingdom of Israel came to an end, some of the Levites had sought refuge in Judah, taking with them their sacred traditions. Among these was the legislative part of Deuteronomy (the deuteronomical code, that is, Dt. 12-26). This brief document was to have a powerful and far-reaching effect—but not just yet. The great power which had destroyed Israel menaced Judah too, but the latter, thanks in large measure to the efforts of Isaiah, managed to survive. A century later Assyria, while still at its apogee, collapsed and disappeared with dramatic suddenness. In the short period that covered the decline of Assyria and the rise of the Neo-Babylonian Empire, Judah was granted a brief respite and the young and pious King Josiah was able to set on foot a religious reform. One of the first works to be undertaken was the restoration of the Temple, which had been sadly neglected during the long and disastrous reign of Manasseh. During the work of renovation the "Book of the Law" was discovered (2 Kgs. 22:8-10). This was the deuteronomical code which had been brought to Jerusalem by the refugees from Israel one hundred years before and which had been reverently deposited in the Temple, only to be at first disregarded and ultimately forgotten. Now providentially coming to light again, it became the charter of the reform and was published in the framework of a discourse of Moses; this first edition of the work corresponds to chapters 5-28 of our Deuteronomy. Even though the reform of Josiah failed, the book was now at last known (Jeremiah gives evidence of his knowledge of it).

The capture of Jerusalem by Nebuchadnezzar in 587 B.C. marked the end of the kingdom of Judah and the beginning of the Babylonian Exile (587-538 B.C.). During the Exile Deuteronomy was re-edited: the other discourses of Moses were added. The first four chapters of the book, which envisaged the conquest of the Promised Land, held out to the exiles the prospect of return, a reconquest. And at the close, the long canticle of chapter 32 will henceforth stand as a witness against Israel and as a criterion of the people's conduct.

A striking feature of Deuteronomy is that it looks back to the time of the Exodus. Doubtless, the Northern origin of the tradition explains a certain lack of concern with David—though in Judaean surroundings this was speedily redressed—but this "rediscovery of Moses" in the seventh century B.C. is a significant development in

Judah. There was at that time a conscious effort to recapture both
the letter and the spirit of Mosaism. "Ask now of the days that
are past" is a characteristic appeal of Deuteronomy (cf. Dt. 4:32).
This nostalgic revival of interest in the past had close parallels in
the contemporary literature of neighboring peoples. The deuteronomic
reaction was not merely local, but was part of a general tendency
which reached to all the lands of the ancient Near East. "The sun
of the ancient Orient was beginning to set and its people could not
help but be obscurely and unhappily conscious of the approaching
darkness."[3] Divine Providence, however, bends circumstances and
trends to its purpose, and if the eyes of the deuteronomists, in common
with the people of their time, were turned to the past, it is in very
great measure thanks to the achievement inspired by this tendency
that the religion of Moses was able to come through the dark days
of the close of the monarchy and survive the great trial of the Exile.

As a prelude to a brief assessment of Deuteronomy we may set
out the plan of the book:

FIRST DISCOURSE OF MOSES (DT. 1:1–4:40)
SECOND DISCOURSE OF MOSES (DT. 4:41–28:64)
THIRD DISCOURSE OF MOSES (DT. 29–30)
APPENDICES
1) The Testament of Moses (DT. 31-33) 2) The death of Moses (DT. 34)

The oldest part of Deuteronomy is the Second Discourse. This is
the first edition of the work and was made during the reform of
Josiah; though it may well be that the document brought from
Israel and deposited in the Temple had already contained not only
the code (Dt. 12:1–26:15) but also the discourse framework.

The Decalogue is set at the head of the discourse (Dt. 5:6-21),
and is followed by the celebrated passage which still dominates the

---

[3] W. F. Albright, *From the Stone Age to Christianity* (New York: Doubleday, 1957[2]), p. 316.

piety of Judaism: "Hear, O Israel: The Lord your God is the only Lord. You shall love the Lord your God with all your heart and with all your soul and with all your might" (Dt. 6:4 f.). The love of the Chosen People for Yahweh must be exclusive, for he is a "jealous God" (Dt. 6:15) who will brook no rivals. As Hosea would have put it, Israel must be a faithful wife.

The deuteronomic code (Dt. 12:1–26:15) breaks the discourse; or, if one prefers, it is framed by it. Insistence on one, central sanctuary is the most notable feature of this code; it is a point that is set in relief at the very beginning. This centralization of cult, which was not in force at the time of the Judges (Jgs. 6:28; 13:16), nor even under Solomon (1 Kgs. 3:4), is an essential trait of the deuteronomical legislation. It was paid very special attention in the reform of Josiah and it is because of their violation of this law that the kings of Israel are condemned—in Kgs.—while the kings of Judah, too, are judged in the light of it.

The rest of the laws are similar to those of the other Pentateuch codes, though there is a notable development in social customs. But the greatest change is one of spirit and outlook witnessed to by the exhortatory tone of the prescriptions and by the constant appeal to the heart. At the end of the code, in the ritual of the presentation of the firstfruits, is a little liturgy which has been aptly described as "the heart of the Pentateuch."[4] It takes the shape of a profession of faith, a creed, which the worshiper is to recite when he comes to offer his gifts in the Temple (Dt. 26:5-10). It is significant, and very much in the spirit of Deuteronomy, that this profession of faith in Yahweh's mighty act of deliverance from Egypt (because that is what it amounts to) should be solemnly renewed each year.

The first and third discourses (together with the appendices) were added during the Babylonian captivity and are really addressed to the exiles. The typical phrase, "ask now of the days of old," bids the Israelites look at their history in order to find in it the unequivocal proofs of God's love, a love which no accumulation of infidelities on their part can quench or even lessen. Once again the events of the Exodus provide the supreme proof (Ex. 4:37-39). The last dis-

---

[4]B. W. Anderson, *Understanding the Old Testament* (Englewood Cliffs, N.J.: Prentice-Hall, 1957), p. 7.

course, in conclusion, sets before Israel two ways: the way of the commandments, which is the way of life; or the way of faithlessness, which means death (Dt. 30:15). The final chapters give the last acts and words of Moses, his testament to his people. The book closes with a noble tribute to the great leader (Dt. 34:10).

When we read these splendid pages we are quite carried along by the majesty and beauty of the prose and, all the while, we are listening to the authentic voice of Israel's unshakable faith. Men may fail, and have failed miserably, but Yahweh cannot fail, the great God who loves his people still despite the long centuries of infidelity. There is much that is salutary here, much that finds a ready echo in the Christian heart. It would be well for us to be as candidly aware of our personal failure as the deuteronomists were of the national betrayal and, at the same time, to be as serenely confident as they in the love of our God.

3. THE DEUTERONOMICAL HISTORY

The Book of Deuteronomy, or that part of it which was brought to Jerusalem at the time of the destruction of Samaria in 721 B.C., was destined to inspire a very important literary movement—though this was not until a century later—during the reign of Josiah. In the fresh atmosphere of the young king's reform program the spirit of the deuteronomical writing was contagious; but we should not exaggerate its influence. The aftermath shows that the majority of the people had given no more than superficial assent to the new, radical policy, though it is nonetheless clear that a certain element greeted the reform with enthusiasm and pressed it forward wholeheartedly; to these, the "Book of the Law" was a veritable source of strength and consolation and life.

The history of the Chosen People obviously did not end with Moses and the men of the seventh century B.C. would have inherited a mass of traditions centered around Joshua, the Judges, and the monarchy. In the latter period there were also the royal archives. But these traditions were isolated; there was no obvious link between the various units and, above all, there was no clear lesson to be drawn from the whole of it. We owe it to the deuteronomists that they not only collected and edited this material but that, in setting it out, they made manifest to all the one striking lesson of their history. The books from Joshua to Kings bear the stamp of the deuteronomists, even if, admittedly, in certain parts the influence is not very marked, due to deliberate policy, as we shall see.

Deuteronomy is the first volume of this great religious history:[5] it justifies historically the doctrine of the choice of Israel by Yahweh and outlines the theocratic constitution that is demanded by this divine election. Joshua presents the installation of the Chosen People in the Promised Land and Judges traces the immediate aftermath, the succession of its apostasies and conversions. Samuel points out how the theocratic ideal was at last realized under David, after the initial failure of Saul. Kings describes the decline that set in even during the reign of Solomon, which eventually led to the fall and disappearance of the monarchy. Deuteronomy, which is the introduction to the whole, at a later date was detached from the work and was added on to the first four books of the Bible, for the obvious reason that it forms a fitting climax to the story of Moses.

But we must be careful how we understand the unity of the books Deuteronomy-Kings. On the one hand we speak of a deuteronomical *edition* of oral traditions and written documents which, generally speaking, had already been grouped in collections. Furthermore, this material was not everywhere retouched to the same extent, and whole books, or large sections within books, preserve their individuality. On the other hand, the books show traces of more than one edition in a deuteronomical context. There were at least two editions of Kings, for example, one during the reform of Josiah and the other after the Exile. It was during the Exile, in fact, that the final edition of the great history was made.

4. THE BOOK OF JOSHUA

The story of the conquest as presented to us in Joshua is complex—inevitably so, because it is really an amalgam of varied sources. There is enough evidence to show that, at the death of Joshua, the Promised Land was still far from being conquered; this is abundantly borne out by the Book of Judges apart from the many references in Joshua. The Israelites, for the most part, held only the hill regions and were quite unable to dislodge the better armed Canaanites

---

[5]See De Vaux, *op. cit.*, p. 215.

from the plains. They must wait for two centuries before the whole land was theirs.[6] The editorial additions, however, give a very different picture of the conquest. According to the deuteronomic view, Joshua, the leader of a united people, won mastery of the whole country in a few lightning campaigns. The "whole land" fell into the hands of Joshua "because the Lord, the God of Israel, fought for Israel" (Jos. 10:42; 11:23).

1) Division

PROLOGUE: God has given the Promised Land to his people, but the conquest demands fortitude and fidelity to the divine law (chap. 1).

OCCUPATION OF CANAAN (2–12)	
1) The spies saved by Rahab in Jericho	2
2) The miraculous crossing of the Jordan	3–4
3) Circumcision and Pasch in Gilgal	5:1-12
4) Destruction of Jericho and Ai	5:13–8:29
5) Sacrifice and reading of the Law on Mt. Ebal	8:30-35
6) Treaty with the Gibeonites	9
7) Conquest of the south of Palestine	10
8) Conquest of the north of Palestine	11
9) General view of the occupation of Canaan	12

DIVISION OF CANAAN (13–21)	
1) Land still to be conquered	13:1-7
2) Territory of Transjordan tribes	13:8-33
3) Territory of Judah, Ephraim, and Manasseh	14–17
4) Territory of the remaining tribes	18–19
5) Cities of refuge and levitical cities	20–21

FULFILLMENT OF THE DIVINE PROMISES (21:43-45)

EPILOGUE (22:1–24:28)	
1) Withdrawal of the Transjordan tribes	22
2) Last discourse of Joshua	23
3) The great assembly at Shechem	24:1-28

APPENDICES (24:29-33)

---

[6]See pp. 19 f. The historical outline of Chapter One should be kept in view throughout this chapter.

2) Literary Analysis

Joshua was compiled from different sources. The work of the deuteronomical editors has not smoothed over the seams between the various units of tradition.

THE OCCUPATION   In chapters 2-9 we have a group of traditions,
OF CANAAN   sometimes parallel (and all literarily independent
of the four Pentateuch traditions),[7] which are connected with the Benjaminite sanctuary of Gilgal. This unit was most likely constituted at the beginning of the monarchic period; chapter 24 belongs, substantially, to the same tradition. The narrative of the passage of the Jordan and of the entry into Canaan is a conscious parallel of the account of the Exodus. Yahweh stopped the course of the Jordan (Jos. 3:7-4, 18) as he had opened a passage in the Red Sea (Ex. 14:5-31); the Ark of Yahweh guided the crossing (Jos. 3:6-17; 4:10 f.), like the pillar of smoke or of fire (Ex. 13:21 f.; 14:19 f.); Joshua (Jos. 3:7; 4:14) played the same role that Moses had earlier played; circumcision was renewed (Jos. 5:2-9) and the Pasch was celebrated at Gilgal (Jos. 5:10) as it had been after the crossing of the Red Sea.[8]

Chapters 10-11 differ from the preceding traditions. They link the conquest of the whole of the South and then of the whole of the North of the Promised Land with two expeditions of Canaanite kings: the battles of Gibeon and Merom. The campaign against these kings is depicted as having been carried out with the participation of all the tribes and under the leadership of Joshua. This is not in agreement with other passages in the book (cf. Jos. 13:1-6; 14:6-13; 15:13-19; 17:12,16), nor with the picture presented in Jgs. 1. From these it appears that the conquest was gradual and incomplete and that each tribe acted on its own; and this view is in conformity with historical facts.[9] But Joshua anticipates later events in order to present a complete picture of the conquest.

THE DIVISION   The passage Jos. 13:1-7 lists the territories which
OF CANAAN   never became Israelite, though they were included

---

[7]Though eminent scholars have argued that the Pentateuch traditions continue into Joshua—hence they speak of a Hexateuch—M. Noth (*Das Buch Josua* [Tubingen, 1953²]) has shown that the Joshua traditions are distinct.
[8]See BJ, p. 223.
[9]See pp. 23 f.

in the ideal picture of Jos. 1:4 (cf. Nm. 34:1-12). It is a deuteronomical introduction to the following geographical document. This
document localizes the tribes of Reuben, Gad, and the half-tribe of
Manasseh, already installed by Moses in Transjordan. Chapters 14-19
combine a description of the boundaries of the tribes that is earlier
than the monarchic age, with a list of towns which, since it is more
detailed concerning the kingdom of Judah, must be, at least in part,
later than the political schism. To complete the picture, chapter 20
indicates the cities of refuge (an ancient institution [cf. Ex. 21:13]
to protect those guilty of involuntary homicide) and chapter 21 lists
the levitical cities.

EPILOGUE   Chapter 22 is a special tradition of uncertain age. It
tells of the withdrawal of the Transjordan tribes and of the altar
which they raised on the river bank; the episode is probably from
the time of the Judges. The Ephraimites, who possessed the Ark in
the sanctuary of Shiloh, were opposed to the multiplication of sanctuaries. Chapter 24 preserves an old tradition of the assembly at
Shechem and of the religious covenant entered into by the tribes.

THE   Verses 28-31 of chapter 24 are found again at the
APPENDICES   beginning of the second introduction to Jgs. (2:6-9).
This suggests the redactorial unity of the books.

3) *The Deuteronomical Redaction*

All these traditions, to some extent combined before the deuteronomical redaction, have been retouched here and there in a deuteronomical
spirit. More particularly, we may attribute to the editors: chapter 1
(at least the introduction 1:1-9); the profession of faith attributed
to Rahab 2:9-11 (cf. Dt. 4:39); the insertion of 8:30-35—an account
of the assembly at Mt. Ebal (most likely a parallel tradition of the
Shechem assembly, chapter 24) which is clearly inspired by Dt. 27;
the perspective of chapters 10-11; and the list of chapter 12. Chapter
23 is a deuteronomical composition, a doublet of chapter 24, and
was meant to replace it in one of the editions of the book.

In general, we may say that the deuteronomists have carefully
collected and presented the varied traditions and have done so with
scrupulous honesty. But upon this material they have superimposed
a simplified and idealized picture of the conquest, and have projected

back to the time of Joshua the final realization achieved by David. This foreshortening of the historical perspective was justified in their eyes because the outcome was ultimately the work of God. For these editions "the taking of Canaan is not a profane event, it is a theological event."[10] The conquest is an episode in the history of salvation, an essential element of God's plan for his people. When the edition was being made the plan seemed in jeopardy: the Northern Kingdom had disappeared and Judah was in mortal danger. In this context the picture of the whole nation united under Joshua took on a prophetical significance, in harmony with the outlook of Jeremiah and Ezekiel: God himself will bring about the unity of his people.[11]

True to the spirit of Deuteronomy this ideal is set in the golden age of the Exodus. Joshua completed the work of Moses, the ideal of a people united under a leader who is entirely dedicated to the law of Yahweh; this alone could win the divine blessing. Where the prophets looked to the future the deuteronomists looked to the past, but the result was the same. The modest achievement of Joshua was already the seed of the ultimate triumph of God and that truth was expressed by attributing to him the success of later times. The ideal conquest of Joshua will be repeated on a grander scale when the people learn to observe the Law of Yahweh with all their heart and with all their soul and with all their might.

5. THE BOOK OF JUDGES

The Book of Judges bears the unmistakable print of the deuteronomic stamp and affords perhaps the best example, in this complex history, of the editorial method. The main part of the book (Jgs. 3:7–16:31) is a compilation of quite distinct traditions concerning various "Judges"—local charismatic heroes. These traditions are presented from a definite and clearly-expressed viewpoint, a point of view that is set out in the original introduction to the work (Jgs. 2:6–3:6); it is repeated further on (10:6-16) and is also indicated in the formulas which recur at the beginning of the story of each of the "greater" Judges. The viewpoint is this: The Israelites have

---

10Roland de Vaux, RB, 61 (1954), 261.
11Cf. J. Delorme, IB, pp. 399-401.

been unfaithful to Yahweh; he has delivered them up to oppressors; the Israelites have repented and have called on Yahweh; he has sent them a savior, the Judge. This is a cycle of infidelity, punishment, repentance, and deliverance. But when the trials and the oppression have ceased, after a short period of tranquillity, the infidelities recommence and the cycle begins all over again.

1) Division

HISTORICAL INTRODUCTION: Summary account of the installation in Canaan (1:1—2:5)	
DOCTRINAL PROLOGUE: Moral of the book (2:6—3:6)	

HISTORY OF THE JUDGES (3:7—16:31)	
1) Othniel	3:7-11a
2) Ehud	3:11b-30
3) Shamgar	3:31
4) Deborah and Barak	4—5
a. The campaign	4
b. Canticle of Deborah	5
5) Gideon and Abimelech	6—9
a. Vocation of Gideon	6
b. Career of Gideon	7—8
c. Kingship of Abimelech	9
6) Tola	10:1-2
7) Jair	10:3-5
8) Jephthah	10:6—12:7
9) Ibzan	12:8-10
10) Elon	12:11-12
11) Abdon	12:13-15
12) Samson	13—16

APPENDICES (17—21)	
1) Migration of Danites and the Sanctuary of Dan	17—18
2) Crime of Gibeah and war against Benjamin	19—21

2) Literary Analysis

THE   The first introduction (Jgs. 1:1—2:5) is an ancient
INTRODUCTIONS   tradition of the installation in Canaan. This installation is presented as slow and difficult; each tribe acts on its
own and only the mountain regions are fully occupied. This is the
true picture of the state of affairs and is opposed to the idealized
one of Joshua. The introduction is a later addition, and the ending
(Jgs. 2:1-5) is deuteronomical. The beginning of the second introduction (Jgs. 2:6-9) reproduces the end of Joshua (Jos. 24:28-30);
this indicates that the works followed each other, though the continuity was broken by the insertion of Jgs. 1:1—2:5. This second
introduction (the first in time) gives the moral theme of the whole
book, the above-mentioned cycle (cf. Jgs. 2:7,10-12, 14 f., 16-18,19).
The book teaches the Israelites that oppression is the punishment
of impiety and that victory is a consequence of conversion.

The note on Shamgar is out of place between Ehud and Deborah
and Barak; the activity of the Philistines suggests the end of the
period of Judges, and indeed some manuscripts give it after Jgs.
16:31. The introduction to the history of Jephthah (Jgs. 10:6-16) is
a preface to the second part of Judges. Further additions to the
book are the story of Abimelech (chapter 9) and the appendices
(chapters 17-21). These represent very old traditions which shed
light on the social and religious history of Israel. They are foreign
to the first deuteronomical edition of Judges and were possibly taken
over to link the book with Sm.: Abimelech's attempt at kingship
and the words of Jotham prepare the way for the dispute on the
institution of the monarchy (cf. 1 Sm. 8-12), while the appendices
describe the cultic and moral anarchy of the epoch "when there
was no king in Israel" (Jgs. 17:6; 19:1).

3) The Achievement of the Editors

The varied traditions describe conditions in Israel after the conquest
and show the people in conflict with the nations round about. In
Palestine itself these were first the Canaanites and later the Philistines.
This situation is quite in agreement with the picture provided in
Joshua, when one abstracts from the editorial presentation. The different traditions have not been worked over, but have been merely
set in the general framework and thus given an appearance of homo-

geneity which they do not, in fact, possess, and the editors have achieved their purpose with the minimum of adaptation, if, indeed, with any at all. Once again the deuteronomists have made the point that everything depends on fidelity to Yahweh. This jealous God demands the undivided love of his people: he demands obedience to his Law. The Israelites of a later age can see in these stories of olden times the anticipation of their own graver problem, and the key to it. If they also repent and turn to Yahweh he will quickly take pity on them and raise up a deliverer.

6. THE BOOKS OF SAMUEL

The influence of Deuteronomy is less marked in the Books of Samuel. It is noticeable in some earlier chapters (1 Sm. 7 and 12) and in retouches to the Nathan prophecy (2 Sm. 7). On the other hand, we are given, more clearly than elsewhere, striking proof of the editors' respect for the ancient traditions. Though 2 Samuel 9-20 is a unit, the rest of the work (that is to say, 1 and 2 Samuel, which form one book) is composite. The very importance of the institution of the monarchy meant that it was variously judged in different circles. Similarly, the tragic figure of Saul was seen in both bad and good light. Above all, David, the people's king, was the subject of many traditions regarding his origin and his exploits. In the work of editing, the particular characteristics of the sources were preserved; we get juxtaposition rather than harmonization, with a consequent lack of logical sequence; on the whole, the various traditions are readily discernible.

This is especially obvious in the distinct presentations of the origin of the monarchy. The antimonarchist tradition (1 Sm. 8; 10:17-25; 12) can be clearly distinguished from the monarchist tradition (1 Sm. 9; 10:1-16; 11). Similarly, the lack of cohesion between the two traditions of David's entry into the service of Saul (1 Sm. 16:14—18:2) is even more obvious and, indeed, there are many such doublets in 2 Samuel. Though this method causes a somewhat disjointed narrative it increases our confidence in the deuteronomists. They did not take liberties with the material at their disposal, but treated it with such respect that they were prepared to sacrifice none of it, even for the sake of a more coherent presentation.

1) Division

SAMUEL	
1) The childhood of Samuel	1 Sm. 1–3
2) The Ark captured by the Philistines	4–7
SAMUEL AND SAUL	
1) Institution of the monarchy	8–12
2) Beginning of the reign of Saul	13–15
SAUL AND DAVID	
1) David at Court	16:1–19:7
2) Flight of David	19:8–21:16
3) David chief of an outlaw band	22–26
4) David with the Philistines	1 Sm. 27–2 Sm. 1
DAVID	
1) David king of Judah	2 Sm. 2–4
2) David king of Judah *and* Israel	5–8
3) The Court History	9–20
a. Meribbaal (Mephibosheth)	9
b. Ammonite war: birth of Solomon	10–12
c. Absalom	13–20
SUPPLEMENTS (21–24)	

The Court History is continued, and concluded, in 1 Kgs. 1-2.

2) Literary Analysis[12]

Chapters 1-3, containing the narrative of the birth and childhood of the Prophet, introduce the cycle of Samuel. The canticle of Hannah (1 Sm. 2:1-10) is a later addition, put in the mouth of Hannah because of the reference to the barren woman in verse 5b. The story of the capture of the Ark by the Philistines (chapters 4-6) has

---

[12]See Roland de Vaux, *Les Livres de Samuel* (BJ).

merely external links (mention of Shiloh and of Eli and his sons) with the preceding chapters; the Ark and not Samuel is the principal subject. Chapter 7 is not the logical sequence of chapters 4-6. Samuel is presented as the last of the Judges, and in this it differs also from chapters 1-3 where he is a prophet.

In chapters 8-12 two traditions are clearly distinguished:

1. The antimonarchist tradition: 1 Sm. 8; 10:17-25; 12.

2. The monarchist tradition: 1 Sm. 9; 10:1-16; 11. These two traditions are combined in 1 Sm. 8:22b; 10:26 f.; 11:12-14. In 1 Sm. 13:16—14:46 Saul appears as a pious king who consults Yahweh and is aided by him. The account of the rejection of Saul (1 Sm. 13:8-15) is an anticipation of his actual rejection (chapter 15)—a literary doublet.

It appears that in 1 Sm. 1-15 we may distinguish two strata of traditions:

1. *Primitive stratum.* After the account of the capture of the Ark (1 Sm. 4-6) we get the monarchic version of the institution of the kingship (1 Sm. 9; 10:1-16; 11), which leads to the war of liberation (chapters 13-14). The sequence is: 1 Sm. 4-6; 9:1—10:16; 11; 13-14; 15; (16:1-13). (Samuel is depicted as an inspired instrument of Yahweh in the election of Saul. The cycle of Samuel has been completed by the account of the childhood of the Prophet [1 Sm. 1-3] and of the rejection of Saul [chapter 15], which prepares the way for the anointing of David [1 Sm. 16:1-13].)

2. *Later stratum.* A later stratum presents Samuel as the last of the Judges (chapter 7). This leads to the antimonarchist version of the institution of the kingship. The sequence is: 1 Sm. 7-8; 10:17-24; 12.

The episode of the anointing of David (1 Sm. 16:1-13) seems to come from a prophetical tradition and has no connection with the rest of the narrative. David will be anointed by the people of Judah (2 Sm. 2:4) and by the elders of Israel (2 Sm. 5:3); the anointing here related will not be mentioned again (cf. 2 Sm. 17:28). In the passage 1 Sm. 16:14—18:2 there are two traditions of the entry of David into the service of Saul:

1. David is called as a minstrel to the court of Saul and becomes his shield bearer (that is, his aide) (1 Sm. 16:14-23). In this capacity he accompanies the king in the Philistine war (1 Sm. 17:1-11) and

distinguishes himself in single combat (1 Sm. 17:32-53—combination of the two traditions).

2. David is a young shepherd unknown to Saul, who visits his brothers in the army at the moment when the Philistine champion challenges the Israelites (1 Sm. 17:12-30—v. 31 is a link verse); after the single combat (1 Sm. 17:32-53) Saul has the young hero brought to him and takes him into his service (1 Sm. 17:55—18:2).

Summarily, then, the entry of David into Saul's service is like this:
1. 1 Sm. 16:14-23; 17:1-11; 17:32-53.
2. 1 Sm. 17:12-30; 17:32-53; 17:55—18:2.

The narrative of the relations of Saul and David abounds in doublets:

1 Sm. 18:10 f. and 19:9 f.:	attempt on David's life.
1 Sm. 18:12-16 and 18:28-30:	success and popularity of David.
1 Sm. 18:17-19 and 18:20-27:	promises of marriage to a daughter of Saul—verse 21 has a harmonizing gloss.

Interventions on David's behalf:

1 Sm. 19:1-7—Jonathan intercedes for David. This episode is not in accordance with the narrative of chapter 20 where, in verse 2, Jonathan knows nothing of his father's murderous intent. The intervention of Michal (1 Sm. 19:11-17) is parallel: in one case the daughter, in the other case the son of the king, saves David. Therefore 1 Sm. 19:1-7 and 20:1—21:1 are *separate* traditions of the intervention of Jonathan; 1 Sm. 19:11-17 and 20:1—21:1 are *parallel* traditions of interventions for David. In the second narrative of Jonathan's intervention, the verses 1 Sm. 20:40-42 are an addition, otherwise the stratagem of the arrows would be meaningless. The passage 1 Sm. 23:15-18 belongs to the traditions of the friendship of David and Jonathan (cf. 1 Sm. 20:11-17).

Further doublets:
1. 1 Sm. 23:1-13 and 23:19-28—David twice betrayed.
2. 1 Sm. 24 and 26—David twice spares Saul.
3. 1 Sm. 2:11-16 and 27—David twice seeks refuge with Achish of Gath.
4. 1 Sm. 31:1-3 and 2 Sm. 1:1-16—two traditions of the death of Saul.

The concluding chapters of 1 Sm. are in some disorder. The account of the battle of Gilboa and the death of Saul (1 Sm. 31:1-13) follows immediately on chapter 28; in other words, 1 Sm. 28:3-25 breaks the continuity of 1 Sm. 28:1 f. and 29:1 f. The passage 2 Sm. 1:1-16 follows immediately on 1 Sm. 30. The logical sequence from 1 Sm. 27 is:

1. 1 Sm. 27:1–28:2; 29:30; 2 Sm. 1.
2. 1 Sm. 28:3-25; 31.

The chapters 2 Sm. 2-6—the kingship of David in Hebron, the Philistine war, the capture of Jerusalem, and the installation of the Ark—form a tradition similar to the primitive stratum of the first book. 2 Sm. 7—the prophecy of Nathan—is ancient and many times retouched; chapter 9 is a redactorial summary of the wars of David. The long section 2 Sm. 9–1 Kgs. 2 is the history of the family of David and of the struggle for succession to his throne. Written by an eyewitness to the events, early in the reign of Solomon, it is the prose masterpiece of the Old Testament. The narrative has been reproduced, virtually untouched, by the editors of Samuel. However, the supplements (2 Sm. 21-24) interrupt the long narrative. The six units of these appendices may be arranged in pairs:

1. 2 Sm. 21:1-14 (three years of famine): 2 Sm. 24 (pestilence for three days);
2. Heroic anecdotes: 2 Sm. 21:15-22; 23:8-39;
3. Poetic pieces: 2 Sm. 22; 23:1-7.

Logical sequence: 2 Sm. 21:1-14 + 24; 21:15-22 + 23:8-39; 22 + 23:1-7.

3) *The Deuteronomical Redaction*

The Court History is certainly from the early days of Solomon and it is possible that the other collections were made in the first centuries of the monarchy: a primitive cycle of Samuel; two stories of Saul and David. These traditions, coming from the North and South, were joined together at a date much later than the events related in them (cf. 1 Sm. 27:6). This date would be after 721 B.C. The destruction of Samaria and the end of Israel provided an occasion for exalting the Dynasty of David and a means of completing the Southern traditions by those of the North.

The Northern bias of the original deuteronomical outlook was, naturally, modified in its Judean development. Thus David, the ideal king, took his place beside Moses. And in 2 Sm. 7 the editors set in further relief the import of Nathan's prophecy, that first of a whole series of messianic prophecies. Samuel, as it now stands, is the story of the establishment of a kingdom of God on earth, and bears witness to the great difficulty of the task. The deuteronomists, writing with sad experience of the failure of the monarchy, looked back to David. They seized upon the prophecy of Nathan and dwelt on it, and found their messianic hope bolstered up by the divine promises made to the great king.

7. THE BOOKS OF KINGS

The hand of the deuteronomists is very evident in the Books of Kings. These books (in reality only one) continue the history outlined in Samuel; indeed, 1 Kgs. 1-2 is the conclusion of the family history of David, and describes the inauguration of Solomon as king. After this introduction, and apart from the lengthy insertions of the Elijah and Elisha cycles (1 Kgs. 17–2 Kgs. 13), the books are entirely taken up, first with the history of Solomon and then with the parallel histories of the kingdoms of Israel and Judah—until the fall of Israel when the story of Judah is carried on and brought to its conclusion. Three main sources are explicitly named: a History of Solomon; the Annals of the Kings of Israel; and the Annals of the Kings of Judah. Independent of these are the traditions underlying the cycles of Elijah and Elisha and the description of the Temple (1 Kgs. 6-7).

Where not interrupted by these other sources, the events of the history of the two kingdoms are fitted into a stereotyped framework. Each reign is treated individually and fully (in its religious aspect), and each is introduced and rounded off by formulas that are more or less constant. The essential part of these formulas is the judgment passed on each king. All the kings of Israel are condemned because of the "original sin" of Jeroboam I: the setting up of schismatic sanctuaries at Bethel and Dan.[13] Only eight of the kings of Judah are praised for fidelity to the prescriptions of the Law of Yahweh; six of them, however, with the qualification that they had failed to

---

[13]See Roland de Vaux, *Les Livres des Rois* (BJ), pp. 14 f.

remove the "high places." Hezekiah and Josiah alone merit unreserved approval. This judgment is clearly inspired by the law of Deuteronomy on the unity of the sanctuary, and that book is undoubtedly the "Law of Moses" referred to in 1 Kgs. 2:3; 2 Kgs. 14:6; it is the "Book of the Law" found in the Temple during the reign of Josiah (2 Kgs. 22:8). "One God, one sanctuary" is a fundamental article of that Law, a concrete way of demanding undivided loyalty to a "jealous God" and unwavering fidelity to his commands. But the polemic against the "high places" also has in mind the historical fact that the scattered local shrines—often on the site of former Canaanite shrines—were open to the intrusion of Canaanite cultic elements and, in many cases, became centers of idolatrous worship.

1) Division

THE SUCCESSION OF DAVID (1 KGS. 1-2)

HISTORY OF SOLOMON (1 KGS. 3-11)

1)	Solomon the Wise	3:1—4:14
2)	Solomon the Builder	4:15—9:25
3)	Solomon the Merchant	9:26—10:29
4)	The Darker Side	11

POLITICAL AND RELIGIOUS SCHISM (1 KGS. 12-13)

THE TWO KINGDOMS TO ELIJAH (1 KGS. 14-16)

THE CYCLE OF ELIJAH (1 KGS. 17—2 KGS. 1)

1)	The Great Drought	17—18
2)	Elijah at Horeb	19
3)	Aramean Wars	20
4)	The Vineyard of Naboth	21
5)	Another Aramean War	22:1-38
6)	After the Death of Ahab	22:39—2 Kgs. 1

THE CYCLE OF ELISHA (2 KGS. 2-13)

1)	The Beginnings	2
2)	The Moabite War	3
3)	Miracles of Elisha	4:1—6:7
4)	Aramean Wars	6:8—8:29
5)	History of Jehu	9—10
6)	Athaliah to the Death of Elisha	11—13

THE TWO KINGDOMS TO 721 B.C. (2 KGS. 14-17)

THE KINGDOM OF JUDAH (2 KGS. 18:1—25:21)

1)	Hezekiah—Isaiah and Assyria	18—20
2)	Manasseh and Amon	21
3)	Josiah—the Religious Reform	22:1—23:30
4)	The Fall of Jerusalem	23:31—25:21

APPENDICES (2 KGS. 25:22-30)

2) Literary Analysis

The main sources of Kings are explicitly cited (History of Solomon; Annals of the Kings of Judah; Annals of the Kings of Israel), but there were other sources that are readily discernible.

1 Kgs. 1-2 is the close of the Court History of David (2 Sm. 9-20). 1 Kgs. 6-7, set in the history of Solomon, is a description of the Temple, of priestly origin. In that history, 1 Kgs. 3:2 f.; 11:1-13, 41-43, and much of chapter 8 are due to the deuteronomical editor. Chapters 12-16 are based on the Annals, but the passages 1 Kgs. 12:33—13:33 (the cursing of the altar at Bethel) and 1 Kgs. 14:1-18 (the oracle of Ahijah against Jeroboam) come from prophetical traditions. In the latter text, 1 Kgs. 14:7-11 is a deuteronomical addition.

The cycle of Elijah (1 Kgs. 17—2 Kgs. 1) is itself composite; at least it is interrupted by two accounts of Aramean wars (1 Kgs. 20; 22:1-38). The cycle of Elisha (2 Kgs. 2-13) is much less homogeneous; indeed it is an anthology, popular in style and with complacent stressing of the miraculous. The history of Hezekiah (2 Kgs. 18-20) gives great prominence to Isaiah; the whole passage 2 Kgs. 18:13—20:19 is reproduced in Is. 36-39 and is probably due to a disciple of the Prophet.

3) The Editions of Kings

The first edition of the Books of Kings was surely made in the days, full of promise, of Josiah. The eulogy of the king (2 Kgs. 23:25)— less the final words—would have been the conclusion of this first work: "There was no king before him whom more than he had turned to the Lord with all his heart and with all his soul and with all his strength, in perfect faithfulness to the Law of Moses."

A second edition, also deuteronomical, was made during the Exile; this may have been before 562 B.C. (date of the release of Jehoiachin), because 2 Kgs. 25:21 has all the appearance of a conclusion.[14] In this case, 2 Kgs. 25:22-30 forms an appendix.

Though the later editors must bear witness to the tragic failure of Josiah's great effort and must record the dark days leading to the catastrophe of 587 B.C., the book, in its very last words, sounds a note of hope. It closes on the favors granted to Jehoiachin (2 Kgs.

---

[14]See *loc. cit.*

25:29 f.) who was, in Jewish eyes, the last reigning successor of David. It is the dawn of redemption.

8. CONCLUSION

The deuteronomical history closes with the Books of Kings, but the influence of Deuteronomy does not end there. The idea, which it emphasizes so strongly, of a revealed and written Law, dominated postexilic Judaism. It inspired, to a notable extent, the great work of the Chronicler, and its echoes linger in Daniel and Maccabees. Its spirit served as a balance and as a corrective to an outlook that tended to be excessively legal, for it is essentially a law of love and not of minutiae. "Thou shalt love the Lord thy God with all thy heart and with all thy soul and with all thy strength" is singled out by Christ, and the love of the neighbor which completes this precept is also typical of the book.

But the real importance of Deuteronomy and the deuteronomical history is that it helped, in very great measure, to make postexilic Judaism possible. Its theology gave new hope, the hope of survival. By facing up courageously to the tragedy of Israel's history and in resolutely defending the fidelity of Yahweh it became a great treatise on grace; it is precisely because everything depends on God that there can be no room for despair. In the gloom of the Babylonian Exile the people hear the reassuring words: "In your distress, when all these things shall have come upon you, you shall finally return to the Lord your God and obey his voice, for the Lord your God is a merciful God who will not fail you or destroy you and who will not forget the covenant which, under oath, he made with your fathers" (Dt. 4:30 f.).

FOUR	*The Prophetical Books*

Though in its earliest form prophetism in Israel was little different from the same phenomenon in Mesopotamia—and especially in Phoenicia and Canaan—it developed into something distinctive, into something unique in fact, becoming one of the most significant factors in the history of the Chosen People. Indeed the prophetic movement by itself goes far to answering a major problem:

> Why did the Jewish nation survive at all, when so many of the smaller nations of antiquity sooner or later lost their identity in the melting-pot of the great empires of the Middle East? Few nations were to all appearances more effectively put down: exhausted by successive defeats in war, reduced to a mere remnant, deported to distant countries, subjected to the long-continued domination of alien and highly civilized Great Powers. And yet they survived, reconstructed their community, and handed down a continuous and developing tradition which exerted a creative influence upon the whole of subsequent history. Why was it? The only answer that explains the facts is that the great prophets worked out a particular interpretation of the course of history, and induced their people to accept it, at least in sufficient numbers to give a new direction to their history for the future.[1]

But the prophets did more than insure the survival of a people. They carried on a religious tradition which they had inherited,

---

[1]C. H. Dodd, *The Bible Today* (New York: Cambridge University Press, 1960[2]), pp. 50 f.

fostered its development between the eighth and fourth centuries B.C., and passed it on, immeasurably enriched, to Judaism. They were entirely faithful to the dogma fixed in the Mosaic age—ethical monotheism[2]—and exploited it to the full. They were guides, carefully chosen and specially raised, along a vital and precarious stage of the spiritual journey that led to Christ. We shall try to explain the meaning and significance of prophecy and to indicate the personal contribution of the prophets whose teaching has been preserved.

1. THE PROPHETICAL MOVEMENT

1) *The Name*

In Hebrew the current appellation of the prophet was *nābî*. The origin of the word is uncertain.

1. Some derive it from *nāba‘*—"to gush out," "to pour forth."

2. Most commonly it is derived from a root *nb'*—"to seek," "to announce"—which has fallen into disuse, but which is found in other Semitic languages.

3. W. F. Albright proposes a third explanation, which appears to be the correct one. He associates *nābî* with the Akkadian *nabû* —"to call"; therefore *nābî* is "one who is called." He writes:

> The current explanation of the word *nabî* as "speaker, announcer" is almost certainly false. The correct etymological meaning of the word is rather "one who is called (by God)," "one who has a vocation (from God)," as appears from the fact that this is almost always the sense which the verb *nabu*, "to call," has in Accadian. . . . This interpretation of the word suits its meaning exactly; the prophet was a man who felt himself called by God for a special mission, in which his will was subordinated to the will of God, which was communicated to him by direct inspiration. The prophet was thus a charismatic spiritual leader, directly commissioned by Yahweh to warn the people of the perils of sin and to preach reform and revival of true religion and morality.[3]

Another term used in *rō'eh*—"seer"; but already in 1 Sm. 9:9 this word was regarded as archaic. A synonym is *hōzéh*—"visionary" (2 Sm. 24:11)—which is also found in parallelism with *nābî* (Am. 7:12; Mi. 3:6 f.).

---

[2]Ethical monotheism: belief in one God who imposes a moral order; the one God of Israel is a just God who demands of his people obedience to his righteous law.

[3]*From the Stone Age to Christianity* (New York: Doubleday, 1957[2]), p. 303; cf. p. 17.

In the Septuagint (LXX) *nābî'* is always translated *prophētēs*. The etymology of the Greek word presents no difficulty, though the word has been misunderstood. The word is from the verb *phēmi*— "to say," "to speak," plus the prefix *pro*. This *pro* is not temporal (foretell) but substitutive (to speak in the place of, in the name of, another). The prophet is a spokesman, a herald, who speaks in the name of God; he is one called by God to be his spokesman.

We must beware of understanding the terms "prophet" and "prophesy" according to their common usage in everyday English—a prophet being one who "predicts," and to prophesy meaning "to foretell." The biblical prophets were indeed predictors of the future, but to a limited extent; they were more concerned with the present and often just as much concerned with the past. In other words, "prophet" and "prophecy," in the Bible, have a technical sense that differs widely from current usage. This is not the end of the matter, however, for the term *nābî'* is bewildering in its range: it can designate a great figure like Jeremiah or a member of a group that seems little different from Muslim dervishes. The verb "to prophesy" can describe the sublime oracles of an Isaiah or the ravings of Saul before Samuel (1 Sm. 19:23 f.). We shall need to sort out the different meanings of the word as it occurs in different contexts.

2) *The Prophetical Groups*

THE EARLY   In the eleventh and tenth centuries B.C. in
PROPHETICAL GROUPS[4]   Israel we meet with a certain prophetical
movement and a form of prophecy known as ecstatic prophecy. It was a time of crisis. Guilds of prophets offered a resistance to the dangers that threatened to destroy the nation spiritually (1 Sm. 9-10). They lived in groups near the sanctuaries of Yahweh (1 Sm. 19:20); they may have had a cultic role, though this is by no means certain. They "prophesied" by working themselves into a state of frenzy; this state was induced by music and dancing and was contagious (1 Sm. 10:5 f.).

In many ways this institution resembled that of the Phoenician and Canaanite prophets of Baal, as we know it from profane docu-

---

[4]See A. Gelin, IB, pp. 469-76. This whole chapter owes much to Gelin's fine treatment of the prophets (IB, pp. 467-82).

ments and from biblical references (for example, 1 Kgs. 18). But the resemblance was external only. We may say that a Canaanite-type institution was transformed into a charismatic institution of Yahwism. The prophets were, in fact, the champions of anti-Canaanism. At a later date the great prophets acknowledged their humble predecessors (cf. Am. 2:10 f.; Jer. 7:25).

Yet, at first sight it does surprise us that Israelite prophecy should have had such a humble, and seemingly inauspicious, beginning. When we look at it more closely we find that it exemplifies the constant development within the Old Testament, and that it is not as singular as it appears. The following has been established:

> The prophetic movement takes root in group-ecstaticism, that is, in dances or other physical motions repeated so often by the members of a group that they finally succumb to a kind of hypnotic suggestion, under the influence of which they remain unconscious for hours. In this state the subconsciousness may be abnormally active, and persons of a certain psychological type may have visions and mystical experiences which thereafter control, or at least affect, their entire life. This phenomenon is universal among mankind, being found among savages, in antiquity, and among the highest religions of today.[5]

God deals with men patiently, that is, according to their mentality, culture, and education.

THE "SONS OF In the ninth century B.C. we find confraternities of THE PROPHETS" "the sons of the prophets"; the designation is a Semitic idiom meaning the members of prophetic groups. These were not quite the same as the earlier groups, though they also had their centers at the sanctuaries of Bethel, Jericho, and Gilgal (2 Kgs. 2; 4:38-41; 6:1-7); or if they were direct descendants of the others the ecstatic element in their "prophesying" was severely curtailed or had disappeared. They were spontaneous groupings of those who wished to defend Yahwism against the prevalent Baalism. Thus Elijah, the champion of Yahweh, made common cause with these prophets (1 Kgs. 18:22; 19:10,14), and Elisha associated with them and employed them in his mission (2 Kgs. 2:3,15; 4:38; 9:1-3). However, neither Elijah nor Elisha came from the number of these prophets.

---

[5]Albright, *op. cit.*, pp. 301 f.

INSTITUTIONAL OR
PROFESSIONAL PROPHETS
During the monarchy, side-by-side with the classical prophets, there was another type of prophetism which may be called institutional or official. These prophets accompanied the king (1 Kgs. 22); they were an integral part of the nation (Jer. 18:18; 2 Kgs. 23:2); they spoke their oracles in the Temple enclosure (Jer. 28; Neh. 6:12). This prophetism was not in itself a bad or degraded thing, but the prophets were, by their position, constantly tempted to identify the cause of Yahweh with that of the king. In fact, the vocational prophets often opposed them (cf. Am. 7:14; Jer. 28), and Zech. 13:1-6 tells of their disappearance. The rules for the discernment of spirits given in Dt. 13:1-5; 18:21 f. clearly envisage these prophets —for there were indeed false prophets among them.

THE CLASSICAL
PROPHETS
The classical prophets are not a group but individuals. They are, in short, those whom we commonly mean when we speak of "the prophets."

3) The Vocational Prophets

Vocational prophets are commonly divided into "preaching" prophets and "writing" prophets. This distinction is arbitrary and inaccurate for there were no "writing" prophets until the eighth century B.C. and always the message of the prophet was first delivered by word of mouth. Since, however, the best-preserved oracles of Amos, Hosea, and Isaiah are poetic addresses couched in perfect literary form, we may speak, from Amos onwards, of "literary" prophets. Hence a legitimate division would be: "preliterary" prophets and "literary" prophets. The latter group is our main concern throughout this chapter, and we shall be content to give a brief sketch of the prophetical movement from Samuel to Amos.

Samuel may be regarded as the first of the vocational or individual prophets. David had as advisers two representatives of the theocratic ideal, heirs of Samuel: Nathan (2 Sm. 7:1-17; 12:1-5; 1 Kgs. 1-2) and Gad (1 Sm. 22: 2 Sm. 24). Under Solomon, apparently there was a prophetical opposition, represented by Ahijah of Shiloh, who foretold the schism of 931 B.C. (1 Kgs. 11:29-39). In both reigns the intervention of these prophets was inspired by a common motive: they wanted to maintain the old values of equality and justice which were menaced by the royal policy, the peace which was threatened by division, and the ritual and cultic unity. Therefore Ahijah condemned the house of Jeroboam for its cultic schism (1 Kgs. 14:1-19). Shemaiah forbade Rehoboam to reconquer the North (1 Kgs. 12:21-24). Under Jeroboam an unnamed prophet cursed the altar of Bethel (1 Kgs. 13:11-32). Jehu ben Hanani foretold the end of the usurper Baasha (1 Kgs. 16:1-4, 7-13).

The dynasty of Omri marks a very important period in the history of the prophetical movement; it is the eve of the age of the great prophets. There were many interventions of religious and national bearing (1 Kgs. 20:13 f., 28, 35 f.; etc.). That of Micaiah ben Imla is significant because of his opposition to the professional prophets (1 Kgs. 22).

The vocation of Elijah was to affirm the exclusive and ethical Yahwism of his ancestors. He opposed the nature religion, whose influence was now accentuated by the introduction of the Tyrian Melcarth (Baal) by Jezebel, and was the herald of a religious revival whose spirit was that of the desert where he had relived the experience of Moses (1 Kgs. 19:1-18). From his fidelity to Yahweh flowed his proclamation of social justice (1 Kgs. 21), his political intervention against Ahab and Jezebel, and his warnings to the people. His work, both political and religious, was completed by his disciple Elisha who, through the instrumentality of Jehu, brought about the downfall of the Dynasty of Omri.

Practically no oracles of these two men have survived, perhaps because their sayings were few, since they were men of action rather than men of words. But we can know how they must have spoken by turning to those who were their spiritual heirs. "If we want to know how Elijah and Elisha reacted to the evils of the ninth century, we have only to read what Amos, Hosea, and Isaiah said in the eighth, though they may have expressed themselves differently."[6] The first of the literary prophets began to appear in the eighth century B.C. They continued throughout the following centuries until the prophetical movement came to an end with deutero-Zechariah in the fourth century B.C. We are concerned here with

---

[6]*Ibid.,* p. 306.

these prophets or, more precisely, with those among them whose message (or part of it) has been preserved for us in writing.

2. THE PROPHETICAL WRITINGS
1) *The Prophet and Prophecy*

PSYCHOLOGY OF   The vocational prophet is a man who has received
THE PROPHET[7]   a divine call to be a messenger and an interpreter
of the divine word; he is a man who has had a personal and extra-ordinary encounter with God. The word which has come to him compels him to speak: "The Lord has spoken, who can but prophesy?" asks Amos (Am. 3:8). Jeremiah, despondent because of his unchanging message of woe to the people he loved, would stifle the word: "If I say, 'I will not mention him, or speak any more in his name,' there is in my heart as it were a burning fire shut up in my bones, and I am weary with holding it in, and I cannot" (Jer. 20:9). Not only the words of the prophet, but his actions, even his life, is prophecy. The marriage of Hosea is a symbol (Hos. 1-3); Isaiah and his children are signs (Is. 8:18); Ezekiel multiplies the prophetic gestures (Ezek. 4:3; 12:6,11; 24:24).

What really matters is the relationship between the prophet and the word of God, for the prophet is a man who has had immediate experience of God and who feels himself constrained to speak what— he is convinced—is the divine word. In short, the prophet is a mystic, but a "constructive mystic." This perhaps helps to explain the true dimension of the phrase *kôh 'āmar Yahweh*—"thus says Yahweh"— which so often introduces or closes the prophetic oracle. It does not, each time it occurs, imply a direct revelation. Rather, one should see in this frequently-repeated formula the normal development of an initial vocation.[8] The prophet's vision of God has penetrated the whole manner of his thought, so that he sees things from God's point of view, and he is convinced that he so sees them.

> [The prophets] were not philosophers, constructing a speculative theory from their observation of events. What they said was, "Thus saith the Lord." They firmly believed that God spoke to them (spoke to an inward ear, the spiritual sense). He spoke to them out of the

---

[7]See W. J. Harrington, *Record of Revelation: The Bible* (Chicago: The Priory Press, 1965), pp. 29-34.

[8]See Gelin, *op. cit.*, p. 478.

events which they experienced. The interpretation of history which they offered was not invented by process of thought; it was the meaning which they experienced in the events, when their minds were opened to God as well as open to the impact of outward facts. Thus the prophetic interpretation of history, and the impetus and direction which that interpretation gave to subsequent history, were alike the Word of God to men.[9]

The immediate experience of God, the revelation of God's holiness and of his will, makes of the prophet one who "judges the present and sees the future in the light of God and who is sent by God to remind men of God's demands and to lead them along the road of obedience to God and love of him."[10] For the prophet's message is always primarily to his contemporaries; he is a preacher who speaks to the men of his own generation. He does so even when he predicts the future. This is an important observation because it implies that any interpretation of a prophetic text that would have no meaning for the prophet's contemporaries is certainly a misinterpretation.

CRITERION OF THE   The prophet claimed to speak in the name
TRUE PROPHET   of God; this claim is explicit in the formula
kôh 'āmar Yahweh. But the phrase alone is not sufficient to authenticate the message, for those whom we call "false prophets" could— and did—declare: "Thus says Yahweh." Jer. 28 is illuminating on this score. Hananiah is called a *nābî'*; he spoke in the name of God (Jer. 28:2) and yet his words are not true. He may have been deluded (confusing his own mind with Yahweh's [Ezek. 13:2 f.]), though Jeremiah would seem to suggest that he deliberately deceived the people (Jer. 28:15). In either case, the hearers of Hananiah and Jeremiah could not discriminate between them merely from their words and formulas. Hence Jeremiah gives two criteria: (1) the fulfillment of his prediction (Jer. 28:9, 16 f.); (2) the conformity of his teaching to the traditional doctrine (Jer. 28:7 f.)—what we might call the "analogy of faith."[11] Deuteronomy gives these criteria: one is the fulfillment of prophecy (Dt. 18:21 f.); the other and more important criterion is the doctrine and life of the prophet (Dt. 13:1-5), which should be in the line of pure Yahwism.

---

[9]Dodd, *op. cit.*, p. 51.
[10]Roland de Vaux, BJ, p. 973.
[11]See Harrington, *op. cit.*, p. 114.

Prophecy is inseparable from the religion of Israel that antedated it and brought it into being. In the last analysis, the criterion of true prophecy was its accord with known revelation. . . . The prophet spoke to the conscience of Israel. The Israelite who had stopped his ears to conscience could abide no comminatory word of any prophet. To him the prophets could be only what Elijah was to Ahab, "troublers of Israel." For him there was the soothing syrup of false prophecy, which troubled no conscience. . . . Only the Israelite who held to the faith of his fathers heard in the prophets the authentic ring of the voice of God. True Israelite and true prophet stood in the same tradition and understood each other.[12]

2) *Literary Forms of Prophetic Literature*

The prophets were primarily preachers who delivered their oracles and sermons by word of mouth, with the original oral character still stamped on the written record of their sayings. In exceptional cases the prophets did write (cf. Is. 8:1-4; 30:8; Ezek. 43:11 f.; Jer. 36:2,28). It may be that the work of Second Isaiah is a sustained literary composition; though even this is more likely to be a collection of oracles originally delivered orally, for despite a remarkable unity, there is a certain lack of sequence in the arrangement.[13] There can be little doubt that the last part (chapters 40-48) of the Book of Ezekiel is a literary composition. But these are the exceptions and, by and large, the prophets were certainly speakers rather than writers. This means that the units which make up the prophetic collections are short and many, and that the literary forms are varied. It is absolutely essential for an intelligent reading of the prophets that the limits of these units be determined and their literary forms identified.[14] While we list the most notable of these literary forms,[15] it should be kept in mind that the greater part of Old Testament prophecy is in poetic form.[16]

THE LITERARY   1. *The oracle.* The oracle is a solemn declaration
FORMS   made in the name of God and is determined by
the conviction that God has communicated his word to the prophet
(cf. Jer. 19:11; 28:16). These oracles are generally marked by for-

---

[12]B. Vawter, *The Conscience of Israel* (New York: Sheed & Ward, 1961), p. 27.
[13]See D. R. Jones, PCB, n. 447 c.
[14]This is one of the many notable features of the *Bible de Jérusalem*.
[15]See Gelin, *op. cit.*, pp. 479-82; J. Muilenburg, PCB, n. 413.
[16]For a treatment of Old Testament poetic forms see pp. 281-83.

mulas of introduction (*kōh 'āmar Yahweh*—"Thus says Yahweh")
and of conclusion (*ne'ûm Yahweh*—"oracle of Yahweh").

2. *Exhortation* (cf. Am. 5:4 f.; Zeph. 2:3). Here the tone is that
of a preacher who seeks to convince his audience; the first word is
"Hear!"

3. *Autobiography.* The prophets describe a profound spiritual experience or important incidents in their career (Is. 6; Jer. 1:4-10;
Hos. 3:1-4).

4. *Description* (especially description of visions and dreams). This
form began to predominate after the Exile (Ezek.; Zech.).

5. *Narrative biography*: Jer. 26-29; 32-45; Am. 7:10-17.

6. *Hymn*: Is. 42:10-13; Hos. 6:1-6; Jer. 14.

7. *Confession*: Is. 53:1-9; Jer. 11:18—12:6; 15:10-21; 18:18-23; 20:7-
18.

8. *Invective and threat*: Is. 5:8-25; Jer. 7:16-20; Hos. 7:8-16; Am.
1:3—2:16.

9. *Allegory*: Ezek. 17:2-24; 19:2-14; 23:2-35.

10. *Symbolic actions.* Not infrequently the prophet was not content
with speaking the word, but dramatized it by acting it out symboli-
cally before the people (cf. 1 Kgs. 11:29-40; Jer. 13:1-9; Ezek. 4:1-3,7).

11. *Symbolic life.* In some cases the life of the prophet was symbolic (Hos. 1-3; Ezek. 24:22-24).

COMPOSITION   It has become clear that the oracles and sermons
OF THE BOOKS   of the prophets were preserved by their disciples
and eventually edited by them. These words must soon have been
written down and we may visualize a primitive prophetical literature
circulating in the form of short and separate writings. In the gradual
work of collecting and editing, elements were added: earlier collections were sometimes broken up, and the material was finally arranged
according to a plan—sometimes very vague—that must be determined
(if possible) for each book. The complex genesis of the prophetical
books (or many of them) goes far to explain the disconcerting dis-
array that can confuse and exasperate the reader. The realization,
for instance, that the Book of Isaiah bridges several centuries and
really is an anthology of sermons and oracles, puts the reader on
his guard and enables him to follow the work intelligently. Otherwise,
his consternation must be that of one who would regard Palgrave's
Golden Treasury as a single poem.

3) The Prophetical Books in Chronological Order

1. Prophets of the eighth century B.C.:
   Amos
   Hosea
   Isaiah 1-39
   Micah
2. Prophets of the seventh century B.C. and beginning of the sixth century B.C.:
   Zephaniah
   Nahum
   Habakkuk
   Jeremiah
3. Prophets of the Exile:
   Ezekiel
   Second Isaiah (40-55)
4. Prophets of the sixth century B.C.:
   Isaiah 56-66
   Haggai
   Zechariah 1-8
5. Prophets of the fifth century B.C.:
   Isaiah 34-35; 24-27
   Malachi
   Obadiah
6. Prophets of the fourth century B.C.:
   Joel
   Zechariah 9-14

3. PROPHETS OF THE EIGHTH CENTURY

1) Amos

THE PROPHET   Amos is the earliest of the Old Testament prophets whose words have been preserved for us in book form. The heading of this book (Am. 1:1) tells us that Amos was a peasant of Tekoa (about six miles south of Bethlehem) and that he was active during the reign of the contemporary kings, Uzziah of Judah and Jeroboam II of Israel. Since his ministry was clearly set in the height of Israel's prosperity, it must have been well into the reign of Jeroboam II (783-743 B.C.), in other words, around the year 750 B.C.

The passage of Am. 7:10-15 gives a more detailed picture of Amos' background. He spent part of his time as a shepherd and part as a "dresser of sycamore trees"—this expression refers to the puncturing of the fig-like fruit so that the insects which form inside may be released.[17] The mission of a prophet of Judah in Israel is a striking indication that a common religious tradition bound the divided kingdoms. When Amaziah, the priest of Bethel, warned Amos that he should earn his living in Judah (by accepting fees like the professional prophets [cf. 1 Sm. 9-8; 1 Kgs. 14:3; 2 Kgs. 8:8]), Amos replied that he was not a *nābî* of that kind, nor was he one of the "sons of the prophets": he had received a special vocation.

THE   The Book of Amos is a compilation, made by his disciples
BOOK   or in prophetical circles, of oracles and sermons of the Prophet
spoken in various situations. Though his message was primarily to Israel, as a Southerner he did not altogether neglect Judah (Am. 6:1; 8:14). The book seems to have grown in this fashion:

1. The primary elements.
    a) The oracular material: short, forceful passages (for example, Am. 1:3–2:8; 4:6-12).
    b) Autobiographical passages: the cycle of five visions (Am. 7:1-9; 8:1-3; 9:1-4), which would come more naturally at the beginning of the book. The fifth vision, however, took place in Bethel just before Amos was expelled from Israel.
    c) A biographical passage (Am. 7:10-17), probably taken from a collection of traditions about Amos.
2. The work of compilation.
    a) The earlier units were grouped by mnemonic techniques. Some groups begin with "Hear this word" (Am. 3:1; 4:1; 5:1; 8:4); others with "Woe" (Am. 5:7,18; 6:1b).
    b) The arrangement of Am. 7-9 is strange: the biographical passage of Am. 7:10-17 breaks the series of visions.
    c) Later additions:
        1) The oracle against Judah (2:4 f.) is a deuteronomical fragment.

---

[17]See B. W. Anderson, *Understanding the Old Testament* (Englewood Cliffs, N.J.: Prentice-Hall, 1957), p. 228.

2) The doxologies (4:13; 5:8 f.; 9:5 f.) differ in style from the rest of the book and reflect later theology.

3) The epilogue (9:8b-15) is in sharp contrast to the otherwise pessimistic message of the Prophet.

3. Division.

TITLE (AM. 1:1 f.)
ORACLES AGAINST THE NATIONS AND ISRAEL (AM. 1:2–2:16)
WARNINGS AND WOES (AM. 3-6)
THE VISIONS (AM. 7:1–9:8a)
EPILOGUE: THE RESTORATION (AM. 9:8b-15)

THE MESSAGE   Amos is the great champion of justice. He took his stand on the essential justice of God and vindicated the moral order established by God and enshrined in the Covenant. Thus he mercilessly castigated the disorders that prevailed in an era of hectic prosperity. To his eyes the symptoms of social decay were glaring: wealth, concentrated in the hands of a few—the leaders of the people—had corrupted its possessors; oppression of the poor was rife; the richly-endowed national religion, with its elaborate ceremonial, provided a comfortable atmosphere of self-righteousness. "The ordinary Israelite, we may be sure, felt that he had the privilege of belonging to an uncommonly religious nation, which was properly rewarded for its piety by this unwonted prosperity."[18] It is this dangerous complacency that the Prophet set out to shatter.

The series of oracles (Am. 1:2–2:16) shows how dramatically he could accomplish this. The people listened, doubtless with approval, to the threatened punishment of God on six neighboring nations: Damascus, Gaza, Tyre, Edom, Ammon, and Moab. Then comes the climax, the seventh oracle (the oracle against Judah—Am. 2:4 f.—is a

---

[18]Dodd, *op. cit.*, p. 39.

later addition), and out of the blue the Prophet's thunderbolt strikes Israel! Yahweh is clearly shown to be master of all peoples (cf. Am. 9:7), but he has chosen one people: the whole family which he brought up out of Egypt (Am. 3:1). With the privilege of that choice goes a corresponding obligation: "You only have I known of all the families of the earth, therefore I will punish you for all your iniquities" (Am. 3:2). Israel has received more, and of her more will be required; divine justice demands it.

Amos saw that nothing short of a radical change of life could save Israel (Am. 5:4-6, 14 f.) and he feared that it would not come. He warned those who looked to the "Day of the Lord" as the time of the triumph of God's people over all her enemies that the Day would be darkness and not light (Am. 2:18). He saw that the slumbering Assyrian giant would soon waken and destroy Israel (Am. 3:9-11). There was only one way to avert that wrath to come: "Hate evil, and love good, and establish justice in the gate; it may be that the Lord, the God of hosts, will be gracious to the remnant of Joseph" (Am. 5:15).

2) Hosea

THE
PROPHET Hosea was a younger contemporary of Amos who preached during the latter years of Jeroboam II and during the turbulent years that preceded the fall of Samaria in 721 B.C. (though there is no evidence that he witnessed the final disaster). We may fit his ministry between 745 B.C. and 725 B.C. He was a Northerner and a man of higher social position than Amos. We have little information about Hosea; in fact we are provided just enough data to establish one of the thorniest problems in the Old Testament. This is the problem of the prophet's marriage.

The picture is unclear because Hosea was not primarily interested in giving biographical details, since it was the symbolism of the marriage that occupied his attention. The marriage is described in biographical style (Hos. 1) and in autobiographical style (Hos. 3). From this arrangement two questions emerge: Do chapters one and three represent successive stages of the Prophet's experience with one woman, Gomer? Is the woman of chapter three—she is unnamed— another woman and not Gomer? If the second alternative is correct, then chapter one describes the real marriage and chapter three is the description of a prophetic symbol: the purchase and seclusion of a cult-prostitute as a symbol of God's plan for his unfaithful people.

It is much more probable that both chapters recount Hosea's experience with Gomer, for if the woman of chapter three were another, we should expect more explicit mention of it. The analogy with Israel (Hos. 3:1b) suggests that the Prophet is to be reconciled with Gomer, just as Yahweh will take back to him the Israel he had rejected. "In chapter one the theme is the faithlessness of Israel; in chapter three it is the steadfastness of Yahweh's love in the face of infidelity. These themes are not based on one event of Hosea's life, but on a sequence of events in his relations with Gomer."[19]

Am. 1:2 is best regarded as an introduction to the chapter written in the full knowledge of the events. The woman whom Hosea married was not yet a harlot; only later did her true character appear. It is even more likely that his call to prophesy came through his personal experience, and had not preceded it. He came to see that his life mirrored the tragic relationship of Yahweh and Israel and he realized that what had happened to him was guided by a divine purpose. Then, too, the meaning of his broken marriage became clear: "for the land commits great harlotry in forsaking the Lord." As Isaiah will do (Is. 7:3; 8:3), Hosea gave meaningful names to his children, so that he and they become living signs of God's word to Israel. In chapter three we read that the Prophet took back his unfaithful wife. Gomer appears to have become one of the cult-prostitutes mentioned in Hos. 4:13 f. Hosea brought her back and kept her shut off from her lovers until she turned to him: it is thus that Yahweh will treat Israel—a reference to the Exile of Israel (721 b.c.).

The symbolism of the events is clear enough. The marriage with a prostitute signifies that Yahweh is the spouse of a people which worships the Baals—in prophetical language idolatry is "prostitution." The corrective seclusion of Gomer symbolizes the purification of the Exile; the names of woe given to the children point to the chastisement of Israel; the renewed marriage life of Hosea and Gomer promises the restoration of good relations between Yahweh and his people. Of course the whole story has not been told, but it is obvious that Hosea had suffered as husband and father. Out of his

---

[19]Anderson, *op. cit.*, p. 242.

own personal experience he realized the aptness of the marriage image to describe the relations between Yahweh and his people.[20]

THE The book of Hosea is better ordered than that of Amos and
BOOK contains little, if any, later material. But it too is composed of short sermons and oracles spoken in different times and circumstances.

1. *Analysis.* Chapters 1-3 give the married life of Hosea and its prophetic symbolism. Chapter three is autobiographical and chapter one is biographical, while chapter two is less an explanation of the narratives than a development of their theme. The passage Hos. 2:1-3 (1:10 f. plus 2:1) should come after chapter three. The whole is dated from the second half of the reign of Jeroboam II, for the Dynasty of Jehu is still in power (Hos. 1:4) and the nation is prosperous (Hos. 2:4-15).

The rest of the book (Hos. 4-14) is somewhat later and refers to later events. It comprises (1) threats and invective against the cult and politics of Israel (Hos. 4:1–9:9); (2) poems (Hos. 9:10–14:9) which recall and meditate on the history of Israel—this is a feature which stresses the link with Deuteronomy. The absence of additional material would indicate that the collections were made at an early date. The text of Hosea is poorly preserved, and differences in translations often reflect the efforts of scholars to establish the original readings.[21]

2. *Division.*

TITLE (HOS. 1:1)
THE MARRIAGE OF HOSEA AND ITS SYMBOLISM (HOS. 1-3)
CRIMES AND CHASTISEMENT OF ISRAEL (HOS. 4-13)
CONVERSION OF ISRAEL (HOS. 14)

THE Hosea was profoundly aware of the Mosaic past. He looked
MESSAGE back with nostalgia to the beginning of Israel's tradition; to

---

[20]See Gelin, *op. cit.*, pp. 395 f.
[21]See *ibid.*, p. 494.

the desert, to the "days of her youth" (Hos. 2:17 [15]) and to the Covenant (Hos. 13:5). The baneful influence of a materialistic society had caused Israel to forget Yahweh (Hos. 13:6), so Yahweh will bring her back into the desert and speak to her heart (Hos. 2:16 [14]; 12:10). Here the decisive event in Israel's history—the Exodus—comes to the fore. The Prophet reminds the people of the divine intervention that called Israel into being and set it apart from all nations—Yahweh had called his *son* out of Egypt (Hos. 11:1).

Hosea was the first to represent the Covenant relation of Yahweh with his people as a marriage. It would, of course, have seemed natural enough that the Covenant, a treaty between God and Israel, might have been likened to the marriage contract between man and wife. The singular fact is that it is not the contract aspect that was exploited, but rather the love aspect, and especially the love of a husband for his wife. It is out of his own personal experience that the marriage image came to Hosea and that he realized its aptness in describing the relations between Yahweh and his people. He understood that the psychology of human love can wonderfully illustrate the mystery of God's relations with men, the reality and depth of his love. The divine Husband has been betrayed by his wife who has given herself to adultery and prostitution. Yet he seeks only to win her again to him, and if he chastises her it is with that sole end in view. As a last resort he determines to bring her back once more to the conditions of the Exodus, the honeymoon period of their love (Hos. 2:16 f.). In fact, he ultimately goes beyond this and promises to bring her into the harmony of a new garden of Eden (Hos. 2:18) where their love will be the crowning and fulfillment of the mutual love of the first human couple:

"I will betroth you to me forever,
I will betroth you to me in righteousness and in justice, in kindness and in love.
I will betroth you to me in faithfulness,
  and you shall know the Lord" (Hos. 2:21 f.).

Hosea has to speak of judgment too; he warns of the approaching Assyrian danger (Hos. 13:15). It will come like a whirlwind (Hos. 8:7) and soon (Hos. 10:15), bringing destruction (Hos. 8:14; 12:12) and death (Hos. 14:1) in its wake. But his lead idea remains the divine goodness (*hesed*), which explains the origin of Israel (Hos.

11:1-9) and which will have the last word (Hos. 2:21 [19]). This divine *hesed* is demanding; what God asks is "steadfast love (*hesed*) and knowledge of God" (Hos. 6:6). True religion is a practical, loving acceptance of God, an affair of the heart. "The word *hesed* evokes a relation similar to that denoted by *pietas*: it implies a dedication to Someone."[22]

3) Isaiah 1-39

THE   Isaiah seems to have been an aristocrat and, apparently, PROPHET   a native of Jerusalem. In 740 B.C., the year of the death of King Uzziah, he had his inaugural vision in the Temple. Yahweh appeared to him like an oriental monarch, surrounded by a corps of seraphim who proclaimed the holiness of God. The Prophet's first reaction was fear and trembling (Is. 6:5); but then, cleansed of his sins, he responded without hesitation to the divine call (Is. 6:8). His mission was to be difficult, for the people would refuse to listen to his preaching (Is. 6:9 f.). There was a ray of hope, however: a "Remnant" will remain faithful (Is. 6:13).

Judah had been prosperous under Uzziah and continued so under Jotham (740-736 B.C.). Like Amos before him, Isaiah attacked luxury and social abuses; this is the burden of many of the oracles of chapter 1-5. The Prophet's mission continued under Ahaz and to the end of the reign of Hezekiah. But he seems to have withdrawn from public life during most of the reign of Ahaz (from 734 B.C. onwards). Jewish legend has it that he was martyred under Manasseh. The historical background of Isaiah is given above in Chapter One.

Isaiah was one of the most gifted poets of Israel and a man of deep religious sensibility. A measure of his stature is the fact that more than any other prophet he inspired his disciples, so that an "Isaian school" carried on his ideas and produced oracles in his name until the fifth century B.C.

THE   In the Book of Isaiah modern criticism has distinguished BOOK   a number of different groupings or sections, and these date from different epochs. The three main parts are: Isaiah (chapters 1-39), Second Isaiah (chapters 40-55), and Isaiah 56-66. Though the book has been divided up, modern criticism also takes account

---

[22]*Ibid.*, p. 498.

of certain constant elements running through the whole. Thus throughout the book God is the "Holy One of Israel" and his transcendence is strongly emphasized. The whole is pervaded by a messianic and eschatological atmosphere, which makes this book the classic of hope.

Isaiah 1-39 is very complex. It is, to a notable extent, an anthology of prophetical sermons and oracles, with selections even from the sixth and fifth centuries B.C. However, the great bulk of the material of these chapters is the work of the eighth-century Prophet. The genuine prophecies of Isaiah are: 1-11; 14:24—23:18; 28-32—though even here some short passages may be postexilic.

1. *Division.*

ORACLES AGAINST JUDAH AND JERUSALEM (IS. 1-12)	
1) Oracles before the Syro-Ephraimite War	1-5
2) The Book of Immanuel	6-12
ORACLES AGAINST THE NATIONS (IS. 13-23)	
ESCHATOLOGICAL ORACLES—THE GREAT APOCALYPSE (IS. 24-27)	
THE COLLECTION OF "WOES" (IS. 28-33)	
ESCHATOLOGICAL ORACLES—THE LITTLE APOCALYPSE (IS. 34-35)	
HISTORICAL APPENDIX (IS. 36-39)	

2. *Analysis.*[23] Chapters 1-12, the oracles against Judah and Jerusalem, are made up of five groups:

a) Is. 1: Typical preaching of the Prophet, collected by his disciples.

b) Is. 2-4: The first preaching of Isaiah.

c) Is. 5:9; 7—11:16: Many different fragments.

d) Is. 6:1—9:6: The Book of Immanuel—a complete literary unit.

e) Is. 12: Psalm which forms a doxology; added by a later compiler to round off this section.

Many of the oracles against the nations (chapters 13-23) date from the period which preceded and followed the destruction of Samaria (721 B.C.); but the *collection* was certainly completed after the Exile

---

[23]See *ibid.*, pp. 503-5.

because there are a number of non-Isaian oracles (for example, the oracles against Babylon [Is. 13; 14:22 f.] and the oracles on the return from the Exile [Is. 14:1-21]).

In the collection of "Woes" (chapters 28-33) the Assyrian cycle (chapters 28-31) contains the oracles which were pronounced between 713-701 B.C. However, the passages Is. 29:17-24; 30:18-26; 32:1-8 are postexilic, and chapter 33 is a late prophetic liturgy. The apocalypses (Is. 24-27; 34-35) will be treated below.[24]

The historical appendix (Is. 36-39—borrowed from 2 Kgs. 18:13—20:19) has, like Jer. 52, an apologetic purpose: history has proved Isaiah right. It was added by the disciples of the Prophet. The events are not given in the proper chronological order, which is: illness of Hezekiah (Is. 38); embassy of Merodach-baladan (Is. 39); campaign of Sennacherib (Is. 36-37).

It is likely that the book of Immanuel and the Assyrian cycle were the first collections to be made, and this nucleus grew by additions and insertions. The great apocalypse concluded the oracles against the nations and the little apocalypse concluded the oracles of hope (Is. 32-33). The historical appendix was the last to be added.

THE MESSAGE[25]   The God of Isaiah is the "Holy One." This holiness, thrice proclaimed by the seraphim, indeed expresses the moral perfection of the divinity; above all, however, it indicates his inaccessibility and his majesty. Furthermore, for Isaiah, Yahweh is the "Holy One of Israel": this transcendent God is a God who acts in history on behalf of his Chosen People. The title itself expresses the mystery of an all-holy God who yet stoops down to frail and sinful man.

Isaiah insists on faith—the practical conviction that Yahweh alone matters; one must lean on God alone (Is. 8:13; 28:16; 30:15). He vainly sought, in Ahaz, the faith which would turn the king from human alliances and enable him to stand, unperturbed, in the face of threats and even in the presence of hostile armies. Bluntly, he warned him: "If you will not believe, surely you will not be established" (Is. 7:9). One result of this faith was that, in the Prophet's eyes, Sion, the dwelling place of the holy God, was inviolable (Is.

---

[24]Pp. 212 f.
[25]See Gelin, *op. cit.*, pp. 505-7.

28:16); thus he could encourage Hezekiah when Sennacherib had overrun Judah and had shut up the king "like a bird in a cage."

Perhaps Isaiah's most important contribution to the development of the religion of Israel was his founding of a prophetical party (Is. 8:16). A spiritual society was set up within, and distinct from, the national society. This was the first concrete expression of that small "Remnant" which the prophets envisaged as the bearers and the heirs of the divine promises. Ever afterwards, though the nation might go to destruction, a handful would stand firm, ready to make a new beginning, or to receive the Messiah at last, like the few who "looked for the consolation of Israel" (Lk. 2:25).

4) Micah

THE PROPHET The little information we have about Micah comes from two brief notes, one in his own book and the other in Jeremiah. In Mi. 1:1 we learn that Micah was a native of Moresheth (a town of the Shephelah near Gath [cf. Mi. 1:14]) and preached during the reigns of Jotham, Ahaz, and Hezekiah, that is, between 740 B.C. and 687 B.C.; this makes him a contemporary of Hosea and Isaiah. From Jeremiah we learn that the preaching of Micah under Hezekiah was efficacious and played its part in the religious reform of that king (Jer. 26:18-20; cf. Mi. 3:12). His mission, primarily to Judah, did not exclude Israel, whose end he witnessed. His blunt language is like that of Amos and he has that Prophet's approach to social injustice and the same insistence on the justice of God. He saw that the rot, condemned by Amos, had spread to Judah and he proclaimed, in uncompromising terms, the fearful judgment of Yahweh. The fate of Samaria added weight and urgency to his words.

THE BOOK Some scholars would argue that the genuine prophecies of Micah are found in chapters 1-3 only—but this is hypercritical. Many, however, would claim that chapters 4-5, at least, are later, for they are concerned with the salvation of God's people and the destruction of its enemies, themes that are largely postexilic. However, it may well be that these two chapters "date from the period of messianic enthusiasm that resulted from the rout of Sennacherib's army, and therefore can be the work of Micah."[26] There

---

[26]Vawter, *op. cit.*, p. 131.

are some later additions, but the bulk of the work is quite conceivable
in the setting of the Prophet's own time.

1. *Analysis*.[27] This analysis distinguishes the various units and
seeks to date some of them. The final arrangement of the book is
artificial and follows no chronological order.

a) Oracles of doom: Mi. 1-3.

    1:2-7—prediction of the fall of Samaria (before 721 B.C.).

    1:8-16—against Judah (701 B.C.; cf. Is. 10:24-34).

    2:1-11—against social injustice.

    2:12 f.—promise of restoration (authenticity contested).

    3:1-12—against judges, prophets, and tyrannical leaders.

b) Oracles of weal: Mi. 4-5.

    4:1-4—Yahweh's reign in Sion (cf. Is. 2:2-4—apparently of Tem-
ple origin).

    4:6-8—reign of Yahweh and return from exile.

    4:9-14—triumph of Sion.

    5:1-5—the liberator born at Ephrathah.

    5:6-8—the Remnant (perhaps postexilic).

    5:9-14—oracle against Judah.

c) Oracles of doom: Mi. 6:1—7:6.

    6:1-8—Yahweh's trial of his people (after 701 B.C.).

    6:9-16—oracle against Jerusalem (or against Samaria before
721 B.C.).

    7:1-6—lamentation for Jerusalem. Verse 7—hope of the Prophet
—is the conclusion of his book.

d) Oracles of weal: Mi. 7:8-20 (postexilic addition).

2. *Division.*

TITLE (MI. 1:1)
JUDGMENT OF ISRAEL AND JUDAH—ORACLES OF DOOM (MI. 1-3)
PROMISES TO SION—ORACLES OF WEAL (MI. 4-5)
ORACLES OF DOOM (MI. 6:1—7:7)
ORACLES OF HOPE (MI. 7:8-20)

---

[27]See Gelin, *op. cit.*, pp. 499 f.

THE   Like Amos, Micah viewed social injustice as a crime
MESSAGE   that cried to heaven for vengeance (Mi. 2-31; 6:9-11),
and he stresses the impending divine judgment on this and similar
crimes. He does go beyond Amos by looking past the day of reckoning
to the reign of Yahweh and the triumph of Sion (Mi. 4-5). In his
most famous saying (Mi. 6:8) he presents his message as a synthesis
of the preaching of his predecessor and contemporaries: "He has
showed you, O man, what is good; and what does the Lord require
of you but to do justice [Amos], and to love kindness [*hesed*—Hosea]
and to walk humbly [Isaiah] with your God?"[28]

4. PROPHETS OF THE SEVENTH CENTURY AND BEGINNING OF THE SIXTH CENTURY

1) *Zephaniah*

THE   The little we do know of Zephaniah is gleaned from his
PROPHET   short writing. His genealogy (Zeph. 1:1) is traced back
to a certain Hezekiah, who may be the king of that name. The
object of the genealogy probably is to make clear that, despite the
name of his father (Cushi means "the Ethiopian"), the Prophet
was a Judean. He prophesied under Josiah. The tone of his preaching
indicates that his mission fell during the minority of that king and
before the reform; most likely between 640 B.C. and 630 B.C., just
prior to the ministry of Jeremiah. His oracles give us an idea of
affairs in Judah on the eve of Josiah's great task: the cult of foreign
deities (Zeph. 1:4 f.); foreign customs (Zeph. 1:8); false prophets
(Zeph. 3:4); violence and social injustice (Zeph. 3:1-3; 1:11). His
work must have prepared the ground for the coming reform.

THE   Today it is almost universally acknowledged that the whole
BOOK   of the writing—apart from two or three small retouches—is
authentic.

1. *Analysis.* The book falls into three parts: 1) threats against
Judah and Jerusalem (Zeph. 1:2—2:3); two descriptions of the Day
of Yahweh (Zeph. 1:2-13, 14-18)—Zeph. 1:14 f. inspired the *Dies
irae.* The call to conversion (Zeph. 2:1-3) is remarkable for the
emergence of the class of '*anāwim*—the "poor"—the humble who

---

[28]*Ibid.,* p. 500.

patiently put their trust in Yahweh alone and were faithful to his law. 2) The oracles against the nations (Zeph. 2:4-15) are typical prophetical utterances (Zeph. 2:11 seems to have been inspired by Second Isaiah) and the threats against Judah come as a climax like Amos' oracle against Israel (Am. 2:6-16). 3) The promises (Zeph. 3:9-20) include later additions: Zeph. 3:9 f. ecno Second Isaiah, and the passage 3:18b-20, which looks to the return of the exiles, doubtless dates from the Exile.

2. *Division.*

TITLE (ZEPH. 1:1)
THE DAY OF YAHWEH (ZEPH. 1:2–2:3)
ORACLES AGAINST THE NATIONS AND JERUSALEM (ZEPH. 2:4–3:8)
PROMISES (ZEPH. 3:9-20)

THE
MESSAGE
Like Amos, Zephaniah warned his hearers of the "Day of Yahweh," a universal catastrophe that will sweep away Judah and the nations. The chastisement of the nations should be a warning to Judah (Zeph. 3:7), but the "shameless nation," defiled by pagan practices and proudly rebellious (Zeph. 3:1,11), will not take heed. But a Remnant will be faithful, a people "humble and lowly" (Zeph. 3:12 f.), the *'anāwim*—the "poor of Yahweh" who will inherit the kingdom of God (Mt. 5:3).

2) Nahum

THE
PROPHET
We know nothing of Nahum, not even his place of origin, since Elkosh has not been identified. It is clear that he prophesied not long before 612 B.C. (date of the fall of Nineveh), and perhaps soon after 616 B.C. when the downfall of Assyria was imminent. Nahum was a poet of unusual talent and his words ring with a passionate patriotism. The fall of the great oppressor is contemplated with uninhibited satisfaction; but Nahum believes that Nineveh's fall will mean the restoration of Israel and Judah.

THE
BOOK
The book opens with an alphabetic psalm (from *aleph* to *kaph* only) (Na. 1:2-9), which develops the theme of the Wrath of God. In Nahum 1:9–2:3 short oracles of weal for Judah

(Na. 1:12 f.; 2:1,3) are mingled with oracles of woe for Nineveh (Na. 1:9-11,14). The poem Na. 2:4—3:19 has the power and movement of the Song of Deborah (Jgs. 5).

Division.

TITLE (NA. 1:1)
THE WRATH OF YAHWEH (NA. 1:2-8)
ORACLES OF WEAL AND WOE (NA. 1:9—2:3)
THE FALL OF NINEVEH (NA. 2:4—3:19)

THE MESSAGE Behind the patriotic outburst at the doom of a tyrannical foe we find the conviction that the destruction of Nineveh is an expression of God's justice: it is the punishment for accumulated crimes (Na. 3:1,4; 3:19). Besides, Nineveh had become the image of a world that stood opposed to Yahweh; its downfall was his triumph and the triumph of his people.

3) Habakkuk

THE PROPHET Unlike the earlier prophetical books, the title of Habakkuk does not indicate the date of the Prophet's mission; the *midrash* in Dn. 14:33-39 is no help to us.[29] In fact, we know nothing whatever about the person of the Prophet. Some have argued that the oppressors of Judah are the Assyrians and that the date of the book would be about 615 B.C. It is more reasonable to maintain that the Chaldeans (Babylonians) named in Habakkuk 1:6 are in view throughout and that the oracles fall between Nebuchadnezzar's victory at Carchemish (605 B.C.) and the first siege of Jerusalem (597 B.C.). This would make Habakkuk a contemporary of Jeremiah.

THE BOOK The Book of Habakkuk has all the appearance of having been carefully composed; and though the unity of the work has been contested, a strong case can be made in its favor. It is significant that W. F. Albright regards the book as "substantially the work of a single author."[30]

---

[29]See p. 386.

[30]H. H. Rowley, editor, *Studies in Old Testament Prophecy* (Naperville, Ill.: Allenson, 1957), p. 2.

1. *Analysis.* The book opens with a dialogue between God and the Prophet: a first complaint (Hb. 1:2-4) regards the prevalence of injustice in Judah, and a first divine response (Hb. 1:5-11) foretells the coming of the Babylonians as agents of divine justice. A second complaint (Hb. 1:12-17) concerns the tyranny of the Babylonians, now masters of Judah, and the divine response (Hb. 2:1-4) promises that God's intervention will not fail to save those who trust in him. Next, a series of five woes is hurled at the oppressor (Hb. 2:5-20)—and Habakkuk 2:5-6a form a prelude and Habakkuk 2:20 forms a transition to the following psalm. The Prayer of Habakkuk (chapter 3) is a psalm which (as the musical directions in vv. 1,3,9,13,19 indicate) was adapted for use in the Temple liturgy. Its theme is the final triumph of God.

2. *Division.*

TITLE (HB. 1:1)
DIALOGUE BETWEEN THE PROPHET AND YAHWEH (HB. 1:2—2:4)
FIVE 'WOES' AGAINST THE OPPRESSOR (HB. 2:5-20)
HYMN: THE TRIUMPH OF YAHWEH (HB. 3)

THE MESSAGE Habakkuk faces up to the scandal of God's action in history and of his treatment of Israel. How can he, who hates sin, use the ruthless Babylonians, "guilty men, whose own might is their god" (Hb. 1:11), to chastise his own people who, though far from guiltless, are at least "more righteous" than their oppressors (Hb. 1:13)? "It is the problem of evil on an international plane and the scandal of Habakkuk is also the problem of many men of our day. To him and to them the same divine answer is given: by strange and paradoxical means the all-powerful God prepares the way for the final victory of right, and 'the righteous man shall live by his faith.'"[31] (Cf. Rom. 1:17; Gal. 3:11; Heb. 10:38.) Among the scrolls found at Qumran (Cave I) was a *pesher* (commentary) on Habakkuk 1-2. The book is interpreted as though it were a prophecy of events in the history of the Qumran Essenes.[32]

---

[31]Roland de Vaux, BJ, p. 986.
[32]See Harrington, *op. cit.*, p. 78.

4) *Jeremiah*

THE   Jeremiah was born (c. 645 B.C.) of a priestly family in
PROPHET   Anathoth, a village three miles northeast of Jerusalem.
The prophetic call came to him in 626 B.C. (Jer. 1:2) while he was
still quite a young man, and his mission stretched from Josiah to
Zedekiah and outlasted the reign of the latter; that is to say, he
lived through the days full of promise of the young reformer king
and through the aftermath, the tragic years that led to the utter
destruction of his nation.[33] Jeremiah is better known to us as an
individual than any of his predecessors (or successors, for that
matter), for his book contains many passages of personal confession
and autobiography (for example, Jer. 15:10 f., 15-21; 20:7-18). He
stands out as a lonely, tragic figure and his mission seems to have
failed utterly. Yet that "failure" was his triumph, and the following
splendid tribute to Jeremiah does justice to the man.

> When he tried to arrest the course of a nation, only to be thrown
> down and trampled underfoot, when he cried out in bitterness of
> heart against the inexorable Will that compelled a poet to become a
> prophet, and a lover of men to be counted their enemy, he little
> knew that the development and record of his own lonely experience
> of failure was to be a success of the highest rank and influence.
> For if we want to know the meaning of personal religion at its
> finest and highest in the Old Testament, we must become, like Baruch,
> disciples of Jeremiah. In this respect there is no figure comparable
> with his, nor any of whom the revelation is so intimate and full.
> The only parallel within the Bible is the Apostle Paul. If religion
> means at last fellowship with God—and what else can it mean?—
> then Jeremiah can both show and tell more of it than any other under
> the Old Covenant—and did he not see from afar the New? Other
> prophets had their place and portion, and their measure of success;
> it was with him as with the poet of Schiller's poem, who thought of
> God whilst others secured his gifts, and so had nothing left but—
> God himself.[34]

THE   The LXX (Septuagint) text of Jeremiah is about one-eighth
BOOK   shorter than the Hebrew; the Greek text is perhaps based
on an earlier edition of the book. In the LXX the oracles against

---

[33]See pp. 63-67.
[34]H. Wheeler Robinson, *The Cross in the Old Testament* (London: S.C.M.
Press, 1960²), p. 121.

the nations are found after Jer. 25:13c, while the Masoretic Text has them at the end of the book. Besides, the book is very disordered: many doublets occur; there is a haphazard mixture of the three classic literary forms (oracle, biography, autobiography); and there is a lack of sequence in the chronological indications.

1. *Analysis.*[35] a) The nucleus of the book appears to have been the scroll of 605 B.C. dictated by the Prophet to his disciple and secretary Baruch, and containing the oracles spoken since the beginning of his ministry "against Israel and Judah and all the nations" (Jer. 36:2,32). It comprises: Jeremiah 1:4–6:30 (under Josiah); Jeremiah 7-20—less the complements indicated in b) below (under Jehoiakim); Jeremiah 25; 46:1–49:33 (less 46:13-28).

b) Complements of the scroll. In Jeremiah 36:32 it is stated that the fresh scroll written by Baruch contained all the matter of the first, with the addition of "many similar words." These oracles, added after 604 B.C., appear to be the following: Jeremiah 10:17-22; 12:7-14; 13:12-19; 15:5-9; 16:16-18; 18:1-12; 46:13-28; 49:34-39; as well as chapters 24; 27; 35. Jeremiah 21:11–23:8; 23:9-40 may have been added after 587 B.C. Finally, after the death of Jeremiah, Baruch inserted the "Confessions": Jeremiah 11:18–12:6; 15:10-21; 17:12-18; 18:18-23; 20:7-18.

c) The biography of Jeremiah. Baruch also wrote a partial biography of Jeremiah—the story of what he had suffered through fidelity to his prophetic vocation between 608 B.C. and 587 B.C. These passages, in chronological order, are: Jeremiah 19:2–20:6; 26; 36; 45; 28-29; 51:59-64; 34:8-22; 37-44.

d) Edition during the Exile. The book took final shape in Babylon. Certain collections within the book had already been formed by this time, notably, chapters 27-29 (message to the exiles), chapters 30-33 (the "Book of Consolation"), and Jeremiah 21:11–23:40 (words against the kings and prophets). Some additions were made during the Exile, especially Jeremiah 10:1-16; 33:14-26; 50-52.

2. *Division.* Despite the anthological nature of the work and its indifference to chronological order, the Book of Jeremiah does fall into four rather well-defined parts:

---

[35]See Gelin, *op. cit.*, pp. 522-24.

TITLE (JER. 1:1-3)
ORACLES AGAINST JUDAH AND JERUSALEM (JER. 1:4–25:13B)
ORACLES AGAINST THE NATIONS (JER. 25:13C-38; 46-51)
PROPHECIES OF SALVATION (JER. 26-35)
THE SUFFERINGS OF JEREMIAH (JER. 36-45)
APPENDIX: THE FALL OF JERUSALEM (JER. 52)

THE MESSAGE   It is possible to trace the spiritual progress of Jeremiah and to see in him the purifying and strengthening effect of suffering, for the real message of the Prophet is his own life. He was a man of rare sensitivity, with an exceptional capacity for affection. His mission was "to pluck up and to break down, to destroy and to overthrow" (Jer. 1:10), and to cry out, without respite, "violence and destruction" against the people he loved (Jer. 20:8). Jeremiah's efforts to bring his people to their senses failed, but it is the greatness of the man, and the grandeur of his faith, that precisely during the most tragic moment of his life he spoke his optimistic oracles, notably those of chapters 30-33. He saw that the Old Covenant will be replaced by a new one (Jer. 31:31-34), when God will act directly on the heart of man, when he will write his law on that heart, and when all men will know Yahweh.

That is one of the epoch-making utterances in the history of religion. Jeremiah, we may recall, had in his youth been a witness of the reformation under Josiah, and had no doubt shared the enthusiasm with which it had been greeted by idealists of the time. It seemed that at last the aim for which good men had striven for a century and a half had been attained. The nation had returned to the Lord their God and sealed their repentance by the solemn acceptance of a high code of social morals such as the prophets had taught. But in the period of disillusion that followed he came to the conclusion (trite enough by now) that "you cannot make people good by Act of Parliament." It was not enough to write good laws into the statute-book. They must be written "on the hearts" of men. In other words, the only adequate basis for right relations of men with God is an inward and personal understanding of his demands, an inward and personal response to them. It would not be true to say that Jeremiah first discovered the role of the individual in religion; for it is implicit in all prophetic teaching. But his clear emphasis upon it at the moment when the whole apparatus of public "institutional" religion had been swept away, was of the first importance for all subsequent development.[36]

The greatest tribute to Jeremiah was paid by the One whose way he had prepared. On that night before the Suffering Servant went to his death, he brought the most solemn promise of the Prophet to fulfillment: "This cup is the New Covenant in my blood" (Lk. 22:20). God had set his seal on the life and message of his servant.

APPENDIX: The Hebrew Bible has this little book among the
LAMENTATIONS   Writings. The Septuagint (LXX) and the Vulgate (Vg.) place it after Jeremiah, with a title which attributes it to him. The traditional attribution is based on 2 Chr. 35:25, and is supported by the content of the poems which does fit the time of Jeremiah— at least the last days of the Prophet. Nevertheless Jeremiah is not the author of Lam. He could not have stated that prophetic inspiration had ceased (Lam. 2:9), nor have praised Zedekiah (Lam. 4:20), nor have hoped in Egyptian help (Lam. 4:17); and his spontaneous poetic talent would not have been bound by the artificial form of these poems. Then, too, the influence of Ezekiel is noticeable in chapters 2 and 4.

The poems are laments for a fallen Jerusalem and ruined Temple, composed by some of those who had been left in Judah after 587 B.C. Undoubtedly they were designed for a simple liturgical service in the ruins of the Temple (cf. Jer. 41:5 f.; Zech. 7:3 ff.; 8:18 f.).

Analysis. The first, second, and fourth lamentations are alphabetical: each stanza begins with a different letter of the alphabet and the stanzas follow one another in alphabetical order. The third is also alphabetical, but here the verses of each group of three verses begin with the same letter, and the groups follow in alphabetical order. The fifth poem, though not alphabetical, has the same number of verses—22—as there are letters in the Hebrew alphabet. Basically the poetic form of all five poems is the *kināh* (Lam. 3:2) meter. Lamentations 1, 2, and 4 are in the literary form of funeral chants; 5 is a communal lament; 3 is a communal lament, but with notable

---

[36]Dodd, *op. cit.*, pp. 46 f.

individual characteristics. Despite their artificial plan, the lamentations, especially the fifth (in Vg. entitled the "Prayer of Jeremiah"), strike a high poetic level and convey intense emotion. Through all of them runs a sentiment of invincible confidence in God and an air of profound repentance.

5. PROPHETS OF THE EXILE
1) Ezekiel

THE **PROPHET**   Ezekiel, the son of Buzi and a priest in Jerusalem, was (with Jehoiachin and other prominent citizens of Judah) carried off to Babylon in the first captivity of 597 B.C. (Ezek. 1:1-3). He lived in the community of Tel-Abib on the banks of the Chebar, a canal which conducted water from the Euphrates through Nippur. He was called to be a prophet five years after the deportation (that is, in 593 B.C.). His ministry falls into two periods: from 593 B.C. to the fall of Jerusalem (587 B.C.); and from the fall of the city to 571 B.C., the date of his last recorded prophecy (Ezek. 29:17-20).

Ezekiel was by temperament a visionary; four great visions dominate his book: Ezekiel 1-3; 8-11; 37; 40-48. The vivid imagination displayed in these descriptions is also evident in the allegories: the sisters Oholah and Oholibah (chapter 23); the Shipwreck of Tyre (chapter 27); the Crocodile (chapters 29 and 32); the Great Cedar (chapter 31); and the Denizens of Sheol (chapter 32). At the same time, however, simple everyday things could inspire him: a sentry mounting guard (Ezek. 3:17-21); a wall being built (Ezek. 13:10-16). His own personal experiences could move him: the death of his wife (Ezek. 24:15-24); a mysterious and prolonged illness (Ezek. 4:4-17). Ezekiel used the prophet's technique of symbolic gesture more often and more elaborately than any other; for example, the symbols of Jerusalem under siege (Ezek. 4:1-3,7); of years of exile (Ezek. 4:4-8); of exile and siege (Ezek. 12:1-20); of the union of Judah and Israel (Ezek. 37:15-28).

As for his literary style, W. F. Albright has written:

> As a poet, Ezekiel was even inferior to Jeremiah, and neither of them ever touch the lyric and dramatic heights reached almost casually by Amos, Hosea, and Isaiah; the strength of the great exilic prophet lay in his vivid imagination and profound moral earnestness,

in both of which he is surpassed by no other rhapsodist [that is, as distinct from the earlier "ecstatic"] prophet.[37]

According to the present form of the book, the whole mission of Ezekiel was to the Jews in Babylon between 593 B.C. and 571 B.C. However, the oracles of the first part (Ezek. 1-24) are addressed to the inhabitants of Jerusalem, and Ezekiel gives the impression of being physically present in the city (cf. Ezek. 11:13). Thus a hypothesis of a double ministry of the Prophet has been put forward: he remained on in Palestine and preached there until the disaster of 587 B.C.; only then did he join the exiles. The vision of the scroll (Ezek. 2:1–3:9) marks the initial vocation of the Prophet in Palestine; the vision of the divine chariot (Ezek. 1:4-28; 3:10-15) marks his arrival among the exiles and the beginning of a new phase in his career. This hypothesis does not really dispose of existing difficulties; indeed it raises fresh ones. It involves a considerable rearrangement of the text and, furthermore, must now explain the "transportation" of the Prophet to Jerusalem (Ezek. 8:3; 12:24) and the mutual silence of Ezekiel and Jeremiah with regard to the (on this hypothesis) contemporary Jerusalem mission of the other. Besides, Ezekiel sufficiently distinguishes the exiles, whom he apostrophizes in the second person, from the people of Jerusalem whom he threatens in the third person, and his schematic picture of the city is not that of an eyewitness. It appears that the double ministry hypothesis is untenable and unnecessary.

THE BOOK 1. *Division* At first sight the Book of Ezekiel seems to display remarkable homogeneity and unity of plan, and it is arranged according to a clear outline.

INTRODUCTION (EZEK. 1-3)
ORACLES BEFORE THE SIEGE OF JERUSALEM (EZEK. 4-24)
ORACLES AGAINST THE NATIONS (EZEK. 25-32)
ORACLES DURING AND AFTER THE SIEGE (EZEK. 33-39)
THE "TORAH" OF EZEKIEL (EZEK. 40-48)

---

[37]*Op. cit.*, p. 326.

On closer examination the impression of striking unity is dissipated. Many doublets come to light: Ezek. 3:17-21 = 33:7-9; Ezek. 18:25-29 = 33:17-20; etc. The vision of the divine chariot (Ezek. 1:4–3:15) is interrupted by the vision of the scroll (Ezek. 2:1–3:9). The description of the sins of Jerusalem (Ezek. 11:1-21) follows on chapter 8 and breaks the narrative of the departure of the divine glory (Ezek. 10:18-22; 11:22-25). The chronology of chapters 26-33 is not in correct sequence. It follows that the situation in Ezekiel is really no different from Is. 1-39 and Jer.; it is a compilation made by the disciples of the Prophet.

2. *Analysis.* We are able to distinguish three stages in the progressive formation of the book:[38]

a) The stage of detached fragments. Like his predecessors, Ezekiel was not primarily a writer but a preacher. However, he did write down his ecstatic experiences, his symbolic actions, and certain of the communications of Yahweh.

b) Formation of collections. The different pieces were grouped according to origin, around catchwords ("idols" in chapter 6; "sword" in chapter 21), or more often according to their related content. The result is a haphazard arrangement of material that is complex and diversified.

c) In the final stage a superficial order was imposed on the earlier collections. On the whole, the chronological and logical order of this plan does represent the development of Ezekiel's ministry. There appear to be no later additions in Ezekiel and the book was given its final shape by disciples of the Prophet before the end of the Exile.

THE MESSAGE[39] During the first part of his ministry, Ezekiel's message was very like that of Jeremiah. We might summarize it thus:

1. The people of Judah are gravely culpable.

2. God is just and is preparing to punish them.

3. Very soon the siege of Jerusalem and the great deportation will show what such an intervention of Yahweh means. The Prophet

---

[38]See Gelin, *op. cit.,* pp. 537-39; cf. A. Robert and A. Tricot, editors, *Guide to the Bible,* trans. E. P. Arbez and M. R. P. McGuire (New York: Desclee, 1960[2]), I, p. 331.

[39]See P. Auvray, *Ezéchiel* (BJ), pp. 15-20.

seeks to justify the action of Yahweh by insisting on the culpability of Israel.

At this time the old conception of solidarity in guilt was proving inadequate (cf. Jer. 31:29; Ezek. 18:2). The celebrated vision of the sins of Jerusalem (Ezek. 8-11) provided Ezekiel with the elements of the solution; he developed these and proclaimed the moral principles in chapter 18 (cf. chapter 33). From these principles a fundamental religious truth, belief in retribution after death, will one day be deduced—but that day is centuries later. In the meantime the Prophet showed himself the great champion of individual responsibility.

> Unlike his prophetic predecessors Ezekiel could not lay his principal emphasis on collective guilt, since Israel and Judah were no longer nations and every Israelite group had to fend for itself. It is not surprising, therefore, that the idea of individual responsibility, explicit . . . from the beginning of Yahwism in Israel and emphatically reiterated by the deuteronomists, receives powerful expression in Ezekiel's words: "The soul that sinneth, it shall die. The son shall not be responsible for the iniquity of the father, neither shall the father be responsible for the iniquity of the son; the righteousness of the righteous shall be his (alone) and the wickedness of the wicked shall be his (alone)" (18:20).[40]

After the fall of Jerusalem Ezekiel's preoccupation changed. Exiled in a foreign land, without a temple and without an organized cult, the people of Israel not only have the impression that their God has forgotten them, but they also feel that he has remained on in Jerusalem and that the Israelites still left in Palestine are now the sole objects of his solicitude. At the same time, the destruction of Jerusalem and the deportation of its inhabitants have finally disabused those who had hoped for the salvation of the city. Until then one could still have looked for the conversion of the people and the divine pardon; now that Jerusalem had been treated like Samaria it was felt that this was likewise the end of Judah. Ezekiel answered this double temptation:

1. The vision of the chariot of Yahweh (chapter 1)—whatever its date—is meant to prove to the Prophet and to his hearers that Yahweh is not attached to Palestine, that he is essentially mobile, that he can follow (indeed has followed) his people in order to dwell with them.

---

[40]Albright, *op. cit.*, p. 326.

2. The vision of the dry bones (Ezek. 37:1-10) with its commentary (Ezek. 37:11-14) teaches that the chastisement is not final, that God can raise up what appears to be dead, and that he promises a triumphal return to Palestine.

The messianism of Ezekiel is distant and rather obscure, but it is real. He has an unshakable faith in a future salvation (Ezek. 5:3; 20:40-44). His portrait of the faithful shepherd, the new David, who tends his sheep with justice and love (chapter 34), is not only the inspiration of the image in Jn. 10, but expresses an ideal that will find its realization in Christ. In the promise of a new heart and a new spirit (Ezek. 36:23-28) the Prophet echoes Jer. 31:31-34. In the last nine chapters of his book (Ezek. 40-48) he not only describes exactly the New Temple and its rites, but goes on to describe the division of the country among the sanctuary, the prince, and the twelve tribes. These chapters, from our viewpoint neither very interesting nor very intelligible, have really had more influence than the rest. They express a political and religious ideal that, in large measure, set the pattern for the restoration of Israel.

Ezekiel is often named the father of Judaism. Sometimes the title is a reproach, as if he were responsible for the imperfections of decadent Judaism. He is certainly not to blame for pharisaism as it was at the beginning of the Christian era, but, by many of his ideas, by a certain ideal of aloofness and of legal sanctity, he contributed to the emergence of many aspects of postexilic Judaism.

2) *Second Isaiah*

AUTHORSHIP AND DATE   Since the end of the eighteenth century, and especially from the late nineteenth century, scholars have come to separate Is. 1-39 (which, in the main, goes back to the Prophet of the eighth century B.C.) from the remainder of the book. In this second part, chapters 56-66 are regarded as postexilic, while, for the rest, "the general opinion of scholars is that Isaiah 40-55 forms a unit, coming from the period just before and just after Cyrus' victory over Nabonidus of Babylon (539 B.C.)."[41] The author of these chapters, an anonymous prophet of the Exile, is, for convenience,

---

[41]*Ibid.*, pp. 326 f.

named Second Isaiah (or Deutero-Isaiah). We have no inkling of the identity of this man, one of the foremost poets and theologians of Israel. All we do know is that he certainly belonged to the "Isaian school" and found his inspiration in the work of his eighth-century master.

The sixth-century date of Isaiah 40-55 can be established on historical, doctrinal, and literary grounds.[42]

1. The field of interest of Second Isaiah is the end of the Exile between the victory of Cyrus over Lydia (546 B.C.) and the fall of Babylon (539 B.C.). We may well ask what significance the fall of Babylon could have for Israelites of the eighth century B.C. (facing the Assyrian threat and conscious of the power of Nineveh). Then, it would be surprising, to say the least, that a prophetic work of this caliber should have remained unknown until the sixth century B.C. —for there is no earlier trace of it. In practice, a prophet's message is always addressed to his contemporaries and must mean something to them. Refusal to accept an eighth-century B.C. date for Isaiah 40-55 is not a denial of the possibility of prediction of the future on the part of inspired prophets; it is simply the vindication of a commonsense approach to the Bible and is supported by the evidence of the other prophetical books.

2. The formulation of monotheism is perfectly clear-cut; and the new precision of expression presupposes a gradual theological development. The messianic doctrine of Second Isaiah marks a definite advance and follows a fresh line. The universalist outlook is accentuated and the emphasis on the conversion of the Gentiles is something novel.

3. In language and style Isaiah 40-55 differs notably from Isaiah 1-39; the difference is obvious in a good translation. The contrast is similar to that between the discourses of the Fourth Gospel and the sayings of Christ in the Synoptics.

Yet between Isaiah and Second Isaiah there are many resemblances and constant links. It is significant that Is. 1-39 contains a notable proportion of later material, some of it much later than Second Isaiah. This is why we can speak of an Isaian school of thought

----

[42]See Gelin, *op. cit.*, pp. 550 f.

and see in Second Isaiah the outstanding exponent of that school. It is true that Jewish tradition ascribes the whole work to the eighth-century B.C. Prophet; ben Sirach (c. 200 B.C.) witnesses to that belief (Sir. 48:23 f.) and the New Testament inherited the same outlook. But such acknowledgement of a traditional attribution does not purport to solve a problem of literary and historical criticism. It is just as today a man might, for instance, refer to Thomas á Kempis without committing himself on the issue of the authorship of the *Imitation of Christ*.

THE BOOK

1. *Division.*

ISRAEL IN BABYLON (IS. 40-48)	
1) The mission of the Prophet	40
2) The Liberator from the East	41
3) *The First Canticle of the Servant of Yahweh*	42:1-7 (1-9)
4) Oracles on the liberation of Israel	42:10–44:23
5) Cyrus, the Liberator	44:24–45:25
6) The majesty of Yahweh	46
7) Lament for Babylon (satirical)	47
8) Yahweh alone is God	48
THE RESTORATION OF SION (IS. 49-55)	
1) *The Second Canticle of the Servant of Yahweh*	49:1-6 (1:9a)
2) Yahweh will not reject his people	49:14–50:3
3) *The Third Canticle of the Servant of Yahweh*	50:4-9 (4-11)
4) Fourfold exhortation to confidence in Yahweh	51:1–52:12
5) *The Fourth Canticle of the Servant of Yahweh*	52:13–53:12
6) The New Jerusalem	54
7) Messianic salvation	55

2. *Analysis.* Isaiah 40:1-11 is an introduction and Isaiah 55:10-13 is the conclusion; between these passages, the book falls into two main parts: Isaiah 40-48—centered around Israel exiled in Babylon (and including the cycle of Cyrus [Is. 44:24–48:12]); Isaiah 49-55— centered around the restoration of Sion. Within this general plan the book is made up of a large number of literary units: oracles (Is. 40:1 f.; 43:18; 48:1-11); exhortations (Is. 51:1-8); visions (Is.

40:3-5, 6-8); etc. The Canticles of the Servant of Yahweh are regarded by all scholars as distinctive; there is no agreement concerning their authorship or concerning whether they should be separated from their context.[43]

The message of Second Isaiah was preached in Babylon. The collection may have been made by the Prophet but, on the analogy of the other prophetical books, it is more likely that the work was published by his disciples.

THE   Second Isaiah cast Israel in the role of witness and
MESSAGE[44]   mediator. It stands at the center of world history as a witness to monotheism (Is. 40:18,25; 43:11; 45:5 f., 18-22; 46:5-9). Israel is a mediator too because it will be the means of the conversion of all nations (Is. 40:5; 42:10; 45:14; 52:10; 54:5); the universalist outlook is strikingly expressed in Isaiah 45:22-24; 44:5. The Israel entrusted with this responsible role is a qualitative Israel: the "Remnant" (Is. 41:14; 46:3), the "poor of Yahweh" (Is. 49:13), the servants of the Lord (Is. 44:1; 54:17).

The Assyrians and Babylonians had been the scourges of God in the punishment of his people; now appears one who is a deliverer. Isaiah 41:2 f., 25 present in veiled terms the conqueror, who is expressly named in Isaiah 44:28—45:13—Cyrus, Yahweh's "messiah" (Is. 45:1), his shepherd (Is. 44:28), his loved one (Is. 48:14). This is the man, raised by God, who will set the exiles free (Is. 45:13) and rebuild Jerusalem and its Temple (Is. 44:28; 45:13). The anti-Babylonian oracles of Isaiah 13-14, looking to the capture of Babylon by Cyrus, belong to this same epoch.

The triumphal advance of the liberator opened up a perspective of return. Israel, led by Yahweh (Is. 52:11 f.), will journey in solemn pilgrimage along a *Via Sacra*, a processional way, across the Syrian desert (Is. 40:3 f.). At that passage the desert will be transformed (Is. 40:3-5; 41:17-19; 43:19 f.) and Yahweh will reign in Sion (Is. 52:7). The return is a new Exodus, another decisive intervention of Israel's God. This is not all poetic imagery, for the restoration is a sign of salvation; it is a redemption, a new Creation.

---

[43]See pp. 234-36.
[44]See Gelin, *op. cit.*, pp. 552-55.

The presentation of the return as an Exodus reflects that consciousness of the Mosaic past so prominent in Deuteronomy. In two respects Second Isaiah can be said to mark the culmination of the Mosaic movement: ". . . in his clear-cut and sweeping definition of the concept of ethical monotheism and in his doctrine of vicarious suffering."[45]

6. PROPHETS OF THE SIXTH CENTURY[46]

1) Isaiah 56-66

AUTHORSHIP   According to the generally-accepted view, Isaiah 56-66 is the work of a postexilic prophet, or prophets, of the Isaian school, and was produced in Palestine shortly after the return from the Exile (538 B.C.). Several reasons indicate that these chapters are distinct from Is. 40-55. The subject matter is no longer deliverance and restoration; in many passages the people are regarded as already settled in Palestine and social injustice has had time to make itself felt (Is. 58:3-6; 59:3 f.; 56:10-12). In Is. 40-55 the Prophet's attention is fixed on the immediate future—the fall of Babylon and the deliverance, but this is no longer the perspective of Isaiah 56-66. It is also generally held that these chapters are the work of different writers.

> The last part of the book, chapters 56-66, is composite. Chapter 67 may be prior to the Exile, but the tone of chapters 56, 58, and 66 presupposes the return from the Exile; chapters 63-65 are markedly apocalyptic. The thought and style of chapters 60-62 are very close to those of 40-55 and, in general, all the third section appears to be a natural sequel to the second; it is the work of the disciples of the consoler-prophet of the Exile.[47]

It seems better not to employ the designation Trito-Isaiah. For one thing, chapters 56-66 are composite. Then the relationship of these chapters to Second Isaiah is not at all that of the latter to Isaiah; the title Trito-Isaiah would seem to suggest some such equivalence.

---

[45]Albright, *op. cit.*, p. 327; see below p. 234.

[46]While Ezekiel and Second Isaiah obviously lived in the sixth century B.C., they stand apart from the other, later, sixth-century prophets because their mission was to the exiles in Babylon.

[47]Roland de Vaux, BJ, p. 978.

DIVISION

CALL TO PROSELYTES (IS. 56:1-8)
REPROACHES AND PROMISES (IS. 56:9–57:21)
FASTING: FALSE AND TRUE (IS. 58)
PSALM (IS. 59:1-14)
FRAGMENT OF AN APOCALYPSE (IS. 59:15-21)
HYMN ON THE FUTURE GLORY OF JERUSALEM (IS. 60)
MISSION OF THE PROPHET (IS. 61)
SECOND HYMN ON THE FUTURE GLORY OF JERUSALEM (IS. 62)
DIVINE VENGEANCE—APOCALYPTIC (IS. 63:1-6)
PSALM (IS. 63:7–64:11)
AGAINST IDOLATRY; ESCHATOLOGICAL SERMON (IS. 65)
ORACLE; APOCALYPTIC POEM; ESCHATOLOGICAL DISCOURSE (IS. 66)

THE MESSAGE[48]   Isaiah 56-66 is influenced both by Second Isaiah and by Ezekiel. From the latter these chapters take the notion of a city sanctified by its Temple, and their insistence on fasting and the sabbath observance. To Second Isaiah they owe their interest in the Gentiles and their preoccupation with interior religion, and the idea of the glory of Sion. From both of these prophets comes the idea of a new and purified Jerusalem. Here, for the last time in the prophetical books, idolatry is denounced.

2) Haggai

THE PROPHET   The first return from Babylon in 538 B.C., under Sheshbazzar, was on a very small scale and the returned exiles soon became disillusioned. A later group under Jerubbabel and the priest Joshua gave new hope, and the task of rebuilding the Temple

[48]See Gelin, *op. cit.*, p. 569.

was warmly urged and supported by the Prophets Haggai and Zechariah who seem to have come with Zerubbabel.[49] We have no information concerning Haggai beyond that of his book and the brief references of Ez. 5:1; 6:14. His recorded prophecies are dated from August to December, 520 B.C. (Hag. 1:1,15; 2:1,10,20); the construction of the Second Temple was begun in August of that year, and the immediate concern of these prophecies is the rebuilding of the Temple.

THE 1. *Analysis.* The brief discourses which make up the book
BOOK obviously represent no more than a selection of the Prophet's preaching. As it stands, there are five precisely-dated exhortations:

a) 1:2-11—call to rebuild the Temple—August, 520 B.C. A note (Hag. 1:12-15a) indicates that the call was effective.

b) 1:15b—2:9—the future glory of the Temple—October, 520 B.C.

c) 2:10-14—a priestly decision—December.

d) 2:15-19—past distress and future blessing; should probably be attached to Haggai 1:15a (2:18b is a misleading gloss).

e) 2:20-23—promise to Zerubbabel—probably August.

2. *Division.*

TITLE (HAG. 1:1)
THE REBUILDING OF THE TEMPLE (HAG. 1:2-15A; 2:15-19)
THE GLORY OF THE TEMPLE (HAG. 1:15B—2:9)
A PRIESTLY DECISION (HAG. 2:10-14)
PROMISE TO ZERUBBABEL (HAG. 2:20-23)

THE The Prophet addresses Zerubbabel the governor and
MESSAGE Joshua the high priest and all the "people of the land" (Hag. 2:4)—the "Remnant" (Hag. 1:12-14; 2:2) in the prophetical sense. He exhorts them to rebuild the Temple, for this will mark the beginning of the messianic era. Thus messianic hope takes flesh again around the sanctuary and around Zerubbabel, the Davidic prince, the Lord's "signet ring" (Hag. 2:23).

---

[49]See pp. 72 f.

3) *Zechariah 1-8*

Scholars are agreed that chapters 9-14 of Zechariah are not authentic; indeed they are much later than the time of the Prophet.[50]

THE   Zechariah was a contemporary of Haggai, and apart from
PROPHET   the references in Ez. 5:1 and 6:14 we have no independent information concerning him. Obviously he was greatly influenced by Ezekiel and was probably a priest-prophet. His oracles are dated from November, 520 B.C., to December, 518 B.C. Zechariah, like Haggai, was preoccupied with the rebuilding of the Temple, and also, and more emphatically, with national restoration and the demands of ritual purity and morality.

THE   The main part of the book (Zech. 1:7–6:15) is the series
BOOK   of eight visions interspersed with prophetic sayings by way of comment, and followed by the symbolic crowning of Zerubbabel (Joshua)—Zechariah 6:9-14. Chapters 7-8 are collections of prophetic sayings.

1. *Analysis.*[51]

a) 1:1-6—calls to conversion (November, 520 B.C.).

b) 1:7–6:8—eight visions and their interpretation:

    1) 1:7-17—the Four Horsemen: judgment on the nations.

    2) 2:1-4—the Four Horns: judgment on the destroyers of Judah.

    3) 2:5-9—the Measuring Line: protection of Jerusalem.
      2:10-17—two appeals to the exiles.

    4) 3:1-7, 9a—the Apparel of Joshua: revival of the priesthood. (Zech. 3:8-10—the Branch.)

    5) 4:1-6a + 10b-14—the Lamp and the Olive Trees: Zerubbabel and Joshua, the two "anointed." (Zech. 4:6b-10a—three sayings on Zerubbabel.)

    6) 5:1-4—the Flying Scroll: punishment of sinners in Palestine.

    7) 5:5-11—The Woman in the Ephah: sin is transported to Babylon.

    8) 6:1-8,15—The Four Chariots: destruction, especially of Babylon.

c) 6:9-14—the symbolic crowning of Zerubbabel. (The text has

---

[50]See p. 217.
[51]See Gelin, *op. cit.*, pp. 564-66.

"Joshua," but vv. 12 f. make it clear that this is a later substitution for Zerubbabel.)

d) 7:1-3 + 8:18 f.—a question about fasting.

e) 7:4-14—the lesson of the past.

f) 8—oracles of messianic salvation.

2. *Division.*

INTRODUCTION: CALL TO CONVERSION (ZECH. 1:1-6)
THE VISIONS (ZECH. 1:7—6:8)
THE CROWNING OF ZERUBBABEL (ZECH. 6:9-14)
A QUESTION ABOUT FASTING (ZECH. 7:1-3 + 8:18 f.)
THE LESSON OF THE PAST (ZECH. 7:4-14)
ORACLES OF MESSIANIC SALVATION (ZECH. 8)

THE MESSAGE   Zechariah is concerned with the rebuilding of the Temple,
but he regards this event as the prelude to the messianic
age that is his principal concern. He sees Zerubbabel as the Davidic
Messiah (Zech. 3:8-10; 6:12 f.) but, true to the spirit of Ezekiel,
he also exalts the high priest Joshua (Zech. 3:1-7). Indeed, the two
"anointed ones" (Zech. 4:14) will rule together in perfect accord
(Zech. 6:13). This is not to say that these are two Messiahs—as two
Messiahs were later expected at Qumran—but Zechariah resurrected
the idea of royal messianism and linked it with the priestly perspective
of Ezekiel.

7. PROPHETS OF THE FIFTH CENTURY
1) Isaiah 34-35; 24-27

ISAIAH 34-35: THE   It is not strictly accurate to describe these
"LITTLE APOCALYPSE"   chapters (and the same is true of Is. 24-27)
as apocalypse—though some features of the apocalyptic form are
present (for example, universal judgment, the triumph of God's
people).

1. *Authorship and Date.* The two chapters, which form a unit,
are inspired by Is. 40-66 (cf. Is. 34:6-8 and 63:1-6; 35:10 and 51:11).

Chapter 35 is written throughout in the style of Second Isaiah: Yahweh's final salvation is depicted as a New Exodus. The chapters are patently a product of the Isaian school, and though it is not possible to fix a precise date, the early fifth century B.C. seems probable.

2. *Ideas.* "The two chapters, probably by the same hand, constitute a sort of diptych: an Inferno followed by a Paradiso."[52] Chapter 34 describes the Day of Yahweh, the final judgment of God—for Edom is a type of the enemies of God's people. Chapter 35 is the redemption of Israel. Prominent are the transformation of nature and the Holy Way along which God leads his people home. A vast return of the Diaspora is presented as a solemn pilgrimage to Sion.

ISAIAH 24-27: THE "GREAT APOCALYPSE" 1. *Authorship and Date.* These chapters are a collection of originally independent eschatological prophecies and hymns brought together to form a unified composition. In view of this arrangement it is not easy to posit unity of authorship for the various pericopes. In thought, style, and language the section is postexilic, but it is impossible to fix a precise date. A fourth-century B.C. date is not impossible, but it seems better to settle for the fifth century B.C. At any rate, Isaiah 24-27 is the last product of that prolific Isaian school which had so long kept alive the spirit of the great eighth-century B.C. Prophet.

2. *Ideas.* Hymns and oracles differ in outlook. The theme of the hymns is the ultimate triumph of the City of God. The apocalyptic oracles have in view all humanity and the whole universe: God will chastise the host of heaven and the kings of earth (Is. 24:21), and he will destroy Leviathan, symbol of the forces of evil (Is. 27:1). Then all nations will be invited to the great messianic feast (Is. 25:6-8) and the dispersed of Israel will be gathered together (Is. 27:12 f.).

2) Malachi

AUTHORSHIP AND DATE The Book of Malachi is really an anonymous writing, because the name "Malachi" comes from Malachi 3:1 where the word is a common noun meaning "my messenger." The title of the writing (Mal. 1:1) corresponds to Zech. 9:1 and 12:1;

----

[52]J. Bright, PCB, n. 445 a.

it is likely that originally these were three anonymous collections. Malachi is later than 516 B.C., the date of the renewal of cult in the Second Temple (cf. Mal. 1:13) and seems to be earlier than the interdiction of mixed marriages by Nehemiah in 445 B.C. (cf. Mal. 2:10-12). A date shortly before 445 B.C. is likely.

THE   This book is composed of six sections, each opening with
BOOK   a statement which calls forth a deprecating question; then the theme of the statement is briefly developed.

1. 1:2-5—The Love of Yahweh for Israel.
2. 1:6—2:9—Yahweh dishonored by his priests.
3. 2:10-16—Against mixed marriages and divorce.
4. 2:17—3:5—The Day of Yahweh.
5. 3:6-12—Neglect of the Temple tithes.
6. 3:13-21—Reward of the just.

Appendices: 3:22—an exhortation to observe the law of Moses; 3:23 f.—the return of Elijah to herald the day of the Lord (an exegesis of Mal. 3:1).

THE   The Book of Malachi is strongly influenced by Deuter-
MESSAGE   onomy (cf. Mal. 1:2; Dt. 7:8; Mal. 1:9; Dt. 10:17; Mal. 2:1,4,33; Dt. 18:1; Mal. 2:6; Dt. 33:10; Mal. 4:4; Dt. 4:10), and is preoccupied with the cultic faults of priests (Mal. 1:6—2:9) and people (Mal. 3:6-12). The Day of Yahweh is presented in a cultic setting and the world to come will see the perfect cult (Mal. 3:4). By his criticism of mixed marriages (Mal. 2:10-16) the Prophet hits at current abuses and anticipates the reforms of Nehemiah and Ezra. The contribution of the writing to messianic doctrine is restrained but significant: the "pure offering" of Malachi 1:11 is the perfect Sacrifice of the messianic era, and the forerunner of the Messiah is indicated in Malachi 3:1,23 f.—the Gospels tell us that this new Elijah was John the Baptist (Lk. 1:17; Mt. 11:10-14; 17:12).

3) Obadiah

THE   We know nothing of Obadiah apart from the fact that
WRITING   he was a man of intense nationalistic outlook. This prophecy, the shortest Old Testament writing, falls into two parts, and the differences between these parts raises the question of the unity of the work.

1. Obadiah 1-14 + 15b: A curse on Edom because of her treatment of Judah after 587 B.C.

2. Obadiah 15a + 16-21: The destruction of Edom is the presage of the judgment of Yahweh on all the enemies of God's people, and of the final restoration of Jerusalem.

Part One reflects the threats against Edom of Lam. 4:21 f.; Ezek. 25:12 f.; 35:1 f.; Mal. 1:2 f., and verses 2-10 are found, with some small variants, in Jer. 49:7-22. The downfall of Edom is in view, and we know that the country was conquered by the Nabataeans in 312 B.C.; however, Mal. 1:3 seems to indicate an invasion of Edom at an earlier date (c. 450 B.C.). The prophecy of Obadiah probably took place a short while before this date. Part Two, which is close to Joel in outlook, would support this relatively early date. Comparison with the plan of Jl. would also speak in favor of unity of authorship.

THE An appreciation of the situation in Judah from 587 B.C.
MESSAGE to the mission of Nehemiah will help to explain the bitter resentment of Obadiah.[53] Here is no trace of the universalism of Second Isaiah; instead we find that narrow nationalistic outlook so brilliantly satirized in Jonah—indeed the author of Jonah might have modeled his prophet on somebody like Obadiah![54] This writing must be seen as a footnote to the great volume of prophetic literature —while we should not overlook the fact that it exalts the power and justice of Yahweh.

8. PROPHETS OF THE FOURTH CENTURY

1) Joel

AUTHORSHIP Joel is mentioned nowhere else; all we learn of him
AND DATE from his book is that he was a postexilic prophet of Judah. As in the case of Obadiah, the two parts of the book (chapters 1-2 and 3-4) might indicate dual authorship, but the date of the work is not affected by this possibility since both parts are closely associated. The book is, in all probability, a product of the early fourth century B.C. This date is indicated by borrowings from late

---

[53]See pp. 71-73.
[54]See p. 357.

writings (for example, Jl. 2:11 and Mal. 32; Jl. 3:4 and Mal. 3:23), and by the particularist and cultic mentality of the writing. The apocalyptic style of chapters 3-4 is also in favor of a late date. On the other hand, the changed perspective of these chapters does not demand another author: the description of a calamitous plague of locusts could easily lead to a picture of the final plague of God, his judgment on sinners. While we cannot be certain, it is reasonable to regard the book as the work of one author.

THE BOOK 1. *Analysis*. The book is divided into two parts. Part One (Jl. 1:2–2:27) describes a particularly severe plague of locusts, which occasions a liturgy of mourning and supplication and the proclamation of a national day of fasting and prayer (Jl. 1:2–2:17). Yahweh's gracious response to the nation's penitence is given in Joel 2:18-27. Part Two (Jl. 3-4) is a description of the New Age and of the Day of Yahweh. Joel announces that, in the messianic age, the gift of the Spirit will be poured out on all the people of God (Jl. 3:1 f.): Pentecost was the beginning of fulfillment (Acts 2:16-21). The gift of the Spirit will be followed by cosmic portents of the Day of Yahweh—not directed at an Israel safe in Sion (Jl. 3:3-5). The judgment of Yahweh on the nations will take place in the valley of Jehoshaphat (Jl. 3:1-17). The book closes with an oracle on the restoration of Jerusalem (Jl. 4:18-21).

2. *Division.*

TITLE (JL. 1:1)	
PART ONE: THE PLAGUE OF LOCUSTS	
1) Liturgy of mourning and supplication	1:2–2:17
2) The Response of Yahweh	2:18-27
PART TWO: THE DAY OF YAHWEH	
1) The Prelude	
a) Outpouring of the Spirit	3:1 f.
b) Cosmic Portents	3:3-5
2) The Judgment of the Nations	4:1-17
3) The Restoration of Israel	4:18-21

THE Joel marks a transition from prophecy to apocalyptic,
MESSAGE but it is essentially a prophetical book. The Prophet not
only, in typical prophetic fashion, interpreted a terrible plague as
a punishment of sin, but also saw it as a symbol of the Day of
Yahweh. "Joel is the prophet of Pentecost (cf. Jl. 3:1 f.). He is
also the prophet of penance, and his invitation to fasting and to
prayer, borrowed from the ceremonies of the Temple or modeled
on them, fit quite naturally in the Christian liturgy of Lent."[55]

2) *Zechariah 9-14*

AUTHORSHIP The second part of the Book of Zechariah consists
AND DATE of two groups of material (chapters 9-11 and 12-14)
introduced by the term *massa* ("burden"—oracle of woe). In the
traditional order of prophetical books Mal.—which has the same
heading (Mal. 1:1)—comes last, immediately after Zechariah; it appears that Zechariah 9-11; 12-14, and Mal. were three collections
of prophetic material which were placed at the end of the prophetical
writings, by way of appendix. Later, the third of these collections
was regarded as a separate book (Mal.) and the other two were
attached to Zechariah 1-8; this obtained the significant number of
twelve Minor Prophets.

The center of interest of Zechariah 9-14 is certainly not that of
the first part of the book: there is no mention of Zerubbabel or of
Joshua, nor any word on the rebuilding of the Temple. Assyria and
Egypt appear only as symbols of all oppressors and, on the other
hand, the Greeks are mentioned in Zechariah 9:13. The conquest
alluded to in the oracle of Zechariah 9:1-8 would seem to be the
action taken by Alexander the Great to safeguard his flank after
the battle of Issus (333 B.C.). It would seem that Zechariah 9-14—
an anonymous compilation—was given final shape at the close of
the fourth century.

THE Zechariah 9-14 is an anthology of prophetic material which
BOOK combines, in no given order, passages of widely varied
character.

1) 9:1-8—an oracle of Judgment and Promise.
2) 9:9 f.—a royal and humble Messiah.

---

[55]Roland de Vaux, BJ, p. 988.

3) 9:11-17—the restoration of Israel.
4) 10:1 f.—fidelity to Yahweh.
5) 10:3—11:3—Deliverance and return of the Exiles.
6) 11:4-17—the faithful Shepherd and the worthless.
7) 12:1—13:6—Deliverance and purification of Jerusalem
8) 13:7-9—messianic oracle.
9) 14—the eschatological combat and the New Age.

THE   Zechariah 9-14 is important for its messianic doctrine.
MESSAGE The oracle of Zechariah 12:1—13:6 speaks of the re-
establishment of the house of David. This restoration is linked
with the death of a mysterious personage: ". . . he whom they have
pierced" (Zech. 12:10); doubtless we should look to the Suffering
Servant of Is. 53. The Messiah is presented as a royal figure, but
he is not clothed in worldly pomp (Zech. 9:9 f.). In the messianic
age all things in the land of Israel will be sacred to the Lord
(cf. Ezek. 40-48). Quotations from, or allusions to, Zechariah 9-14
are frequent in the New Testament (for example, Mt. 21:4 f.; 27:9;
26:31; Jn. 19:37).

9. MESSIANISM

Any study of the Old Testament would be sadly incomplete without
a treatment of messianism. While the theme is not exclusively prophetical, it was so notably developed in prophetical writings that we can
fittingly deal with it at the close of this chapter. However, we
shall have scope for little more than a sketch of that distinctive
feature of Israel's religious heritage.

1) Development of the Messianic Idea[56]

Israel had broken with the prevalent cyclic conception of time: in
the biblical view history was meaningful; it had a beginning and,
tending towards a God-given goal, it will have an end. It is a view
that was particularly applicable to the history of Israel, dominated

---

[56]See A. Gelin, "Messianisme," *Dictionnaire de la Bible* (Supplement) (Paris:
Letouzey et Ané, 1961), V, cols. 1165-1212 (further references to this work will
be abbreviated DBS); J. L. McKenzie, *Myths and Realities* (Milwaukee: Bruce,
1963), pp. 203-50; P. F. Ellis, *The Men and the Message of the Old Testament*
(Collegeville, Minn.: The Liturgical Press, 1963), pp. 312-42; J. Obersteiner,
"Messianismus," *Bibeltheologisches Wörterbuch*, J. B. Bauer, editor (Graz-Wien-
Köln: Verlag Styria, 1962²), I, pp. 848-69 (further references to this work will
be abbreviated BW); Bonnard-Grelot, "Messie," VTB, pp. 608-14.

by the idea of covenant and presented in the Bible as *Heilsgeschichte*. This original conception of history is the basis of messianic hope. Messianism, in the widest sense of the word, is Israel's expectation of a glorious destiny. More precisely, it is the expectation of an ultimate era of salvation that involves the manifest inauguration of the kingdom of God. This reign of God will first be established over Israel and then, through Israel, it will extend to all mankind.

It is to be noted that messianism consists essentially in confident expectation of the establishment of God's reign; there was, at first, no mention of a Messiah. And even when, with the passage of time, the figure of a Messiah did emerge, he was always regarded as God's instrument in the bringing in of his kingdom—an event that called for a special intervention of God in person. The Messiah was never the object of Israel's messianic expectation; he was the one through whom that expectation was to be fulfilled. Instinctively we think first of the Messiah who has come and we measure all the past by him. But Israel looked to a future that was vague even to the prophets who were granted a glimpse into it, and to eyes not fully enlightened the Messiah of the future did not stand out as a sharply-defined figure.

Messianic expectation ran through the whole of Israel's history; the essential feature of that hope was there from the beginning, but the centuries and events brought clarification and refinement. While hope remained constant there was a steady growth in the appreciation of the election of Israel and her true destiny. The figure of the Messiah emerged and began to assume an increasingly important role in the nation's hope. We may trace three clearly-defined stages in the development of messianic doctrine.

1. GENERAL MESSIANIC EXPECTATION   Messianic expectation has its roots in the historical beginning of the people of Israel. The call of Abraham—the first moment in the election of a people—already explicitly looked to the destiny of that people and to its universal mission (Gn. 12:1-3). The succeeding patriarchs heard the same promise and were links in a line that reached into the future. Israel's hope was confirmed by the events of the Exodus and by the Sinai Covenant; the seed of Abraham had at last grown into a people, and the Promised Land was in sight. Possession of that land marked another step forward, but the slow and painful conquest

brought home to the people that fulfillment would come only through sweat and tears—history would prove how high the cost was to be. In the meantime Israel, precariously established in Canaan, did not lose hope when, under Philistine pressure, the plan of God seemed in jeopardy. As it turned out, the weathering of that crisis carried the messianic expectation on to a new level.

2. DYNASTIC   The first attempt at kingship under Saul had failed,
MESSIANISM   but his successor, David, brought Israel to the most powerful political position she was to achieve. It was a moment of high hope and great expectation. God was patently with the king, and the oracle of Nathan (2 Sm. 7:8-16) linked the destiny of Israel to the family of David, and the people continued to look hopefully and steadfastly to the dynasty. This faith explains the different outlook on royal succession in the Northern Kingdom and in Judah. In the North there was nothing sacrosanct about any royal family; indeed usurpation was the order of the day. In Judah, however, though assassination was not unknown, the principle of Davidic succession was rigidly adhered to: none but a son of David might sit on the throne of David.

The Davidic king had become the representative of the people, and the father-son relationship that had been established between Yahweh and Israel on the basis of the Sinai Covenant (Ex. 4:22) now existed, in a more personal way, between Yahweh and the king (2 Sm. 7:14). But the divine promise had been made to the dynasty as a whole and the individual king owed his privileged position to his membership of that dynasty. Individuals might fail, but the divine plan would not be thwarted for it was guaranteed by an unconditional divine promise. Yet, as it turned out, not only did individual kings prove wanting, but the dynasty itself ended in disaster.

It is not clear when the prophets had grown disillusioned with the historical Davidic kings: it seems that Jeremiah was the first (though he may have been anticipated by Isaiah) who looked to the future and realized that the special intervention of God which would usher in the messianic age called for one, specially raised up, standing in contrast to the historical kings. At any rate, the disaster of 587 B.C. and the end of the monarchy in Judah forced men to take stock of the situation. From the conflict of two discordant facts—

an irrevocable divine promise of perpetuity to the house of David, and the actual failure of the monarchy—a new refinement of messianic thought emerged, and the third stage of development was reached.

3. PERSONAL   When the ultimate failure of the monarchy was evi-
MESSIANISM   dent, and when it did in fact come to an end, Israel's prophets and theologians looked again at the facts. The one constant element was the unconditional promise to the Davidic dynasty—that could not fail. But since the monarchy was no more, the only possibility now was that God would, in the future, raise up a son of David and through him bring about his reign over Israel and over mankind. Messianic expectation was no longer centered on a dynasty but on a person. True, this man was still a son of David, but he was not just one of a line: he was an extraordinary personage of the future. This Messiah was seen as a king, but he was presented too as a prophet—the Suffering Servant of Yahweh—and as the glorious Son of Man of the end time. And while Jesus was greeted by the people as son of David, he preferred to present himself as one who, through suffering, would enter into his glory.

MESSIANISM WITHOUT   We should not forget that messianic expecta-
A MESSIAH   tion looked to the coming of the kingdom of God. This was the essence of it, and the role of the Messiah in the establishment of the reign of Yahweh could, in practice, slip into the background. Particularly in postexilic times, when the monarchy had ceased, men could look again straight at Yahweh, the King of Israel, and celebrate his kingship; they came to live in vivid expectation of the future kingdom of God. The idea of the kingship of Yahweh is presented with great clarity in Second Isaiah (for example, Is. 41; 21; 43:15; 52:7) and is exclusively the theme of the Kingship of Yahweh psalms.[57] Here we cannot do more than draw attention to this important aspect of messianism, but it is well to recall that what Jesus proclaimed was not primarily the coming of the Messiah, but the presence of the kingdom of God.

2) Messiah

It may seem a singular procedure to have treated, however briefly, of the development of the messianic idea before turning to an ex-

---

[57]See pp. 307-9.

planation of the term "messiah." However, it was important to make the point that messianic expectation predated the expectation of a messiah and could exist without direct reference to a messiah. We believe that our procedure is justified when it is seen against the background of historical messianism.

The noun "messiah" (*mashiah*) comes from a verb meaning "to anoint," "to rub with oil," a verb that in the Old Testament is reserved almost exclusively for sacred anointing, consecration by oil. The derived substantive (messiah) designates the subject of anointing and is applied only to persons:[58]

1. In ancient Israel there is frequent mention of royal anointing (Jgs. 9:8; 1 Sm. 9:16; 10:1; 15:1; 16:3, 15 f.; 2 Sm. 2:4; 12:7; 1 Kgs. 1:34 f.; 5:1; 2 Kgs. 9:3-12; 11:12; 23:30). It is certain that, before the Exile, the king was the Anointed One *par excellence*. From the moment that the oracle of Nathan (2 Sm. 7:12-16) had fixed the hope of Israel on the Dynasty of David, each king of that line became in his turn the actual "messiah" through whom God would accomplish his purpose in regard to his people. And the accession of each new king brought renewed hope and the expectation of peace and justice and prosperity—the blessings of the messianic age— and eventual rule over the whole world.

2. No text prior to the Exile speaks of the anointing of priests. After the Exile the priesthood grew in prestige: now that there was no king the high priest became the leader of the community. The high priest had become the Anointed Priest (Lv. 4:3,5, 16—these are postexilic additions—[2 Mc. 1:10]); therefore an actual "messiah" as the king had formerly been.[59]

3. The prophets were not anointed. The apparent exception in 1 Kgs. 19:16, which has reference to the anointing of Elisha, is explained by 2 Kgs. 2:9 where Elisha is to receive "a double share of the spirit" of Elijah. This metaphorical anointing by the Spirit is expressly indicated in Is. 61:1.

After the Exile the high priest had inherited the royal anointing and had become the focus of messianic expectation. True enough the oracles of Zech. 4:8 and 6:12 give Zerubbabel the title of "Branch"

---

[58]See C. Larcher, *L'Actualité Chrétienne de l'Ancien Testament* (Paris: Cerf, 1962), pp. 93-96.

[59]See Bonnard-Grelot, *art. cit.*, 610 f.

(cf. Is. 4:2; Jer. 23:5; 33:15), but it is already significant that Joshua and Zerubbabel are associated in Zech. 4:11-14 and are called the two "sons of oil," that is, anointed ones. A clear development in the same line is the substitution of Joshua for Zerubbabel in the symbolic coronation (Zech. 6:9-14). In Dn. 9:25 f. the "anointed one" is the high priest Onias III. The failure of the later Hasmonaeans—who had assumed the office of high priest—brought about a return to the old Davidic hope. The Psalms of Solomon (apocryphal), especially Ps. 17, are a witness to this trend.[60]

Jewish eschatology gave an important place to the expectation of a messiah: a royal messiah everywhere; a priestly messiah in certain milieux. The agent of salvation appeared also as the Servant of Yahweh and the Son of Man, while the promises always looked to the inauguration of the kingdom of God. It was not easy to coordinate all the data; the coming of Jesus alone shed full light on the prophecies and reconciled apparent contradictions.[61]

3) Interpretation of the Messianic Texts

It is impractical to deal with all the relevant messianic texts in short compass; besides, we have space for no more than a hurried explanation of selected texts. Our purpose is to show how constant was the messianic hope of Israel and what a wealth of texts can be massed in its support and serve to illustrate it. We feel that over-emphasis on certain classic texts (for example, Gn. 3:15; Is. 7:14) has given the impression that the doctrine of messianism stands or falls by the interpretation of these and a few other passages. It is well to realize once and for all that messianism is an essential feature of the Bible and pervades the whole of it.

GENERAL MESSIANIC EXPECTATION

1. *The promises to the patriarchs.*

a) Gn. 12:1-3. The beginning of Israel's messianic expectation can be set sometime in the nineteenth or eighteenth century B.C. when Abraham was singled out by God and became the recipient of divine promises. "The promises look to the future, to a people

---

[60]See Larcher, *op. cit.*, p. 94.
[61]See Bonnard-Grelot, *art. cit.*, 611.

(Israel, the posterity of Abraham), a land (Canaan), and a blessing (good things for the people and through them for all mankind)."[62]

b) The promises repeated to the other patriarchs, the successors of Abraham, seen in the general perspective of Genesis, witness to the choice of a privileged line for the fulfillment of God's plan. The narratives of the Covenant refer to them explicitly (Ex. 3:15; Dt. 6:10), and their terms will be repeated throughout the Bible in the messianic texts (cf. Gn. 12:3 and Ps. 72 [71]:17; Zech. 8:13), until Paul will sketch a theology of the promise (Rom. 4). Both the special perspective of Genesis and the general perspective of the Bible urge us to see in these ancient texts the launching of the patriarchs on the way of salvation: right from the start the tension of that movement is eschatological.[63] It looks, however vaguely, towards the age to come.

2. *The Covenant* (*Ex. 19-20*). With Moses and the emergence of the Israelite nation the divine plan took a more concrete form. The Covenant (*berîth*) was the climax of a mighty intervention of God; it implied a choice: Israel, the nucleus of the great nation promised as a descendance to Abraham, became Yahweh's first born (Ex. 4:22; Jer. 2:2). The Covenant confirmed Israel's messianic hope and turned her eyes resolutely to the future. Deuteronomy, the book which works out most fully the theology of the Covenant, shows Israel reaching for a goal that is labeled "heritage," "blessing," "rest."[64]

3. *Amphictyonic oracles.*[65]

a) The Blessing of Judah (Gn. 49:8-12). It is commonly agreed that the promises of Jacob (Gn. 49:1-28) are a collection of blessings (and curses) from the period of Judges and find their *Sitz im Leben* in assemblies at the amphictyonic shrine. In the blessing of Judah (Gn. 49:8-12) verses 8 and 10 are generally regarded as later still and as referring to David: Judah's primacy over the other tribes and her conquest of the surrounding nations were the achievement of David. These verses probably saw the light at the central shrine as it was becoming clear that David was the man of the hour.

---

[62]Ellis, *op. cit.*, p. 321.

[63]See Gelin, *art. cit.*, 1171.

[64]*Ibid.*, p. 1172.

[65]See *ibid.*, pp. 1172-1174. The amphictyony is the confederation of twelve tribes united in covenant with Yahweh and having a central shrine. See p. 22.

b) Two oracles of Balaam (Nm. 24:3-9; 15-19). Only two of the four oracles of Balaam interest us in the present context. They appear to date from just before the monarchy. In Nm. 24:7 Agag may stand for the Amalekites defeated by David (1 Sm. 30). More significant is the passage Nm. 24:17 f., which refers to David's victories over Moab and Edom (2 Sm. 8:2,13 f.). The star was frequently the symbol of a divinized king; here it refers to the Davidic monarchy, and already we meet with the language of royal messianism. The verses have the same *Sitz im Leben* as Gn. 49:8,10 and more or less the same date. David's accession to the kingship of Judah and Israel justified the oracle.

DYNASTIC   1. *The Oracle of Nathan* (*2 Sm. 7:8-16*). Nathan's
MESSIANISM   oracle to David is the foundation of dynastic messianism and the first link in an unbroken chain that reaches to the New Testament (cf. Mt. 1:1). The setting is dramatic: David, having made Jerusalem his capital and the religious center of his kingdom, contemplated building a Temple to house the Ark of Yahweh; instead, it was Yahweh who took the initiative and made provision for David. In typical Hebrew fashion the oracle is built around a play on the word "house."

> The prophecy is based on a contrast: it is not David who will build a *house* (a temple) for Yahweh (v. 5), it is Yahweh who will establish a *house* (a dynasty) for David (v. 11). The promise bears essentially on the permanence of the Davidic line on the throne of Israel (vv. 12-16). It is thus that David understood it (vv. 19,25, 27,29; cf. 23:5; Ps. 89 [88]:30-38; 132 [131]:11 f.). The oracle, therefore, goes beyond the first successor of David, Solomon, to whom it has been applied by the addition of verse 13, by 1 Chr. 17:11-14; 22:10; 28:6, and by 1 Kgs. 5:19; 8:16-19. But in the *chiar-oscuro* of the prophecy one may divine a privileged descendant of David in whom God will be well pleased.[66]

2. *Gn. 3:15*. The Yahwist, who wrote under Solomon, was aware of the oracle of Nathan; it may be that the oracle has influenced his veiled reference to future salvation in Gn. 3:15—the seed of the woman represents the Davidic Dynasty through which salvation will come, and the woman is the queen-mother of the Davidic king.[67]

---

[66]Roland de Vaux, BJ, pp. 317 f.
[67]See Ellis, *op. cit.*, pp. 323-29.

The argument is attractive but inconclusive, and we prefer to follow a more traditional interpretation.

The serpent of Gn. 3:15 stands for a being hostile to God and an enemy of man. The Book of Wisdom (2:24), the New Testament (Jn. 8:44; Ap. 12:9; 20:2; Rom. 5:12-21), and Christian tradition have seen in this serpent the Adversary, the Devil. A state of hostility is set up between the serpent and the woman; the latter term is universal as in Gn. 2:23. The term "seed," regularly used for "posterity," is also frequently employed in a messianic context: the seed of Abraham (Gn. 12:7) and the seed of David (2 Sm. 7:12-16) are the recipients of a divine promise, and at the time of the Exile "seed" corresponded more or less to "Remnant" (Is. 43:5; 44:3). In the Hebrew text the "seed," in a collective sense (it), will crush the head of the serpent; the Septuagint (LXX), with its *autos* (he), gives an individualistic interpretation; the *ipsa* (she) of the Vulgate (Vg.) has no textual justification in the Masoretic Text or LXX.

> The Hebrew text, proclaiming a hostility between the race of the serpent and the race of the woman, sets up an opposition between man and the devil together with his "seed," and insinuates the final victory of mankind: it is a first ray of salvation, the *protoevangelium*. The LXX, by introducing a personal pronoun in the last phrase, attributes the victory not to the line of the woman in general but to a son of the woman; this explains the messianic interpretation of many of the Fathers. The Mother of the Messiah is associated with him and the mariological interpretation witnessed to by the Latin *ipsa conteret* has become traditional in the Church.[68]

3. *The Messianic Psalms.* The king of Israel was the prince of a theocratic nation, a mediator between his people and God; he is a religious figure, an instrument of the divine plan. In view of his central role in the life of the nation it is natural and fitting that he should play a prominent part in the liturgical worship of Israel; it is not surprising that he became the subject of a group of psalms— the royal psalms.[69] There is no agreement among commentators regarding the date of many (or all) of these psalms. The view adopted here is that most of them are pre-exilic and visualize a

---

[68]Roland de Vaux, BJ, p. 11.
[69]See pp. 303-6.

historical king seated on the throne of David. By the same token they are messianic, since the Davidic king is a member of the messianic dynasty and a messianic figure in virtue of his office: each king was, in his turn, the bearer of the divine promises and the pledge of hope. The extravagant language of some of these psalms can be put down in part to traditional court protocol and in part to the fact that an individual was invested with the hopes and promises of the dynasty, irrespective of his personal qualities. Such a conception of the monarchy "does not of itself imply an eschatological development, nor a view of the future which transcends the historical king and looks to the end time, and to an individual who is not identified with the historical king. . . . What appears in the royal psalms is the present ruler who is endowed with the ideal traits of the future."[70]

a) Ps. 110 (109). This psalm is a prophetic oracle which extols the Davidic prince as king, priest, and conqueror; it seems most at home in the age of David. He is the king of Israel who had a very special right to the priestly dignity: by his taking of Jerusalem and his installation of Yahweh in Sion. In order to substitute the cult of Yahweh for that of *Elyon* (cf. Gn. 14:18), and at the same time to conciliate the Jebusites, David attached to himself the tradition of Melchizedek. The oracle is concerned with a *de facto* situation: David has taken the Ark to Sion; Yahweh, in return, assures the king that he will reign over all the territory of which his God is now master (v. 2). He receives the right and honor of serving Yahweh as a priest—a perpetual right conferred by oath—so that the psalm links up with the promise of perpetuity to the Davidic Dynasty.[71]

After the Exile, when the historical monarchy had come to an end, this and the other royal psalms were applied to the David of the future—a procedure that is not, strictly speaking, a "reinterpretation," though it has been so described. From the beginning these psalms looked to the ideal Davidic king. At first it was felt that the ideal would be achieved in the person of a historical king; later it was realized that the son of David who would bring about the fulfillment

---

[70]McKenzie, *op. cit.*, pp. 329 f.
[71]See Larcher, *op. cit.*, p. 68.

of the promises, beyond the limits of the historical monarchy of Judah, was to be raised up specially for that purpose. But this is a change in perspective, an adjustment, not a reinterpretation: the essential feature of messianic expectation was present all the time. It is only when we move into the New Testament that a decisive step forward is taken and the fuller sense of these texts is perceived.[72] For now, in the revealing light of fulfillment, we can look back and trace beneath the surface of the texts the divine nature and attributes of the Son of David.

b) Ps. 2. Some would date this psalm considerably later than the preceding one, but it too would seem to fit well into the time of David or Solomon. It is a prophetic oracle in which the Davidic prince promulgates to his enemies the prerogatives of power and dominion promised to him by Yahweh. We might regard it as a warning to the vassals of David (or Solomon) that any attempt at revolt is doomed to failure: their rebellion would be against Yahweh himself. Verse 7 is a poetic paraphrase of the Nathan oracle (2 Sm. 7:14): the Davidic prince became the adopted son of God on the day of his accession. The "ends of the earth" (v. 8) describe the ideal limits of the Promised Land (cf. Dt. 33:17; Ps. 18 [17]:44-48).

c) Ps. 45 (44). There can be little doubt that we have here a royal psalm written for the marriage of a king to a foreign princess. Again it is impossible to fix the historical context with certainty, but the marriage of Solomon to the daughter of Pharaoh springs to mind. This event was a highlight in the reign of Solomon, a measure of the international standing of the king, and the hopes raised by the still-fresh promises to David seemed well on the way to fulfillment. The poet has seized the occasion and has made the most of it: he looks with confident expectancy to the continued glory of the dynasty (vv. 16 f.). Late Jewish tradition witnesses to an allegorical interpretation of the psalm: the king is the Messiah and the bride is the Israelite community. Many Fathers, taking their stand on the prophetic marriage imagery (for example, Hos. 1-3; Is. 54:4-10), understood the psalm as directly referring to Christ and the Church. This exegesis, closely linked to a similar view of the Canticle, is questionable.[73]

---

[72]See Harrington, *op. cit.*, pp. 56-59.
[73]See pp. 273-77.

d) Ps. 132 (131). Here we have a prayer for the king which urges the solicitude of David for Yahweh's worship (vv. 1-10) and God's promise of a perpetual dynasty (vv. 11 f.) as grounds for the divine favor. Reference to a reigning king (vv. 10,17), to David's descendants (v. 12), and to the Temple (v. 14) suggest a pre-exilic date.

e) Ps. 72 (71). This psalm is an elaborate prayer at the accession of a new Davidic king. It illustrates the Israelite conception of the king as a channel of divine blessing for his people. His relationship to Yahweh and his maintenance of justice among his people are of fundamental importance. The king is not regarded as a secular monarch, but as a representation of the dynasty to which God had promised perpetuity and through which he will extend his rule over the world. The accession of a new king heightens expectation and raises the hope that this may be the agent who will usher in the new age of peace and justice.

f) Ps. 89 (88). This does seem to be an exilic or postexilic psalm, for its center of interest is the apparent failure, after 587 B.C., of the promise made to David. Its theme is confidence in the faithfulness of God. The messianic oracle (vv. 20-38) is nothing more than a poetic elaboration of Nathan's oracle (2 Sm. 7:9-13). It is a striking witness to faith in the irrevocability of the promise made to David. The historical line of David may have ended but it is impossible that God's word should fail.

4. *Is. 7-11.* In chapters 7-11 of Isaiah three passages especially are concerned with the permanence of the dynastic line. It is true that some would regard them as referring to the Messiah of the future. While the third passage does seem to point in that direction it appears better to set the others within the field of dynastic messianism and to interpret them in that context.

a) Is. 7:10-17: The Sign of Immanuel. The historical setting of this oracle is the Syro-Ephraimite war.[74] Isaiah presented himself before Ahaz and offered him a sign as proof of the truth of his declaration that the king had nothing to fear from the invaders. The king refused the sign and Isaiah bluntly retorted that he should have it whether he liked or not. The promised sign—the birth of a child whose name will be Immanuel ("God with us")—must cor-

---

[74]See pp. 59 f.

roborate the prediction that Judah will stand before the Syro-Ephraimites and must be recognizable to Ahaz. The Hebrew text implies that the 'almāh (the "young woman") soon will be, or (more probably) already is, with child; the birth of the child is imminent.

It should be kept in mind that Isaiah is addressing the Davidic king, who fears for the permanence of the dynasty (Is. 7:1-3,6). The situation was aggravated by the fact that Ahaz had sacrificed his first-born son (2 Kgs. 16:3; cf. 23:10)—possibly the only son of the young king—and the birth of a crown prince would be of the utmost significance. The 'almāh is a wife of the king, and the child to be born, a royal heir, will be a sign that the line of David will continue. Before that child reaches the age of minimal discernment ("knows how to refuse the evil and choose the good") Israel and Syria will be· destroyed (by the Assyrians). While the significance of "curds and honey"—the food of Immanuel—is quite uncertain, verse 17 explicitly refers to the devastation of Judah. The sign is also a sign of calamity, a punishment of the king's incredulity: the dynasty will remain but the kingdom will suffer the disaster of subservience to Assyria.

The Hebrew word 'almāh means a young woman of marriageable age, and not necessarily a virgin (cf. Gn. 24:43; Ex. 2:8; Prv. 30:19; Ct. 6:8); the technical term for virgin is bethulah. In Is. 7:14 the LXX has parthenos (its normal translation of bethulah), but this is not as significant as it might seem, since in Gn. 24:43 the LXX also renders 'almāh by parthenos. Isaiah speaks of ha 'almāh (with the article); this could well designate the queen-mother (who occupied a privileged place in Judah [cf. 1 Kgs. 2:19; 15:13; etc.]), the mother of the crown prince whose birth is announced. Despite a chronological difficulty (but then the chronology of the Israelite kings is uncertain) the Immanuel envisaged by Isaiah may be Hezekiah. At any rate, Immanuel is a Davidic prince and hence the oracle is messianic in the manner of the royal psalms. It is mariological too, for the 'almāh, the queen-mother, as mother of an individual "messiah," is a type of the Mother of the future Messiah.

b) Is. 9:1-6. This oracle forms a sequel to Is. 7:14 and celebrates the birth of Immanuel, the Davidic prince. Significantly the birth is linked with the devastation of Northern Israel—Ephraim is deserted (Is. 7:16). The composite throne name of verse 5 is colored by Nathan's oracle and reflects court language. The name is prophetic.

The child has, to an eminent degree, the virtues of the heroes of his race: the wisdom of Solomon; the valor of David; the religious qualities of Moses and the patriarchs. He is the very ideal of a Davidic king; Christian tradition and liturgy, in applying these titles to Christ, acknowledge that he is the true Immanuel.[75]

c) Is. 11:1-9: The advent of the just king. This oracle appears to date from 701 B.C. (cf. Is. 37:35), when the house of David was on the verge of being overthrown by Sennacherib. Isaiah reaffirms the permanence of the dynasty, but it seems not unlikely that, disillusioned with Hezekiah, he looks to a future Messiah. The oracle in question—some thirty years later than the Immanuel prophecy—perhaps may indicate the step from dynastic messianism to personal messianism, but we cannot be sure. In either event, the essential message of the oracle remains the same.

The messianic poem points to several characteristic traits of the Messiah: he is of Davidic origin (v. 1); he will be filled with the prophetic spirit (v. 2); he will bring a reign of justice (vv. 3 f.); and he will re-establish the peace of paradise, fruit of the knowledge of Yahweh (vv. 6-9). The Spirit of Yahweh will bring to him the eminent virtues of his great ancestors: the wisdom and understanding of Solomon; the prudence and might of David; the knowledge and fear of Yahweh, of the patriarchs, and of the prophets.[76]

5. *Mi. 5:1-5: Distress and glory of the Dynasty of David.* The circumstances of the oracle are those of Is. 11:1-9—the siege of Jerusalem by Sennacherib in 701 B.C. (or 688 B.C.). Sion is threatened and the dynasty is in jeopardy, but salvation will come from little Ephrathah (Bethlehem), the birthplace of David. Another "ruler in Israel" will come from the ancient Davidic line; the dynasty will not end with Hezekiah, despite the threat of Assyria. "She who is in travail" (v. 2)—the mother of the ruler—is possibly an allusion to the '*almāh* of Is. 7:14. At any rate, she is the Mother of the ideal king to come, the Mother of the Messiah—within the perspective of the line of David.

PERSONAL   The step from dynastic messianism to personal mes-
MESSIANISM[77]   sianism may have been taken by Isaiah (cf. Is.

---

[75]See BJ, p. 998.
[76]See *ibid.*, p. 1000.
[77]See Gelin, *art. cit.*, 1184-1188.

11:1-9); it was certainly taken by Jeremiah. His prediction of a
"righteous Branch" to be raised up for David is the turning point
in Israel's messianic expectation. No longer is her hope fixed on
the historical kings and on the dynasty as such; she looks to a
Davidic king of the future who, unlike the kings of the past, "shall
reign as king and deal wisely" and shall "execute justice and righteousness in the land."

1. *Jer. 23:5 f.* As a conclusion to his oracles against the kings
of Judah (Jer. 21:11–23:8) Jeremiah gives three messianic oracles
(Jer. 23:1-4, 5 f., 7 f.). The second of these looks to a personal
Messiah. Its date in the reign of Zedekiah is assured by the play
on the name of that king. The term "Branch" (v. 5), derived from
Is. 11:1, designates the Messiah (cf. Zech. 3:8; 6:12). The new
reign will be marked, to an eminent degree, by wisdom, justice,
and righteousness, and in the days of the new king the reunited
land will again know peace (v. 6). The name of the Messiah is
"Yahweh is our righteousness" in deliberate contrast to the name
of the last king of Judah, Zedekiah ("my righteousness is Yahweh").
This oracle would find its proper setting in the "Book of Consolation"
(chapters 30-31), especially in the perspective of the New Covenant
(Jer. 31:31-34).

2. *Ezekiel.* The allegory of the eagle (Ezek. 17) is aimed at
Zedekiah who had violated his oath of allegiance to Nebuchadnezzar:
his punishment will be defeat and deportation (Ezek. 17:16,20 f.).
Zedekiah, the "willow twig" (v. 5), had replaced the topmost branch
of the cedar (Jehoiachin), carried into captivity in 597 B.C. The
conclusion of the allegory (vv. 22-24) is messianic. Yahweh will
plant in Sion a twig from the top (*semereth*) of the cedar (v. 22).
The same term designates Jehoiachin in verse 3: Ezekiel hopes that
God will raise up a Messiah from the descendants of Jehoiachin.
The contrast between the future Messiah and Zedekiah—the last king
to sit on the throne of Judah—is repeated in Ezek. 21:23. Nebuchadnezzar marches on Jerusalem—the "day" of Zedekiah has come; it
is also the "day" of Jerusalem "until he comes whose right it (the
sovereignty) is"—a phrase that repeats the oracle of Jacob (Gn.
49:10) and applies it, not to David, but to a future son of his.

In Ezek. 34 Yahweh's care of his people is contrasted with the
neglect of the kings. Yahweh himself will bring about the restoration
of his people; then the Messiah will appear (Ezek. 34:23 f.). The

name "David" indicates his origin and his standing: this *David redivivus* will be the only ruler of all Israel, as his ancestor was, though his title is not *melek* (king) but *nāsî* (prince) (cf. Ezek. 45-46). Later, in Ezek. 37:24 f., *melek* is used side-by-side with *nāsî* because the dual monarchy is evoked: the new David, like the old, will be king of Judah and Israel.

3. *Zerubbabel (Hag. 2:23; Zech. 6:9-14).* Zerubbabel, descendant of David through Jehoiachin, and governor of Judah, began the reconstruction of the Temple in 520 B.C.; this, according to Ezekiel, was a messianic work, the prelude to the messianic age, and was so regarded by the contemporary Prophets Haggai and Zechariah. In Hag. 2:23, Zerubbabel, successor of David, links up with the old royal messianism and crystallizes around his person the expectation of fulfillment. God reverses his curse on Jehoiachin (Jer. 22:24) and reiterates his promise to the Davidic Dynasty.

Zech. 6:9-14 describes the symbolic crowning of Zerubbabel. In view of verses 12 f. the name of Zerubbabel must have originally stood in verse 11 and was later replaced by the name of the high priest Joshua, at a time when the priestly office had come to the fore. "Branch" (v. 12)—borrowed from Jer. 23:5—had become an accepted designation of the Messiah. It appears that, with Haggai and Zechariah, we have something like a rebirth of dynastic messianism, for these prophets seemed to have pinned their hopes on Zerubbabel. At least these texts are evidence that the Exile had caused no rift in messianic expectation.

4. *Zech. 9:9 f.* The oracle of Zech. 9:9 f. is influenced by Second Isaiah and Ps. 72 (71) and by Ezekiel's dream of the union of Ephraim and Judah; it dates probably from the fourth century B.C. The messianic king will renounce the pomp of the historical kings and will enter Jerusalem on the mount of the olden princes (Jgs. 5:10; 10-4; etc.). He will be the object of the "justice," the powerful protection, of Yahweh (cf. Is. 45:21-25), the bearer of salvation— that is, victorious by divine help—and humble (*'ānî*); in all this there is an echo of the Suffering Servant. Our Lord fulfilled this prophecy on Palm Sunday.

5. *1 Chr. 17:7-14.* The Chronicler reproduces the text of 2 Sm. 7. The discreet changes he makes in it are revealing. In his time (c. 300 B.C.) the historical monarchy was a distant memory; thus he applies the promise to a future son of David. In verse 13 he omits

the threat, "When he commits iniquity I will chasten him with the rod of men, with the stripes of the sons of men" (2 Sm. 7:14b), which could not apply to the Messiah. In verse 14 he changes "your house," "your kingdom," "your throne" of 2 Sm. 7:16 to: "I will confirm him in my house and in my kingdom forever, and his throne will be established forever." It would be difficult to present more clearly the change in perspective from dynastic messianism to personal messianism and, at the same time, to stress more surely the same fundamental idea that underlies and links both stages.

4) The Suffering Servant of Yahweh

Frequently throughout Second Isaiah[78] Israel is named the "Servant of Yahweh." Yet there are four passages (Is. 42:1-7; 49:1-6; 50:4-9; 52:13–53:12) where the title has a distinctive meaning and can no longer be said to designate Israel in the same manner as elsewhere. We have no intention of going into the vexed question of the relationship of these poems among themselves and to their context, nor do we intend to give a survey of the immense field of interpretation. All we shall do, when we have pointed out some characteristics of the Servant figure, is to outline two main lines of interpretation.

The Servant of the canticles stands in contrast to the Israel-Servant found elsewhere in Second Isaiah. Israel is deaf and blind (Is. 42:19 f.); the Servant hears (Is. 50:4 f.) and enlightens (Is. 49:6). Israel is sinful (Is. 42:18-25; 43:22-28); the Servant is just (Is. 53:9-11). Israel has need of consolation (Is. 41:9 f.); the Servant has a courageous faith (Is. 42:4). The Servant must restore Israel (Is. 49:5 f.).

The Servant is a mysterious figure who has been chosen by Yahweh and filled by his Spirit (Is. 42:1) and who plays a role at once national and universalist. On the one hand, though he seems inseparable from the Israel whose name he bears, from the Remnant "in whom God will be glorified" (Is. 49:3), he must lead back Jacob (Is. 42:6) and reassemble (Is. 49:5 f.) and teach (Is. 50:4-9) Israel. On the other hand he must be the light of nations. Patient (Is. 50:6) and humble (Is. 53:7) he will, by his sufferings and death, accomplish the plan of Yahweh: the justification of sinners of all nations (Is. 53:8,11 f.).

---

[78]See pp. 204-8.

While the identification of the Suffering Servant is, and doubtless will remain, a widely-discussed problem, almost all scholars would agree that he is a messianic figure. No one who acknowledges the unity of the two Testaments and accepts the messianic role of Jesus can doubt this for a moment. Here we shall be content to give two main lines of explanation.[79]

1. *The Servant is an incarnation of the prophetical movement in an eschatological setting.* Second Isaiah had been carried away by the glowing prospect of liberation and restoration and by his vision of a New Exodus. The return from the Exile took place without fanfare and with no wonders, and the number of those who went back was very small—and the nations were not converted. Yet these traits—the Return of Israel and universal redemption—were essential to the divine plan, and Second Isaiah took them up again and presented them in an entirely new perspective.

This time the plan of God—the regrouping of Israel and the conversion of the Gentiles—will succeed (Is. 53:10). The artisan of this success will no longer be Cyrus (Is. 44:28), but one taken from Israel, a man of the future who will incarnate the true Israel (Is. 49:3). He is presented with characteristics of Moses and Jeremiah, and his death is described as a sacrifice of expiation. The religious experience of Jeremiah and Ezekiel had pointed to a mediation other than royal mediation: the Servant is such a mediator, a Messiah-Prophet and not a Messiah-King. Thus the perception of Second Isaiah had sharpened, and these last oracles of his—his testament—were treasured by his disciples and inserted into the framework of his collected oracles.

2. *The Servant is the Israel of the future fulfilling its vocation, ultimately in the person of an eminent representative.* In this type of explanation, the starting point is the reflection of Second Isaiah on the vocation of Israel—a mission that is universalist in scope. His reflection passes through different stages; its development may be traced in the Canticles. Israel is charged with the true religion for the whole world (first Canticle). A purified Remnant alone will be capable of this role, and this Remnant must first of all convert Israel (second Canticle). The mission is difficult and painful for Israel or, at least, it is difficult for the leader who symbolizes

---

[79]See Gelin, *art. cit.*, 1194 f.; IB, pp. 559 f.

Israel (third Canticle). These tribulations will not be incidental to the mission, but the very means of its accomplishment—in the person of one who will surpass, in dignity and in efficacy, any historical figure (fourth Canticle). In him Israel is concentrated, but is not lost to sight—the situation foreshadows the mystery of Christ and the Church.

Perhaps it is true to say that both lines of interpretation do meet in the end. It is hard to deny that the Servant figure has both corporate and personal characteristics; he is, at one and the same time, the Messiah and the messianic people. It is a difficult concept, but no more difficult than Paul's doctrine of the Body of Christ —and no less real. And while we may argue about precise interpretations, we have no doubt that Jesus made his own, and accomplished, the mission of the Servant. He, meek and humble of heart (Mt. 11:29), was in the midst of his disciples "as one who serves" (Lk. 22:27), though he was their Lord and Master (Jn. 12:12-15). He not only gave them the ultimate proof of his love (Jn. 13:1; 15:13), but laid down his life for the redemption of a multitude of sinners (Mk. 10:43; Mt. 20:26). Treated like a common criminal (Lk. 22:37) and condemned to death, he was raised up on a Cross, that he might draw all men to himself. He died, but only to rise again as it was written of him (Lk. 18:31-33); for it was by passing through the suffering and death of the Servant that he entered into the glory of the Son of Man (Lk. 24:26).

5) The Son of Man (Dn. 7:13-14)

The second part of the Book of Daniel (chapters 6-12) consists of visions which portray the movement of historical events towards the consummation, when God will overthrow the empires of men and establish his own kingdom on earth. Four successive empires are depicted: Babylonian, Median, Persian, and Greek; but the interest of the author always concentrates on one king (Antiochus IV Epiphanes), the persecutor of the Maccabaean revolt. In him evil has reached its term; his downfall will herald the messianic age.[80]

In the first of these visions (chapter 7) Daniel saw four beasts rising out of the sea (the abode of things evil); an angel explained that these beasts were four successive empires (Babylonian, Median,

---

[80]See pp. 370-76.

Persian, and Greek [Seleucid]) or the kings who represented the empires. The "little horn" rising from the last of them is Antiochus IV; the phrase, "before which three of the first horns were plucked up," describes him as an usurper who had succeeded his assassinated brother Seleucus IV and supplanted the rightful heirs, his nephews Demetrius and Antiochus. The "mouth speaking great things" refers to his blasphemous arrogance (cf. Dn. 7:25; 11:36).

In a heavenly judgment scene the "Ancient of Days" (God) takes his seat; but other thrones are also set out, because God's saints judge with him. The "little horn" is condemned, while the other empires are no longer a danger since they have lost imperial power. Then, in contrast to the beasts, appears one "like a son of man" (that is, a human figure); again, in contrast to the beasts' origin from the depths of the sea, he appears "on the clouds of heaven"— "on" (LXX, Syr.) is a better reading than "with" (MT) (cf. Ps. 104 [103]:3; Is. 19:1). This "son of man" is presented to the Ancient of Days and receives universal and everlasting dominion. The phrase "son of man" is Aramaic idiom (*bar enash*) for "man"; the figure is "like" a son of man, to mark the symbolic character of the representation. As presented in these verses (13 f.) the figure certainly appears as an individual.

The difficulty is that, in the interpretation (vv. 26 f.), the kingdom, formerly given to the Son of Man, is now given to the "Saints of the Most High," that is, to the messianic people, the purified Remnant of Israel. Their everlasting and universal kingdom will be inaugurated after "a time, two times and a half a time" of the little horn, that is, after three and one-half years, the approximate duration of the persecution of Antiochus (167-164 B.C.). It appears that the "saints of the Most High" and the "Son of Man" must stand for the same reality, at once collective and individual. A study of the context justifies this interpretation.

In Dn. 7:17 we read that "these four great beasts are four kings who shall arise out of the earth." In verse 23 the fourth beast is interpreted as "a fourth kingdom"; hence the beasts represent both the kingdoms and their kings. We find the very same situation in chapter two of Daniel. The composite statue (Dn. 2:32 f.) represents the four empires (cf. 2:39-44); and yet the head of gold is Nebuchadnezzar (Dn. 2:37 f.), who stands for the Babylonian Empire. Again, after the other parts of the statue are interpreted in terms of empires, verse 44 speaks of "the days of those *kings*." It is sufficiently clear that, in Daniel, king and empire are interchangeable: the one symbol may stand for either. The king who incorporates and represents his empire, however, does not lose his own identity, his individuality. The head of gold may describe Nebuchadnezzar, insofar as he may be identified with the Babylonian Empire, but Nebuchadnezzar does not thereby become a mere symbol.

If we apply this reasoning to the Son of Man we find that both the individual and the collective senses indicated in Dn. 7 may be preserved. The Son of Man is certainly the representative of "the people of the saints of the Most High," but he is also an individual, with an identity of his own. "Saints of the Most High" and "Son of Man" are the messianic people and the Messiah who represents and contains them. It is clear from Dn. 7:13 f. that this Son of Man is no ordinary mortal; the reference to the "clouds of heaven" is sufficient by itself to prove this. Throughout the Old Testament, "cloud" occurs about one hundred times—in thirty cases it is the natural phenomenon. In all other cases it accompanies a theophany or an intervention of Yahweh. However, it would be going too far to argue that everything or everybody associated with this cloud must belong to the divine sphere. A New Testament text can be of help here: in Ap. 10:1 a mighty angel, entrusted with a very special mission, comes down from heaven "wrapped in a cloud"; he is a heavenly being and he has come from the presence of God, but he is not divine. Similarly the Son of Man comes, riding on the heavenly vehicle (cf. Ps. 104 [103]:3; Is. 19:1), into the presence of God. He is a heavenly figure, the leader of God's people, but the author of Daniel would not have regarded him as divine.

We may look at the Son of Man passage from another angle and see here two registers of the same tableau:[81] in the higher part, in heaven, the beasts are condemned by the Ancient of Days and dominion is given to the Son of Man (Dn. 7:13 f.); in the lower register we have the earthly repercussions of these heavenly events (Dn. 7:19-27)—the pagan empires are destroyed and the faithful part of the Chosen People (the Saints of the Most High) received

---

[81]See A. Feuillet, "Le Fils de l'homme de Daniel et la tradition biblique," *RB*, 60 (1953), 195.

the kingdom. In other words, while divine judgment has been passed on the beast and while the people of God are assured of ultimate victory, history must run its allotted span. After all, this is our own situation: by his death and resurrection Christ has won the victory over death and sin ("I have overcome the world" [Jn. 16:33]; the prince of this world is already judged [Jn. 16:11; cf. 12:31]) and yet Christians have to struggle with sin and suffer death. But ultimate victory is certain for those who are faithful to Christ.

Among the Jews, "Son of Man" never became a current messianic title, but probably in certain restricted circles a Messiah was awaited who was "Son of Man."[82] What is certain is that Jesus gave himself this title by preference, and, in using it, linked together the two notions of the great Judge of the world and of the Servant of Yahweh—notions that would seem mutually exclusive—and showed that both were united in his person.[83] For he, Son of David, is also the Suffering Servant, the Redeemer of mankind; and he is indeed the glorious Son of Man, Leader of the people of God, Head of his Body, the Church.

---

[82]See Pierre Benoit, *Exégèse et Théologie* (Paris: Cerf, 1961), pp. 133-40.
[83]See W. Harrington, *Explaining the Gospels* (New York: Paulist Press, 1963), pp. 88-91.

| FIVE | *The Wisdom Literature* |

As we read through the Old Testament we must notice that the theme of the Exodus keeps on recurring, often unexpectedly. Indeed, we cannot miss the resonance of that mighty intervention of God which marks the emergence of Israel as a nation; and we cannot fail to realize that this is unquestionably the central event in Israel's memory. But the Exodus is not only a great religious moment, it was essentially a historical experience. Henceforth Yahweh is the God of Israel, and Israel is the people of Yahweh. The literature of the Old Testament bears striking witness to Israel's keen awareness of its unique history. It is all the more surprising, then, to find that in one important and extensive group of writings within this literature the historical sense is almost entirely lacking—only the latest of the wisdom books regard the special destiny of the people of God. This is perhaps the main reason why the wisdom literature stands apart from the rest of the Old Testament writings, though the subject matter and the style also mark its distinctiveness. Nevertheless it is an authentic part of the peerless literary and religious legacy of Israel.

In this chapter we shall first examine briefly the wider setting as well as the peculiar national genius of the Israelite wisdom movement. Then we shall range rather hurriedly through the five wisdom books,[1] and close with a consideration of the developed concept of divine wisdom. It is hoped that the treatment will give a hint of the immense worth of these writings, and a further appreciation of the literary as well as of the religious achievement of the Chosen People.[2]

1. THE WISDOM OF THE EAST

In this matter of wisdom, as in most other respects, Israel was not unique (under certain aspects at least), but fitted into the common pattern of the ancient Middle East. The Bible has many allusions to the wise men of other peoples (cf. 1 Kgs. 5:10 f.; Jer. 49:7; Obad. 8). Archaeology has brought to light extensive remains of a widely-diffused wisdom literature. Nearly all of it is older, and most of it much older, than anything in the Bible. It is also evident that the movement was international, for wisdom writings circulated widely and had an influence far beyond the country of their origin. The sage, as such, was not circumscribed by age or culture; though he was, inevitably, a man of his own epoch and milieu, the problems with which he dealt were human problems, and these, fundamentally, are much the same wherever men dwell.

The Eastern sages are met with especially among the ruling classes or, more precisely, among the court officials: ministers and counsellors, scribes and annalists. They formed an educated and cultured class who readily became teachers: passing on to others the results of their experience, .inculcating the principles which should guide conduct, and pointing out the path to success in an administrative career. Thus they composed wisdom writings: sayings and instructions in Egypt; fables and allegories in Babylon; maxims and picturesque parables in Canaan and Phoenicia. Such writings were intended for those who would follow in the footsteps of the sages or, as we might put it, for the formation of aspiring civil servants. We must not imagine, however, that the wisdom movement did not look beyond such an utilitarian horizon. The sages, we have remarked, were very

---

[1]The canonical wisdom writings are: Proverbs, Job, Qoheleth (Ecclesiastes), Sirach (Ecclesiasticus), and Wisdom; the Canticle of Canticles was edited by wisdom writers. The influence of wisdom is also clearly evident in many psalms and in Baruch, Tobit, and Judith.

[2]See W. Harrington, "The Wisdom of Israel," *Irish Theological Quarterly*, 30 (1963), 311-25. This article forms the basis of the present chapter.

much concerned with human problems; ultimately this meant the problems of the individual. Looming largely in their field of interest was man's anguished search for the meaning of life; and it is not surprising that this quest should have inspired some of the most notable products of the movement, works like the Egyptian *Dispute over Suicide*, the Babylonian *Dialogue on Human Misery*, and the *Book of Job*.

The most important of the ancient Eastern wisdom writings still extant are the following:[3]

1. *Egypt.*
    a) Instructions:
        1) The Instructions of the Vizier Ptah-Hotep: c. 2450 B.C.; pp. 412-14.
        2) The Instructions for King Meri-Ka-Re: c. 2000 B.C.; pp. 414-18.
        3) The Instructions of King Amen-Em-Het: c. 1900 B.C.; pp. 418-19.
        4) The Instructions of Amen-Em-Opet: 10-6th cent. B.C.; pp. 421-24.
    b) Didactic:
        1) A Dispute Over Suicide: c. 2000 B.C.; pp. 405-7.
        2) The Protests of the Eloquent Peasant: c. 2000 B.C.; pp. 407-10.
    c) Observations:
        1) In Praise of Learned Scribes: c. 1300 B.C.; pp. 431-32.
        2) The Satire on the Trades: c. 2100 B.C.; pp. 432-34.
2. *Babylonia and Assyria.*
    a) Proverbs and Counsels:
        1) Proverbs: 1800-700 B.C.; pp. 425-26.
        2) Counsels of Wisdom: before 700 B.C.; pp. 426-27.
    b) Observations:
        1) "I Will Praise the Lord of Wisdom"; pp. 434-37.
        2) Dialogue About Human Misery: 7th cent. B.C.; pp. 438-40.
3. *Aramaic.*
    a) Proverbs and Precepts:
        1) The Words of Ahiqar: 6th cent. B.C.; pp. 427-30.

---

[3]See ANET, pp. 405-40; page references are to this work.

2. THE WISDOM OF ISRAEL

1) *The Origin of Wisdom in Israel*

Just as the Pentateuch was attributed to Moses and the Psalms to David, so also the bulk of Israel's wisdom literature was attributed to Solomon. He is traditionally the author of Proverbs, Qoheleth, Wisdom, and the Canticle of Canticles—and his influence is not reckoned to end with these. While, apart from Proverbs (or certain sections of it), the attribution of these writings to Solomon is consciously pseudepigraphical, a valid basis for the procedure lies in the king's undoubted interest in wisdom. His own reputation for wisdom is illustrated by the popular story of his decision in the case of the two women who claimed the same baby (1 Kgs. 3:16-18). Elsewhere we read that "Solomon's wisdom surpassed the wisdom of all the people of the East and all the wisdom of Egypt," and that people from all other lands came to hear him for "he was wiser than all other men" (1 Kgs. 4:32,31).

Indeed, the Book of Kings goes so far as to claim that Solomon uttered three thousand proverbs and a thousand and five songs (1 Kgs. 4:32); an assured reputation must underlie such a manifest exaggeration. At any rate, he undoubtedly must have played an important part in the development of a wisdom movement in Israel, though his own personal contribution to the wisdom literature or, at least, to the extant literature, is modest. We have no reason to doubt that some of the maxims in the oldest sections of Proverbs are his, but the rest of the sapiential books are much later than the age of the wise king. What is more important is that it was Solomon who first provided the atmosphere in which wisdom could flourish. His own outlook was cosmopolitan and he welcomed foreign currents of thought; his close relations with Egypt and Phoenicia were not, and could not have been, exclusively commercial. Besides, in order to handle his complicated administration, Solomon had to organize a civil service, and in this, the cultured milieu of the day, wisdom thrived. A striking example of Egyptian influence about this time is the literary dependence of Prv. 22:17—24:14 on the *Instructions of Amen-em-opet*. Of course, such dependence is to be expected: coming, as she did, late to the field, Israel had to learn from her neighbors. But soon her sages developed a typically Israelite literature; before long, not only in terms of a higher morality, but also on literary grounds, she had far outstripped her masters.

2) The Nature and Forms of Wisdom in Israel

The court origin of a large element of Hebrew wisdom is manifest. Much of Proverbs and a great deal of Qoheleth and Sirach have to do with conduct in society and, as a rule, the "thing to do" comes in for careful consideration. The scribe should be a man of taste and elegance, a man possessing prudent reserve, one who shuns ostentation—in short, the perfect gentleman. Since the very purpose of the instructions was to form a cultured civil service, their whole tenor could not have been any different. Significantly, respect for constituted authority is repeatedly inculcated.

We must not forget, however, that this is not the whole of it: many wisdom writers searched the deeps of man's heart and weighed his yearnings and his fears. Quite apart from this, nevertheless, the Israelite sages were well aware that true wisdom comes from God only. It is emphasized that the celebrated wisdom of Solomon was a gift which the king had obtained in answer to his prayer (1 Kgs. 3:6-14). It is God alone who gives to man "an understanding mind to discern between good and evil" (1 Kgs. 3:9). The biblical writers are conscious that the first sin was a revolt against this truth and that ever since, the same wily Serpent has held out to man the same false wisdom (Gn. 3:5 f., 1; Wis. 2:24). This is the wisdom of men who judge all things from the human viewpoint, like the scribes who make the law of Yahweh into a lie or like the royal counsellors who follow their own way (Jer. 8:8; Is. 29:15 ff.). But the true human wisdom has a divine source; God can and does communicate wisdom to whom he pleases. This is why the wisdom writers are pleased to contemplate the divine Wisdom: they realize that their own has flowed from it.

In the Old Testament the chief term for the basic literary unit in the wisdom literature is *māshāl*. The simplest type of *māshāl* is a proverb in couplet form, with the lines of the couplet almost always in parallelism. In the oldest sections of Proverbs this form prevails almost exclusively. But the *māshāl* is not exhausted by this simple literary unit—its range is bewildering. The noun meaning "comparison," "parable" is derived from a verb meaning "to become like," "to be comparable to." It is applied not only to proverbs but also to long poems or hymns (Jb. 27:1; 29:1; Pss. 49 [48]:5; 78 [77]:2), and it can designate a "taunt song" (Is. 14:4 ff.; Mi. 2:4 f.; Heb. 2:6 ff.) or a "byword" (Dt. 28:37; Pss. 44 [43]:15; 69 [68]:12 f.; Ezek. 14:8). In view of this complex usage we can best render *māshāl* as "saying," with all the vagueness of that term. It is noteworthy that in the Gospels, *parabolē* is a rendering of the Hebrew word (or of its Aramaic equivalent) and has the same elasticity of meaning.

3. THE BOOK OF PROVERBS

It is clear that the Book of Proverbs, as we know it, is the result of a long process of growth. The cultural and literary activity which produced the work began in the era of Solomon and the book seems to have received its final form in the fifth century B.C. (or perhaps as late as the fourth century B.C.). Thus Proverbs is representative of some five centuries in the life of Israel's wisdom movement; it is, in a true sense, an anthology of wisdom.

1) The Structure of Proverbs

On grounds of internal criticism (attribution to different authors; variety of matters treated; diversity of literary forms) eight sections may be discerned in the Book of Proverbs.

2) Analysis

The basis of the book is the double collection of the "maxims of Solomon" (sections 2 and 4). To these, five appendices were added: one to the first collection (section 3); four to the second collection (5-8). The prologue (first section) is the latest portion of the work. The two major collections (Prv. 10:1–22:16 and 25-29) are attributed to Solomon; with regard to the second it is added that the collection was made in the reign of Hezekiah (716-687 B.C.). There is no reason why Solomon may not have been the author of many of the proverbs in the two collections. However, later additions must be admitted: this is proved by the presence of Aramaisms and the evident influence of the prophets and Dt. Thus the Solomonic collections grew over the centuries; this is particularly true of the second collection.

PRV. 1:1-7	TITLE
1:8–9:18	*Prologue.* Complex literary form. Anonymous —Invitation to acquire Wisdom; the fruits of Wisdom and its praise.
10:1–22:16	Couplets in antithetical (10-15) or synonymous (16-22) parallelism. "Solomon" —Rules of conduct.
22:17–24:34	Quatrains in synonymous paral- "The Sages" lelism. —Duties to neighbor; temperance; laziness.
25-29	Couplets and quatrains. "Solomon" —Various maxims.
30:1-14	Quatrains in synonymous paral- "Agur" lelism. —Divine Wisdom; pettiness of men.
30:15-33	Numerical sayings in synonymous and progressive parallelism. Anonymous —Varied.
31:1-9	Quatrains in synonymous paral- "Lemuel" lelism. —Instruction for kings.
31:10-31	Alphabetic poem in progressive parallelism. Anonymous —Praise of the Virtuous Wife.

The "Sages" can neither be identified nor dated. The passage Proverbs 22:17–23:11 has, without any doubt, been inspired by the Egyptian maxims of Amen-em-opet; but the Egyptian work itself is of uncertain date (between the tenth and sixth centuries B.C.). Agur and Lemuel seem to be sages of the tribe of Massa (Gn. 25:14). Their date is uncertain, but the *meshālīm* attributed to Lemuel would appear to be postexilic.

The last editor of Proverbs added, by way of conclusion, the alphabetical poem in praise of the Virtuous Wife (Prv. 31:10-31), and provided the long Prologue (chapters 1-9). (The consequent late date is to be kept in mind when assessing the doctrine of the prologue.) At the time of ben Sirach (c. 200 B.C.) Proverbs already had its present form (cf. Sir. 47:17 [18]; Prv. 1:6).

3) *The Message*

Proverbs conceives a world divided into two distinct categories: the wise and the foolish. An intermediate category is that of the uncommitted, the simple or inexperienced who have yet to fall under the influence of one of the two groups and join one or other of them. The contrast "wise-foolish" (and not "wise-ignorant") is significant: even the highly-skilled, cultured man is a "fool" if he has not grasped the true meaning and purpose of life. The sages do not waste time addressing themselves to the foolish, but turn to the wise, and to the simple who may yet become wise.

In keeping with the accepted notion of wisdom, the maxims of Proverbs are concerned with right conduct. Self-discipline is urged: sobriety in food and drink; control of the tongue. Many of these counsels strike further into the moral order and regard honesty in business, faithfulness in marriage, impartiality in judgment, and the value of almsgiving. On a still deeper level it is recognized and stressed that religious faith is the necessary foundation of the moral life. Ultimately, the wise and the foolish are identified with the religious and the ungodly, for religion, or the "fear of the Lord," is the one basis of wisdom (Prv. 1:7). Thus it is that, if Proverbs does resemble the wider wisdom literature, especially that of Egypt, it has its own special characteristics. For Israel's wisdom, though much of it is mundane enough and trite enough, is never merely secular. Wisdom does not really come by observing human conduct or by reflecting on the teaching of the sages. It is a fact of course that attentive observation and balanced reflection do play their part in the education of the wise man, but he can attain true wisdom only when he is guided by a reverential fear of God (Prv. 15:33).

In this, wisdom joins hands with the prophetic and priestly traditions and Israel's sages would give unhesitating approval to the declaration of Jeremiah: "Let not the wise man glory in his wisdom . . . but let him who glories glory in this, that he understands and knows me, that I am the Lord who practice kindness, justice, and righteousness in the earth" (Jer. 9:23 f.). The Torah also plays its part; in particular, the deuteronomic doctrine of reward and punishment is now applied to the individual. Where the historians had shown the principle at work in Israel's history, the sages contended that the happiness and misery of every man depended on his fidelity to or disregard of Yahweh's law. But the principle had to be applied within the narrow limits of this life; after a while the logic of the facts troubled men and impelled them, in sweat and tears, to prepare the ground for a new seed, the revelation of an afterlife, with reward and punishment beyond the grave.

4. THE BOOK OF JOB

The Book of Job belongs to the stage when the idea of individual retribution in this life palpably ran up against insoluble practical difficulties. For an understanding not only of this book but of the great bulk of the wisdom literature, it is important to have in mind that the Hebrews had a very vague notion of the afterlife. At death a man did not quite disappear, he continued to exist in some dim, undefined way in Sheol; but in that dismal abode of the dead all, rich and poor, good and bad, were equal. Given this situation, it is inevitable that, throughout most of the Old Testament, retribution of good or evil was seen in an exclusively earthly perspective and was concerned with temporal sanctions only. It was not until the first half of the second century B.C.—a good two centuries later than the Book of Job—that the doctrine of retribution after death made its appearance (cf. Dn. 12:2). Progress, divinely guided, was made by troubled souls (cf. Ezek. 18:2; Jer. 31:29; Mal. 2:17) searching for a solution that was truly the measure of reality. The Book of Job marks the longest stride in that progress.

Job has become a figure of proverbial patience, but anyone who has troubled to read the Book of Job may well be at a loss to understand how he came to win such a reputation. After all, he curses the day of his birth in no uncertain terms, and more than once he practically serves God an ultimatum. But what if there are two Jobs! This, indeed, is more or less the case. The author of the book found his inspiration in a story about a legendary Edomite sheik who, when tried by the Satan—not yet the evil spirit of later

biblical tradition—proved unshakably faithful. On the basis of this
story, Israel's greatest poet built his masterpiece.

1) Division

It is clear that in Job we have a carefully-planned literary scheme.
The central poetic part is made up of three cycles of discussion
(Jb. 3-31), followed by Yahweh's answer from the whirlwind (chapters 38-41). The third cycle (chapters 22-27), however, has been
thrown out of order, either through scribal confusion at an early
stage or, and this is more likely, through the efforts of an editor
who wished to tone down Job's utterances. The poem on wisdom
(chapter 28) has been interpolated by later editors (perhaps by
the original author). The speeches of Elihu (chapters 32-37) are
also an intrusion into the literary scheme. Elihu is not mentioned as
one of Job's friends in either the prologue or epilogue. He has
nothing to say during the three rounds of discussion, and his advice
comes as an afterthought, following the statement that "the words
of Job are ended" (Jb. 31:40). It is generally held that the Elihu
speeches were added by a later Jewish writer who sought to uphold
the traditional doctrine more rigorously than the three friends. (Many
scholars tend to regard Jb. 39:13-18 and 40:15—51:26 as later additions
to the speeches of Yahweh.)

1. The prose Prologue (Jb. 1:1—2:13).
2. Three cycles of discussion.
   a) Job's lament (3).
   b) First cycle:
      Eliphaz (4-5).
      Job's answer (6-7).
      Bildad (8).
      Job's answer (9-10).
      Zophar (11).
      Job's answer (12-14).
   c) Second cycle:
      Eliphaz (15).
      Job's answer (16-17).
      Bildad (18).
      Job's answer (19).

Zophar (20).

Job's answer (21).

d) Third cycle:

Eliphaz (22).

Job's answer (23:1–24:17,25).

Bildad (25,1-6; 26:5-14).

Job's answer (26:1-4; 27:1-12).

Zophar (27,13-23; 24:18-24).

Poem on Wisdom (28).

Job's final defense (29-31).

Speeches of Elihu (32-37).

3. Yahweh's answer from the whirlwind.

a) The first speech (38-39).

Job's submission (40:1-5).

b) The second speech (40:6–41:34).

Job's repentance (42:1-6).

4. The prose Epilogue (42:7-17).

The Book of Job has an undeniable unity but, in its present form, it is equally certain that the literary equilibrium has been disturbed. The relationship between the prose sections and the poetic part is easy to divine. The author had come across a popular writing (*Volksbuch*) which suggested the idea of his work and which served to preface and round off his poem. Into the first part of the traditional story he introduced the three friends of Job (Jb. 2:11-13), and, in the epilogue, he also inserted a reference to the interlocutors (Jb. 42:7-9). Then he composed the poetic dialogue and the discourses of Yahweh. Later, the same author—or, more likely, another—going over the work, introduced the person of Elihu (chapters 32-37) and the praise of Wisdom (chapter 28). (The speeches of Yahweh may likewise have received additions [Jb. 39:13-18; 40:15–41:26]). The book thus has an organic unity. The original work (prose booklet, dialogue, theophany) has *grown* into its present form by the additions of new elements which have been skilfully fitted into the original plan.

2) *Authorship and Date*

The date and authorship of Job are difficult to determine because the writer gives us no hint of the historical circumstances of his time. The hero of the book is an Edomite sheik and the scene of the drama is in Edom, but there is no doubt that the writer was a Jew. "The time—patriarchal age—and the place—Edom—are part of the imaginative setting; the thoughts expressed are those of a Palestinian Jew of the postexilic period."[4]

While modern scholars are agreed that the book belongs to the postexilic period, they may differ as to the precise date within that period. A postexilic date is indicated by the language of the book and by the fact that, in general, the wisdom literature is a product of the postexilic age. The end of the fifth century B.C. would seem to be the most likely date.

The prose narrative is earlier than the poetic composition. Ezekiel mentions Job together with Noah and Daniel (a Phoenician sage) as legendary righteous men (Ezek. 14:14,20); the story of Job (that is, the prose narrative) must have circulated orally for many years before it was written down as we now have it.

3) *The Problem of Job*

In the dialogues Job wrestles with a tormenting problem: he is suffering, yet knows himself to be innocent. The inadequacy of the traditional position[5] has become apparent, but men can close their eyes to a disturbing new truth. Here the three friends are the champions of "orthodoxy"; they have accepted the classic teaching without question and quite refuse to admit that it will not fit the facts of the present case. Their position is very simple: suffering is punishment for sin; if a man suffers it is because he is a sinner—the facts must be made to fit the traditional viewpoint! Hence they proceed to comfort the sufferer by pointing out that he must be a sinner—and a great sinner at that judging by his sufferings—and they grow more and more insistent as he protests his innocence.

For Job does protest. He *knows* that he is innocent; at least he is certain that he has done nothing to deserve such trials. His world has broken in pieces about him, for he too had subscribed to the traditional doctrine. Now he sees that it does not meet his case—but he has no other solution. He struggles manfully with his problem,

---

[4]E. J. Kissane, *The Book of Job* (Dublin: Browne and Nolan, 1939), p. 1.

[5]The traditional doctrine of retribution, in its simplest form, is that the good are rewarded and the wicked are punished *in this life*.

but there is no outlet; his sufferings are now utterly meaningless and he is tempted to question the justice of God. This Job is not the improbable hero of the older tale, but a man of flesh and blood, striving to find a glimmer of meaning in the inscrutable ways of God, a man groping in thick darkness—but it is the darkness of faith. The grandeur of Job is that he can "defy the sufferings which overwhelm him to rob him of his faith in a hidden God."[6] In his agony he may have criticized God and his ways, but this is balanced by his cry for God and his yearning to meet him. And, fittingly, in the climax, God does speak to Job. Then, overwhelmed by the marvels of God's works, he makes his final profession of faith and his submission:

"I had heard of thee by the hearing of the ear,
    but now my eyes see thee;
Therefore I despise myself,
    and repent in dust and ashes" (Jb. 42:5 f.).

Yet, though he speaks of having seen God, the mystery remains, for Job has no knowledge of retribution beyond the grave. God's ways towards him are still inscrutable. But if, theoretically, the problem looms as largely as ever, he has solved it as a practical issue: he has come to accept God as he is and he no longer questions the divine purposes. Hence, though we may have shattered the stained-glass Job—the inhumanly patient man—we have raised instead the real Job, the man of faith. And from him we can learn that faith in a God whose ways we cannot know does lead to patience, and to peace.

5. QOHELETH

The Book of Qoheleth (Ecclesiastes) comes after Job and marks a further development in biblical thought. Once again the problem of personal retribution is taken up, and again the traditional doctrine is criticized. This is not to say that the position of Job is just restated in more emphatic terms—it is not at all a parallel treatment of the matter. Job was able to show that suffering does not presuppose sin in the sufferer and can be quite independent of guilt; but what about the reward of the virtuous man? It is precisely this other side of

---

[6]H. Wheeler Robinson, *The Cross in the Old Testament* (London: S.C.M. Press, 1960[2]), p. 32.

the picture, the view that the just man must be happy, that Qohelet questions. He observes that when a man, even a just man, has all he wants, he is not content. Now, at last, the inadequacy of the accepted position has been well and truly challenged, but the time is not yet ripe for the revelation that will enable theologians to come forward with the final, satisfactory solution. In the meantime, even so gifted a sage as ben Sirach will still take the "orthodox" view for granted. Conservatism can often be a very effective soporific.

Qoheleth is of a very different cast: he refuses to take a mechanical view of Providence. For him God is no accountant keeping a rigid balance sheet and doling out life and death, happiness and misery in strict proportion to man's virtue or guilt; God is in no way answerable to man. In contrast to the naïve optimism of some of the sages, he denies that the human mind can ever understand the ways of God: "I saw all the work of God, that man cannot find out the work that is done under the sun. However much man may toil in seeking he will not find it out; even though a wise man claims to know, he cannot find it out" (Qoh. 8:17). This is very much the final position of Job, but Qoheleth takes the further step of opposing the view that would regard earthly happiness as the goal of life. Life cannot be a mere seeking after pleasure. Happiness is never man's due; his duty is to accept whatever comes from the hands of God: "In the day of prosperity be joyful, and in the day of adversity consider; God has made the one as well as the other" (Qoh. 7:14). Qoheleth does not solve the problem, but he has cleared the way by contesting illusory solutions and by forcing men to face up to the veritable state of affairs. His is a providential role. "Qoheleth did not reach the threshold of the gospel. But it is true to say that before one could understand: 'Blessed are the poor' it was first of all necessary to have recognized that: 'Blessed are the rich' is not true."[7]

1) Authorship and Date

"Ecclesiastes," the name by which the book is usually known, derives by way of the Vulgate from the Greek *Ekklēsiastēs* of the Septuagint (LXX), and is a rendering of the Hebrew *Qōheleth*, a feminine

---

[7]R. Pautrel, *L'Ecclésiaste* (BJ), p. 13.

singular participial form, peculiar to Qoheleth which is connected with the noun *qāhāl*—"assembly." Apparently the Hebrew word refers to "one who speaks to an assembly," that is, a speaker or preacher. Thus Qoheleth (Ecclesiastes) is not a proper name but a description of a function.

The title (Qoh. 1:1) identifies Qoheleth with Solomon (cf. Qoh. 1:12,16; 2:4-10), but this is no more than a literary convention, since many of the wisdom books are similarly attributed to the king. Most scholars agree that Qoheleth comes, chronologically, between Job and Sir. The language of the book is late Hebrew, with many Aramaisms; on the other hand we may not descend too low—fragments of two manuscripts of Qoheleth have been found at Qumran and the oldest of these (4QQoh[a]) has been dated about 150 B.C. Sometime in the second half of the third century B.C. would seem the most likely date of composition.

Qoheleth is influenced by Greek culture, but not in any fundamental way. Its era is that of Ptolemaic dominance, and hence of close contact with Egypt—not the Egypt of the ancient sages but an Egypt very much Hellenized. The atmosphere of Hellenism was all around; hence the author could not escape it. But the most we may legitimately say is that Qoheleth, while remaining essentially Israelitic in outlook, does mark a step towards Greek thought.

The fourth of the five festal *megilloth* (rolls), Qoheleth was read (and still is read) in the synagogue on the third day of the Feast of Tabernacles. It adds a serious note to the festivities by reminding the congregation that the joys of life are transient.[8]

2) Composition and Plan

UNITY   The presence in Qoheleth of inconsistencies and sudden changes of subject has caused some scholars to posit the work of more than one author. However (apart from the epilogue [Qoh. 12:9-14], which certainly seems a later addition), it is not difficult to maintain the unity of the work. One does feel that, though the book presents a loosely connected account of Qoheleth's wisdom, it bears the impress of a strikingly individualistic mind. It is natural enough that the oscillation between an inherited religious faith

---

[8]See B. W. Anderson, *Understanding the Old Testament* (Englewood Cliffs, N.J.: Prentice-Hall, 1957), p. 478.

and a spirit of critical inquiry tends to conflict and to project a certain incoherency. Besides, the author is wrestling with a (to him) insoluble problem, and he approaches it from every angle, looking for a glimmer of light.[9]

DIVISION   No well-defined plan can be discerned in Qoheleth; any division suggested must be to some extent subjective. The plan presented here is at least a help towards an intelligent reading of the book.[10]

INTRODUCTION (QOH. 1:1-3)	
PART I	
PROLOGUE: ENNUI (QOH. 1:4-11)	
Four forms of disillusionment:	
1) The Life of Solomon	1:12–2:26
2) Mortality	3
3) The Individual in Society	4:1–5:8
4) Money	5:9–6:12
PART II	
PROLOGUE: LAUGHTER (QOH. 7:1-7)	
Four forms of disillusionment:	
1) Sanctions	7:8–8:15
2) Love	8:16–9:10
3) Chance	9:11–11:6
4) Age	11:7–12:8
EPILOGUE (QOH. 12:9-14)	

3) *The Outlook of Qoheleth*

Qoheleth is a complex character. He has been differently evaluated according as one or other aspect of his thought has been seized upon and emphasized to the exclusion of other elements. He has been branded a pessimist—an existentialist *avant la lettre*—or again

---

[9]See E. T. Ryder, PCB, n. 400 c-g.
[10]See Pautrel, *op. cit.*, p. 10.

an epicurean, even a hedonist. Most commonly, perhaps, he is regarded as a thoroughgoing sceptic. Each of these views can find
some support in his book, but all of them are far wide of the mark.
He is not a sceptic, but a religious man who has faith in a just
God and who professes, with conviction, his belief in the reality of
Providence (Qoh. 3:11,14 f.; 8:17; 11:5). Nor is he an epicurean.
Understandably he is no Christian ascetic, but he counts the pleasures
of this life as gifts of God (Qoh. 2:24; 3:13; 5:18; 9:7) and condemns the abuse of them (Qoh. 2:1 f.; 11:8,10). He is not really a
pessimist either (although he is a thinker who has written of pes-
simism), for he rejoices in creation (Qoh. 11:7) and has confidence
in the foreknowledge of God, he who is man's last end (Qoh. 6:10;
12:7). In other words, he is a realist. And, in the ultimate analysis,
he is something more. He has plunged more deeply yet into the
dark labyrinth uncovered by Job, and he too, despite his vain search-
ings for an outlet, clings desperately to his faith in God.

> The reflections of Qoheleth, centered on the emptiness of earthly
> joys, constitute one of the last stages in the search that was to
> discover the existence of sanctions in the afterlife. Now the ground
> is sufficiently prepared for the Holy Spirit to sow the seeds of the
> last doctrinal harvest of the Old Testament. The notion of collective
> retribution belonged to a distant past. The emerging idea of a person
> responsible for his own actions had led to the concept of individual
> retribution (Jer. 31:29 f.; Ezek. 18:33). But this was yet within the
> limits of earthly existence and as such was unsatisfactory, and was
> often contradicted by the facts (Job). The only outlet was in the
> yet unexplored regions of eternal sanctions; but a move in that direction
> presupposed that the sages, docile at once to the divine pedagogy
> and to intellectual reflection, had ceased to regard earthly beatitude
> as an unmixed joy and as a last end. This was largely brought
> about by the outspoken author of Ecclesiastes. While accepting earthly
> pleasures, he so powerfully emphasized the ultimate vanity of them
> that, inevitably, he orientated the minds of his disciples towards a
> life beyond the judgment of God (Qoh. 12:13 f.).[11]

6. SIRACH

The problems which were of such concern to the author of Job
and to Qoheleth did not trouble other sages; ben Sirach for one
(writing about 180 B.C.) does not consider them at all. He raises
no doubt regarding temporal reward and punishment; rather he

---

[11]H. Lusseau, IB, pp. 686 f.

expounds the traditional doctrine in calm and concrete fashion (Sir. 1:12 f.; 9:11 f. [16 f.]; 11:14-26; etc.). His is the practical aim of teaching piety and morality and his book is an important witness to the moral outlook and to the doctrine of Judaism shortly before the Maccabaean age. (Sirach must have helped to form those Jews who opposed the advance of Hellenism.) The spirituality of the book is grounded on faith in the God of the Covenant, a faith which shows itself in works of cult and in the practice of justice and mercy towards one's neighbor. Thus ben Sirach exhorts men to humility, kindness to the poor, and almsgiving. He denounces pride, sins of the tongue, adultery, covetousness, and sloth. In general, man must flee sin of every kind. Prudence is highly recommended in one's attitude to women—like most of the sages he is something of a misogynist—and in various social contacts. He repeatedly gives advice on family duties. All this moral instruction is inspired by religion, the service of God, and the book abounds in religious counsels that are entirely practicable.

1) Authorship and Date

The Greek text of the book has the title, *The Wisdom of Jesus, Son of Sirach,* or, *The Wisdom of Sirach.* In Sirach 50:27 the author is named: "Jesus, the son of Sirach, son of Eleazar, of Jerusalem." The Hebrew text of the same verse reads: "Simeon, son of Yashuah, son of Eleazar, son of Sira," but textual critics omit "Simeon." The title *Ecclesiasticus* has come to us via the Old Latin; it indicates that the book, though not everywhere accepted as canonical, was at least "ecclesiastical," that is, it might be read in church. It was, in fact, used as a handbook for the training of catechumens. As a deuterocanonical book Sirach was rejected at the Synod of Jamnia about the year 90 A.D., and though, as part of the Greek Bible it was accepted from the beginning by the Christian Church, it was not regarded as canonical in certain quarters.[12]

The author, named "Jesus" in the Prologue, names himself Sirach in 50:27 (29); what we know about him is gathered from his book and from his grandson's prologue to the Greek translation.

---

[12]See Wilfrid Harrington, *Record of Revelation: The Bible* (Chicago: The Priory Press, 1965), pp. 66-68.

The prologue, and various passages of his book (Sir. 34:9-13; 38:24 [25]; 39:1-5; 50:27 [29]; 51:3-5, 13 [18], 23 [31], 29 [37]), show him as an inhabitant of Jerusalem, a member of the scribal class, with the necessary wealth and leisure to devote himself in his youth entirely to the study of the Scriptures which he loved; as one who in his maturity traveled abroad, mixed with high society, found employment with some foreign potentate (in the course of which he escaped providentially from a mortal danger which a slanderous conspiracy had raised against him); as one, finally, who in later years settled in Jerusalem and opened a school for the scriptural and moral instruction of his younger fellow-countrymen, and composed the present work. With regard to the date at which he wrote, the prologue shows his grandson to have been of mature age "in the thirty-eighth year of the reign of Euergetes." This is best taken as meaning the thirty-eighth year of Ptolemy Euergetes II, that is, 132 B.C. The grandfather, ben Sirach, would have flourished fifty or sixty years previously (190-180 B.C.). This fits in with his reference in Sirach 50:1 ff. to "Simon the high priest, son of Onias" in such a way as to show that he had known him and that he was dead when this was written. The high priest referred to was Simeon II, son of Jochanan II. He held office about 219-196 B.C. This confirms 190-180 B.C. as the date of writing.[13]

2) Text and Versions

Sirach was certainly written in Hebrew, but by the eleventh century A.D. the Hebrew text had disappeared, due no doubt to the fact that the book had been excluded from the Jewish canon. Then in 1896 and the following years a substantial part of the Hebrew text was found in the *geniza*[14] of an old synagogue in Cairo. The Cairo Geniza manuscripts are five, dating from the eleventh and twelfth centuries:

1. 6 pp.: Sir. 3:6–16:26.
2. 19 pp.: Sir. 30:11–33:3; 35:11–38:27; 39:15–51:30.
3. 4 pp.: Sir. anthology of chapters 4-7; 18-20; 25-27.
4. 1 p.: Sir. 36:29–38:1.
5. 1 p.: Sir. 32:16–34:1.

This amounts to about three-fifths of the original.

Critical study of these manuscripts and of quotations in rabbinical literature shows that, already before 132 B.C. (when ben Sirach's grandson translated the work), the Hebrew text existed in at least

---

[13]C. J. Kearns, "Ecclesiasticus," *A Catholic Commentary on Holy Scripture*, B. Orchard, editor (London: Nelson, 1953), n. 369 h.

[14]A *geniza* was a storeroom or hiding place attached to synagogues in which discarded manuscripts were deposited.

two recensions. The evidence of Greek, Syriac, and Latin versions strongly confirms this conclusion. These recensions may be referred to as Primary and Secondary Text; there are two corresponding Greek texts:

1. Primary Greek, made by the author's grandson, represents Primary Hebrew. It is found in A.B.S.C., nearly all printed editions of the LXX, and underlies the Revised Standard Version.

2. Secondary Greek (first cent. B.C.) represents Secondary Hebrew. It is found in 248, in the Complutensian (Alcalá) Polyglot, and underlies the Vulgate, Authorized Version, and Douay Version.

3. Vg. is in fact the Old Latin, left untouched by St. Jerome. It was made from a manuscript of Primary Greek which had been emended to agree with a manuscript of Secondary Hebrew.[15]

The textual tradition of Sirach is complicated. The Greek is longer than the Hebrew and the Latin is longer still. However, the Latin is, on the whole, a translation of a Greek text, and Greek translates a Hebrew original.

> A rough idea of the differences between the Primary and Secondary Texts can be had by comparing RSV (substantially Primary) with AV or DV (substantially Secondary). A number of the differences are purely *scribal*: marginal glosses, explanatory expansions, or doublets of one original text. But there are also many *editorial additions* incorporated in the Secondary Text. A small number of these are *Christian glosses*, adapting Sirach to its function as a church handbook. But the greater number are *pre-Christian supplements* (probably Essene in origin), intended to emphasize a certain theological outlook which the editor or editors thought insufficiently represented in the Primary Text. They stress in particular the spiritual nature of creatures; the value of the individual soul and the human person; the part repentance can play in undoing sin, God's appreciation of such repentance, and his part in bringing it about. Above all, they supplement the rudimentary eschatology of the Primary Text by stressing the ideas of judgment at or after death, of conscious survival in the next world, of the moral aspects of human immortality, of lasting punishment and reward beyond the grave (for example, Sir. 6:23; 15:8; 16:22; 17:25; 18:22; 20:4; 24:46).[16]

The additions of the expanded text are not the work of ben Sirach; indeed they are appreciably later than his time. Not all Catholic scholars regard them as inspired. Those who do so accept them

---

[15]See Kearns, *op. cit.*, n. 396 c-e.
[16]*Ibid.*, n. 396 g.

argue that the Western Church at least has received the longer
text as contained in the Old Latin version, later incorporated into
the Vulgate. Besides, the Council of Trent has declared canonical
all the "parts" of the Vulgate[17] and these additions, in extent and
doctrinal content, are decidedly notable parts; there is at least a
serious case in favor of their inspiration. And, if they are canonical,
Sirach is notably enriched doctrinally and in spiritual depth. Most
of the scholars who regard the additions of the Secondary Text
as inspired deny the inspiration of the Prologue. It is not easy to
see how they can consistently take this view since it too forms
part of the Old Latin and is contained in the Vulgate.

3) *Composition and Plan*[18]

The literary form of the book would suggest that it has no regular
and logical plan. Many commentators are content to distinguish
two parts: a collection of proverbs (Sir. 2:1—42:14); the praise of
God and of the ancestors (Sir. 42:15—50:29). It must be admitted,
indeed, that the various themes follow one another without apparent
order and that some of them are treated two or three times without
any notable development. It is not likely that ben Sirach would
have composed such a work all at once. Most of the material would
have grown up over the years as he carried on his work of teacher,
and the final phase would have consisted largely in the editing of
that composite material. It is along these lines that we may explain
the many repetitions of the book and also the clear mark of one
hand on the whole of it.

It seems possible, however, to distinguish five parts in the book.
Each of these parts is composed in an identical manner: a doctrinal
introduction exalting wisdom (Sir. 1:1-30; 24:1-34; 32:14—33:19) or
God the Creator (Sir. 16:24—18:14; 42:15—43:33), followed by practical teaching in no particular order. A comparison of the five introductions brings to light a parallel structure: they begin with God,
or the divine Wisdom, and lead to the idea of wisdom communicated
to man. The author concludes with a bit of practical advice which
may take the shape of an exhortation to himself to write or of an

---

[17]See EB, p. 45.
[18]See C. Spicq, *L'Ecclésiastique* (Pirot-Clamer, VI) (Paris: Letouzey et Ané,
1951²), pp. 553 f.

invitation to fidelity or to thanksgiving. On the other hand, they exhibit a notable development. Wisdom is first envisaged in its widest acceptation, universal, destined for "all flesh," for "men" in general (Sir. 1:10,25). The second introduction (Sir. 16:24 ff.) represents the doctrine of God the Creator. In chapter 24 (third introduction) Wisdom is communicated to Israel, to Sion. The fourth introduction (Sir. 32:14 ff.) insists on the cult of the Law of Moses. Finally the treatment of the wisdom and power of the Creator God (Sir. 42:15 ff.) introduces the eulogy of the ancestors of Israel. In other words, the book, at first universalist in its outlook, tends to concentrate more and more on the Chosen People, regarded as the true depositary of the divine Wisdom on earth. Ben Sirach shows a particularly profound knowledge of the Pentateuch. It is significant that the development of his book is analogous to that of Genesis which begins with the Creation of the world and ends with the twelve patriarchs—and thus with the twelve tribes of Israel (Gn. 49:28)—after having successively eliminated all other races. If the body of the work does not show the same development, we may suppose that ben Sirach wrote the introductions when he came to publish his book, in this way putting some order into his earlier scattered writings. The plan of the book follows.[19]

PROLOGUE
NATURE AND BENEFITS OF WISDOM (SIR. 1:1–16:23)

1) Introduction	1:1-30 (1-40)
2) *Meshalim*	2:1–16:23

GOD AND CREATION; MAN AND MORALITY (SIR. 16:24–23:27)

1) Introduction	16:24–18:14
2) *Meshalim*	18:15–23:27 (37)

WISDOM IN FAMILY AND SOCIETY (SIR. 24:1–32:13)

1) Introduction	24:1-34 (47)
2) *Meshalim*	25:1–32:13 (17)

---

[19]See *ibid.*, p. 554. *Meshalim*, plural of *mashal* = "sayings."

THE VIRTUOUS LIFE (SIR. 32:14–42:14)	
1) Introduction	32:14 (18)–33:19
2) *Meshalim*	33:20–42:14

MANIFESTATION OF THE DIVINE WISDOM (SIR. 42:15–50:29)	
1) In Nature: Hymn to the Glory of God	42:15–43:33 (37)
2) In History: Praise of the Ancients of Israel	44:1–50:29 (31)

APPENDICES	
1) Prayer of Thanksgiving	51:1-12 (17)
2) Concluding Poem	51:13 (18)-30 (38)

4) Doctrine

The doctrine of Sirach is traditional. The wisdom which the book propounds comes from the Lord; it forms the young and insures the happiness of all who will receive it. The author believes in retribution, but takes his stand on the accepted teaching, and he is unperturbed by the practical difficulties of this view. Here there is no advance, but ben Sirach does break new ground when he identifies wisdom with the Law (Sir. 24:23 f.; cf. 15:1; 19:20). He differs more notably from the earlier sages in his concern with the history of Israel (Sir. 44:1–49:16). But even he is not interested in this history as such; rather he presents the saints of his people as men who were in love with wisdom and who were led along the road of sanctity by her. In his procession of great men the priesthood is conspicuously represented: Aaron and Phinehas have places of honor, and he closes with a eulogy of a contemporary, the high priest Simon.

Ben Sirach was evidently conservative in his views, but his book was ultimately to receive substantial additions which brought it into line with new ideas, especially those on the afterlife. The additions of the secondary or expanded text are largely concerned to supplement the eschatology of the primary text in the light of the new doctrine of retribution beyond the grave. The main point stressed is that there is to be a final, divine judgment of each one: for the wicked that will be a day of wrath and vengeance and unending punishment; for the just it will mean eternal reward in the world to come. At last, then, the problem of Job and Qoheleth has been solved; and Sirach, in its longer form, joins hands more firmly with the last great work of the wisdom movement.

7. THE BOOK OF WISDOM

In Alexandria, the most important center of the Diaspora, Jews were in close and constant touch with Hellenism. Some of the better educated among them sought to present their religion to the pagans. Naturally they strove to show it in the most favorable light possible, and they searched out points of contact between Greek culture and the traditions of Israel. It was in this milieu that the Book of Wisdom appeared. Written in Greek in such an atmosphere, it shows the influence of Greek thought, though the measure of this influence must not be exaggerated. For if the author displays some acquaintance with the various philosophies, this is no more than one would expect from the average cultured Alexandrian; he makes no attempt to syncretize Jewish and Greek ideas as Philo was to do. He is completely loyal to the faith of Israel, but borrows from the Greek thought of his environment whatever can serve him in the expression of his message.

1) Authorship and Date

In the Greek manuscripts (and in Syriac) Wisdom is entitled *The Wisdom of Solomon*. In the Vg. it is called *Liber Sapientiae*. The attribution of the book to Solomon is a literary fiction, common in wisdom writings (cf. Prv. 1:1; Qoh. 1:1; Ct. 1:1). Wisdom was written in Greek and is a deuterocanonical book.[20] The unknown author—who wrote Greek with ease—composed his work almost certainly in Alexandria. The place of origin is indicated by the spirit and outlook of the work as well as by the emphasis the author lays on the Egyptian phase of the Exodus and by his sustained criticism of animal worship (a feature of Egyptian religion).

We can be reasonably sure of the date of Wisdom. It is certain that the author has used the Septuagint, and since this version could scarcely have been completed before the beginning of the third century B.C., Wisdom cannot be earlier than that. The doctrine of the writing would suggest that it is considerably later. On the

---

[20]See Harrington, *op. cit.*, p. 64.

INTRODUCTION: TO SEEK JUSTICE, WISDOM, AND LIFE (WIS. 1:1-15)	

WISDOM AND HUMAN DESTINY (WIS. 1:16—5:23)	
1) Life according to the impious	1:16-2:20
2) Error of the impious	2:21-24
3) The lot of the just and of the impious	3:1—5:23

ORIGIN, NATURE, ACTION, AND ACQUISITION OF WISDOM (WIS. 6-9)	
1) Exhortation to kings	6:1-21
2) Solomon, Doctor of Wisdom	6:22—8:1
3) The Wisdom granted to Solomon	8:2—9:19

THE WISDOM OF GOD IN HISTORY (WIS. 10-19)	
1) The role of Wisdom from Adam to the Exodus	10:1—11:3
a) 1st antithesis: water, chastisement for Egyptians, salvation for the Israelites	11:5-14
Digression I: Mercy of God	11:15 (16)—12:27
Digression II: Folly and malice of the cult of idols	13-15
2) Marvelous action of Wisdom in the Exodus	16:1—19:17 (16)
b) 2nd antithesis: Egyptians tormented by animals Israelites nourished by quails	16:1-4
c) 3rd antithesis: locusts and flies destroy Egyptians bronze serpent heals Israelites	16:5-14
d) 4th antithesis: the elements strike the Egyptians the elements help the Israelites	16:15-29
e) 5th antithesis: horrible darkness afflicts Egyptians blessed light granted to Israelites	17:1—18:4
f) 6th antithesis: Egyptians lose the first born Israelites are spared	18:5-25
g) 7th antithesis: Red Sea swallows the Egyptians Red Sea opens to the Israelites	19:1-9

ISRAEL AND EGYPT (WIS. 19:10-21)	

CONCLUSION (WIS. 19:22 [20c])	

other hand the author shows no knowledge of the ideas of the Jewish philosopher Philo (20 B.C.-54 A.D.)—or of the prephilonian movement: his book would scarcely be later than 50 B.C. A date in the first half of the first century B.C. cannot be far off the mark. Wisdom is thus the last writing of the Old Testament.

2) *Plan*[21]

After an invitation to acquire wisdom (Wis. 1:1-15), the author goes on to show its unique importance in human destiny (Wis. 1:16–5:23). Then he describes its origin, nature, and action, indicating the means of acquiring it (chapters 6-9), and represents it at work in the history of Israel (Wis. 10:1–11:3). From Wisdom 11:4 wisdom gives place to God, to his breath, spirit, word, hand, and arm; Wisdom 19:22 is the conclusion.

Thus the work has three parts: the way of wisdom, opposed to the way of the impious (chapters 1-5); wisdom itself (chapters 6-9); the works of wisdom in the unfolding of Israel's history (chapters 10-19). The first chapters (1-5) depend largely on the prophets, whose style is notably Hebraic; chapters 6-9 use Prv. and some Greek philosophical ideas; but the style is less biblical; the last chapters (10-19) are in a style unlike that of the rest of the Old Testament. (See opposite page for the plan of the book.)

3) *Literary Form*

Wisdom, unlike Prv. and Sir. is a carefully-planned work; in general, however, it keeps close to the style of these writings. Nevertheless, from chapter 10—and more particularly from chapter 16—onwards, where the author points to the role of wisdom in the history of Israel, he introduces another literary form. For he is not content to reproduce the facts of that history but, according to the principles of *midrash*,[22] he strives to discover the deeper meaning of them. In the first place he embroiders the traditional narratives with features borrowed from Jewish legends or suggested by himself. Some of these are merely descriptive and serve the interests of style (Wis. 17:17-20; 18:1 f., 15 f.; 19:9). Others are meant to render a particular event more impressive, more dramatic, and more meaningful (Wis.

---

[21]See E. Osty, *Le Livre de la Sagesse* (BJ), pp. 7-10.
[22]See pp. 323-26.

17:3–6,9; 18:12; 11:11-13; 17:8,18,20; 18:17-19; 16:27-29). On the other hand, he has suppressed or modified whatever might reflect on God's goodness or on the reputation of the Chosen People, such as God's hardening of Pharaoh and the murmuring of the people in the desert.

Elsewhere the author takes the biblical narrative just as it is but, in order to fit it into his plan, he gives it a new interpretation. For instance, according to Exodus (23:28-30), God drove the Canaanites out of the land little by little lest the land should become a desert; the action is intended to benefit the Chosen People. Wisdom, however, regards it as an act of mercy towards the pagans: despite their culpability and their malice, God wished to give them a chance to repent (Wis. 12:3-6, 10 f.). It is a fine thought and a deeply-spiritual rendering of the old text, but it certainly falls outside the viewpoint of Exodus. This freedom of interpretation is best seen in the long parallel treatment of the respective fates of Egyptians and Israelites (Wis. 11:5-14; 16:1–19:9). In a series of seven antitheses the author boldly presents pairings which nothing in the Exodus narrative would suggest (for example: manna and hail; brazen serpent and locusts) and dramatizes the facts in order to heighten the contrast. In all this procedure he is guided by clear-cut ideas: God is essentially merciful and punishes only when he is constrained to do so; all the while he shows special solicitude for his own people. Underlying the method is the belief that the facts recorded in the Bible have a moral and religious value; it is the purpose of *midrash* to bring these to the surface.

4) Doctrine

The God of Wisdom is the God of Israelite tradition: omnipotent Creator; sovereign Master of the destinies of the universe. But the author emphasizes certain of his attributes. God is infinitely wise (Wis. 11:20); he handles all things with justice and always "makes the punishment fit the crime" (Wis. 12:15-18). He is sovereignly good, the friend of men and desirous of their welfare; he loves all his creatures. He has pity on all men (Wis. 11:23) and goes to great lengths to win the conversion of sinners (Wis. 12:20).

The divine attribute on which the author insists above any other is unquestionably the divine *wisdom*. This wisdom is manifestly the same as that of Prv. 8:1—9:6 and Sir. 24, yet here there is a distinct development. Its origin and nature are expressed in more philosophical terms (Wis. 7:25 f.); its relations with God are more intimate (Wis. 8:3 f.; 9:4); its creative activity is more marked (Wis. 7:21; 8:5 f.; 9:2,9) and the same is true of its omnipresence (Wis. 7:23 f.), its omniscience (Wis. 7:23; 8:4), its universal providence (Wis. 8:1), its sanctifying role (Wis. 7:27), its beneficial role in the history of Israel (Wis. 10:1—11:3), its love for men (Wis. 1:6; 7:23), its care for them (Wis. 6:12-16), and its importance in the acquisition of virtue (Wis. 8:7). He attributes to it all the encyclopedic knowledge of the Greek world of the time (Wis. 7:17-21; 8:8).

The teaching of Wisdom serves as a prelude to that on grace in the New Testament. Wisdom dwells in holy souls (Wis. 1:4; 7:27) and it is set on a level with the spirit of God (Wis. 1:4-7; 9:17). It is a treasure which procures the friendship of God (Wis. 7:14,28). Furthermore, since it is God who grants it, one must ask him for it (Wis. 7:7; 9). Even if a man has all other good qualities, without wisdom he is nothing before God (Wis. 9:6). Wisdom assures the observance of God's law and leads to blessed immortality (Wis. 6:17-20; 8:17).[23]

More important than anything else is the new teaching, the new hope, which Wisdom brings: "God created man for immortality" (Wis. 2:23). After death the faithful soul lives on—not in the shadowy existence of Sheol, but in a life of unending happiness before God (Wis. 3:9). This doctrine appears abruptly and briefly in Daniel (12:2); it is treated more fully in the additions of Sir.; but here it is put forward with complete assurance. The bankruptcy of the traditional doctrine of retribution had long been evident to the discerning, for material well-being is no more a sign of God's favor than misery is a sign of reprobation. Now, at last, it is seen that what happens in this life is a preparation for the life beyond, and the sufferings of a just man serve to purify him and win for him a greater recompense. One thing alone matters: to do God's will and to live in his love, for this is the way to eternal life. Paul and John did not disdain to listen to the nameless author of the last Old Testament writing.

---

[23]See Osty, *op. cit.*, pp. 15-22.

5) *Influence of Wisdom*[24]

Though not admitted into the Jewish canon, Wisdom was warmly received by the early Church. There is no explicit citation of the book in the New Testament, but it is certain that Paul and John were influenced by it; this is especially evident in their Christology.

The following comparisons may be made:

1. *Paul and Wisdom.*

Rom. 1:18-20—Wis. 13:3-5: Knowledge of existence and nature of God from the works of creation.

Rom. 2:4—Wis. 11:23,26; Wis. 12:2,10,19: Divine longanimity calls men to repentance.

Rom. 9:20—Wis. 12:12: Absolute power of God.

Rom. 9:21—Wis. 15:7: The potter.

Rom. 1:21-32—Wis. 14:22-31: Depraved morals—punishment of idolatry.

Col. 1:15—Wis. 7:26: Christ is the image of the invisible God as wisdom is of the divine excellence.

Eph. 6:14-17—Wis. 5:17-20: Panoply of God and of the Christian.

1 Cor. 1:24,30: Christ is called "Wisdom of God."

Heb. 1:3—Wis. 7:26: The Son is the reflection of the Father's glory as wisdom is of eternal light.

2. *John and Wisdom.* The influence of Wisdom on St. John is perhaps more profound still. It is no exaggeration to say that, in regard to the presentation of the relationship of the Word towards the Father and towards men, Wisdom has blazed a trail for the author of the Fourth Gospel. Here are some of the more noteworthy contacts:

Jn. 1:1-18—Wis. 8:3; 9:4: Intimacy of the Word with the Father.

Jn. 1:3,10—Wis. 7:21; 8; 6; 9:1,9: Creative activity of the Word.

Jn. 5:20—Wis. 8:4—9:9,10,11,17: Omniscience of the Word.

Jn. 3:16-17—Wis. 1:6; 7; 23; 11; 24; 26: Love of God for men.

Jn. 14:23; 16; 27—Wis. 7:28—The Father loves those only who love the Son.

In general, the Johannine writings understand the history of the world and of souls in the same way: an unending warfare between

---

[24]See *ibid.*, pp. 26 f.

light and darkness, life and death, with the victory of the light assured despite the apparent success of darkness.

6) *Wisdom in the Liturgy*

The Church has given Wisdom an honorable place in her liturgy. Many passages of Wisdom have been chosen to honor the saints (Wis. 3:1-8,13; 4:7-16; 5:1-5; 7:7-14). They turn up in the office of apostles and evangelists, of martyrs, confessors, and virgins (*capitula* of vespers and versicles), in the Mass of martyrs, of All Saints, of St. Thomas Aquinas. The familiar versicle of the office of Corpus Christi—*Panem de coelo praestitisti eis, omne delectamentum in se habentem*—is taken from Wisdom 16:20.

8. THE DIVINE WISDOM[25]

1) *The Source of Wisdom*

From the very first the Israelite sages acknowledged that true human wisdom has a divine source: God communicates wisdom to whom he pleases, and he can do so because he is himself the Sage *par excellence*. Wisdom is a divine reality; she has been from eternity and will endure forever (Prv. 8:22-26; Sir. 24:9). She has come forth from the mouth of the Most High (Sir. 24:3) like his spoken word; she is a "breath of the power of God and a pure emanation of the glory of the Almighty . . . a reflection of eternal light, a spotless mirror of the working of God, and an image of his goodness" (Wis. 7:25 f.). She dwells in heaven seated by the throne of God and lives in closest association with him (Wis. 24:4; 9:4; 8:2).

Wisdom is tireless. She was with God when he created heaven and earth (Prv. 8:27-31), and has remained the ruler of the universe (Wis. 8:1). She resides familiarly with men (Prv. 8:31) and was bidden to make her home in Israel (Sir. 24:8-12). As the providence that guides history (Wis. 10:1—11:4) and the bringer of salvation to men (Wis. 9:18) she has time and again gone forth on divine missions to men. She expresses her absorbing interest in men's welfare by warning them of judgment (Prv. 1:10-33) and by inviting all who will to share her goods and to sit at her table (Prv. 8:1-21, 32-26; 9:4 f.; Sir. 24:19-22). She it is who distributes the gifts of

---

[25]See P. van Imschoot, *Théologie de l'Ancien Testament* (Tournai: Desclée, 1954), I, pp. 226-36; A. Barucq and P. Grelot, VTB, pp. 974-81.

God to men (Prv. 8:21; Wis. 7:11) and, greatest service of all, it is she who makes men friends of God (Wis. 7:27 f.). In short, this presentation of divine wisdom is a prelude to the New Testament doctrine of grace and it is in the light of this doctrine that the Old Testament idea becomes more readily understandable for us.

2) *The Personification of Wisdom*

This striking presentation of wisdom gives rise to a problem of its own. The question is whether the texts indicated in the previous paragraph, and many similar passages, are to be taken in a strict sense, or whether they do not go beyond literary personification. Perhaps we should no longer describe it as a problem, since Scripture scholars agree that it is no more than a figure of speech, and the special interest of the matter now is the realization that a proper understanding of the biblical context points unerringly to the true interpretation; it was the intrusion of later theological ideas which led to confusion. Throughout the sapiential literature, wisdom is consistently practical. The wisdom authors were moralists who couched their teaching in poetic language, not philosophers speculating on the nature of God. If we are not to falsify their thought we must keep in mind the general context and the essentially practical purpose of their writings as well as the poetic quality of their style which abounds in imagery and picturesque touches. Here as elsewhere we may not impose on the Bible the categories of scholastic speculation —or do so at the peril of missing the import of what *God* says in his Scripture.

There is nothing surprising in this personification of wisdom. The figure of speech is common to all ages and to all peoples, and in Israel's literature it is by no means confined to the Wisdom books. No one can fail to appreciate the splendid image of Second Isaiah which describes the joy of the return from the Exile:

"The mountains and the hills before you
shall break forth into singing,
and all the trees of the field shall clap their hands" (Is. 55:12).

Personification is not less conscious when the author of Wisdom declares that Wisdom is of noble birth and dwells with God as his spouse, or becomes the spouse of men (Wis. 8:3; 7:28; 8:2,9); or when Prv. describes her as an infant playing before God (Prv. 8:30). Yet the bold personification of wisdom by the sages of Israel did prepare the way for the full revelation of the New Testament.

3) Jesus and Wisdom

The manner of teaching employed by our Lord resembled that of Israel's sages: he used the same forms as they (sayings and parables—the *māshāl* in all its range), and like them he laid down rules of life (cf. Mt. 5-7). The people were astonished at his wisdom (Mk. 6:2), and he could say of himself: "The queen of the South came from the ends of the earth to hear the wisdom of Solomon, and behold, something greater than Solomon is here" (Mt. 12:42). For it is in his own name that he promised to his followers the gift of wisdom (Lk. 21:15).

The New Testament writers understood that, if Jesus communicates wisdom to men, it is because he himself is the Wisdom of God (1 Cor. 1:24,30). Naturally, then, they apply to him the same terms used by the Old Testament sages: he is the first born of all creation (Col. 1:15-20; cf. Prv. 8:22-31); he is the reflection of the glory of God and bears the very stamp of his nature (Heb. 1:3; cf. Wis. 7:25 f.); he is the Incarnate Word of God (Jn. 1:1-18; cf. Sir. 24:3). The personal wisdom of God is fully revealed in Jesus Christ who has come forth from the Father to dwell with men and to win them salvation. In him all the wisdom of the wise men finds its term and its true significance.

9. THE CANTICLE OF CANTICLES

The Canticle of Canticles is traditionally classed with Jb., Prv., Qoh., Sir., and Wis. to form the "Books of Wisdom"; we shall see that there is a sound basis for this classification. However, the Canticle is distinctive and it is best taken by itself at the close of this chapter on the wisdom literature.

1) The Book

The Canticle of Canticles finds its place in the Hebrew Bible among the Writings, at the head of the festal *megilloth* ("rolls") and was appointed to be read at the Pasch. The title, "Canticle of Canticles," like "Holy of Holies" and "King of Kings," is a Hebrew form of the superlative and means the loveliest song. Jewish regard for the

Canticle was expressed by the Rabbi Aqiba (second cent. A.D.): "All the writings are holy, but the Song of Songs is the Holy of Holies." The book met with some opposition at the Jewish Council of Jamnia (c. 90 A.D.), but was accepted as part of the Jewish canon. Since it is found both in the Hebrew and in the Septuagint (LXX), it passed without question into the Christian canon.

The Canticle is a love poem (or a collection of love poems). Its language throughout is the language of love, and if that language seems daring, perhaps at times even shocking, in its realism, this is because it is the product of another culture. It has undeniable contacts with earlier Egyptian love songs. A notable parallel is the use of the terms "sister" (Ct. 4:10,12; 5:1; cf. Tb. 5:21; 8:4,7,21) and "brother" (Ct. 8:1)—recognized terms in Egyptian love poems; common also are the themes of lovesickness and the absence of the beloved (Ct. 2:5; 3:1 f.; 5:6-8). A single example brings out the correspondence: "Seven days to yesterday I have not seen the sister. And a sickness has invaded me . . . more beneficial to me is the sister than any remedies . . . when I embrace her she drives evil away from me—but she has gone forth from me for seven days."[26] Parallels have been noted between the Canticle and the *wasfs* (songs sung in praise of bride and groom during rural weddings in Syria); such *wasfs* undoubtedly have a long history. But neither ancient Egyptian nor modern Syrian parallels are surprising or really significant, for in the nature of the case we should expect to find similarities of expression. Love is a fundamental human emotion and the language of love sounds much the same in all lands.

2) *Authorship and Date*

The Canticle of Canticles is traditionally attributed to Solomon (Ct. 1:1), but he is no more the author of it than he is of Qoh.; the attribution is based on his reputation as a poet (1 Kgs. 4:32). The language of the Canticle is many centuries later than the time of Solomon; it shows the influence of Aramaic and has Hebraized Persian words (Ct. 1:12; 4:13,18; 6:11) and one Greek word ("palanquin" [Ct. 3:9]). Though some of the basic material may be older, the finished work is certainly postexilic. A date in the first

---

26ANET, pp. 468 f.; cf. P. F. Ellis, *The Men and the Message of the Old Testament* (Collegeville, Minn.: The Liturgical Press, 1963), p. 384.

half of the fourth century—a period of religious and political tranquillity following the reforms of Ezra and Nehemiah—seems indicated. The book was edited by wisdom writers about the same time.[27]

3) The Plan

Though interpretations of the Canticle of Canticles differ widely, it is agreed that the book is, superficially at least, a poem, or a collection of love poems. In fact, unity of authorship seems to be undeniable: the same language and style are found throughout and there is a movement towards a climax, reached in chapter 8. It may be that the poet has used traditional material, but he has dominated it and shaped it to his own ends. At any rate, the position adopted here is that the Canticle is a series of connected poems, the work of a single author—apart from the later addition (Ct. 8:8-14; and perhaps 8:6 f.).

DIVISION

TITLE AND PROLOGUE (CT. 1:1-4)
FIRST POEM (CT. 1:5—2:7)
SECOND POEM (CT. 2:8—3:5)
THIRD POEM (CT. 3:6—5:1)
FOURTH POEM (CT. 5:2—6:3)
FIFTH POEM (CT. 6:4—8:5)
EPILOGUE: HYMN TO LOVE (CT. 8:6 f.)
APPENDICES (CT. 8:8-14)

4) Interpretation

In the course of the centuries the Canticle has been interpreted in many ways, but no explanation has won universal acceptance. Present-day Catholic interpretations may be reduced to three:

---

[27]See J. Winandy, *Le Cantique des Cantiques* (Paris: Ed. de Maredsous, 1960), p. 55.

1. *The allegorical interpretation.* The work is an allegory, immediately signifying the union of Yahweh with Israel.

2. *The literal interpretation.* The Canticle is in praise of human love as God had willed and created it.

3. *The theological reinterpretation.* The Canticle is a poem in praise of human love which, under the influence of the prophetical marriage image, was reinterpreted by an inspired writer in the perspective of divine love.

The allegorical interpretation has been dominant among Jews and Christians; in recent years it has been warmly and competently presented by eminent scholars.[28] Both as a traditional view and on the basis of scholarship it merits serious attention, and yet, on both grounds, it is vulnerable. For one thing, it seems that the earliest evidence we have in support of the allegorical interpretation is a second-century A.D. Jewish tradition.[29] The Canticle was accepted as part of the Jewish canon in 90 A.D., not because it was regarded as an allegory but because of its popularity. On the other hand, this interpretation demands that too much should be read into the text. For instance, the historical and topographical significance attributed to descriptive details is forced and seems arbitrary.[30]

Perhaps the most serious difficulty is that nothing in the poems suggests that they are allegories. Elsewhere (as in Hos., Jer., Ezek.), where nuptial language is used to describe the relationship between Yahweh and his people, the allegorical nature of the language is always made clear. It is noteworthy too that, when the biblical writers have spoken of Yahweh and his people in marital terms, they have displayed an obvious restraint and have set definite limits to the imagery; the boldness of the Canticle's language would surely strike the earlier writers as out of place in this context. Besides, the marriage image is a prophetical theme, whereas the Canticle

---

[28]Read A. Robert, *Le Cantique des Cantiques* (BJ), 1958²; A. Feuillet, *Le Cantique des Cantiques* (Paris: Cerf, 1953); A. Robert et R. Tournay (avec le concours de A. Feuillet), *Le Cantique des Cantiques* (Études Bibliques) (Paris: Gabalda, 1963).

[29]See J.-P. Audet, "Le sens du Cantique des Cantiques," RB, 62 (1955), 200-3; "Love and Marriage in the Old Testament," *Scripture*, 10 (1958), 81.

[30]See, for example, A. Robert, BJ, pp. 857-67. The sustained interpretation is a brilliant *tour de force;* one is impressed but not convinced.

is lyric poetry and—as it is presented by its editors—belongs to the wisdom literature.

Another line of argument in favor of the allegorical interpretation is that the author of the Canticle has employed the "anthological" method, that is, that he has systematically used the words and expressions of earlier biblical writings.[31] Here again the arguments are ingenious, but the "anthological" method has been shown to be a double-edged weapon.[32] All in all, despite its long tradition and its eminent champions, the allegorical interpretation of the Canticle is difficult to maintain. We turn, by choice, to the literal interpretation.

The literal interpretation takes the Canticle at its face value, regarding it as a love poem or a collection of love poems celebrating the love of a man and a woman. It has been urged in the past—and the prejudice still lingers—that the theme of human love is unworthy of Scripture; or, at least, that it is unlikely, unseemly even, that a biblical book should have been wholly dedicated to it. This outlook would appear to miss the true significance of Scripture. The Bible is the word of God, certainly, but (we may ask) to whom is that word addressed? God has not written this work just for his own pleasure; he has destined it for the human beings whom he had created; it is his gift to them. It is he who has made them men and women; it is he who has implanted in them, deep in their nature, the mutual attraction that is meant to culminate in marriage. Like all the gifts of God this may be abused but, in the divine intention, the love which so strongly draws young people, which inspires each of them to dedicate his and her life to the other, and which later enables them, together, to support inevitable cares and troubles, is a good thing—it is part of the work which God himself has called very good (Gn. 1:31). It is eminently worthy of special treatment in the Bible, that word of God *to men*.

If we accept the literal interpretation of Canticles we may ask how the work is to be approached and what we should expect to find there.

---

[31]See Feuillet, *Le Cantique des Cantiques*, *op. cit.*, pp. 193-244.
[32]See A.-M. Dubarle, "L'amour humain dans le Cantique des Cantiques," RB, 61 (1954), 75-81; P. Grelot, "Le sens du Cantique des Cantiques," RB, 71 (1964), 49-51.

We may find in these poems a progression leading to love's consummation in marriage, and the depth and intensity of love itself is acknowledged. We shall not look for any particular man or woman whose love is being described. Rather we shall hear the words of a great poet who has chosen this medium for presenting the simplicity and the greatness, the gentleness and the strength of love. The scenes he describes did not necessarily exist as he speaks of them; neither did the people he referred to have objective reality. . . . For the deepest of all human emotions cannot be treated in abstraction; it is a relationship. The poet therefore has presented love through the medium of a youth and maiden in an appropriate setting, the countryside. He has essayed the profoundly difficult task of conveying the emotions both of the youth and of the maiden and has done so with rare artistry and insight. . . . But the important fact to remember is, that it is a poet whose words we read, and that must determine our interpretation.[33]

It would seem that the obvious sense of the Canticle may be reconciled with the Jewish and Christian allegorical interpretation of it. This reconciliation would be achieved if it were shown that the application of the Canticle to the mutual love of Yahweh and Israel is a *biblical sense*—and not a later rereading of a biblical text (by non-biblical interpreters). This, however, is just the point that is not proved. It has been argued that, at the moment when the Canticle took final form as a love poem, the inspired author could not but have been conscious of the prophetical symbolism of human love. At the same time it is conceded that the marriage image has not influenced Prv. or Sir. and that Tb. refers only to Gn. 1-2.

But here the case is different because it is a question of directly presenting the mutual sentiments of the bridegroom and of the bride; and on the testimony of the prophets, these sentiments are precisely the concrete means which enable us to understand the religious relationship between God and men as a mystery of love. We may say that the words are charged with religious overtones; they are, of themselves, capable of a parallel presentation of the personal relationship of man to woman and of the covenant relationship between God and his people; they are intelligible on two registers.[34]

Is not this to beg the question? Why *must* the inspired author relate his poem to the Covenant relationship and have the marriage image positively in mind? If his intention was—as the literal inter-

---

[33]A. S. Herbert, PCB, n. 406 d, 1.
[34]Grelot, *art. cit.*, 52 f.

pretation maintains—to exalt human love, he can have remained on that level. Our preference for the literal interpretation of the Canticle is obvious; we may have been less than fair to other views. All we wish to say is that there is no place for dogmatism—the whole problem is much too complicated and is still too open. However, it has seemed well to follow a line of interpretation that gives a fresh religious meaning to a fundamental human experience, and one which must appeal to men and women of our day.

Jews of the Christian era interpreted the Canticle as an allegory, signifying the love of Yahweh for his people from the Exodus to the dawn of the messianic age. The allegorical method of interpretation was adopted by Christians who interpreted the Canticle in terms of Christ and his Church; later it was taken as an allegory of the union of Christ with the individual soul or of the Holy Spirit and the Virgin Mary. In the literal interpretation of the book this usage is reduced to accommodation. "Whatever literal interpretation of the Canticle one accepts, it is legitimate to apply it either to the relationship of Christ and his Church or to the union of individual souls with the God of love, and this justifies the admirable use made of it by mystics like St. John of the Cross."[35]

5) The Message[36]

The Canticle of Canticles takes its place in the Bible as the exaltation of human love. Whether it is a collection of songs or whether it is one elaborate poem, it is certainly lyrical. As such it does not "teach," it has no "doctrine" to propound: it is the expression of a state of mind and heart. It is concerned with the mutual love of two young people who, quite obviously, contemplate marriage; if, indeed, they are not already married. Its language is the language of love; if it seems daring to our Western ears, it is surely relevant to note that, throughout the Old Testament, the same Hebrew verb and noun are used for human and divine love, but when we turn to the New Testament we find that Christian authors, writing in Greek,[37] could not use the ordinary word for love in their religious vocabulary,

---

[35]BJ, p. 856.
[36]See W. Harrington, *The Bible on Marriage* (Dublin: Dominican Publications, 1963), pp. 27-31.
[37]See Herbert, *art. cit.*, 406.

because its association had made it unfit for such usage. (The same is very nearly the case today when "love" is so often a synonym of "lust".)

The epilogue of Canticles (or an editorial addition) would indicate that the author (and editors) understood the writing in its straightforward literal sense:

"For love is strong as death,
 jealousy is cruel as Sheol.
Its flashes are flashes of fire,
 a very flame of Yahweh.
Many waters cannot quench love,
 nor can floods drown it.
If a man should offer all the wealth of his house
 as a price for love,
 he would be utterly scorned" (Ct. 8:6b-7).[38]

Such language is reminiscent of Prv. or Sir., and orientates the Canticle in the traditional direction of wisdom literature;[39] the writing was reinterpreted in terms of the mutual love of Yahweh and Israel only after the book had taken its place in the canon. The growing tendency among Catholic scholars to read Canticles according to its obvious sense is due to the realization that the theme of human love is no more out of place in the wisdom literature than is the theme of human wisdom of Prv.

A feature of the Canticle that often occasions surprise is the absence of the divine name; what should really surprise us is the absence of any allusion to a god or goddess of love. Israel did indeed feel the strong attraction of *Ashtaroth* (the Canaanite goddesses of fertility) and did fall into idolatry, but Israel itself never divinized love, it never even personified love. The explanation of this fact, which is truly remarkable when we view it in historical perspective, is to be found in the second chapter of Genesis. There is no essential difference between the admiration that attracted the first man to

---

[38]W. F. Albright comments: "Nowhere in the entire range of world-literature can we find an equal to the praise of the love of man for woman in Canticle 8:6 f." (*Archaeology and the Religion of Israel* [Baltimore: Johns Hopkins Press, 1946], p. 13).

[39]For the same theme as that of the Canticle see Prv. 5:15-19; 31:10-31; Sir. 25:13—26:18.

the first woman (Gn. 2:23) and the mutual wonder of the young couple of the Canticle. There is little difference between the comment of the editor of Genesis: "That is why a man leaves father and mother and cleaves to his wife, and they become one flesh" (2:24), and the reflection of the poet (or editor) of the Canticle: "For love is strong as death. . . . If a man should offer all the wealth of his house as a price for love, it would be utterly scorned" (8:6 f.). Both texts bear witness to the same attitude in face of the same human experience. Marital love belongs to the order of things created by God from the beginning, it is one of the wonders of God which should evoke admiration and gratitude.[40]

It is arguable that the Canticle was originally a collection of espousal songs or songs of the wedding feast; at the very least it has been inspired and colored by such songs. This explains its atmosphere, the springtime joy, the companions, and the young couple immersed in each other. The whole is, admittedly, on a natural plane, but is there anything reprehensible in that? Love is normally awakened by physical beauty, by very human qualities, and God made man's body as well as man's soul. It would be unrealistic, to say the least, to seek to ignore this; logically it ought to lead to a denial of the role of sex in marriage. Besides, and this is more to the point, such an attitude is entirely unbiblical.

> In the biblical view there never is an obligation which has not been preceded by a corresponding gift of God. It is because Yahweh has delivered his people from Egypt that Israel is obliged to adore him alone (Ex. 20:2 f.; Dt. 5:6 f.). In the same way the overflowing happiness of the Canticle, a happiness which will be doled out more sparingly afterwards, is the divine gift which prompts the acceptance of future duties: daily work, painful maternity, persevering faithfulness. A passage which can well be the climax of the work begins with an adjuration and then goes on to formulate, in more abstract terms, the practical conclusion of the poems: unshakable fidelity is the very expression of true love—and this is not a matter of social constraint; it is the inevitable desire of a heart entirely given to another (Ct. 8:6 f.).
> The spontaneous accord of two young people is a more striking introduction to the wonderful harmony of the work of God than is the mutual understanding patiently acquired by the sharing of good and ill over the course of a long life. The joy of love newborn gives a taste of creation in its first unblemished beginning. . . . It is not

---

[40]See Audet, *art. cit.*, 219 f.

by chance that these love poems are accompanied by a feeling for all that is gracious and charming in nature which is more vivid than anywhere else in the Old Testament and which has been equalled only by the Gospel (Mt. 6:29; 23:27).[41]

There is yet another point that is well worth noting. By attracting attention to the personal element in marriage the Canticle has not merely provided a more balanced view, but has enriched the concept of marriage. Love brings out the unique value of the person (cf. Ct. 2:2 f.; 5:10; 6:8 f.) and establishes a real equality between man and woman; it is significant that the latter's freedom of choice is here quite obviously taken for granted. Perhaps even more striking is the fact that, in the context, a monogamous and indissoluble union is manifestly in view.

But there is still more to it. The important fact that a biblical writing has extolled the tender love of a young couple not only restores the balance of marriage but has its place in the development of revelation.[42] It plays its part in the transformation of the essentially communitary Covenant of Sinai into the new Covenant foretold by Jeremiah (Jer. 31:31-34), a Covenant in which the place and dignity of the individual are explicitly affirmed. For, when love had been acknowledged as a constitutive element in marriage, side-by-side with the founding of a family, the individual had ceased to be absorbed in the group. It is a decisive step towards the recognition of the personal dignity of every man and woman.

---

[41]Dubarle, *art. cit.*, 82 f.
[42]See *ibid.*, p. 84.

1. HEBREW POETRY

A large part of the Old Testament is poetry. Some of its books are wholly poetic in form: Psalms, Proverbs, Job, Canticle, Lamentations, Sirach, Wisdom. Most of Isaiah, Jeremiah, and the minor prophets and part of Ezekiel are also written as such, while songs and fragments of songs survive embedded here and there in the historical books. Of course, the Bible does not contain the total output of Hebrew poets. For instance, we find references to three collections of poems which are no longer extant: The Book of the Wars of the Lord (Nm. 21:14 f.)—probably a collection of songs celebrating great events in the history of the nation; the Book of Jashar (Jos. 10:12 f.; 2 Sm. 1:18)—probably a collection of songs celebrating the achievements of national heroes; and a collection of lamentations (2 Chr. 35:25).

1) Elements of Hebrew Poetry

Some elements of Hebrew poetry, such as rhythm and assonance, do not survive in translation. Others, such as strophic structure, the use of refrains, and especially parallelism show through in vernacular renderings.

RHYTHM   Meter in Hebrew poetry is reckoned in terms of ac-
OR METER   cented syllables: the line has a definite number of

accented syllables and the unaccented syllables are not counted. The chief rhythms are 3:3 and 3:2.

1. 3:3—each member of the couplet has three accented syllables:

"He comes fórth like a flówer and wíthers,
 he flées like a shádow and contínues not" (Jb. 14:2).

This is the most frequently used meter.

2. 3:2—The first member of a couplet has three accented syllables and the second has two:

"The Lórd has scórned his áltar,
 disówned his sánctuary" (Lam. 2:7).

This is called the "Qinah" or "Elegiac" meter because it was first identified in Lamentations. It is often employed in laments, but it is also frequently used to express praise and thanksgiving. Other meters are: 4:4; 2:2; 4:3; while occasionally the line consists of three members. As a rule, however, a metrical pattern is not rigidly observed.

STROPHES OR STANZAS   In Hebrew poetry there are no strophes or stanzas in the strict sense of the terms, but we may discern a certain strophic construction based on a unity of thought. A refrain repeated at regular intervals is evidence of a definite strophic form (for example, Is. 9:8–10:4; Ps. 106). Some of the alphabetic psalms[1] are strophic in form (for example, Ps. 118, where the first eight verses begin with the letter *aleph,* the second with *beth,* and so on).

PARALLELISM   The most important and the most distinctive feature of Hebrew poetry is parallelism. This involves a couplet (sometimes a triplet) in which the terms of the first line are balanced by the terms of the second. It is usual to distinguish three forms of parallelism:

1. *Synonymous parallelism.* The second member of a couplet repeats the thought of the first in different words:

"Now, O kings, understand,
 take warning, rulers of the earth;
Serve the Lord with awe,
 and trembling pay him your homage" (Ps. 2:10 f.).

---

[1]Alphabetic psalms follow an artificial pattern in which each verse, or group of verses, begins with a different letter of the alphabet; there are generally 22 verses or units, according to the letters of the Hebrew alphabet. In this chapter, to avoid cumbersome reduplication, we shall list the psalms according to the Vg. numbering only.

2. *Antithetic parallelism.* The terms of the second member of a couplet contrast with those of the first:

"A wise son makes a glad father,
  but a foolish son is sorrow to his mother" (Prv. 10:1).

3. *Synthetic or constructive parallelism.* The sense of the first member is developed in the second:

"Sing to the Lord a new song;
  sing to the Lord, all the earth" (Ps. 95:1).

Parallelism is not always complete, and though parallelism is a general rule in Hebrew poetry, it is not always present.

2) *Literary Characteristics of Hebrew Poetry*[2]

Since the Hebrews were a pastoral and agricultural people, it is not surprising that their poetry gives great prominence to nature. But Hebrew poets found in nature (not exclusively, but often) a manifestation of the attributes of their God and the clear trace of his hand. The heavens proclaim his glory and the firmament shows forth his handiwork (Ps. 18:1). His voice is heard in the raging storm (Ps. 28:5-9); he showers down snow, scatters hoar frost like ashes, casts hailstones like crumbs, and freezes the waters by a touch (Ps. 147:16 f.). He makes the springs to gush forth in the valleys where the beasts of the field may drink and where the birds sing among the branches of the trees (Ps. 103:10-12). He waters the earth, softens it with showers, and blesses its growth so that the meadows are clothed with flocks and the valleys decked with corn (Ps. 64:10-14).

Nature not only mirrors the divine attributes, it can be used to symbolize them. The sky is a symbol of God's steadfast love (Ps. 35:5; 102:11), the mountains of his eternity (Ps. 89:2) and of his righteousness (Ps. 35:7), the sea of his justice (Ps. 35:7), the dew of his goodness (Hos. 14:5), and the bird sheltering its young under its wing of his protection (Ps. 138; Qoh. 12:1-7; Is. 2:2-4; 35; 40; 55; 44:11-13; 60). The vivid imagery of the Hebrew poets was often inspired by nature. The writer of Ps. 101 felt himself "like a pelican in the wilderness, like an owl in desolate places." Leviathan made the deep boil like a pot (Jb. 41:31). When Israel was delivered

---

[2]See T. Henshaw, *The Writings* (New York: Humanities Press, 1963), pp. 86-94.

from Egypt, "the sea fled at the sight: the Jordan turned back on its course, the mountains leapt like rams and the hills like yearling sheep" (Ps. 113:3 f.). Second Isaiah described in similar terms the joy of nature at the glad return from the Exile: "The mountains and the hills before you shall break forth into singing, and all the trees of the field shall clap their hands" (Is. 55:12). It would be difficult to surpass the poetic boldness of the psalmist's exhortation: "Let the rivers clap their hands" (Ps. 97:8).

Hebrew poetry is highly subjective and is marked by intensity of feeling, for the poet is generally striving to give expression to his own feelings and to reveal his inmost thoughts. This also induces simplicity of style; in this very personal poetry there is little place for artificiality or mere ornamentation. Hebrew thought was essentially theocentric: everything began and ended with God, the Creator of the world, the Source of life and the Controller of history. It is natural, then, that Hebrew poetry be marked by an exalted spirituality which gives it a unique position in world literature. On his journey through life the Hebrew, and a fortiori the Hebrew poet, looked for and found the spiritual in the material, the unseen in the seen, the eternal in fleeting time.

2. THE PSALMS

The history of Psalms, like that of most of the Old Testament books, is complex. The collection of 150 psalms that we know was not made all at once and it is not the work of one author or of one age. The Canticle of Deborah (Jgs. 5) is proof of the early origin of religious poetry in Israel, while the apocryphal *Psalms of Solomon* and the Qumran *Hodayoth* (thanksgiving psalms), as well as the *Magnificat* and the *Benedictus* show that the tradition continued to the time of Christ. It is altogether likely that many older psalms have been lost, while others of different dates exist outside the collection of 150 psalms (for example, 1 Sm. 2:1-10; Is. 38:10-20; 44:23-28; Jer. 15:15-25; Lam. 3:5; Dn. 2:20-23; 3:26-45, 52-90; Jon. 2:2-9; Tb. 13). However, the great bulk of extant Hebrew psalms is to be found in the Psalter.

1) *The Name*

The English title of the book comes from the Greek *biblos psalmōn* ("book of psalms") or *psalmoi* ("psalms"). In the LXX, *psalmos*, translating the Hebrew *mizmor*, means a song or hymn accompanied by a stringed instrument. The Codex Alexandrinus (A) has the title *psaltērion*, which means a collection of sacred songs (though originally the word meant a stringed instrument). The Hebrew title of the book is *tehillim* (or *sepher tehillim*)—"hymns of praise" (or, "the book of hymns of praise"). In the Hebrew Bible Psalms stands among the *kethubhim* (the Writings), the third division of the canon. In the LXX and Vg., Psalms stands among the poetical and didactical books (before the prophets) and comes between Jb. and Prv.

2) Division and Enumeration

Psalms, probably in imitation of the Pentateuch, is divided into five books: I: 1-40; II: 41-71; III: 72-88; IV: 89-105; V: 106-150. Each of the first four books ends with a special doxology: 40:13; 71:18 f.; 88:52; 105:48. Psalm 150 is a doxology which closes not only Book V but the whole Psalter.

In the Hebrew and LXX the Psalter contains 150 psalms (the spurious Ps. 151 in the LXX is explicitly stated to be "outside the number"), but the numeration is somewhat different; the discrepancy is reproduced in translations from the Hebrew and from the LXX or Vg. The difference is due to the division into two by the LXX of certain psalms which in Hebrew remain as one psalm, and to the division into two in the Hebrew of others which remain as one in the LXX. The following table shows this difference:

LXX	1-8	9	10-112	113	114-115	116-145	146-147	148-150
Heb.	1-8	9-10	11-113	114-115	116	117-146	147	148-150

In general, Hebrew numeration is one ahead of LXX.

3) The Growth of the Psalter

The division into five books, though early, is not original. Psalms is, in fact, "a collection of collections," composed of several originally independent collections. We shall first consider two major collections and then pass on to smaller groupings.

ELOHISTIC AND   These are so-called from the preponder-
YAHWISTIC COLLECTIONS   ance of one or other divine name:

Book	I	II	III	III	IV	V
Psalms	1-40	41-71	72-82	83-88	89-105	106-150
Yahweh	272	30	13	31	103	236
Elohim	15	164	36	7	0	7

Hence there are three collections; two yahwistic (Pss. 1-40; 89-150); one elohistic (Pss. 41-82). To these must be added the secondary yahwistic collection (Pss. 83-88). The preponderance of one or other divine name is no accident and a division may be made on this basis, but the reason for the varied use is not clear.

OTHER SMALLER   1. Pss. 3-40: the greater Davidic collection. All
GROUPINGS   (except Ps. 32) are attributed to David. Pss. 1 and 2 are clearly introductory to the Psalter.

2. Pss. 50-71: the smaller Davidic collection—the "prayers of David."

3. Pss. 41-48: assigned to the Sons of Korah (cf. 2 Chr. 20:19).

4. Ps. 49:72-82: assigned to Asaph (cf. 1 Chr. 16:4-7; 25:1 f.; Neh. 7:44).

5. Pss. 119-133: the "gradual" psalms or Songs of Ascents.

6. a) 17 Davidic: Pss. 100; 102; 107-109; 121; 132; 137-144.

b) Pss. 91-98: psalms of the kingdom.

c) *Hallel* (halleluiatic psalms): Pss. 103-106; 110-116; 134-135; 145-150.

THE DIVISIONS IN SCHEMATIC FORM:[3]

It appears that the Psalter is made up of three principal strata which correspond to three distinct periods: (1) point of arrival—the division in five books; (2) intermediate stage—the three major collections: one elohistic and two yahwistic; (3) starting point—the existence of smaller autonomous collections.

The greater Davidic collection is the earliest component, followed by the "prayers of David." Together they form the fundamental nucleus of the Psalter. These psalms belong to a collection attributed

---

[3]See G. Castellino, *Libro dei Salmi* (Turin: Marietti, 1955), p. 9.

5 books	I	II	III	IV	V
	Pss. 1-40	Pss. 41-71	Pss. 72-82; 83-88	Pss. 89-105	Pss. 106-150
3 coll.	A	B		C	
elohistic		41-82			
yahwistic	1-40		(83-88)		89-150
gradual					119-133
Asaph			49; 72-82		
Korah		41-48			
David	3-40	51-71 (85; 100; 102; 107-109; 121; 130; 132; 137; 144)			
single	1; 2; 32 etc.				

to David; it does not necessarily follow that he is their author. In the Hebrew, seventy-three of the psalms bear his name. The phrase *le dāwîd* ("of David," "belonging to David") does not prove or even imply Davidic authorship. There is no doubt, however, that it came to be regarded as such: until recent times it was believed that David was the author of all the psalms which bore his name. This view can no longer be sustained since the evidence against it is convincing. It is now generally recognized that, while there is no reason for doubting the presence of Davidic elements in the psalms ascribed to him, the majority of them cannot be his work. Nevertheless, he remains the originator of the psalm form and the organizer of the Israelite liturgy. Thus he is the principal author of the Psalter, that is, the most important and most eminent. But it is not possible to know even approximately how many of the psalms are his. Of the three collections, the elohistic is later than the first yahwistic: two psalms (Pss. 13; 39) of the first collection are repeated in the second (Pss. 52; 69), with Elohim in place of Yahweh.

The Psalter had taken its final shape before the completion of the LXX, that is, well before 200 B.C. The precise dates of the individual psalms cannot be fixed since the internal evidence is indecisive. At the beginning of the century it was customary (among non-Catholic scholars) to assign practically all the psalms to the postexilic period. Of recent years there has been a general tendency to find a large pre-exilic element in the Psalter. Albright "would date the contents of the Psalter in their present form between the eleventh and fourth centuries B.C."

4) The Titles of the Psalms

In the Hebrew text all except thirty-four of the psalms bear titles which vary considerably in extent and in character. These titles, though they are not original, must go back to comparatively early times, for in the third century B.C. the translators of the LXX could not understand them. These titles of the MT (Masoretic Text) have a historical value which must be given due weight, but they are not inspired. They may be grouped as follows:

TITLES DENOTING   1. David: 73 in all (sometimes combined
TRADITIONAL AUTHORS   with an allusion to some incident in David's
life).

   2. Solomon: 2 (Pss. 71; 126).

   3. Asaph: 12 (Pss. 49; 72-82).

   4. Sons of Korah: 11 (Pss. 41-42; 43-48; 83; 84; 86; 87).

   5. Heman the Ezrahite: 1 (Ps. 87; cf. 1 Kgs. 4:31).

   6. Ethan the Ezrahite: 1 (Ps. 88; cf. 1 Chr. 15:17-19; 25:5).

   7. Moses: 1 (Ps. 89).

The LXX ascribes twelve more psalms to David, while others are ascribed to the sons of Jonadab, Jeremiah, Haggai, and Zechariah.

TITLES GIVING THE   1. *Mizmor* (*psalmos*): 57—religious song ac-
LITERARY TYPES   companied by stringed instruments.

   2. *Shir* (song): 30—generally preceded or followed by *mizmor*.

   3. *Maskil* (obscure): 13—probably sapiential psalm.

   4. *Miktam* (obscure): 6—perhaps psalm of atonement (Pss. 15; 55-59).

   5. *Shiggaion* (obscure): 1—perhaps lament (Ps. 7).

   6. *Tehillah* (praise): 1—(Ps. 144) (*Tehillim* = Hebrew title of Ps.).

   7. *Tephillah* (prayer): 5—(Pss. 85; 89; 101; 141; 71).

TITLES CONTAINING   1. *Lamnasseah*: "to the choirmaster" (Vg.
MUSICAL DIRECTIONS   *in finem*)—55 Pss.

2. *Selah*: perhaps a pause; or, raise tone (71 times)—39 Pss.

3. *beneginoth*: "with stringed instruments"—6 Pss.

4. *el han-nehiloth*: "to the flutes"—1 (Ps. 5).

5. *al alamoth*: "for soprano" (literally "for maidens")—1 (Ps. 45).

6. *al hash-sheminith*: "for bass voices" (Vg. *pro octavo*)—2 (Pss. 6; 11).

7. *al hag-gittith* (Vg. *pro torcularibus*): reference to Gath—3 (Pss. 8; 80; 83).

8. *le/al Jeduthun*: name of chief musician—3 (Pss. 38; 61; 76).

TITLES OF   1. According to "Do Not Destroy": Pss. 56-58;
POPULAR MELODIES   74.

2. According to "The Hind of the Dawn": Ps. 21.

We may guess that "According to Muth-labben" (Ps. 9), "According to Lilies" (Pss. 44; 68), "According to Shushan Eduth" (Ps. 59), "According to Shoshannim Eduth" (Ps. 80; RSV, "According to Lilies. A Testimony"), "According to Mahalath" (Pss. 52; 87), "According to the Dove on Far-off Terebinths" (Ps. 55) are names of tunes.

TITLES REFERRING TO THE   1. A Song for the Sabbath: Ps.
LITURGICAL USE OF THE PSALMS   91.

2. *lehazkir*: "for the memorial offering" (cf. Lv. 2:2, 9)—Pss. 37; 69.

3. *lethodah*: "for the thank offering"—Ps. 99.

4. The "gradual" psalms—"Songs of Ascents" (probably sung by pilgrims to Jerusalem)—Pss. 119-133.

5) *The Literary Forms of Psalms*

The application of form criticism to the Old Testament writings has been nowhere more effective than in the study of Psalms. The pioneer worker in this field was H. Gunkel,[4] who sought to supplement analytical literary criticism by the study of literary forms (*Gattungen*) and of their setting in life (*Sitz im Leben*), together with the attempt to trace their history.

Gunkel reasoned as follows: We seek to classify the psalms. Now the psalms are literary products; hence any grouping or classification must be on a literary basis. If we note literary correspondences

---

[4]See H. Gunkel and J. Begrich, *Einleitung in die Psalmen* (Göttingen: 1933).

among different psalms we discover types of psalms. In order to understand each type we must study *how* it was formed, how the circumstances of time and place and the actions which surrounded its composition can explain why the psalm has spontaneously taken on such a literary form. Too often the psalms appear obscure simply because they have come to us from a milieu and civilization which differ on more than one point from those of the twentieth century and our Western culture. This is why we must put our finger on the concrete situation of each type of psalm and decide its function. It will then be enough to replace the psalms of a given family in their proper situation, to restore their natural background, for them to become readily intelligible. The method has shown itself remarkably fruitful.[5]

On the whole, the poetry of Israel is never merely personal, but it is born of the life of the people; it is, in a true sense, a product of the nation. And the principal source of inspiration was the cult (cf. Nm. 10:35; Ps. 67; Jdt. 15:9 f.; Ex. 15) in which, especially, Israel became conscious of its character as the people of God. The Psalter is not only a book of prayers and chants used in the second Temple and in the synagogue, it often reflects the cult before the Exile. (Many psalms were formed in and by the early cult of Israel.) The concrete situation, the *Sitz im Leben* which better than any other explains the origin of the psalms, is beyond doubt the liturgy of Israel.

> The cult of Israel: its great annual feasts, its daily sacrifices, the thanksgiving ceremonies, the days of prayer, the reading of the Law, the renewal of the Covenant—all this is the celebration of Yahweh's saving act and gives thanks to the God of Israel. The liturgy, for Israel as for us, cannot be a mere commemoration of past events. The whole saving deed—and especially the Exodus and all that it involved—was not only commemorated but was, in a certain manner, actualized as the saving act and word of God; thus the faithful could again live this event.[6]

The story of salvation is announced in the community; this authentic pronouncement of the Word of God is operative, it brings salvation.

---

[5] See P. Drijvers, *Les Psaumes* (Paris: Cerf, 1958), p. 5. Throughout this chapter I am constantly indebted to this valuable study.

[6] *Ibid.*, pp. 49 f. For an excellent treatment of the place of the psalms in the Church's liturgy see the series of six articles by Liam G. Walsh, *Doctrine and Life* (July-November, 1963; January, 1964).

This active memorial, itself the fruit of faith, must, at the same time, awaken faith—faith in Yahweh and his works. We may conclude that many of the psalms originated in the cult and liturgical feasts of Israel. In answer to the needs of a given ceremony, someone— king, priest, or prophet—composed suitable psalms. These psalms were repeated and became traditional. Eventually, well-defined styles evolved. A hymn demanded a certain technique; a thanksgiving psalm had its own rules and plan. In other words, definite literary forms had taken shape and were carefully followed.

A particular family of psalms may be discovered by the application of three criteria: (1) an identical concrete situation; (2) a common ground of concepts and sentiments; (3) a similar literary form, with the same style and the same structure. These three factors must be present together; one of them will not suffice to determine a literary form—this is particularly important in psalms of similar content. For example, psalms which develop a historical theme do not necessarily belong to the same family. The exegete, then, must examine not only the content of a psalm but also the concrete situation in which it was formed, and its literary form. In fact, it is the recognition of the *Sitz im Leben* and of the literary form that will enable him to be sure of the content and sense of the psalm.[7]

Of course, not all the psalms owe their existence to the cult; not all have a liturgical origin. This is true especially of the individual supplications which were born of a personal need or danger of the psalmist. But such psalms also became part of liturgical worship, after the Exile, for the Book of Psalms really came into its own in the second Temple where, as one psalmist puts it, Yahweh was "enthroned on the praises of Israel" (Ps. 21:3).

6) *The Classification of Psalms*

PSALMS OF   1. *Individual.* These constitute the largest single SUPPLICATION   class in the Psalter. They appear to have been, originally at least, the immediate concern of individual worshipers rather than of the congregation as a whole; the psalmists deal with their personal troubles. These psalms may be regrouped as:

a) psalms of supplication;
b) psalms of confidence.

---

[7] See Drijvers, *op. cit.*, pp. 49-55.

2. *Communal.* These were sung by the congregation on the occasion of some national calamity or when the community was threatened by some dire peril.

PSALMS OF   1. *Individual.* These were sung by individual worTHANKSGIVING shipers during the offering of sacrifice; they express gratitude for deliverance from trouble or for recovery from sickness.

2. *National.* These express gratitude on a national level.

HYMNS OF These hymns are entirely devoted to extolling the
PRAISE   goodness of Yahweh.

ROYAL   These psalms celebrate an event of the court or a royal
PSALMS   victory; or constitute a prayer for the king.

PSALMS   These psalms glorify the holy city, the dwelling place of
OF SION   Yahweh.

THE KINGSHIP OF   These hymns of praise acknowledge the one King
YAHWEH PSALMS   of Israel and of the world.

OTHER   1. *Wisdom Psalms.* These are psalms influenced by the
GROUPS   Wisdom movement.

2. *Psalms of a Deuteronomical Liturgy.* These comprise a small group which reflect a covenant liturgy inspired by Dt.

3. *Various Prayers.* This is a small collection of postexilic prayers.

3. PSALMS OF SUPPLICATION
1) Psalms of Individual Supplication

With the psalms of individual supplication we associate the psalms of confidence, which do not form a distinct class; in them the motive of confidence in God, present in all the supplication psalms, is predominant.

THE SITZ   The psalms of individual supplication did not originate
IM LEBEN   in the liturgy, but were motivated by individual distress.[8]

1. *Imminent danger of death.* The Israelite feared nothing so much as premature death; his ideal was long life (Ps. 101:25; cf. 90:15 f.). The canticle of Hezekiah is a good example of this (Is. 38:10,12). Premature death was regarded as punishment for sin (Ps. 54:24). The reason for this attitude is that the Old Testament (before the

---

[8]See *ibid.,* pp. 101-11.

second half of the second century B.C.) had an imprecise and incomplete idea of an afterlife. Sheol, the abode of the dead, is located beneath the earth (Pss. 21:29; 68:15 f.) and is sometimes referred to as the "Pit." It is thought of as a place of silence (Ps. 114:17), of darkness and forgetfulness (Ps. 87:12). There the dead, ghostly replicas of men lived a dreary existence, deprived of everything that made life desirable, and cut off from fellowship with God (Ps. 87:5). There is no praise of God (Pss. 6:6; 87:10-13). The psalmist, in describing the danger of death, often has recourse to hyperbole: he is about to enter Sheol; he is already there (Pss. 68:15; 87:4). His thanksgiving for deliverance celebrates a return from the dead (cf. 1 Sm. 2:6).

Here we must forget our distinction between soul and body. For a Semite, *soul* is a synonym of life or, often, the equivalent of the personal pronoun: "my soul" = "me." "My soul goes down to Sheol" = "I go down to Sheol" (Ps. 85:13; cf. 15:10; 29:4; 48:16; 88:49). It is not *a part* of man—what we call the soul—that survived after death, but a shadow of the *whole man*. It was only in the Hellenistic era, due to the influence of Greek philosophy, that the dichotomy soul/body was introduced into biblical thought; the principal witnesses of this evolution are 2 Mc. and Wis.

2. *Sickness.* The psalms have given us an excellent idea of the mentality of Old Testament man in face of sickness. It is Yahweh who has sent it and it is he who must cure it—secondary causes remain in the background (Pss. 37:3; 68:27; 101:11; Is. 38:12; 29:3). The psalms often mention the reasons why God sent the sickness: it is most often a punishment for sins (Ps. 37:4; 40:5). The prayer frequently includes a highly-colored description of the illness (Ps. 37:101; Is. 38:14). The sickness also gave the enemies of the stricken one an occasion of asserting themselves (Pss. 34:13-15; 40:6,9). Three kinds of enemies are distinguished:

a) Friends and relatives who regard the illness as the chastisement of a hidden fault (Ps. 37:12; Jb.; cf. Jn. 9:2): his friends have become his enemies.

b) The impious and blasphemers. The sufferer's virtue is ridiculed (Ps. 68:11-13). These men are really opposed to Yahweh and his providence.

c) Former enemies who take advantage of the stricken one's helplessness; besides, their previous charges against him are now vindicated: Yahweh has punished him (Pss. 30:12-14; 34:15 f.; 68:27; 108:22-25).

3. *False accusation.* Litigation was very common in Israel, while at the same time there was widespread corruption in the administration of justice. Here the distinction between rich and poor was glaring; too often the poor were oppressed by the ruling class (cf. 2 Sm. 12; 1 Kgs. 20; Dn. 13; Is. 1:23; 5:7; 11:3 f.; Am. 5:12; Jer. 5:26; 22:3). The situation was no better at the time of our Lord (cf. Lk. 18:2-5). The legislation of Israel had to take measures against false testimony and unjust sentences (Ex. 20:16; 23). The *lex talionis* was invoked (Dt. 19:18-20; cf. Ex. 21:23-25). Cases were generally tried before the gate of a town so that the phrase "before the gate" is often a synonym of "before the tribunal." A process could also take place in the royal palace (cf. Ps. 121:5). Before sentence the witnesses of both parties were heard: for acquittal a majority vote was necessary (cf. Ps. 126:5). Yahweh was often the best witness (Ps. 106:31). In default of witnesses a man might take an oath (Ps. 7:4-6). False witnesses and accusers are often indicated by metaphors: hunters (Pss. 7:16; 34:7; 56:7; 63:6; 139:6); robbers (Pss. 16:9-12; 55:7); lions (Pss. 7:3; 16:12; 56:5); dogs (Ps. 58:15 f.); snakes (cf. Ps. 57:5 f.).

In order to understand the background of the supplication psalms it is necessary to grasp the significance of anthropomorphisms in the Bible. For the Israelite, Yahweh was a living and personal God, never a first unmoved mover far apart from man and creation. The faith of Israel was not founded on philosophical reflection on the spirituality of Yahweh, but on the concrete experience of his active personality and of his nearness. This is why he is so easily represented anthropomorphically. He is approached as one approaches a man, with a surprising familiarity. We have only to read how men of God conversed with Yahweh: for example, Moses (Nm. 11:11-14); Joshua (Jos. 7:7-9); Elijah (1 Kgs. 17:20); Jeremiah (Jer. 15:17 f.; 20:7). But this does not mean that his transcendence was lost sight of; the prohibition to make any image of him is proof of that. It is, however, these anthropomorphisms that bring out the specific element in the Israelite concept of God: they emphasize the truth that the

Holy One of Israel is near and living. Thus we find that, in these psalms, Yahweh is called upon with insistence, for the appeal is addressed not to some distant divinity but to a living and personal God. This is why the pleading is at once so human and so poignant. It is especially in extreme need that one discovers in Yahweh a Person who is all-powerful and close at hand and ready to help.

THE   Ideally, the supplication psalms are composed of four ele-
STRUCTURE   ments: invocation, complaint, supplication, and motives.[9]

1. *The invocation.* The first words of the psalm are usually an appeal to God—often no more than the mention of the divine name. Sometimes the invocation is a little more developed, recalling, for example, the habitual goodness of God towards those who call upon him (Pss. 50:3; 70:2 f.; 85:5). It is noteworthy that it is sufficient to pronounce the name of Yahweh without the long string of epithets characteristic of pagan prayers; the invocation of the name is enough to bring one into his presence.

2. *The complaint.* The psalmist mentions his need and describes it in detail (Pss. 21:13; 30:14). He repeats the threats uttered against him (Pss. 21:9; 108:8). Often he concludes by insisting on his weakness and asserting that Yahweh alone can save him.

3. *The supplication.* This is the heart of the psalm. It is here especially that we note the simple, spontaneous attitude of the psalmist towards his God. He calls upon God: hear me, help me, protect me, save me, have pity on me. If Yahweh delays, the cry becomes bolder. awake, rise up, turn towards me, give me an answer (cf. Pss. 7:7; 43:24,27). The questions can become daringly insistent: How long will you forget me? Why do you remain so far away? When are you going to look on me again?

4. *The motives.* The psalmist puts forward reasons which guarantee that his prayer will be heard.

a) The attributes of Yahweh: mercy, kindness, justice, knowledge. These can be expressed by a title: Yahweh, my help, my savior, my strength. Or they may be developed in a phrase: You hear those who call upon you; you save the poor from the oppressor.

b) The confidence of the psalmist—based on the Covenant and the divine choice. It is *impossible* that the just man should be con-

---

[9]See *ibid.,* pp. 111-15.

founded, because this concrete deliverance for which he hopes is but the application to his particular case of national salvation and the redemption of the whole people of God. The God of the Covenant demands of men surrender and confidence; and when and where this confidence exists Yahweh will intervene.

c) Many other motives include: penance by fasting and mortification; the frailty of man; the brevity and precariousness of human life; a promise of thanksgiving; the psalmist's fidelity to Yahweh and his commandments; his innocence.

Psalms of supplication: 5; 6; 7; 12; 16; 21; 24; 25; 26; 27; 30; 34; 37; 38; 40; 41; 42; 50; 53; 54; 55; 56; 58; 60; 63; 68; 69; 70; 85; 87; 101; 108; 119; 129; 139; 140; 141; 142.

Psalms of confidence: 3; 10; 15; 22; 61; 130.

2) *Psalms of Communal Supplication*

These have the same structure as the individual supplications but they are the prayer of the whole nation. Here there is greater emphasis on the Covenant and the divine interventions of the past. Days of prayer and penance in Israel form the *Sitz im Leben* of these psalms. Such days of prayer were decreed on the occasion of national calamities, like war, a defeat in battle, a drought, a bad harvest, a pestilence, or an invasion of locusts. On the appointed day the people would assemble in the Temple (cf. 1 Kgs. 8:33-40; 2 Chr. 30:9; 1 Mc. 4:37), not to celebrate a feast but to do penance in sackcloth and ashes (1 Sm. 7:6; 1 Mc. 3:47; Jdt. 4:8-15). Joel has described a ceremony of this kind (Jl. 1:13 f.; 2:15-17).

The public supplication of the leaders of the people is to be seen in the same ritual context: Moses (Dt. 9:25-29); Joshua (Jos. 7:7-9); Jehoshaphat (2 Chr. 20:6-12); Ezra (Ez. 9:6-15; Neh. 9:6-37); Nehemiah (Neh. 11:5-11); similarly, the prayer of the people in 1 Mc. 3:50-53.

In these psalms one motive is stressed beyond others: Yahweh, this is your people—this is therefore your affair (Ps. 43:13; 73:2; 78:1; 79:16).

Psalms of communal supplication: 43; 57; 59; 73; 76; 78; 79; 81; 82; 84; 89; 107; 124; 136.

4. PSALMS OF THANKSGIVING[10]
1) *Psalms of Individual Thanksgiving*

THE SITZ   Like the rest of the Psalter, these psalms have their
IM LEBEN   place in the worship of Israel, but what is of particular
interest is that most of the thanksgiving psalms came into being
precisely as a liturgy. This is their *Sitz im Leben,* the concrete,
historical situation in which they took shape. Clear traces of this
origin are visible in many of them. There is, surely, a liturgical nuance
in the following passages: Psalms 9:15; 91:1-4; 115:14-19; 117; 137:1 f.
Regularly, the psalmist addresses the bystanders (we may infer that
he is thinking of worshipers in the Temple): Psalms 9:12; 29:5; 31:11;
33:4; 106:1-3; 117:1-4. Some psalms speak of a liturgical reunion
in the Temple: Psalms 39:10 f.; 106:32; 115:18 f. The Temple is
indicated by references to sacrifices in fulfillment of vows: Psalms
106:22; 115:17.

Admittedly, these psalms are very nearly the only evidence we
have for the existence in Israel of a liturgical ceremony of thanksgiving, but this evidence is compelling; the passages indicated do
not exhaust the relevant texts. We may go further and assert that a
close study of the thanksgiving psalms will enable us to reconstruct
the ceremony, at least in its broad outlines. It would have been
something like this: An Israelite, who had come safely through a
great danger, went up to the Temple, often accompanied by his
family and friends, there to be met by a priest or priests. He brought
a victim for sacrifice, usually in fulfillment of a vow. He gathered
about him a group of worshipers and recounted what Yahweh had
done for him. Here we have all the essentials of the thanksgiving
psalm. The whole was concluded by the offering of sacrifice. Psalm
117 has preserved a remarkable description of such a thanksgiving
liturgy.

It seems clear that an individual's act of thanksgiving, at least
when it was performed in the Temple, was not regarded as a private
devotion. Moreover, the ceremony was not always carried through
by, or on behalf of, just one man. In this regard Psalm 106 is illuminating because it shows us a communal thanksgiving ceremony which

---

[10]See W. Harrington, "Thanksgiving," *The Furrow*, 14 (1963), 225-33.

is obviously a carefully-organized liturgy. It is natural that many Israelites chose one or other of the great feasts—doubtless the joyous Feast of Tabernacles was especially favored—as an occasion when they could most fittingly give thanks to God. Hence it would happen that many would wish to perform the ceremony on the same day and then the priests would arrange them in groups according to the favors they had received; Psalm 106 distinguishes four such groups: travelers (vv. 4-9); prisoners (vv. 10-16); the sick (vv. 17-22); and sailors (vv. 23-32). The psalm opens with a liturgical invitation to those present, those who have come from many lands, urging them to give thanks to the merciful Lord (vv. 1-3). Then, corresponding to the four groups, come the four main sections of the psalm, all built on an identical plan. First, the particular predicament is described, after which we are told:

"Then they cried to the Lord in their need
and he rescued them from their distress" (6, 13, 19, 28).

Next the deliverance is outlined and each group is exhorted:

"Let them thank the Lord for his love,
for the wonders he does for men" (8, 15, 21, 31).

The ceremony concludes with a general recalling of God's benefits to men (vv. 33 f.).

Thus it appears that the thanksgiving psalm was originally the product, or rather the accompaniment, of such a religious ceremony, a ceremony that could have involved an individual or which may have been communal. But soon a distinct literary form emerged and psalms may have been composed without reference to the Temple or to any special ceremony. It follows that not *all* the thanksgiving psalms necessarily grew in the manner we have described; some of them may well be the spontaneous and personal outpourings of a grateful spirit. But, once gathered into the Psalter, they became community prayers, and that too is the role they play in the liturgy of the Christian Church.

THE
STRUCTURE
Most of the thanksgiving psalms follow a rather clearly-defined pattern of *proclamation, narrative,* and *invitation*—the last urging those present to join in giving thanks. The opening formula (the proclamation) always mentions gratitude to God or praise of him:

"I will praise you, Lord, with all my heart" (Ps. 9:2).

"I will bless the Lord at all times" (Ps. 33:2).

"It is good to give thanks to the Lord" (Ps. 91:2).

Sometimes the introduction is longer and the proclamation is developed into a short hymn (cf. Pss. 62:2-6; 91:2-7; 117:5-18). The body of the thanksgiving psalm is the narrative, normally done in three parts: description of the danger; anguished prayer; account of the gracious intervention of God. Psalm 114 will serve to illustrate this procedure:

1. *The danger.*

    "They surround me, the snares of death,/with the anguish of the tomb; they caught me, sorrow and distress."

2. *The Prayer.*

    "I called on the Lord's name:/'O Lord my God, deliver me.' "

3. *The intervention.*

    "How gracious is the Lord, and just;/our God has compassion. The Lord protects the simple hearts;/I was helpless so he saved me."

The danger in question may be of any kind, but often it is danger of death through illness or, not infrequently, through the machination of enemies. Whatever the danger may have been, the psalmist relives it—and nothing is lost in the telling. Thus, if his life had been threatened, he pictures himself as already dead, crying out from the depths of Sheol. At the same time, however, he makes it clear that he had never lost confidence in Yahweh, and if he does perhaps exaggerate the danger now, it is to emphasize the vigor of his confidence and to underline the significance of the divine intervention:

"You have been my help;/in the shadow of your wings I rejoice. My soul clings to you;/your right hand holds me fast" (Ps. 62:8 f.; cf. 137:7).

Finally, these psalms end with an invitation to those present; though this may also occur repeatedly within the psalm:

"Rejoice, rejoice in the Lord,/exult, you just!

O come, ring out your joy,/all you upright of heart" (Ps. 31:11).

This, in general, is the plan of the thanksgiving psalms. They may not, in every case, be worked out so elaborately and the different parts are not always clearly distinct, but on the whole they are readily recognizable.

Psalms of individual thanksgiving: 4; 9:1-21; 17; 29; 31; 33; 39; 62; 91; 106; 114; 115; 117; 137.

2) *Psalms of National Thanksgiving*

Thus far we have considered individual thanksgiving: hymns of gratitude for favors granted to individual Israelites, even though these benefits were regularly celebrated by a liturgical ceremony which could have taken a marked communal form. Now we may glance briefly at a smaller class of psalms: psalms of national thanksgiving. The *Sitz im Leben* of these psalms is to be sought in feasts of a national character, whether these are annual and recurring or whether they were extraordinary celebrations. Some of the psalms of this type have been occasioned by a victory or, more probably, by deliverance from imminent danger on a national scale (cf. Pss. 65; 123; 128). Others, like Psalm 64 and Psalm 66, thank God for a bounteous year of healthy stock and abundant harvest:

"The hills are girded with joy,/the meadows covered with flocks, the valleys are decked with wheat./They shout for joy, yes, they sing" (Ps. 64:14).

Thus the nation, no less than the individual Israelite, acknowledged the great goodness of its God. Surely these psalms must blend, with conspicuous ease, into the Christian cult, the thanksgiving and praise of the whole new Israel.

5. HYMNS OF PRAISE[11]

1) *The* Sitz im Leben

The hymn of praise has its roots in the beginning of Israel's history. The song of Miriam (Ex. 15:21)—which is the source of the later canticle of Moses (Ex. 15:1-19)—was a spontaneous celebration of the saving power of God manifested in the crossing of the Red Sea. The introduction to the ancient song of Deborah (Jgs. 5:3) also has a hymnal form, again in praise of a divine intervention. In short, each time that Yahweh shows himself in a terrifying theophany or in an event of history a hymn must follow (cf. Jdt. 16:1 f., 13). These canticles of praise, springing spontaneously from the recognition of a liberating intervention of Yahweh, receive a new value, one might say a "sacramental" quality, in that encounter of Yahweh

---

[11]See Drijvers, *op. cit.*, pp. 57-69.

with his people which is the liturgy. For it is in the liturgy that the *qahal*, the "church," relived the high deeds which God had wrought for the former generations; it is there that the old traditions of the Exodus and of Sinai were celebrated. It is there too that Israel became more conscious of being the people of the Covenant.

It is, therefore, in the framework of the feasts of Israel that we must generally set the origin of the psalms of praise. Hence we find that Elkanah went each year to Shiloh to offer sacrifice and "to worship the Lord of Hosts" (1 Sm. 1:3). The Prophet Amos, in condemning religious hypocrisy, mentions disdainfully "the noise of your songs . . . the melody of your harps" (Am. 5:23). Song was a constant factor in the feasts of Israel. For example, we find evidence of choral chants in the psalms: 135; 117:2-4; 134:19 f. Psalm 150 reminds us of a conductor of an orchestra inviting each instrument in turn to join in.

The active participation of the people took the form of rhythmical handclapping (Pss. 46:2; 97:8) and cries and exclamations of joy (1 Kgs. 1:39 f.; 2 Chr. 23:11-13; 29:30). The principal exclamation was the divine name "Yahweh," generally in its shortened form "Yah." (*Allelu-Yah* = "Praise Yahweh.") Another exclamation of joy was "Amen" (cf. 1 Chr. 16; 36; Jdt. 15:10; Pss. 40:14; 17:19; 88:53; 105:48). The phrase, "for his love has no end," occurs not only in the psalms but in several other places (for example, 2 Chr. 5:13; 7:3,6; 20; 21; Jer. 33:11). The participation of the people expressed itself also in certain rites and gestures: lifting up of hands (Pss. 27:2; 76:3; 133:2; 140:2); bowing low (Pss. 94:6; 95:9); kneeling (Ps. 94:6); prostrations (Pss. 5:8; 94:6). Other examples are: 2 Chr. 6:12–7:3; 29:28 f.; Ez. 3:11; 1 Mc. 4:54-59.

2) *The Structure*

What characterizes the hymn is not only the tone of praise and glorification but the fact that this praise is essentially disinterested. There are no personal petitions, no thought of self: the hymn is wholly theocentric. Besides, most of the hymns have a similar structure and are, ideally, composed of three parts: (1) an invitation to praise God; (2) the development, indicating motives for this praise; (3) a conclusion—often a repetition of the introductory invitation.

1. The *invitation* is a call to praise God. It is addressed in the first place to those present (Pss. 32:1-3; 67:5; 112:1). But all nations can be summoned to render praise (Pss. 99:1 f.; 116); as well as the angels (Pss. 28:1 f.; 148:2) and inanimate nature (Pss. 18:2 f.; 28; 148:3-10). Indeed, psalms like 148 and 150 are an invitation to nature to join in mighty orchestra with the feeble praises of men (cf. the Benedicite [Dn. 3:57-88]). In some hymns the invitation is addressed to the psalmist himself (Pss. 102:1 f.; 103:1; 145:1).

2. The central part of the hymn lists the *motives* for praising Yahweh: his power, goodness, love, and solicitude for his people. Most often the section is introduced by "for" or "because" (see Pss. 32:4; 134:3-5; 135; 149:4). Yahweh is the center of this praise. The psalmists celebrate the works of his providence and his interventions in history; they rejoice in the creation of the universe and of man and in the deliverance from Egypt. Yahweh is praised for his promised salvation (Ps. 28:10).

3. A formal *conclusion* is not always present. When it exists it is usually a repetition of the introductory invitation (Pss. 8:10; 102:22; 103:35) or a short prayer (Pss. 18:15; 32:22).

The variety achieved within this framework may be judged by comparing some "cosmic" hymns: Psalms 8; 18; 28; 103.

Psalm 28 is a sort of litany of the storm-God. After a brief invitation to give glory to God (vv. 1 f.), the author enumerates and describes the characteristic manifestations of this "voice of Yahweh" which manifests his glory and terrifies the proudest creatures (Ps. 3:10). A brief conclusion mentions the people of Israel for whom God reserves his blessing.

Psalm 18 is a hymn to the beauty of the heavens, with particular emphasis on the splendor of the sun, which proclaims the glory of God (vv. 2-7). It ends with a long meditation on the Law (vv. 8-15) which also illuminates and warms men. (This is perhaps a later addition.)

Psalm 103 is the great cosmic hymn; it brings to mind Gn. 1 and Jb. 38-40. The starting point of the three passages is the same: the contemplation of nature by a man of observant disposition who finds in it order and harmony. But while Gn. 1 is a didactic presentation in rhythmic prose and Jb. 38-40 is a grandiose "theodicy" cast in epic form, Psalm 103 takes a middle course. It has neither the somewhat cold rigor of the first account of creation nor the vivid fantasy of Job: it is a typical example of religious lyrical poetry. The author addresses God and expresses his admiration as he describes, with a rare sense of the picturesque, of color, and of movement, the world that God has made. The author is an optimist who loves nature and sees it as a means of drawing near to God.

Psalm 8 marks a transition from the "cosmic" hymn to the "human"— which is more interested in man than in things and goes from man to God without passing by other creatures. Thus the psalm mentions God's work: his heaven; the moon and the stars (v. 4)—only to lead to the contemplation of man made "a little less than a god" and established lord of creation (vv. 6-9).

Psalm 112 is a typical "human" psalm. It does mention the glory of God "above the heavens," but its real interest is on the one hand the praise of God in the mouth of man and on the other hand the gifts of God to men. One has the impression that God's glory resides especially in his mercy: God has manifested his greatness more in raising up Job from his dunghill than by creating heaven and earth.

At first sight Psalm 102 seems very like Psalm 103, but fundamentally the attitude of both psalmists is quite different. The one, a poet of nature, proceeds from the outer things to the inward things— from the world to God. The other has a mediocre feeling for nature, but is a searching observer of the human and moral world. He finds the greatness of God in man's humility and in all the manifestations of the divine mercy. Though Psalm 102 is less poetic than Psalm 103, it outstrips it in psychological and religious depth.[12]

Hymns of Praise: 8; 18; 28; 32; 67; 99; 102; 103; 110; 112; 113; 116; 134; 135; 144; 145; 146; 147; 148; 149; 150.

6. ROYAL PSALMS

A number of psalms are concerned with the king of Israel. There is no question of any new literary form; these are hymns, thanksgiving psalms, supplications, but the place which the king occupies in them gives them a special character. For the king of Israel had a privileged role in the religion of Israel: he is not the profane leader of a people called to a supernatural destiny; rather, he is himself the

---

[12]See P. Auvray, IB, pp. 599-601.

instrument of the divine plan; he participates in the promises and in the supernatural character of the history which he helps to shape. He is at once the representative of God who leads the people, and the people's spokesman before God. But, above all, the king is the representative of a dynasty which is the object of divine favor and the recipient of the divine promise (2 Sm. 7). The royal psalms, or most of them, are messianic.

1) *The* Sitz im Leben

The setting of these psalms is to be sought in the court of the kings of Israel. It must be kept in mind that the king of Israel was the prince of a theocratic nation and not an autonomous sovereign. Yahweh was the true King of the nation and his earthly representative was his "anointed"–"chosen to sit upon the throne of the kingdom of the Lord over Israel" (1 Chr. 28:5). He must walk before Yahweh as David did (1 Kgs. 9:4; 2 Chr. 7:17). When the day of his accession, or its anniversary, was celebrated, when a royal marriage was solemnized or when an exultant procession went to meet his triumphal return after a victory, when prayers were offered for the success of a campaign—it was never forgotten that he was the Lord's anointed. On such occasions the royal canticles were sung in the palace or Temple.

2) *Characteristics*

These psalms have a certain number of common characteristics, due, no doubt, to the court ceremonial.

1. Description of the king in his magnificence (Ps. 44:2,4,6,9). The other royal psalms complete this image: the king is enthroned in Sion, in majesty and glory, wearing a crown of gold, honored by all. The righteousness of the monarch is extolled.

2. The blessing and prosperity of his reign are presented as consequences of the favor of Yahweh. The king is not only the anointed of Yahweh, he is his son (Pss. 2:7; 109:3); this is why Yahweh blesses him and hears his prayers, leads him in battle and grants him victory. The first of the royal line, David was the well-beloved of Yahweh in a special way, the pledge of the blessings to be granted to his line (Pss. 88:20-38; 131:11-18; 143:10).

3. Prayers for the king—at his accession, when setting out on a campaign, or simply in order to obtain a happy and peaceful reign

(Pss. 17:1 f.; 19:3,5,10; 44:5; 143:12-14). On his part the king promises Yahweh that he will uphold his justice and truth (Ps. 100).

4. A short oracle indicates Yahweh's attention to the prayer of the king and people, and the assurance of his fidelity to his promise (Pss. 2:7-9; 19:7-9; 88:20-38; 109:5-7; 131:11-18).

The royal psalms: 2; 19; 20; 44; 71; 88; 100; 109; 131; 143.

3) Messianic Psalms[13]

The royal psalms are ancient poems dating from the monarchic age and reflect the court language and ceremonial. In their original composition they speak of a contemporary king and they visualize directly a king seated on the throne of David. But the king of the Chosen People is an "anointed one," a "messiah," and the promises made by God to the Dynasty of David envisaged a privileged descendant in whom God will be well-pleased and whom he will employ to bring his saving plan to fulfillment. These psalms are messianic from the beginning.

> It has been maintained that Psalms 2, 71, and 109 were at first royal psalms, and were modified after the Exile in a messianic sense; but it is very hard to say what the revisions were. It is more reasonable to suppose that these psalms, like Nathan's prophecy and other texts referring to royal messianism, had a twofold meaning from the moment of their composition: every king of the Davidic line is a figure and a shadow of the ideal king of the future. In fact, none of these kings attained this ideal, but at the moment of enthronement, at each renewal of the Davidic covenant, the same hope was expressed, in the belief that one day it would be fulfilled. All these texts, then, are messianic, for they contain a prophecy and a hope of salvation, which an individual chosen by God will bring to fulfillment.[14]

Certain psalms, or parts of psalms, are recognized as messianic in the New Testament:[15]

1. *The royal psalms.* Psalms 2; 44; 71; 88:20-38; 109; 131:11-18.

2. Psalms 15; 21 (cf. Mt. 27:39,43,46; Jn. 19:24; Heb. 2:12; Acts 2:25,28; 13:35).

---

[13]See pp. 226-29.

[14]Roland de Vaux, *Ancient Israel, Its Life and Institutions,* trans. John McHugh (New York: McGraw-Hill, 1961), p. 110.

[15]See Drijvers, *op. cit.,* p. 211.

3. Parts or verses of the following psalms are referred to the Messiah.

8 (Heb. 2:6; 1 Cor. 15:27; Eph. 1:21; Phil. 3:21; 1 Pt. 3:22)
15 (Acts 2:25-28)
18 (Rom. 10:18)
30 (Lk. 23:46; Mt. 26:34)
40 (Jn. 15:25)
67 (Eph. 4:8)
68 (Mt. 27:34,38; Mk. 15:36; Jn. 2:17; 15:25; 19:28; Rom. 15:3; Acts 1:16-20)
77 (Mt. 13:34 f.)
96 (Heb. 1:6)
101 (Heb. 1:10-12)
108 (Acts 1:16-20)
117 (Mt. 21:42; Mk. 11:9; Jn. 10:24; Acts 3:11; 1 Pt. 2:4-7)

It does not follow that in every case the original text is strictly messianic: it may be that the New Testament writer is using the Old Testament passage in an accommodated sense. The precise intention of the New Testament writer has to be determined.

7. PSALMS OF SION

When David had captured the Jebusite stronghold of Jerusalem he first of all made it his capital and then, by transporting the Ark there, established it as a religious shrine. With the building of the Temple of Solomon, Sion became very definitely the religious center of the kingdom, the place which Yahweh had chosen (Pss. 77:68 f.; 67:17). Later, when Jerusalem alone had withstood the assaults of Sennacherib, belief in the inviolability of Sion assumed the nature of a dogma, and Jeremiah, in vain, tried to break down that presumptuous confidence (cf. Jer. 7:4-7). Nebuchadnezzar proved that the Prophet's threats were not empty words. During the Exile, ruined Sion became the center of messianic hopes (Is. 60; 66; Zech. 8). Though the Second Temple was not built according to the ideal specifications of Ezekiel (chapters 40-43), it was raised in the atmosphere of his teaching and looked to the future, to the new Jerusalem, the spiritual capital of all men. It is to be expected that there are psalms, both before the Exile and after the restoration, which sing of the city and its Temple.

1) *The* Sitz im Leben

These psalms of Sion are particularly in place on the lips of pilgrims to the holy city. If not all of them were composed precisely for this purpose, at least the pilgrimage must speedily have become their natural liturgical setting. The Law prescribed three annual pilgrimages —Pasch, Pentecost, and Tabernacles—which all adult Israelite men were bound to attend (Ex. 23:17; 34:23; Dt. 16:16); in practice, those who lived at any distance from Jerusalem chose one or other of the feasts. Jews of the Diaspora made a valiant effort to visit the holy city at least once in a lifetime. It is clear that pilgrimages to Sion were frequent and were accompanied by special ceremonies (cf. Pss. 23; 83; 14).

Some of the psalms of Sion can be fitted, with a high degree of probability, into a definite historical setting. Psalm 23 was likely composed on the occasion of David's solemn translation of the Ark of Jerusalem. Psalms 45, 47, and 75 would seem to celebrate the deliverance of Sion from Sennacherib in 701 B.C. or 688 B.C. The other three, of their nature, cannot be placed in a determined historical background: Psalm 83 extolls the Temple as the dwelling place of Yahweh and the center of the cult, while Psalm 86 looks to an idealized Sion as the spiritual capital of mankind. Psalm 121 is patently a pilgrim song.

2) *The Structure*

The psalms of Sion are hymns and have the structure of hymns; but, like many of the hymns of praise, the format is not rigidly applied. Ideally they contain (1) an invitation to praise Sion, or Yahweh who has chosen Sion; (2) the motives for this praise; (3) a conclusion which is usually a repetition of the introductory invitation.

Psalms of Sion: 23; 45; 47; 75; 83; 86; 121.

8. THE KINGSHIP OF YAHWEH PSALMS

Israel's conception of God as the King of Israel is found early in sacred history: Ex. 15:18; Nm. 23:21; Dt. 33:5; Jgs. 8:22; 1 Sm. 8:7; 12:12. This God was enthroned in their midst, on the Ark of the Covenant; more precisely, he was seated between the cherubim, or upon them, above the Ark: "The Lord is enthroned on the cherubim" (Pss. 17:11; 79:2; 98:1; Dn. 3:55; 1 Kgs. 19:15). Yahweh said to Moses: "From above the mercy seat, from between the two cherubim that are upon the ark of the testimony, I will speak with you" (Ex. 25:22). Ex. 37:1-9 gives a description of the Ark: the "mercy seat" or "propitiary" was the golden cover of the Ark and the cherubim were the two sphinx-like creatures placed at either end of the cover; the whole resembled an elaborate throne. In the gloom of the tent of assembly and later in the darkness of the Holy of Holies, Yahweh was enthroned invisibly upon the Ark. Alternatively, the Ark is called the footstool of Yahweh (Ps. 131:7; cf. 98:5).

1) *The* Sitz im Leben

The *Sitz im Leben* of the psalms of the Kingship of Yahweh is found in the liturgical feasts of Israel. This, we have seen, is the setting of the hymns of praise, but these psalms, too, are hymns of praise. S. Mowinckel[16] has posited the existence of a New Year ceremony of the enthronement of Yahweh, on the model of the Babylonian annual enthronement of Marduk. The existence of such a feast in Israel cannot be demonstrated; it remains a hypothesis and, seemingly, a doubtful one. Others have suggested that, in celebrating the Kingship of Yahweh, the intention was to extol the universal kingdom of the future; the emphasis is eschatological.

The true position may be quite simply that the Kingship of Yahweh, acknowledged from the earliest history of the people, was spontaneously honored in the liturgical celebrations. The liturgy of Israel should be taken on three levels, for present, past, and future were united in one actual celebration. The Covenant of the past is regarded as still at work, and the present generation enters into it consciously and freely, while it looks already, full of confidence, to the full realization on the day when Yahweh will appear as King over the whole earth. It is, doubtless, in the background of such a liturgy that we must recognize the background of our psalms of the Kingship of Yahweh.[17]

---

[16]*The Psalms in Israel's Worship*, trans. D. R. Ap-Thomas (Nashville, Tenn.: Abingdon, 1962), I, pp. 106-92.

[17]See Drijvers, *op. cit.*, pp. 154 f.

2) The Structure

These psalms are hymns of praise and have the characteristic form of hymns.

1. *The invitation* (cf. Pss. 46:2,7; 95:11 f.; 96:1; 97:5 f.). This invitation is always a call to praise and joy, motivated by the royalty of Yahweh.

2. *Presentation of the King.* Terrible, majestic, Yahweh is seated on his throne (Pss. 92:2; 96:2; 98:6; 46:8-10).

3. *The manifestation of the royalty of Yahweh* is effected in creation and redemption and is renewed in Israel at each liturgical celebration (Pss. 46:4 f.; 92:3 f.; 97:2 f.).

3) Characteristics

Yahweh reveals himself as Master and King, either in the elements or in the slow formation of his people and his benevolent protection of them. This royalty of Yahweh is actualized in the cult; hence the exclamation which we encounter five times in these psalms: "The Lord is king" (Pss. 46:9; 92:1; 95:10; 96:1; 98:1); while at the same time there is an eye to the future, to that longed-for age when he will reign manifestly over all. The influence of Second Isaiah is marked in this universalist perspective (cf. Pss. 96:6-8; 95:8-10). When he does come to establish his kingdom over the whole earth, Yahweh will appear as Judge (Ps. 95:12 f.).

The Kingship of Yahweh Psalms: 46; 74; 92; 95; 96; 97; 98.

9. OTHER GROUPS

1) Wisdom Psalms

It is to be expected that the Wisdom movement would have inspired some, at least, of the psalms.[18] In fact, quite a large number are markedly sapiential in treatment. These psalms may be grouped according to their stand on the question of retribution.[19] Many of them take for granted, either more or less, the traditional position that virtue is rewarded and wickedness punished in this life. Other psalmists, like Job and Qoheleth, are painfully aware that this facile

---

[18]See pp. 243-45.
[19]See Castellino, *op. cit.*, pp. 729-31.

solution does not answer the problem, while a few seem to glimpse
the true answer.

The greatest number of wisdom psalms represent the traditional
teaching and thus do not really face up to the problem of retribution
at all. In a second group the anomaly of the suffering of the just
and the prosperity of the wicked is keenly felt, and God is asked
to restore the equilibrium by punishing sinners and restoring well-
being to the just. The psalms of a third group take a step towards the
ultimate solution when they question the contentment of the wicked
in their prosperity and when they underline the true good of the
just: the possession of God, and his approval, despite their trials.
Finally, three of these psalms (together with the supplication Psalm
16) reach, or at least very nearly attain, the ultimate solution. It is
seen that retribution is not a matter of prosperity or the lack of it;
it is not spelled out in terms of the things of this world:

> "Let your hand, O Lord, rescue me from men,
>   from men whose reward is in this present life. . . .
> As for me, in my justice I shall see your face
>   and be filled, when I awake, with the sight of your glory"
>   (Ps. 16:14 f.).

> "What else have I in heaven but you?
>   apart from you I want nothing on earth. . . .
> To be near God is my happiness" (Ps. 72:25,28).

Wisdom psalms: a) 1; 14; 51; 111; 118; 126; 127.
               b) 9; 11; 13; 52; 93.
               c) 35; 90; 138.
               d) 36; 48; 72; (16).

2) *Psalms of a Deuteronomical Liturgy*[20]

Five psalms (80; 94; 77; 104; 105) are closely related to Deuteronomy
(especially to Dt. 5-11) and appear to form a special "liturgy."

It is notable that the same principal motifs recur frequently in
Dt.; these are: (1) the observance of the statutes and ordinances

---

[20]See *ibid.*, pp. 677-81.

(for example, Dt. 5:1 f.; 6:1-9); (2) an admonition to fidelity to the true cult of Yahweh (for example, Dt. 6:10-16; 8:11-18). The admonition is accompanied by threats (for example, Dt. 4:26-29; 8:19 f.), and promises of easy conquest (for example, Dt. 6:18 f.; 7:16-24) and great fertility (for example, Dt. 7:13-15; 8:7-10); (3) commemoration of the events of the Exodus (for example, Dt. 6:6-9; 11:18-21) by a "commemorative discourse."

This group of psalms not only reflects these motifs but reflects also a liturgical function which gave concrete expression to the prescriptions of Dt. After an initial invitation to praise Yahweh (Pss. 80:2-4; 94:1 f.) the motifs of Dt. recur:

1. Recall of the law and statutes (Pss. 80:5 f.; 77:5 f.; 104:8-10).
2. The "commemorative discourse" (Pss. 80:7 f.; 104).
3. The admonition (Pss. 80:9-13; 94:8-11; 77; 105).
4. The promises (Ps. 80:14-17).

The liturgical action suggested by these psalms fulfilled the prescription of Dt. 27:32 (cf. Jos. 8; 24) that the commandments should be reiterated and the events of the Exodus, and the Covenant, should be recalled at an assembly of the people. In practice, this would have taken place at the great feasts.

3) Various Prayers

Five of the gradual psalms (120; 122; 125; 132; 133) form a small collection of postexilic prayers. Though they might have been attached to some of the greater groups, it seems best to consider them apart. Psalm 120 treats of the continual and loving protection of God, while the theme of Psalm 122 is the humble expectation of mercy. The wonder and deep joy of the restoration are beautifully caught in Psalm 125. Psalm 132 would seem to reflect the first harmonious relationship of the returned exiles. The group is suitably rounded off by the invitation, to priests and levites, to praise the Lord in his sanctuary through the hours of the night.

10. DOCTRINAL ASPECTS OF PSALMS
1) The Problem of Suffering in the Supplication Psalms

For a long time the problem of individual suffering was not prominent in Israelite thought. The religion of Israel was always theocentric:

attention was riveted on the action of God, and the consequences of this action for the people or the individual were secondary considerations. Besides, the thought of Israel was collective; hence for a time the sufferings of the individual were overlooked. Nobody could count himself innocent because, as a member of the community, each was responsible for the sins of others. On the other hand, if the individual did not receive earthly reward—the only conceivable retribution— the community would be recompensed by the blessings of Yahweh. The religious psychology of the individual was eclipsed in great measure by that of the community.

The people of God had had long experience of suffering and had come to interpret it as a punishment for sin or as the providential means of preparing an obedient people. Each individual has to walk the same road; each is tried by God, by means of enemies, sickness, and mortal dangers. His anguish and personal suffering, like the salvation which comes to him from Yahweh, constitute the elements of a history of salvation that is intimate and personal but which reflects the great redemptive drama in which God has cast his people. So it is that the concrete experience of the psalmist is not something exclusively individual; it is a particularly eloquent image of the great event which concerns the whole people.

The suffering of the just man seems to have been taken for granted (cf. Pss. 33:20; 137:7; 36:39; 49:15), but Yahweh saves him from it all at last (Ps. 125:5). Suffering and pain lead to happiness and joy because they enable one to make expiation for sin, since they are a process designed to purify us and to open our hearts to God. But suffering has a deeper meaning still. Many times the psalms speak of the "poor"—the *'anawim* (for example, Pss. 9; 10; 21; 24; 27; 33; 36; 68:33 f.; 73:19; 85:1 f.; 131:15; 149:4). These were humble and pious Jews, from all strata of society; most often, perhaps, from the less fortunate classes, without necessarily being poor in the strict sense. They were men whom suffering had tried and matured and who had learned the true attitude of humility and abandonment before Yahweh. This is why, even in the midst of suffering, the psalmist is confident that Yahweh is near (Pss. 25:2; 108:21 f.; 138:23); and he realizes that the divine consolation will be in proportion to his suffering (Ps. 93:19).

Jesus Christ is the *'anaw* par excellence. The four evangelists, in describing his passion and death, have explicitly referred to the psalms of supplication, notably Psalms 21; 30; 37; 68; 87. In these psalms the primitive Church has recognized the voice of Christ addressed to his Father. The other psalms speak to us of Christ or are addressed to Christ; but here it is his own voice that we hear, with its expression of immense confidence in his Father. Christ himself has had full experience of suffering (Lk. 24:26; Heb. 4:15). In abandonment and love, he has willed to accept the ultimate consequences of his Incarnation; he has endured the pains that are the lot of sinful humanity. The mystery of the passion and death of Jesus, of his dereliction, but also of his love, takes life when we recite the psalms of supplication.

2) *The Old Testament Notion of Thanksgiving*

When we turn to the Bible we soon perceive that the *Heilsgeschichte*, the salvation history, is throughout dominated by the realization of God's free choice of Israel and by the awareness that this was no isolated act but a continual grace which tends to fulfillment—fulfillment in Christ. And in the light of this awareness it is felt, more or less confusedly, that each particular gift of Yahweh, even his benefits to individual men, is a consequence of that choice and, in its own modest way, a moment of this great history. Therefore the Israelite spontaneously reacted to the divine generosity, towards the nation or towards himself, by wonder at the unbounded goodness of God, by praise and thanksgiving. Even beyond the horizon of Israel the biblical view is that any man who comes to the knowledge of God must react in the same way: it is the proper and the only reasonable attitude of the creature. Failure to act so was, in Paul's eyes, the capital sin of paganism: "Though they knew God, they did not honor him as God or give thanks to him" (Rom. 1:21).

Old Testament thanksgiving is never merely gratitude for past favors; it ever looks to the future and to a higher grace; and indeed, in the time of fulfillment, thanksgiving dominates the prayer of Christians, as we may readily learn from Acts and from the New Testament epistles. Yet gratitude does remain, in Israel, the distinctive feature of this prayer. Thanksgiving, we have noted, always goes along with profession of faith in God and with the recognition of his glory and of his goodness, because the acknowledgment of God inevitably gives rise to praise of him and calls forth gratitude for his generosity. Above all else, it is the merciful and saving work of God that fills the heart of the Israelite with overflowing gratitude. For him, thanksgiving is the public confession of determined divine acts; to thank God is to publish his greatness, to proclaim the marvels he has wrought, to bear testimony to his works.

It should be noted, however, that the psalms of thanksgiving by no means exhaust the Bible's stock of thanksgiving hymns. The attitude of thankfulness to God is, as we have seen, characteristically biblical, and once the distinctive literary form of the thanksgiving psalm had evolved it is natural to expect that it would have been rather widely exploited. An excellent representative of the form is the canticle of Hezekiah (Is. 38:10-20) and, significantly, it has an unmistakable liturgical suggestion: "The Lord will save me,/and we will sing to stringed instruments all the days of our life,/at the house of the Lord" (v. 20). We may cite as further examples the canticle of Hannah (1 Sm. 2:1-10) and the prayer of Jonah (Jon. 2:2-9)—this last is of special interest. Though obviously not placed in a liturgical setting— Jonah prays "from the belly of the fish"—yet it still looks to the Temple: "When my soul fainted within me,/I remembered the Lord; And my prayer came to thee/into thy holy Temple" (v. 7). This is surely an echo of the origin of such psalms, while at the same time it offers striking evidence that the Israelite, while maintaining that Yahweh could be adequately worshiped only in Jerusalem, nevertheless believed that he might pray anywhere and offer thanksgiving in any circumstance, and that his prayer would be heard. Nor is the thanksgiving psalm confined to the Old Testament. The *Benedictus* and *Magnificat* are much influenced by the form and, outside of the Bible, we have the *Hodayoth*, the hymns of the Essene community of Qumran.

We have remarked that the most significant feature of the thanksgiving psalms is the relating of the benefit received, precisely because this was a manifestation of God's goodness and redounded to his glory. Here we find that close association of praise and thanksgiving so characteristic of the Bible. It is in his great works and because of his great goodness that God appears worthy of all praise, and it is for the same reason that he must be thanked. This situation quite satisfied the Hebrews, but if we, in our Western way, would like to be more precise (and Western precision is not always an improvement on biblical language) we might say that praise regards God in himself, whereas thanksgiving looks to his gifts.

An important element of the thanksgiving ceremony is that the Israelite, by openly acknowledging the benefit received, bears witness to the goodness of God. He can point to one more instance of God's solicitude for his people; it is precisely because he is conscious of being one of God's people that he feels urged to go up to the Temple and there praise God with his brethren:

"I will tell of your name to my brethren

and praise you where they are assembled" (Ps. 21:23).
The man who has so experienced the goodness of the Lord becomes a witness of that goodness, an apostle of his fellowmen.

3) *Redemption and Creation in the Hymns of Praise*

The hymns of praise may be regarded as the reaction, the *amen* of the Israelite community to the revelation of God. And, in the Bible, God's revelation, the proclamation of his Word, is never the presentation of a doctrine, of a system, of philosophical reflections on divine realities: its object is facts, *events*. It is of these events that the hymns of praise sing. The reaction of the Chosen People as revealed by these hymns is always a reaction to facts—to the experience of God. An analysis of the central part of the hymn, the motives, shows that this experience of God rests above all on two events: creation and redemption, but on redemption primarily. In fact, two psalms celebrate exclusively the one and the other of these themes: Psalm 103 sings of creation and Psalm 104 of redemption. Usually, however, the motives are more varied. Thus creation dominates in Psalms 8; 18; 28; 32; 148; it also appears in Psalms 134; 135; 144; 145. Redemption dominates in Psalms 134 and 135; and it is present in Psalms 110; 144; 145; 147; 148.

In studying *how* Israelites understood creation and redemption we must begin by noting that this spiritual experience was first and foremost an experience of salvation and that their concept of God was founded on the events of sacred history, on the fact that God had drawn near to his people. Only later, as a result of further reflection, did they become aware of their relation of creatures vis-à-vis the Creator. The Bible does not begin with a philosophy to end in a theology; on the contrary, the data which it possesses on being, on the cosmos, and on creation are the fruit of a reflection which presupposed the consciousness of belonging to the people of God, of having been chosen by Yahweh.[21]

> When the psalms speak of *redemption* they have especially in view the establishment of the people of God by the deed of the Exodus and of Sinai. The marvels of Yahweh, the *miribilia et prodigia Dei*, are, above all, the deliverance from Egypt, the crossing of the Red Sea, the journey through the desert, the legislation of Sinai and the possession of the Promised Land. By these events Israel was constituted the people of God. In them Yahweh showed himself to be the Savior, the *Go'el* of Israel: he delivered his people from slavery. He had willed to play the part of one who pays the ransom, like the member of a family who undertakes to honor the debts of his poorer relations. But this family link was not based on blood relationship; it was based on a call, on a free choice. And the ransom was not a sum of money but the sovereignly free will of him who is Lord of Israel and of all peoples, and who redeemed from slavery his Chosen People.[22]

The idea of *creation* is the second principal theme of the psalms of praise, but in this context we take creation in a broad sense. It is a matter of the activity of God as Master of nature, as Providence. It is only later, after mature reflection on that idea, that the more formal notions of Creator, of creation, and of creature were arrived at. The starting point of this reflection was the encounter of Israel with the living God. It was seen that Yahweh, the God of Israel, was powerful in the world of nature and of men—the psalms extol this providence (cf. Pss. 146:7-9; 110:4 f.). Eventually the idea of creation in the strict sense emerged: we find it in the narrative of Gn. 1 (in contrast to the more primitive concept of Gn. 2) and in the promise of Is. 54:5 (cf. Jer. 31:35-37; Ps. 52:6,9). Yahweh, the God of Israel, is the Creator-God; but he remains the God who has called Israel into being and has surrounded her with his love. A psalm which presents the might of Yahweh revealed in the storm ends with reassuring words to his people (Ps. 28:10 f.; cf. 94:7).

---

[21]See Drijvers, *op. cit.*, pp. 70 f.
[22]*Ibid.*, pp. 72 f.

4) The Kingship of Yahweh

The nearness of God and the kingdom of God are the two principal themes of the Kingship of Yahweh psalms.[23] The end of all revelation is communion between God and man. God wills to draw near to man, he wills to establish his kingdom in the midst of humanity. God's dominion over man is aimed at elevating man to communion with God and hence, mercifully, the reign of Yahweh was progressively manifested. The earlier prophets visualized this kingship as the "Judgment" of Yahweh on Israel and on the wicked. The more recent prophets contemplated a re-created world standing in the shadow of God's presence; while the authors of the apocalypses described the establishment of the kingdom in the scenario of a cosmic catastrophe. In the wisdom literature the kingdom of God was presented as the fruit and the progressive realization of the plan of the divine wisdom. The New Testament announced the kingdom as imminent, thanks to the death and resurrection of Christ, or as already come in his person, and put the accent on its essential interior character, founded on charity. Our Christian world lives in the expectation of the full manifestation of this kingdom at the end of time. All these aspects are covered by the one concept of "kingdom of God." There is no conflict between them, nor do they differ entirely from one another, though they are not the same. They go together, closely linked, one depending on the other as they constitute so many progressive realizations of that communion of life which God has willed to establish between himself and humanity.

The people of Israel first conceived the Kingship of Yahweh as an actual reality, valid for the present—though already it was vaguely felt that one day it would transcend time (Pss. 9:39; 28:10; 73:12; 102:19; cf. 5:3; 23:7 f.; 34:5; 144:1,11). Thus envisaged, the Kingship of Yahweh was linked to the destiny of Israel, for it was in his people that Yahweh was present. His presence was even localized in the Temple, above the Ark of the Covenant. It was this presence which gave Israel its cohesion and made it a people.

But this first community of God was only the prefiguration of another community, of a new kingdom of God, more interior and

[23]See *ibid.*, pp. 155-59.

more universal. Not only will God be present in his people as a people, but he will henceforth be present to each of its members; more, he will be *in* them, under the regime of a New Covenant. Any man—and not only a son of Abraham—may henceforth be joined to him. It is in the crucible of the Exile that Israel acquired this new comprehension of her destiny: when the glory of Yahweh had abandoned the Temple (Ezek. 10:18 f.), when the Ark had disappeared, and when the Temple itself had been destroyed. In God's plan these bitter facts were a purifying trial destined to mature the mentality of the people in view of new graces and richer blessings. Before the ruins of the abolished monarchy, Israel gained a deeper understanding of the faithfulness and of the tenderness of Yahweh. A spiritual Israel was born, and grew in the awareness of a nearness to God that was more real than ever. Jeremiah, Ezekiel, and Second Isaiah prepared the people for the coming of a renewed and enlarged kingdom. Henceforth the Kingship of Yahweh appeared as a reality of the world to come, not limited to Israel but embracing all peoples (Jer. 31:31-34; Ezek. 37:26; Is. 60:2 f.; cf. Pss. 21:29 f.; 47:3; 67:30; 86:4).

The psalms of the Kingship of Yahweh have particularly underlined the future coming of the kingdom of God. It is Yahweh in person who will establish his kingdom on earth—no allusion is made to the Messiah. It is Yahweh who will reign, clothed in majesty; it is he who will come to judge nations. For the coming of Yahweh and the establishment of his kingdom will take the form of a terrible *judgment*, but the divine coming will signify at the same time *grace and salvation*: Yahweh will reign in justice, in peace, and in goodness. That is why, in these psalms, despite the awesomeness and the terror of his majesty, joy always accompanies the coming of Yahweh.

After centuries of preparation, the Jewish people lived at last in vivid expectation of the kingdom of God. Most often this expectation took a political turn: they looked for the restoration of the Davidic monarchy. But the more deeply religious visualized a reality that was essentially interior: in obeying the Law, "the just man took on himself the yoke of the kingdom of God." Therefore it is surprising, especially given the place which the preaching of the kingdom of God holds in the Gospel of Jesus, that we attach more importance to the proclamation of the Messiah-King than to the proclamation of the kingdom of God. It is surprising, seeing that Jesus is God and that in him God has come on earth, that one does not learn to find in him the accomplishment of the promises which proclaim the coming of Yahweh in order to establish his kingdom.[24]

---

[24]See A. Gelin, "Messianisme," DBS, V, col. 1192. Throughout this chapter, by permission of The Grail (England), psalm-texts have been quoted from *The Psalms: A New Translation* (London: Collins [Fontana Books], 1963).

SEVEN

The Chronicler's History

We have seen that the deuteronomical school produced a great historical work, marked by a distinctive theological outlook. In the postexilic age another major historical work saw the light, one that reflects the priestly interests and that is also dominated by the theological views of its author. This unknown writer is conveniently named the Chronicler—after the title of the first part of his work.

1. 1 AND 2 CHRONICLES

1) The Book

TITLE   It is generally agreed that 1 and 2 Chronicles, Ezra, and Nehemiah form one work. This is borne out, in the first place, by the language and style of all these books. Then too, the same intense interest in the Temple is found throughout, and a penchant for genealogies and statistics is evident from first to last. It is also significant that the closing verses of 2 Chronicles (36:22 f.) are reproduced in the introduction of Ezra (Ez. 1:1-3a)—this is a manner of indicating that Chronicles and Ez.-Neh. are one book.

The Hebrew name for Chronicles is *dibre hayyamim*, which means literally "the things of the days," that is "the events of the past." St. Jerome, in his *Prologus Galeatus*, comments that the work might well be called *Chronicon totius historiae divinae*, that is, "the chronicle of the whole of sacred history." In the LXX the title is *Paraleipomena* or "the things omitted," because the translators viewed the work as a supplement to Sm. and Kgs; this view and name were adopted by the Vg. Chronicles is the last book of the Hebrew Bible and comes after Ez. and Neh. This position of the work seems to be indicated by Christ in Mt. 23:25 and Lk. 11:51 (cf. 2 Chr. 24:20-22): the murder of Zechariah is the last mentioned in Scripture, as that of Abel is the first.[1]

DATE   In determining the date of Chronicles we must keep in mind the continuation of the work in Ez.-Neh.; consequently a date later than Ezra is certain—in other words, later than 428 B.C. The genealogy of the Davidic line given in 1 Chronicles 3:19-24 descends to at least six generations after Zerubbabel (that is, to c. 350 B.C.). The language of the work, the priestly preoccupations, and its position as the last book in the Writings all point to the late postexilic period. We may reasonably date the Chronicler's history about 300 B.C.

DIVISION   There are four clearly marked divisions in Chronicles:

I. FROM ADAM TO DAVID (1 CHR. 1-10)	
1) Genealogical lists	1-9
2) Saul	10
II. DAVID, FOUNDER OF THE TEMPLE CULT (1 CHR. 11-29)	
1) The Kingship of David	11-14
2) The Ark in the City of David	15-20
3) Towards the Building of the Temple	21-29
III. SOLOMON AND THE BUILDING OF THE TEMPLE (2 CHR. 1-9)	
IV. THE KINGS OF JUDAH (2 CHR. 10-36)	
1) The First Reforms	10-27
2) The Great Reforms	28-35
3) The End of the Monarchy	36:1-21
EPILOGUE: THE DECREE OF CYRUS (2 CHR. 36:22 f.)	

[1]See A. S. Herbert, PCB, n. 309 a.

SOURCES   The canonical books, from Gn. to Kgs., are the main sources of Chronicles:

1. Gn.-Jos. for 1 Chr. 1-9.
2. Sm.-Kgs. for 1 Chr. 10—2 Chr. 36.

In 1 Chronicles 1-9 the source material is resumed in the form of genealogies; for the rest of the work the sources are, as a rule, quoted literally. In addition to the canonical books the Chronicler refers by name to a large number of other works which served his purpose. These sources may be classified as historical and prophetic.[2]

1. *Historical sources.*

a) The Book of the Kings of Israel and Judah (2 Chr. 27:7; 36:8).
b) The Book of the Kings of Judah and Israel (2 Chr. 16:11; 25:26; 28:26; 32:32).
c) The Book of the Kings of Israel (2 Chr. 20:34).
d) The Chronicles of the Kings of Israel (2 Chr. 33:18).
e) The Midrash (Commentary) on the Book of Kings (2 Chr. 24:27).

It seems most likely that these titles really represent the same work: a midrashic[3] history of the kings of Israel and Judah.

2. *Prophetic sources.* The Chronicles of Samuel the Seer (1 Chr. 29:29; 2 Chr. 27:7; 36:8); Nathan the Prophet (1 Chr. 29:29; 2 Chr. 9:29); Gad the Seer (1 Chr. 29:29); Shemaiah the Prophet and Iddo the Seer (2 Chr. 12:15); Jehu the son of Hanani (2 Chr. 20:34); the Seers (2 Chr. 33:19); The Visions of Iddo the Seer (2 Chr. 9:29); Isaiah the Prophet (2 Chr. 32:32); The Prophecy of Ahijah the Shilonite (2 Chr. 9:29); The Acts of Uzziah written by Isaiah the Prophet (2 Chr. 26:22); The Midrash of Iddo the Prophet (2 Chr. 13:22).

It is possible that these writings are parts of a single collection; but it can be just as easily maintained that they are independent sources. Nor may the possibility of pseudepigraphy be excluded; it may be that these documents are really of late date, like the apocalyptic and apocryphal literature.[4]

---

[2]See T. Henshaw, *The Writings* (New York: Humanities Press, 1963), pp. 294-96.
[3]See below, p. 323.
[4]See T. Lusseau, IB, p. 721.

We can check the attitude of the Chronicler towards his sources by a comparison of his work with the canonical writings on which it is based. We find that, in general, he reproduces verbatim whole passages of his basic text. On the other hand he can display remarkable freedom, particularly in his choice of material, but also in adapting his sources to suit his own outlook and presentation. We may assume that he used the noncanonical material in much the same way. This procedure calls for a study of the literary form of Chronicles.

2) Literary Form

A comparison of Chronicles with Sm.-Kgs. carries the conviction that the Chronicler intends to write a history; a closer look at the work gives the further assurance that he has planned to set a religious doctrine in full relief. It becomes clear that, despite a wide material agreement, the outlook and object of the deuteronomical history and of the Chronicler are not the same. In the latter a constant tendency is manifest: to justify, from history, the solutions which, in the post-exilic era, had been given to complex problems, and notably to refer back to David the basic element of the Jewish community. The writer desires to establish the continuity between the past and the present and to make the old relevant to the new. This procedure is an aspect of a certain literary form which is characteristic of the epoch—the *midrash*.[5]

MIDRASH[6]   *Midrash* is at once a method of exegesis and a special literary form. In accordance with the meaning of the term it is an investigation, a search of Scripture or ancient tradition, which takes the form of an explanation or amplification of the data. The method is not concerned with determining when or in what circumstances the writing or the tradition arose, but rather it seeks to learn what they have to say to us *here and now*. The whole point of *midrash* is to actualize a biblical theme, a work or word of God, in face of a new situation. It is rewarding to look to the etymology of the word and the antecedents of the form.

---

[5]See *ibid.*, pp. 721 f.
[6]See R. Bloch, "Midrash," DBS, V, cols. 1263-1281.

1. *In the Old Testament.* The word *midrash* occurs twice only: 2 Chronicles 13:22; 24:27, and designates noncanonical sources used by the author; Sir. 51:23 has the expression *beth ha-midrash.* On the other hand, the verb *darash* ("to search," "to examine") occurs very frequently. Most often it is used in a religious sense: it means to frequent a place of cult, to seek God, to seek the response of God in the cult and in personal prayer (Am. 5:5; 2 Chr. 1:5; Dt. 12:5; Pss. 34 [33]:5; 69 [68]:33; 105 [104]:4; etc.). But, above all, one searches the Scriptures. This last meaning is current in the postexilic age: one turns to Scripture to find the responses of God. *Darash,* therefore, signifies the study of the Torah (in the wide sense of all divine revelation considered as a norm of life): Ps. 119 [118]:45,94,155; 1 Chr. 28:8; or of the great interventions of God in the history of Israel: Ps. 111 [110]:2—"Great are the works of the Lord, studied (*derushim*) by all who have pleasure in them." Is. 34:16 (a postexilic text) is significant in this respect: it is an invitation to seek in "the book of the Lord" the prophecies concerning Edom (Is. 13:20-22) in order to show their realization.

Since the meaning of *darash* is fixed in the postexilic period, we can have little doubt about the meaning of *midrash* in the Scripture passages mentioned above. Admittedly the nature of the writings which have served as the Chronicler's sources remains uncertain but, since the meaning of the verb *darash* is clear, it is probable that, when the Chronicler employs the term *midrash* he refers to works which gloss and amplify the Scriptures for the purpose of instruction and edification. As for the *beth ha-midrash* of which ben Sirach speaks, it is doubtless a place where Scripture was studied and interpreted.

2. *In rabbinical literature.* Here *midrash* has the general sense of "search" or "research," with the double nuance of study and explanation. More specifically, *midrash* designates a writing whose object is the interpretation of Scripture, normally on a homiletic level, like the *midrash rabbah* which is a commentary on the Pentateuch. In short, in the rabbinical literature, *midrash* has acquired a technical sense: it is always used in relation to Scripture, and means to search out, to strive to understand the content of a scriptural text—to explain and to expound the sense of Scripture.

THE CHARACTERISTICS   Midrashic literature has four distinctive
OF MIDRASH   characteristics:

1. *Its starting point is a Scripture text or a sacred tradition.* It involves a meditation on a text or tradition, a "search" of Scripture. Hence *midrash* is a literary form proper to Israel.

2. *It is homiletic. Midrash* is not a scholastic method but a popular form, and it is notably homiletic. The origin of much of it may be found in the liturgical assemblies: it is the commentary on, and an interpretation of, the text read in synagogue worship. In this it is not far removed from the homily on the Gospel as required by the Constitution on the Liturgy.[7]

3. *Midrash is generally a study of a scriptural text in the light of other biblical passages.* This procedure is based on the conviction that the Bible is a unity and that it is everywhere the word of God.

4. *Adaptation to the present.* The practical purpose of *midrash* is to bring out the lessons of faith and of moral and spiritual bearing which the text or tradition contains; hence the interpretation, the "actualization," of Scripture, which is the essential feature of *midrash.* It applies an older text or tradition to later and different circumstances and draws out a lesson that is valid in the changed situation.

THE FORMS   *Midrash* is extremely varied; still the method may
OF MIDRASH   be reduced to three main types:

1. The form of *midrash* that is most limited in its scope is the *halakah.* It is based on the legal texts and its purpose is to find in them rules of conduct and of action that fit later times and circumstances. While this method could find a place in synagogal sermons, it is understandable that it developed more fully among the rabbis and priests by way of commentaries on the Torah.

2. The most widely-occurring and elastic form of *midrash* is the *haggadah.* This was the designation of every commentary on Scripture which aimed at the spiritual formation of its hearers. The viewpoint was varied (moral exhortation, explanation or justification of liturgical feasts, doctrinal commentary) and the methods diverse (varying from a simple explanation of a text to a free narrative built on a text

---

[7]Nn. 51 f.

or tradition), but always it sought to make an older text or tradition applicable here and now. It is not surprising—given this wide field—that haggadic *midrash* flourished.

3. The third form of *midrash* is known as *pesher midrash* after a term which figures in many Qumran texts.[8] It is an interpretation of prophetical texts which makes them relevant to later circumstances and shows their accomplishment in events of another age. Dn. 9 is a characteristic example of *pesher*.[9]

We believe that the nature and purpose of *midrash*—particularly of haggadic *midrash*—will be clearer when we have studied concrete examples of the method, notably Dn. 1-6. For our purpose in the present chapter it is enough to observe that Chronicles has a marked haggadic element. This fact has to be kept in mind when assessing the historical character and contribution of the writing. The realization that the Chronicler has adopted this literary form will help us to understand his deviations from the plain meaning of Sm.-Kgs. and will warn us to weigh carefully the details of a historical nature that are proper to him. "The Chronicler admits certain objective data: in this respect he is a historian. But he sometimes arranges and adapts the data in order to press them into the service of his thesis: in this regard he is a midrashic writer."[10]

3) The Purpose of Chronicles

The Chronicler is interested not only in the meaning of history but in the lesson of history and in the relevance of the pre-exilic age to his own time. His work may be more aptly described as a theology of history than as history, and he himself is a theologian rather than a historian. He has written for his contemporaries, not to present a summary of past events, but to offer them a reinterpretation of Israel's past. He has done this in order to bring them to an awareness of their status as God's people and to urge them to live in fidelity to God by obeying his Law and by rendering him true and meaningful cult. This, we have seen, is the object of haggadic *midrash*. An

---

[8] See Wilfrid Harrington, *Record of Revelation: The Bible* (Chicago: The Priory Press, 1965), p. 78.
[9] See p. 380.
[10] See Lusseau, *op. cit.*, p. 723.

understanding of this literary form points the way unerringly to the real purpose of the Chronicler.

This is not to say that the data brought forward by the Chronicler, beyond those furnished by his canonical sources, lack historical reliability. We have to examine each item of this additional material on its merits, while noting that recent archaeological discoveries and historical investigations have repeatedly vindicated the trustworthiness of the author.[11] But keeping in mind the literary form he has adopted, we must also acknowledge that, by studied selection and by deliberate insertions and omissions, he has consciously modified the picture of events drawn in Sm.-Kgs. He selects material that would emphasize certain aspects of the tradition, as for instance, those actions of the kings of Judah which affected the religious life of their people and their attitude towards the Temple. A notable addition is the long account of David's preparations for the building of the Temple and the organizing of its services (1 Chr. 22-29). Events had shown that God's plan would be fulfilled in the Davidic line and in Judah; thus the author omits altogether the history of the Israelite kings. Modifications are usually inspired by a more refined theological insight: in 2 Sm. 24:1 Yahweh moved David to number Israel, whereas in 1 Chronicles 21:1 the action was instigated by Satan; 1 Chronicles 17:11-14 deftly adapts the dynastic oracle of 2 Sm. 7:12-16 to fit the later stage of messianic expectation.[12]

In short, the author is "a theologian who in the light of the experiences of the past and especially of the Davidic experience, 'thinks' the conditions of the ideal kingdom. He brings together in one synthesis past, present, and future; he projects into the age of David the whole cultic organization of his own time while he omits everything that might lessen the standing of his hero, now become the type of the messianic king for whom he yearns. Apart from some additional information whose reliability can be checked his work is less important as a reconstruction of the past than as a picture of the situation and of the preoccupations of his own epoch."[13]

---

[11]See W. F. Albright, *From the Stone Age to Christianity* (New York: Doubleday, 1957²), pp. 273 f.

[12]See p. 233.

[13]Roland de Vaux, BJ, p. 404.

From his study of the past and his knowledge of the postexilic situation, the Chronicler was fired by one dominating conviction: Israel was called to be a holy community. He had read the deuteronomists aright and had imbibed the spirit of Ezekiel and the priestly writers. The true Israel, brought into being by God, was an Israel gathered about one central shrine, a "kingdom of priests and a holy nation" (Ex. 19:6); a people "whose whole life was to be a 'liturgy' or divine service."[14] In practice, this meant a community which had its center in the Temple where priests and levites assured that fitting cult would be paid to God on behalf of his people.

The Chronicler was anxious to demonstrate that the community, living in the spirit of the reforms of Nehemiah and Ezra, was in fact the kind of community that God had willed from the beginning. He wanted to show that the Exile had not meant a break and had not led to the emergence of something entirely new. After all, it did look like that: the monarchy had been the accepted shape of Israel's life for centuries and the new state of Judah had been built on different lines. So he looked again at the past and found in it the seeds of the future—he saw fulfillment, not rejection. Forms were different, but the essential features of God's people had persisted.

He took his stand on the Nathan prophecy (2 Sm. 7) and on the divine choice of the Davidic dynasty. From this standpoint he viewed the political schism as a rebellion against the divine plan: the Northern Kingdom had broken with the divinely-chosen king and had turned its back on the one shrine where legitimate worship might be offered to God. Jeroboam and his people had cut themselves off from the Covenant—logically, they may be left aside. It is no more than a development of the judgment passed on the Northern kings by the deuteronomists. The author's stand on the choice of the Davidic Dynasty also explains his idealization of David, while his preoccupation with the cult leads him to exaggerate the cultic role of his ideal king. Basing himself on David's bringing of the Ark to Jerusalem, on his desire to build a Temple, and on his reputation as a psalmist, the Chronicler has given him credit for

---

[14]B. W. Anderson, *Understanding the Old Testament* (Englewood Cliffs, N.J.: Prentice-Hall, 1957), p. 437.

drawing up the plans of the Temple, for making all necessary preparations for its construction, and for organizing the liturgical worship of the nation. This is a striking way of bringing out the essential link between the kingdom of David and the little Judaean community. The monarchy has gone, but the work begun by David has developed: Judaism is a worshiping community gathered around a central shrine and living in expectation of the coming of a new David.

> History had demonstrated that the Lord's people were in fact narrowed down to those for whom Jerusalem, the Temple, and the Davidic line were central to their loyalty. To deny this was apostasy. Not to know this was heathenism. For these were of Yahweh's choosing, and through their media his people acknowledge his rule. Yet it is an important element of the Jewish faith, as reflected in this book, that the apostate might return and the heathen acknowledge the one true God, the sole ruler of all history who is known in his dealings with his Chosen People. All historical success or failure are the direct product of Divine reward for loyalty to the Torah or punishment for apostasy.[15]

The Chronicler has brought about the marriage of dynastic messianism with the priestly ideal of Ezekiel. His David, king and priest, is not only an idealization of the historical king, he is the ideal David of the future, the Messiah. Unhappily, his stress on the primacy of the spiritual and on the essentially religious nature of the kingdom of God did not have the impact it deserved and a more materialistic outlook prevailed. But the Chronicler was vindicated by the King he had dimly foreseen, by him who declared: "My kingship is not of this world" (Jn. 18:36).

2. EZRA AND NEHEMIAH

We have noted that the Chronicler did not lay down his pen at the close of 2 Chronicles. Although in modern versions Ezra and Nehemiah constitute two books (in the Vg. they are 1, 2 Esdras) they are really sections of the Chronicler's one work. The position of Ez.-Neh. before 1, 2 Chronicles in the Hebrew indicates that it was the first to be regarded as Scripture, probably because Chronicles seemed to be no more than a summary of the earlier histories.

---

[15]A. S. Herbert, *op. cit.*, n. 310 b.

The Book

PLAN AND CONTENTS

1. *Plan.*

Return from the Exile and Reconstruction of the Temple	Ez. 1-6
Organization of the Community by Ezra and Nehemiah	Ez. 7-Neh. 13
1. Mission and Personality of Ezra	Ez. 7-10
2. Nehemiah and the Rebuilding of the Walls of Jerusalem	Neh. 1-7
3. Religious Reforms of Nehemiah and Ezra	Neh. 8-13

2. *Contents.* The book opens with the decree of Cyrus (538 B.C.) authorizing the Jews to return to Jerusalem and permitting them to reconstruct the Temple. The return took place at once, but the building of the Temple was interrupted by the opposition of the Samaritans; it was eventually completed in 515 B.C. In the following half-century efforts to build the walls were blocked by the Samaritans (Ez. 1-6). In the reign of Artaxerxes, Ezra, a scribe who had charge of Jewish affairs at the Persian court, arrived in Jerusalem with a new group of returning exiles. He had authority to impose on the community the Law of Moses—officially recognized by the Persians as the state law of Judah. He took stern measures against mixed marriages (Ez. 7-10).

Nehemiah, cupbearer (a position of rank) to Artaxerxes, was commissioned to return to Jerusalem and to carry out the rebuilding of the city walls. The work was speedily finished, despite opposition, and the city was repopulated (Neh. 1:1–7:72a). In the meantime Nehemiah had been named governor of Judah. The Law was solemnly read by Ezra to the assembled people who confessed their guilt and undertook to observe the Law (Neh. 7:72b–10:40).

The passage Neh. 11:1–13:3 contains a list of names, further measures of the reformers, and the dedication of the fortifications. Nehemiah, who had gone back to Persia, returned on a second mission. He had to take action against certain disorders (Neh. 13:4-30).

SOURCES Just as in the first part of his work the Chronicler has here, too, depended on a number of documents. The chief sources used in the compilation of Ez.-Neh. are the following:

1. *The Ezra narrative*: Ez. 7:1—10:44; Neh. 7:73b—9:37. This narrative is based on the Ezra memoirs: Ez. 7:27—9:15.

2. *The memoirs of Nehemiah*: Neh. 1:1—7:73a; 11:1 f.; 12:27-43; 13:4-31 + chapter 10 (2nd mission).

3. *Aramaic sections*: Ez. 4:8b—6:18; 7:12-26. These are official documents to and from the Persian king.

4. *Lists*: These are mostly the names of persons (for example, Ez. 2:1-67; 8:1-14; Neh. 11:3-36; 12:1-26), and were apparently copied from records preserved in the Temple.

The Chronicler seems to have utilized his sources in this fashion:[16] he interrupted the memoirs of Ezra by removing the section which ought to follow Ez. 8:36 (reading of the Law, Feast of Tabernacles, confession of sins) and inserting it in the Book of Nehemiah (Neh. 7:73b—9:37). Probably he composed the prologue (Ez. 7:1-11). In view of its marked biblical tone he must have edited or rewritten the decree of Artaxerxes (Ez. 7:12-26).

Apart from the fact that Neh. 12:33-36, 41 f. appear out of place, the memoirs of Nehemiah do not seem to have been retouched. However, the Aramaic source has been reproduced in a wrong chronological order. The opposition to the fortification of the city (Ez. 4:6-23) is manifestly later than the reconstruction of the Temple —the names of the Persian kings are sufficient indication of that. In Ez. 3:2,8 and 4:1-3 Zerubbabel seems to have been substituted for Shesh-bazzar (cf. Ez. 5:2) and the bitter opposition of the Samaritans has been anticipated (cf. Ez. 5:3). Perhaps the Chronicler wished to play down the inertia of the returned exiles, which Haggai has pilloried (Hag. 1:14 f.).

CHRONOLOGY One of the most perplexing problems in the history of Israel is the relationship of the careers of Ezra and Nehemiah. Happily, we do not need to go into the matter here since we have examined it sufficiently in an earlier chapter.[17] On the basis of the

---

[16]See Lusseau, *op. cit.*, pp. 711 f.
[17]Pp. 74-76.

hypothesis which we regard as the most satisfactory we reconstruct the order of events as follows:[18]

1. 538-520 B.C. Several caravans of returning exiles arrived in Jerusalem. The first of these was led by Shesh-bazzar, prince of Judah, who restored the altar of holocausts and laid the foundations of the Temple (Ez. 1:1—3:13).

2. 520-515 B.C. The rebuilding of the Temple, a work encouraged by Haggai and Zechariah (Ez. 5:1; cf. Hag. 1-2; Zech. 2:5-17) was completed by Zerubbabel; the Temple was consecrated and the Pasch celebrated (Ez. 5:1—6:22).

3. 515-445 B.C. The Samaritans successfully impeded the restoration of the fortifications under Xerxes I (486-465 B.C.) and Artaxerxes I (465-424 B.C.) (Ez. 4:6-23).

4. 445 B.C. (twentieth year of Artaxerxes I). Beginning of the first mission of Nehemiah. The walls were rebuilt and the fortifications were dedicated (Neh. 1:1-4,17; 6:1-73a; 11:1-20,25a; 12:27-32, 37-40,43).

5. 433 B.C. (thirty-second year of Artaxerxes I). Nehemiah, after twelve years of governorship (Neh. 5:14), went back to Susa. He returned on a second mission before the death of Artaxerxes (424 B.C.) —most likely before the mission of Ezra (Neh. 13:4-31; 10).

6. 428 B.C. (thirty-seventh year of Artaxerxes I). Arrival of Ezra who busied himself with the organization of the religious life of the community (Ez. 7:1—8:36). He read the Law to the people (Neh. 7:73b—8:12), presided at the Feast of Tabernacles (Neh. 8:13-18), sought to suppress mixed marriages (Ez. 9-10), and moved the people to true repentance (Neh. 9:1 f.).

Despite the uncertainty of the chronology, the data of Ez.-Neh. are worthy of every respect. The main sources go back directly to the two great figures of the epoch and, in fact, the accuracy of many of the details can be checked. We find that the administrative organization of the Persian state is correctly presented, even to precise references to the relations of governors among themselves and with the king (Ez. 4:7-23; 5:3-17; 6:1-13). The description of events and circumstances in Judah fits in with what we happen to know of the situation. Apart altogether from his contribution to our

---

[18]Cf. Lusseau, *op. cit.*, pp. 713 f.

historical knowledge of these times, we are grateful to the Chronicler for the glimpse he has given us into the formative stage of Judaism.

FATHER OF   Perhaps we today would be inclined to follow ben
JUDAISM   Sirach who eulogized Nehemiah ("The memory of Nehemiah also is lasting; he raised for us the walls that had fallen" [Sir. 49:13]) but did not mention Ezra; for it does seem that Ezra's contribution would not have been possible without the long and careful preparation of the other. But we can be certain that the Chronicler would not have shared our view. For him Ezra is the father of Judaism; and his judgment has the support of later Jewish tradition which witnesses to a continual growth in the stature of Ezra. The Chronicler could evaluate the contribution of the man more accurately than we.

Ezra brought with him from Babylon "the book of the Law of Moses" (Neh. 8:1). It seems certain that the title designates the Pentateuch in its final form, or in something very nearly its final form. This "Book of the Law" was accepted by the people as the law of the community, and Ezra, by his cultic and moral reforms, brought the life of the community into conformity with this norm. From his time the life and religion of Jews was directed and moulded by the Torah and Judaism assumed its distinctive characteristic of strict adherence and fidelity to the Law.

This does not mean that Ezra is responsible for the often extreme legalistic outlook of pharisaism; though it is not altogether surprising that his reform should have led to legalism and isolationism—it is not easy to maintain a balance in such matters. If we are to judge Ezra's role aright, we shall need to make certain observations.[19] Ezra did not introduce the emphasis on obedience to the Law: this went back to Moses and the Sinai tradition. Then there is Israel's attitude to the Law to be taken into account: the Torah was not regarded as a code to be obeyed, a long list of commands and prohibitions. Rather it was seen as the expression of the will of a Lawgiver who is the Redeemer of Israel; the goodness of this God moved the Israelite to serve him freely and to obey him gladly. It follows that the Law was not counted as a burden: it was a gracious gift of God and a source of delight (cf. Pss. 1; 19 [18]:7-14; 119

[19]See Anderson, *op. cit.*, pp. 457-60.

[118]). Nor does attachment to the Law conflict with the prophetic outlook and spirit. The long prayer of Ezra (Neh. 9) shows that the postexilic priestly view was quite in sympathy with the prophetic demands.

In the light of these observations we may appreciate Ezra's attitude to the Law and to the cult and realize the true place of the Torah in Judaism. If for many the elaborate Temple ritual became an empty form and if devotion to the Law lapsed into legalism, these deviations were due to the weakness of Judaism, to the weakness inherent in any community of men. But to lay later abuses at the door of Ezra is no more justified than to blame the Founder of Christianity for the failure of Christians.

3. THE MESSAGE OF THE CHRONICLER[20]

Chronicles is a history of the theocracy. The genealogies of the opening chapters lead to David, but the emphasis is not so much on him as on the plan of God in which he plays a role. God will establish a kingdom, a kingdom of which he is King and in which the king of Judah is his vicar (1 Chr. 17:14,22). The first recorded event of David's reign is his capture of Jerusalem (1 Chr. 11:4-9), the dwelling place of God. The transport of the Ark (chapter 13) heralds the building of the Temple and opens the way for the prophecy of Nathan (chapter 17). The close of 1 Chronicles (chapters 21-29) is concerned with preparations for the building of the Temple and with the organization of the cult and clergy by David; the principal act of the reign of Solomon is the building of the Temple (2 Chr. 1-9).

The break-up of the united monarchy on the death of Solomon was more than a religious schism, it was an apostasy on the part of the Northern Kingdom. Judah had remained faithful to the ideal of the theocracy founded on Jerusalem, the Temple, the levitical priesthood, and the Davidic Dynasty. Israel, by turning its back on all this, had placed itself outside the pale of sacred history, and in the discourse of Abijah (2 Chr. 13:4-12) the Chronicler justifies his exclusion of Israel from his history. But he has to admit that most of the successors of David were little better than the kings of the North. In fact only three (Jehoshaphat, Hezekiah, and Josiah) walked

---

[20]See A. M. Brunet, "Paralipomènes," DBS, VI, cols. 1256-1260.

in the steps of David and Solomon. Yahweh was at last forced to punish his ungrateful people (2 Chr. 36:14-16).

It is chastisement, not destruction, for God must be faithful to his promises. Just as he had moved Nebuchadnezzar to chastise his people (2 Chr. 36:17 ff.) he will raise up the king of Persia to deliver them and to permit them to return to the holy land (2 Chr. 36:22 f.; Ez. 1:1-4). Ez.-Neh. tell the story of the return, the reconstruction of the Temple and of the walls of Jerusalem; they tell of the religious formation of the new community that is yet the prolongation of the old, firmly linked to it by bonds of blood and by the same faith. But the Chronicler is aware that this re-establishment of his people is not the full realization of the prophecies (Neh. 9:36). Israel is still subject to foreign nations and the house of David has not been set up again at the head of the people. Hence there is an attitude of expectation in a spirit of hope and faith; in the time of waiting, Judah, a people separated from other nations, must group itself around the Temple and live according to its own Law.

The Chronicler has wished to present a history of the theocracy, but he has done so in a literary form that does not quite square with our modern notion of history. Indeed, his work is more truly a theology of history and to his religious teaching everything else in his work is subordinated. Even the historical facts themselves, whether he has found them in the Bible or in extrabiblical sources, are pressed into the service of his teaching. In his great work he brought to life again before the eyes of his contemporaries the history of the Davidic theocracy, both in its vicissitudes before the Exile and in its restoration, and he did so as a lesson for his readers. The recalling of the glories and of the woes of the Davidic Dynasty would help them to ponder on their vocation and on their standing as God's people. The story of the historical restoration, coming after the disastrous failure of the monarchy, would show how God had remained faithful to his promises; as a new beginning, it would turn their hope towards the perfect establishment of God's kingdom.

The Chronicler's recourse to history is not unlike that of ben Sirach and of the Book of Wisdom. Like the eulogy of the ancestors of Israel (Sir. 44-50) the passages of Chronicles consecrated to David and to the faithful kings have a generous element of idealization; and like Wis. 10-19 the Chronicler, despite his great respect for and his vast knowledge of the biblical writings, does not hesitate to draw new interpretations from their text. The parallel with Wis. is particularly striking since, as we have seen,[21] Wis. 10-19 is a *midrash*. All three authors are concerned with instructing and edifying their readers.

The Chronicler has adopted a literary form in which historical facts are subordinated to the presentation of doctrine and to moral exhortation. We should not thereby conclude that the work has nothing to offer the historian—we have made this point before, but it bears repetition. In Chronicles the author has added many details which give every guarantee of historicity. The books of Ez.-Neh. are based on the narrative of Ezra and the memoirs of Nehemiah—immediate and even firsthand sources. If we wish to grasp the message of the Chronicler in its entirety we must pay attention to the contributions of great historical value which his work contains. He has traced the progress of sacred history from the Exile to the beginning of the fourth century B.C., and he has also preserved many details of the earlier phases of that history. But his work, with its definite purpose and its distinctive theological outlook, is anything but a *paraleipomena*—a mere supplement.

The Chronicler has taken his stand on the past—the Davidic Dynasty —and is concerned with the present—the contemporary postexilic community—but his eyes are ultimately fixed on the future. Though not himself a prophet (in the classic sense), he is the heir of the prophets and has learned from them. More than any other of the Old Testament historical books, the work of the Chronicler turns the eyes of his readers toward him whom Ezekiel called the "one shepherd," "my servant David" (Ezek. 34:22), and Jeremiah the "righteous Branch" (Jer. 23:5). He turns their eyes towards Christ, the final term of Israel, who by his life and by his death laid the foundation of a theocracy which no adversary can ever henceforth destroy.[22]

21Pp. 265 f.
22Cf. A. Noordtzij, "Les intentions du Chroniste," RB, 49 (1940), 168.

| *The Books of the Maccabees*

1 MACCABEES

2 MACCABEES

The Books of Maccabees take their title from the name Maccabaeus, the surname of Judas the leader of the revolt against Antiochus IV. The meaning of the name is uncertain; it is frequently explained as a derivative of *maqqabah*—"hammer." Judas is by no means the only hero of these books and 1 Mc. covers the whole of the Maccabaean movement to the accession of John Hyrcanus I.

Though 1 Maccabees was written in Hebrew it has come to us only in a Greek version; 2 Maccabees was written in Greek. Both books are represented in A (Codex Alexandrinus—5th cent.), V (Venetus—8th cent.), and a great number of minuscules; S (Sinaiticus —4th cent.) has 1 Maccabees only; B (Vaticanus—4th cent.) has neither. The Old Latin versions are important—the Vg. text is a mediocre representative of the Old Latin.

The Books of Maccabees are deuterocanonical, and theirs is the common history of the deuterocanonical writings.[1] Besides there are two apocryphal books of Maccabees. 3 Maccabees is a pseudo-historical account of a persecution of Alexandrian Jews in the reign of Ptolemy IV (221-204 B.C.). It is the work of an Alexandrian Jew and dates from about the beginning of the Christian era. 4 Maccabees was written by a Jew imbued with Stoic ideas who wished to prove that reason guided by piety can control the passions. He illustrated

---

[1]See Wilfrid Harrington, *Record of Revelation: The Bible* (Chicago: The Priory Press, 1965), p. 64.

his theme by the example of Eleazer and the seven brothers of 2
Maccabees. The date is first century A.D., before the year 70.

1. 1 MACCABEES

1 Maccabees covers the period from 175 to 134 B.C., that is, from
the beginning of the reign of Antiochus IV to the death of Simon,
the last of the sons of Mattathias. In other words, it is the history
of the Maccabaean revolt up to the establishment of the Hasmonaean
Dynasty.[2]

1) *Division*

PRELUDE (1 MC. 1-2)	
1) The advance of wickedness	1
2) The growing resistance	2
JUDAS MACCABAEUS (1 MC. 3:1–9:22)	
JONATHAN (1 MC. 9:23–12:54)	
SIMON (1 MC. 13-16)	

2) *Contents*[3]

In his introduction (chapters 1-2) the author contrasts the progress
of wickedness with the hardening of resistance. On the one hand
Hellenism, implanted by Alexander the Great, is the root of all these
evils; an impious branch of the same line has brought matters to
the breaking point. The Wrath of God has fallen on Israel (1 Mc.
1:64). On the other hand, the priest Mattathias, zealous for the Law,
inspires and typifies the Jewish resistance. His last message to his
sons was an impassioned exhortation to fight to the death for the
people and the Law; faithful Jews would check the unleashed anger of
God (1 Mc. 2:49-68). The sons of the old hero were worthy of him
and proved faithful to his legacy.

Judas was the mighty warrior. The religious flame of his exhortations and prayers before battle (1 Mc. 3:18-22, 58 f.; 4:8-11, 30-33;

---

[2]For the history of this period see pp. 86-94.
[3]See A. Lefèvre, IB, pp. 754-56; DBS, V, cols. 598-600.

7:4 f.) animated his troops with indomitable courage. After a series of brilliantly successful campaigns he entered Jerusalem in triumph and purified the Temple (chapters 3-4). Then he carried out punitive expeditions along the frontiers of Judaea, everywhere coming to the aid of his persecuted countrymen (chapter 5). Antiochus died miserably on an expedition against the Parthians (1 Mc. 6:1-6), but the struggle continued under his successors Antiochus V (1 Mc. 6:16-63) and Demetrius I (chapter 7). Judas won a resounding victory over Nicanor (1 Mc. 7:39-49). The feasts of the Dedication (1 Mc. 4:59) and of the Day of Nicanor (1 Mc. 7:49) preserved the memory of his exploits. The author gives an account of his diplomatic contacts with Rome (chapter 8) before describing his glorious death in a desperate battle (1 Mc. 9:1-22).

Jonathan proved an able successor to Judas, but his qualities were of a different cast and his tactics followed another course. He favored guerilla warfare and proved himself a clever politician. He was able to "judge" the people (1 Mc. 9:73) in comparative peace from 159 B.C. to 152 B.C. He took advantage of the struggle for power of Demetrius and Alexander Balas and, by playing one against the other, he won the high priesthood and the official title "Friend of the King." When Alexander emerged victorious, Jonathan gained the right to wear the purple and received the titles of *stratēgos* (general) and *meridarchēs* (governor) of Judaea (1 Mc. 10:1-66). In 145 B.C. Demetrius II replaced Alexander; Jonathan maintained all his privileges and had his brother Simon named *stratēgos* of the whole Palestinian coast. The brothers took advantage of their office to fortify strategic sites (1 Mc. 10:66–12:38). As in the case of Judas, the author gives the diplomatic activity of Jonathan just before describing his end (1 Mc. 12:1-23). The end was sad: the wily Jonathan—perhaps overconfident at last—was tricked by Trypho, captured, and put to death (1 Mc. 12:39-54; 13:23).

Simon became leader of the Jews as soon as his brother had been captured. Though he did not save Jonathan, he did drive Trypho from Jewish territory; he was formally recognized as chief of the Jewish nation by Demetrius II. It was 142 B.C., henceforth regarded as the year of Jewish independence: "The yoke of the Gentiles was removed from Israel, and the people began to write in their documents and contracts, 'In the first year of Simon the great high priest and commander and leader of the Jews'" (1 Mc. 13:41 f.). That same year the Acra fell; the hated symbol of foreign domination was gone at last (1 Mc. 13:43-53). In his eulogy of such a savior of his country the author does not hesitate to use expressions reminiscent of messianic hope (1 Mc. 14:1-15). As before, the diplomatic advances of Simon are given: Sparta, Rome, and Antioch recognized the sovereignty of Simon, ethnarch of the Jews (1 Mc. 14:16—15:24). A skirmish with Cendebeus, general of Antiochus VII, gave the sons of Simon a chance of proving their valor (1 Mc. 16:1-10). Though Simon was treacherously murdered by his son-in-law, the book closes with the acclamation of his son John Hyrcanus, the first of the Hasmonaean kings.

3) Date and Authorship

The eulogy of the Romans (chapter 8) proves that the book was written before 63 B.C., the year in which Pompey took Jerusalem and which marked the beginning of a bitter hatred of Rome. The closing formula, 1 Maccabees 16:23 f., modeled on the formula which closes each reign in Kgs., indicates that the author wrote after the death of John Hyrcanus I (134-104 B.C.). A date early in the reign of Alexander Jannaeus (103-76 B.C.) seems most likely; the book was written during the promising years of the king in order to glorify the ancestors of the dynasty.

The author is unknown. All we can say is that he was a Palestinian Jew, well versed in the Scriptures, who wrote in Hebrew, the sacred language, and was concerned to a notable extent with contemporary events. He was an ardent supporter of the Hasmonaeans and he was convinced that they alone could lead Israel along the right road. He has no difficulty about accepting the fact that these princes, though not of the Aaronitic family, should be high priests as well as civil rulers. It does seem that his outlook was close to that of the later Sadducees.

4) Sources

The author would have been familiar with most of the events recorded in his book and could have had firsthand knowledge of some of them. At the same time he would have been able to consult various documents, like the Chronicles of the high priesthood of John Hyrcanus (1 Mc. 16:24). He includes the copy of an inscription honoring Simon (1 Mc. 14:27-45) which had been deposited in the treasury (1 Mc. 14:49). He must have turned to the state archives for the twelve official letters he has reproduced (1 Mc. 5:10-13; 8:23-32; 10:18-20, 25-45; 11:30-37,57; 12:6-18,20-23; 13:36-40; 14:20-23; 15:2-9,16-21). It has been argued that the last three chapters of 1 Maccabees (from 14:16 onwards) are not authentic, on the grounds that Josephus, who had followed the book up to that point, thereafter turned to a history by Nicholas of Damascus. This is not a very weighty argument when balanced against the fact that the chapters in question are a normal development of the foregoing narrative and show the same style. We must certainly maintain the integrity of the work and we can feel confidence in a writer who stands on familiar ground and has access to authentic documents.

5) *Literary Form*[4]

The author has consciously imitated the literary forms of the older historical books (Jgs., Sm., Kgs.). His history too is fragmentary; it is concerned with certain episodes rather than with providing a continual sweep of events. Such statements as "not even one of them was left" (1 Mc. 7:46), "not one of them had fallen" (1 Mc. 5:54), and the grossly exaggerated numbers are to be seen as echoes of a traditional style and should be evaluated accordingly. This is not the language of a modern historian, anxious about exact figures and details, but testifies to a vivid impression of events that are still fresh, balanced by a familiarity with traditional historiography.

The author has reproduced documents where these were available to him. On the other hand he has not hesitated to put speeches in the mouth of his heroes; this, most likely, indicates a certain Greek influence, though the procedure is by no means unknown in earlier biblical writings (cf. Gn. 49:1-27; Jos. 23). Again true to his scriptural background he has striven to bring out the religious meaning of events. We may say, in short, that 1 Maccabees belongs to the same historical literary form as the deuteronomical history and Ez.-Neh.

---

[4]See IB, pp. 756 f.

6) Teaching

Though the name of God is not mentioned (a reflection of the growing postexilic tendency to avoid pronouncing the Holy Name) 1 Maccabees is a religious history. The course of events is governed by divine Providence, and God himself is spoken of under the titles Savior of Israel (1 Mc. 4:30), Heaven (1 Mc. 3:18 f., 60), or is indicated simply as "He" (1 Mc. 2:61; 3:22). The Jews turn to God for help before battle and thank him for victory (1 Mc. 4:24,33; 13:47,51). His interventions in the past (1 Mc. 4:9,30; 7:41) are a firm foundation of hope.

The author has been influenced not only by the style of the deuteronomical history, he has also been inspired by the same outlook towards the Law and its observance. In his history too the Law is the center of everything; it is that which divides men into two camps. "The struggle is not between Seleucids and Hasmonaeans, nor even between pagan kingdoms and the Jewish state; it is between the upholders of the Law and its adversaries."[5] The sons of Mattathias are not less zealous than their father and do not betray his last testament when they treat with pagan princes; they are conscious that such action will effectively guarantee the free observance of the Law. On the other hand, confidence in the unfailing promise of God must not end in quietism. The author is not in sympathy with the attitude of those who allowed themselves to be massacred on the sabbath (1 Mc. 2:36-38); and he manifestly approves the decision of Mattathias that it is a far better thing to fight for the Law on the sabbath (1 Mc. 2:42-48); the greatest glory is to die, sword in hand, for the Law (1 Mc. 2:50,64). "This history exalts, at one and the same time, human values and supernatural values: faith engenders heroism and service of the fatherland becomes one with service of the only God."[6]

Yet, when all is said and done, it is plain that 1 Maccabees does not attain the religious stature of the earlier biblical histories. Here there is no influence of the prophets; we note instead a further step towards a legalism that will eventually become excessive; already the Law seems to be more important than God himself. The victory

[5]*Ibid.*, p. 757.
[6]*Loc. cit.*

of the Maccabees seems to satisfy the aspirations of the people and the eulogy of Simon is almost messianic in tone. Then there is the fact that the revolution was so soon betrayed—by the immediate successors of John Hyrcanus I—and so utterly; the seeds of that betrayal must have been planted at an early date.

On the other hand, despite these shortcomings, the message of 1 Mc. remains valid and its appeal persists. We are shown what faith and confidence can achieve and we once again witness an intervention of God on behalf of his people. And knowledge of the subsequent history of the Hasmonaeans warns us that success and power can corrupt with devastating ease. Where persecution had engendered heroes and martyrs, worldly success had brought a decline in religious fervor. The book continues to utter its message of hope, and the failure of men to remain true to the faith on which that hope was built continues to be a warning to us.

2. 2 MACCABEES

The Second Book of Maccabees is not the sequel of the first. It deals in part with the same history—from 176 B.C. to the victory of Judas Maccabaeus over Nicanor in 160 B.C.—and is a résumé of a work in five volumes by Jason of Cyrene.

1) Division

INTRODUCTION (2 MC. 1-2)	
1) Letters to the Jews of Egypt	2 Mc. 1:1—2:18
2) The Author's Preface	2 Mc. 2:19-32
FIVE TABLEAUX WITH THE TEMPLE AS CENTER OF INTEREST	
1) Heliodorus: the Holiness of the Temple	2 Mc. 3
2) Persecution of Antiochus IV: Profanation of the Temple	2 Mc. 4-7
3) Victory of Judaism: Purification of the Temple	2 Mc. 8:1—10:9
4) Judas' Struggle: Freedom of Cult	2 Mc. 10:10—13:26
5) Fight against Nicanor: the Day of Nicanor	2 Mc. 14:1—15:36
EPILOGUE (2 MC. 15:37-39)	

344 ───── *Record of the Promise* ─────

2) Contents[7]

The book opens with copies of two letters of the Jews of Jerusalem inviting their brethren in Egypt to celebrate, together with them, the Feast of Dedication (Hanukkah) on the twenty-fifth of Chislev and giving the traditional story of the feast (2 Mc. 1:1–2:18). In his preface (2 Mc. 2:19-32) the author explains his intention and his method: he wishes to write a pleasing narrative and is satisfied to give an epitome of the work of Jason.

The book proper falls into five sections, each of which centers, in one way or another, on the Temple. Under a great high priest like Onias III, the holy Temple could not be profaned—as Heliodorus learned to his cost (chapter 3). The scandalous intrigues of the false priests Jason and Menelaus led to the profanation of the Temple by Antiochus IV. But the death of the martyrs, an acceptable sacrifice of expiation, turned aside the divine anger (chapters 4-7). Thus it came about that Judas defeated the pagan persecutors. Antiochus himself, before his death, acknowledged that he had been justly struck by God. The Temple was purified (2 Mc. 8:1–10:9). Judas extended the measures of purification and religious liberty to the towns of Palestine. The peace of the fifteenth of Xanthicus formally recognized the Jewish way of life and the Temple cult (2 Mc. 10:10–13:26). But it was still possible that an utterly unworthy person, like Alcimus, could have himself appointed high priest. Nicanor, who had blasphemed against the Temple, was defeated and killed by Judas; the victory was celebrated by an annual feast (2 Mc. 14:1–15:37). The author concludes his work with a word of farewell to the reader (2 Mc. 15:38 f.).

3) Date, Authorship, and Sources

The opening letter is dated 124 B.C., and this letter—an invitation to the Jews of Egypt to celebrate the Feast of Dedication—seems to have led to the composition of the work. We may date 2 Maccabees to the last quarter of the second century B.C.—and hence a little before 1 Mc.

The author has not named himself. Since he wrote in Greek and used a Greek history as his source, it is likely that he was an

---

[7]See *ibid.*, pp. 758-60.

Alexandrian. Unlike the author of 1 Mc. he is no champion of the Hasmonaeans; Judas is for him the man who saved the Law and purified the Temple, and he does not follow the later fortunes of the family of Mattathias. His outlook and his theology also serve to mark him as one who, if not a Pharisee, was in that tradition. We know nothing of Jason or of his work apart from the references of this book.

In his preface the author has stated that the history of Jason has been his main, and seemingly his exclusive, source: "All which has been set forth by Jason of Cyrene in five volumes, we shall attempt to condense into a single book" (2 Mc. 2:23). The letter of 2 Maccabees 9:19-27 and the four letters of chapter 11 most likely came by way of Jason. The two introductory letters, however, were originally written in Hebrew or Aramaic and were probably translated by the author of 2 Maccabees.

4) Literary Form[8]

The purpose of the author was to persuade his fellow Jews to celebrate the Feast of the Dedication of the Temple; hence each of the five tableaux of his work is composed in oratorical style: the whole is meant to move the reader and give him a sense of involvement. In the first episode we taste something of the peace and joy of the Temple service under the saintly Onias; we share the anguish of the high priest when the sacred place is threatened and again rejoice with him when Heliodorus is compelled to acknowledge the holiness of the God who dwells there. The next two episodes form a contrast. Impiety develops from Jason to Menelaus—from the pillage of the Temple to its profanation, from a massacre of the inhabitants of Jerusalem, to a general violent persecution of Jews. But, in the third discourse, the death of the martyrs, a sacrifice of expiation, turned aside the divine anger and Judas rescued his people and purified the Temple. We feel that hopelessness has given place to hope and confidence. The fourth discourse strikes the same optimistic note and dwells on the further successes of Judas. The last discourse is particularly dramatic and builds up to a climax: the death of Nicanor and the establishment of a commemorative feast.

---

[8]See *ibid.*, pp. 760 f.; DBS, V, cols. 605-7.

Five times the same movement is repeated—not the chaotic movement of history which follows the pattern of events but an oratorical movement. Each discourse is a drama with three actors: the pious Jew (Onias, the martyrs, Judas and his followers), the renegade Jew (Simon, the intriguing high priests), the pagan (Heliodorus, Epiphanes, Eupator, Nicanor); and each actor must proclaim, in his own way, the holiness of the Temple and the glory of the God who dwells in it. At first the situation is relatively peaceful. The source of trouble is the ambitious intrigues of unfaithful Jews; then pagan arrogance rears itself against God, and God strikes a devastating blow which reveals his power. Each discourse closes with a hymn to his glory (2 Mc. 3:38 f.; 7:37; 10:7; 13:23; 15:34).[9]

It is clear that 2 Maccabees belongs to a literary form then popular in the Hellenistic world and known as "pathetic history"; its characteristic was its appeal to the imagination and emotions of the reader. Impassioned discourses, forceful language, enormous numbers, contrived contrasts, flowery style—all are part of the form and all are typical of 2 Maccabees. The intention is to move the reader and the means employed are accepted literary conventions. Therefore the author of 2 Maccabees seeks to bring out the significance of the events he relates, but he neglects the details that scientific history would demand. Chronology yields to oratorical expediency and the orator reserves the right to choose, and to magnify, certain aspects. The "help which comes from Heaven" (1 Mc. 16:3) here takes the form of celestial manifestations (2 Mc. 3:24-26; 10:29 f.; 11:8; cf. 12:22; 15:11-16). The apparition of gods come to aid warriors in battle was a current feature of pathetic history; the Jewish author simply substituted angels for the gods.

Obviously 2 Maccabees may not be judged by the standards of modern scientific historical writing, but despite the liberties permitted by the special form, it remains a work of history. The author's plea and exhortation are based on facts, on facts of the recent past. Many of these facts can be checked by parallel texts of 1 Mc., while the long work of Jason of Cyrene is still nearer to the actual events— and we have no reason to suspect the competence and integrity of Jason. In two important matters 2 Maccabees has filled out the brief data of 1 Mc.: the part played by the high priests in the attempts at Hellenization (2 Mc. 4) more effectively explains the

_____

[9]DBS, V, col. 606.

origin of the conflict, while the agreement reached with Lysias (2 Mc. 11) places the purification of the Temple in a more understandable historical context.[10]

However, something must be said about the second introductory letter (2 Mc. 1:10–2:18). It is presented as a document of 164 B.C., the year of the Dedication of the Temple. In it rumors of the death of Antiochus are linked to traditions about Nehemiah and Jeremiah taken from apocryphal writings (2 Mc. 2:1,13). The narrative is, in short, the "legend" (in the sense of the second nocturn lessons of the Roman breviary) of the Feast of Hanukkah, and the author of 2 Maccabees, while inserting it at the beginning of his work, does not guarantee its historical accuracy.

The story of the "hidden fire" (2 Mc. 1:18-36) is designed to show that the Temple has lost none of its privileges: it has even preserved the sacred fire of the first Temple. The narrative combines a memory of the Persian cult of fire (cf. 2 Mc. 1:33 f.) with some knowledge of the properties of naphtha—natural oil. In the passage 2 Maccabees 2:1-12 (from an apocryphal work about Jeremiah) many of the details are not historical. Thus the tabernacle no longer existed after the building of Solomon's Temple and the Ark disappeared at the destruction of the Temple in 587 B.C. But the intention of the narrative is to affirm the continuity of the legitimate cult (2 Mc. 1:18), despite the absence of the tabernacle and the Ark, and to link this Dedication with those of Solomon and Moses (2 Mc. 2:8-12).[11]

5) Teaching

The author of 2 Maccabees is more interested in theology than in history (or, rather, in politics); hence in religious stature and in doctrine this book far surpasses 1 Mc. The issue is not clouded by political motives; the struggle is a stark combat of Judaism (the word appears for the first time [2 Mc. 2:21; 8:1; 14:38]) with Hellenism, and it is war to the death. Compromise can lead only to ruin (2 Mc. 4:7-17) and it is unthinkable that the high priesthood should be obtained by the favor of a pagan king (2 Mc. 11:2 f.).

---

[10]See Lefèvre, *op. cit.*, p. 761.
[11]See Roland de Vaux, BJ, pp. 571 f.

Though fidelity to the Law is inculcated at all times, the legalistic tendency of 1 Mc. has been avoided; this has been achieved by insistence on the holiness of the Law and on its interior aspect. It is this deeper appreciation of the Law that saves the author from the consequence of a seemingly intransigent attitude. Thus, for instance, the sabbath rest may never be transgressed—not even in view of self-defense (2 Mc. 5:25; 6:6; 15:3). He has also linked the sanctuary, the holy place, with observance of the Law. The "holy One, Lord of all holiness" (2 Mc. 14:36) can tolerate no defilement of his land, his city, his dwelling, no stain on his holy people. That is why the piety of Onias can guard the Temple more effectively than an army, and that is why the impious Jason and Menelaus bring disaster on the holy place. In the dream of Judas the avenging sword which he received from Jeremiah was given to him at the prayer of Onias (2 Mc. 15:16); the intercession of the just high priest was the means of victory over Nicanor.

This religion of the Law and of the Temple is firmly centered on God. It is significant that 2 Maccabees (unlike 1 Mc.) names God continually; he is the Creator of the universe, the All-Powerful, the Lord of the World, and the King of kings; he is the "Lord who has manifested himself" (2 Mc. 15:34); this last title, at the close of the book, is a deliberate challenge to the arrogant claim of Antiochus Epiphanes. Yet this great God is near his people, ready to help them; the earnest prayers illustrate the point in a striking way. There can be no doubt that the spirituality of 2 Maccabees is profound and living.

One point perhaps more than any other serves to underline the difference in outlook of these two books: it is their attitude towards the martyrs. For the author of 1 Mc. their death is a result of the divine anger that has fallen on Israel (1 Mc. 1:64); it has no positive significance. The divine anger is averted by armed resistance, by the resolute action of Judas (1 Mc. 3:8). For the other writer, though the sufferings of the martyrs are still a chastisement, their willing acceptance is an expiation which turns aside the anger of God. If Judas wins victories it is because God has accepted the sacrifice (2 Mc. 7:36; 8:5).[12]

---

[12]Lefèvre, *op. cit.*, p. 762.

An important feature of 2 Maccabees is its confident teaching on the afterlife. Here the influence of Dn. 12 is manifest and the contrast with 1 Mc. is sharp—a contrast that reflects the Pharisaic and Sadducean tendencies of the two authors (cf. Mt. 22:23; Acts 23:6-8). We learn that the living can pray for the dead and make sin-offerings on their behalf (2 Mc. 12:42-45); this is the scriptural basis for the doctrine of Purgatory. On the other hand, the just who have passed beyond the grave can intercede for those who still live on this earth (2 Mc. 15:11-16). Here we have for the first time, explicitly stated, the doctrine of the communion of saints. It is not surprising that the resurrection is taken for granted (2 Mc. 7; 14:46). These doctrines are the climax of the sure faith and unswerving hope that characterize the book; at the same time they highlight the loving mercy of God and his care for those who are faithful to him.

NINE	*The Writings*
	RUTH—JONAH
	TOBIT—BARUCH
	DANIEL—ESTHER
	JUDITH

In the Hebrew division of the sacred books the third grouping, after the Law and the Prophets, is that of the *kethubhim,* the Writings. The title of this chapter does not refer to that collection of inspired books and is not meant to have a precise technical sense. It is obvious indeed that *kethubhim* is a deliberately broad designation, calculated to accommodate a variety of books that do not belong in the other categories. In a similar fashion the works that fall outside the determined groups we have studied may be gathered here under the same vague title. The advantage of this procedure is that miscellaneous writings can be treated in a single chapter, while the question of literary forms is not begged in advance.

1. RUTH

1) The Book

The Book of Ruth, one of the shortest of the Old Testament writings, takes its name from the Moabitess whose story it relates. In the Hebrew Bible it is found among the *kethubim* and is the second of the five festal *megilloth* or "rolls"; it was read at the Feast of Pentecost. In the LXX and Vg., Ruth comes immediately after Judges. It is quite unlikely that, if Ruth had ever formed part of the Former Prophets (Jos.-Kgs.), it would have been detached and inserted in the later collection of Writings. It is noteworthy that the book shows no signs of editing in a deuteronomical sense. We may take it that Ruth originally took its place in the Bible among the Writings.

Its position (in the LXX and Vg.) between Judges and Samuel is explained by its opening words: "In the days when the judges ruled" (Ru. 1:1).[1]

2) Analysis

CONTENTS   In the days of the Judges a Bethlehemite named Elimelech was constrained, by famine, to emigrate to Moab, together with his wife Naomi and their sons Mahlon and Chilion. There Elimelech died and his sons married Moabite wives: Orpah and Ruth; before very long Mahlon and Chilion also died. When Naomi had learned that the famine was ended she decided to return to her own country. She advised her daughters-in-law to stay on in Moab; Orpah remained, but Ruth was determined to accompany her mother-in-law.

It happened to be the beginning of the barley harvest when the two women arrived in Bethlehem and Ruth went to glean after the reapers. She was shown great consideration by Boaz, owner of the fields where she gleaned (he was a kinsman of Elimelech). Following the advice of Naomi, Ruth made bold to request of Boaz that he should be her go'el,[2] her champion (in this case involving the right of levirate): he should take her to wife on condition that their first son should be legally regarded as the son of her former husband and have claim to that husband's property—in practice to the property of Elimelech. Boaz was agreeable to marrying Ruth, but he was aware that another, closer relative had prior rights; this man, in

---

[1]See H. Lussęau, IB, pp. 667 f.

[2]The go'el was a redeemer, a protector, a defender of the interests of the individual and of the group (cf. Lv. 25:47-49). If an Israelite had to sell his patrimony, the go'el had priority over all other purchasers (Lv. 25:25). The story of Ruth is an illustration of this custom, but here the purchase of the land is complicated by a case of levirate (see Roland de Vaux, *Ancient Israel, Its Life and Institutions,* trans. John McHugh [New York: McGraw-Hill, 1961], p. 21). For levirate (Latin *levir* = brother-in-law) see Dt. 25:5-10: if brothers live together and one of them dies without issue, a surviving brother marries the widow and the first born of this marriage is regarded as the son of the deceased. The law of Dt. 25 does not apply in the case of Ruth, for she had no more brothers-in-law (Ru. 1:11 f.). "The fact that some near relative must marry her, and that this obligation proceeds in a certain order (Ru. 2:20; 3:12), no doubt indicates a period or a *milieu* in which the law of levirate was a matter for the clan rather than for the family in the strict sense. In any case, the intentions and effects of the marriage were those of a levirate marriage, for it was made 'to perpetuate the name of the dead' (Ru. 4:5,10; cf. 2:20), and the child born of it was considered the son of the deceased (Ru. 4:6; cf. 4:17)" (De Vaux, *ibid.,* p. 38).

public, renounced his right. Thereupon Boaz acquired the property of Elimelech and married Ruth. A son was born to them: Obed, the grandfather of David. Ruth, the Moabitess—and not one of the Chosen People—had become an ancestress of the great king of Judah and Israel.

PLAN

RUTH AND NAOMI (RU. 1)
THE MEETING OF RUTH AND BOAZ (RU. 2)
NAOMI'S PLAN FOR RUTH AND BOAZ (RU. 3)
THE MARRIAGE OF BOAZ AND RUTH (RU. 4:1-17)
EPILOGUE: GENEALOGY OF DAVID (RU. 4:18-22)

3) *Authorship and Date*

The Aramaisms and neologisms of Ruth are sufficient indication that it is not possible to sustain the Talmud's attribution of the writing to Samuel. In fact, the author of Ruth is unknown and the date of the writing is likewise uncertain. The language would suggest a postexilic date. Also to be taken into account is a certain polemic intent, for it cannot be by chance that the author insistently names his heroine "Ruth the Moabitess": he is at pains to emphasize the fact that the grandmother of David himself was a foreigner. He does so, surely, because he wishes to oppose the view expressed in Ez. 9-10 and Neh. 13:1-3, 23-27. But the problem of mixed marriages would have been felt before it had been so radically attacked by Nehemiah and the calm atmosphere of Ruth would appear to indicate a time before the matter had come to a head. It seems that the writing may be dated about 450 B.C.[3]

> The late date in no way impugns the antiquity or the authenticity of the material. We may see that both are necessary for the author's purpose. . . . It is the telling of a well-known story, which may have existed in oral form and derived from pre-exilic days. What the writer has done is to use this well-known and often repeated story and give

---

[3]See BJ, pp. 147 f.

it a point. He has effected this (1) by drawing attention to the connection between this story and Israel's messianic hope (Ru. 4:17, 18-22); (2) by gently underlining the Moabite background of Ruth (Ru. 1:22; 2:2,6,21, etc.); (3) by emphasizing the divine intention that is fulfilled in the literary climax of the story (Ru. 4:13-18). Perhaps also it is deliberately intended that the action of Boaz "goes beyond" the tradition suggested by the Judah and Tamar story and that is required by the law of Dt. 25:5-10. It is by such fulfilling of the Law that Judaism is saved from becoming a legalistic religion, and that Israel enters into the divine purpose.[4]

4) Literary Form

While it is reasonable to suppose that Ruth is based on a pre-exilic tradition, a study of the writing convinces one that its literary form is close to that of the modern novel.[5] The author, skillfully and with charm, presents an idyll of simple family devotion and of country life. We see that the virtues of generosity and piety are rewarded and we discern the guiding hand of divine Providence over all. The very names suggest that the writing is fiction: Naomi—"my gracious one"; Mahlon—"weakness"; Chilion—"pining"; Orpah—"stiffnecked"; Ruth—"friend." Still, the existence of a tradition that David's ancestress was a woman of Moab is significant; and David's care to seek asylum for his family in Moab (1 Sm. 22:3 f.) perhaps points to a family link with that country.

5) The Message

The author of Ruth cleverly exploited the ancestry of David to make a point that had special relevance to the postexilic Jewish community. In the tiny Jewish state the struggle to preserve national identity was a painful one.[6] Some came to regard mixed marriages as a mortal danger to the continued existence of the people as the people of God; an excessively nationalistic and exclusive outlook tended to develop. The author of Ruth (like the author of Jon.) struck a blow on behalf of a more liberal and more universalist outlook. (It is noteworthy that both of them are unusually gifted writers.) Ruth the Moabitess (this foreigner) had accepted Yahweh as her God (Ru. 1:16) and had entered so wholeheartedly into

---

[4]A. S. Herbert, PCB, n. 271 c.
[5]See BJ, p. 148.
[6]See p. 72.

the Jewish way of life that she is lauded by Boaz for her earnestness in seeking the one kind of marriage that would perpetuate the family name (Ru. 3:10). Her attachment to Naomi is beautifully touching. The divine favor had come upon her; she had become an ancestress of David, an essential link in the messianic line.

> If the author has insisted so deliberately on the Moabite origin of Ruth, is it not to underline at the same time the universalist scope of his writing? The writing led to David because, after the Exile, the name of that king conjured up the messianic expectation of the people. This St. Matthew perceived, in a perspective still more universalist, when, in the genealogy of our Lord (Mt. 1:5) he inserted the name of Ruth, together with those of two other foreign women.[7]

Ruth brings out two complementary truths: the revelation which the Jewish people had received from God must be carefully preserved from contamination and must, at the same time, be made available to all. The danger was that, in the effort to maintain the purity of Judaism the door should be firmly barred to the Gentiles. Here is a reminder, and a striking one, that the Gentiles too should be received into the community of Israel (cf. Is. 2:3 f.; 45:22 f.). The known Moabite ancestry of David adds point to the story of the Moabitess who recognized the God of Israel and entered wholly into an Israelite family.

2. JONAH

The Book of Jonah, though listed among the twelve minor prophets, is not a prophetical book. The realization of this fact and the establishment of its true literary form and its purpose set the little writing in its proper light and underline its real significance.

1) *Analysis*

CONTENTS   Called by Yahweh to preach penance in Nineveh, Jonah rebelled and fled to the west. A violent storm was sent by Yahweh. The sailors learned that Jonah was the occasion of the storm; they cast him into the sea which immediately grew calm (chapter 1). A great fish swallowed the Prophet, who remained within the fish for three days. There he recited a thanksgiving psalm. Finally, the

---

[7]BJ, p. 149.

fish vomited him out on the shore (chapter 2). God again ordered
Jonah to go to Nineveh; this time he obeyed. The people of Nineveh
repented at his preaching and God pardoned them (chapter 3). The
Prophet was extremely annoyed by this manifestation of divine fore-
bearance. He was taught a salutary lesson by Yahweh who, at the
same time, made clear the moral of the story (chapter 4).

It should be noted that the thanksgiving psalm (Jon. 2:2-10),
composed largely of appropriate verses taken from the Psalter, is a
later addition. The psalm was put in the mouth of Jonah because of
references to "the belly of Sheol," "the deep," "the heart of the seas,"
"thy waves and thy billows"—language that is typical of thanksgiving
(and supplication) psalms.[8]

PLAN

A REBELLIOUS PROPHET (JON. 1)
THE DELIVERANCE OF JONAH (JON. 2)
REPENTANCE OF THE NINEVITES AND GOD'S PARDON (JON. 3)
DISAPPOINTMENT OF THE PROPHET AND GOD'S LESSON (JON. 4)

2) Date and Literary Form

Jonah is described as the "son of Amittai"; in 2 Kgs. 14:25 we read
of a prophet of the same name who flourished in the eighth century
B.C. Many have thought that this prophet was not only the hero of
the book but its author as well. In the eighth century B.C. the mighty
Assyrian Empire was near the height of its power and the capital,
Nineveh, must have reflected its splendor. According to Jonah an
Israelite prophet was sent to this great city with the mission to
preach repentance. And when the unknown prophet of a despised
nation appeared, the king and all his people not only listened to him
but were immediately converted and did penance. There is no trace
in any of our records of such an occurrence, which is remarkable
since the conversion of Assyria would have changed the course of

---

[8]See pp. 297-300.

history. It cannot be objected that the conversion was no more than a temporary one. In that case it would have been no real conversion, whereas it is formally stated that the people of Nineveh believed God (Jon. 3:5), and God himself acknowledged the sincerity of their conversion (Jon. 3:10). A miracle of this magnitude not only eclipses that of the great fish, but it has no parallel.

We have a problem on our hands, if the Book of Jonah is a historical work. This problem vanishes when the book is taken for what it really is, a work of fiction, and when it is realized that the fictional hero of Jonah has nothing in common with the prophet of the eighth century B.C. except the name. The Hebrew of Jonah and the many Aramaisms in the writing demand a date not earlier than the fifth century B.C. By that time Nineveh, which had been utterly destroyed in 612 B.C., was only a distant memory. This is borne out by the fantastic dimensions given to the city: "Nineveh was an exceedingly great city, three days' journey in breadth" (Jon. 3:3); Jonah felt that he had not arrived inside the city until he had walked for a whole day (Jon. 3:4)! Needless to say, this is popular description; the site of Nineveh has been excavated and it is evident that it was quite a modest town by our standards.

Jonah echoes earlier prophetical literature and has close contacts with Jeremiah.[9] For instance, Jonah 3:8 echoes Jer. 25:5; 26:3; 36:3,7; and Jonah 3:2 presents a situation similar to that of Jer. 36. Jonah's wish that he might die (Jon. 4:3,8) suggests a parallel with Elijah (1 Kgs. 19:4-8), but with a touch of irony since the two men are so different. Especially noteworthy is a passage of Jer. (18:7 f.) which may well have been the inspiration of Jonah.

> The book may be described as a written sermon in story form based on Jer. 18:8: "If that nation, concerning which I have spoken, turns from its evil, I will repent of the evil that I thought to do to it." This is clearly alluded to in Jonah 3:10. In the course of the sermon the author not only demonstrates the possibility of a heathen city repenting and turning to God, but draws attention also to the love, mercy, and forgiveness of God, and, in the person of Jonah, strongly rebukes those who would be unwilling to see God's mercy extend beyond Israel.[10]

[9]See A. Feuillet, *Le Livre de Jonas* (BJ), pp. 16-18.
[10]L. H. Brockington, PCB, n. 549 c.

3) *The Message*

The milieu in which Jonah was written would have been the same, or much the same, as that in which Ru. took form. It is understandable that, among the returned exiles, in view of all they had gone through and were still suffering, a certain exclusiveness should have appeared—at least in some circles. Those who shared this outlook wished to cut themselves off from contact with other peoples and looked with impatience for the vengeance of God on the Gentiles—for they were the Chosen People and all others were accursed. Jonah is nothing other than a criticism of this view and a bold declaration that God is the God of all peoples. It is no naïve collection of improbable miracles, but it is a highly-sophisticated writing, a brilliant satire. For all its brevity it is one of the masterpieces of literature and, from the point of view of doctrine, it is in advance of its time, for its universalist outlook anticipates that of the Gospel. We can understand this if we glance again at the contents of the book.

Jonah is presented as an authentic prophet of the Chosen People, one entrusted with a divine mission. This mission is to preach to the Assyrians, the hated oppressors of his people. The Prophet well knows the mercy of God and he suspects that, in fact, the Assyrians will repent and God will not carry out his threat against them. The thought of the divine mercy extended to the great enemy is more than Jonah can stand. Hence, instead of setting out for Nineveh in the east, he flees to the west (Jon. 1:1-3).

With splendid artistry the author contrasts the narrow, unforgiving disposition of the Israelite Prophet with the open and sympathetic attitude of the other characters of his story—all Gentiles. The pagan sailors are horrified to learn that anyone can bring himself to disobey a divine command (Jon. 1:10) and they are loath to cast him into the sea (Jon. 1:13). The king of Nineveh and his people at once believe the word of the Prophet and are converted and do penance (Jon. 3:6-9). The irony is unmistakable: the preaching of the reluctant Jonah meets with an immediate and universal response in the pagan city, whereas the great prophets had, over the centuries, preached to the Chosen People in vain!

God did accept the sincere conversion of the Ninevites; but what of Jonah? "It displeased Jonah exceedingly, and he was angry" (Jon.

4:1). However, he did not give up hope that the Lord might yet change his mind, and so he sat outside the city, waiting for the longed-for destruction (Jon. 4:5). Then God, who was all patience and mercy even towards his stubborn Prophet, taught him a lesson in a gentle but effective way. He caused a plant to spring up and give shade to Jonah, and then he permitted it to wither just as quickly—and this angered the Prophet (Jon. 4:6-9). Now the moral of the story becomes clear: If Jonah felt that he had a right to be annoyed because the plant had withered up, should not God pity Nineveh in which there were more than 120,000 helpless infants ("who do not know their right hand from their left" [Jon. 4:11]) —and so necessarily innocent—as well as many animals, and not seek to destroy it? The loving mercy of God extends to all peoples and to all his creatures.

Understood in this way the Book of Jonah makes delightful reading. The miracles are no longer an embarrassment, but serve to embellish the story, leaving us free to appreciate its satirical humor. At the same time, however, we must not forget the sublime teaching of the book, a doctrine that is valid for all time, even though it was largely overlooked in the following centuries until it was emphatically restated by Christ.

There is perhaps one point that may appear to conflict with our presentation of Jonah as a work of fiction. In Mt. 12:41 and Lk. 11:29-32 Jesus brings forward the conversion of the Ninevites as an example; and in Mt. 12:40 he presents Jonah in the belly of the fish as a type of his own sojourn in the tomb. But these references are to the *Book* of Jonah: the Ninevites, as there described, are an example; and Jonah, as there represented, is a type—it does not follow that they or he are historical. The argument is strictly scriptural; it is confined to the biblical Jonah and to the Ninevites as portrayed in this one writing.

It is not surprising that our Lord referred to Jonah, for it was he who brought to fulfillment the sublime doctrine of that book. Jonah had declared that God was the God of all peoples, a merciful God who had pity on his creatures; St. John is able to go far beyond that and can assure us that God "so loved the world that he gave his only Son" (Jn. 3:16). And this Son tells us that he is the Shepherd who desires to gather all his scattered sheep into one flock (Jn. 10:16).

3. TOBIT

1) The Book

The Greek manuscripts group Tobit with Judith and Esther and place them either immediately after the historical books or immediately after the wisdom books. Of the three, Esther alone is found in the Hebrew Bible. Tobit and Judith have suffered the usual vicissitudes of the deuterocanonical books.[11]

Tobit is extant in four main recensions:

1. *Greek.* (1) Vaticanus (B) and Alexandrinus (A); (2) Sinaiticus (S).

2. *Latin.* (1) Old Latin; (2) Vulgate.

In practice, we get down to two main forms of the text:

I: represented by B and A;

II: represented by S and Old Latin.

Today the text II is more and more preferred. It is somewhat longer than the other, but contains less certain corruptions. Also in its favor are a superior literary style and more obvious coherence and originality. St. Jerome translated Tb. only at the insistence of the Bishops Chromatius and Heliodorus. He had access to an Aramaic copy of the work but, as he was not yet proficient in that language, he used an interpreter. A Jew who knew both languages gave a verbal Hebrew rendering of the Aramaic; Jerome, on the spot, dictated his Latin translation of the latter. The job was completed in a single day.[12]

Tb. was originally written in Hebrew or Aramaic. At Qumran fragments of three manuscripts in Aramaic and of one in Hebrew have been found. The impression from these fragments is that the book was written in Aramaic and translated into Hebrew.[13] Both Aramaic and Hebrew texts correspond to the longer text of S and Old Latin.

---

[11]See Wilfrid Harrington, *Record of Revelation: The Bible* (Chicago: The Priory Press, 1965), p. 64.

[12]See Migne, *PL*, cols. 29, 23-26; cf. A. Lefèvre, IB, pp. 740 f.

[13]See J. T. Milik, *Ten Years of Discovery in the Wilderness of Judaea* (Naperville, Ill.: Allenson, 1959), p. 31; cf. Harrington, *op. cit.*, p. 64.

2) Analysis

CONTENTS Tobit, a pious Jew, found himself transported to Nineveh along with his wife Anna and their son Tobias. He prospered in exile and was in a position to give generous alms to his needy brethren; he also made a practice of giving honorable burial to Jews who would otherwise have been deprived of it. One evening, returning from such an errand of mercy, he slept in his open courtyard and was blinded by droppings from a sparrow's nest. Like Job before him, he patiently accepted this painful trial and turned in earnest prayer to God.

At that self-same moment the prayer of another afflicted soul went up to God. In the city of Ecbatana a Jewish maiden named Sarah—daughter of Raguel and Edna—was insulted by one of her father's servants who accused her of having strangled her husbands. The trouble was that Sarah had been betrothed seven times, but each time the evil demon Asmodeus had slain the unfortunate fiancé. Cut to the quick by the cruel words, she was tempted to end it all; but she overcame the temptation by turning to the Lord and putting her trust in him.

The author then proceeds to link these two episodes with superb literary skill. Tobit recalled that he had, many years before, entrusted a sum of money to his friend Gabael and now decided to send Tobias to claim it. Just like Polonius, he gave his son good advice, but the maxims here are reminiscent of the Book of Proverbs; and to be his son's companion on the journey he engaged a Jew named Azarias—in reality the angel Raphael in human form. The angel encouraged the young man in face of danger and helped him to procure remedies for his father's blindness and against the machinations of evil spirits. Moreover he extolled the charms of Sarah so effectively that Tobias "fell in love with her and lost his heart to her hopelessly" (Tb. 6:18).

At Ecbatana they visited the home of Raguel; Tobias wasted no time in seeking Sarah's hand. Despite the apprehension of Raguel (who had prudently prepared a grave—just in case) this time the demon was vanquished. The mutual affection of the young couple is love in the deepest and truest sense, and the writer is at pains to put the matter beyond doubt. It is not in the least surprising that our marriage liturgy has been colored by the Book of Tobit, for Tobias and Sarah do indeed stand as an example to Christian husbands and wives. And in the same writing we are shown that a deeply-religious concept of marriage can go hand-in-hand with the realization that marriage is a happy occasion, to be celebrated with joy and gladness (Tb. 8:19-21; 11:17 f.). Then follows the glad return to Nineveh and further rejoicing, made all the greater by the restoration of Tobit's eyesight. Raphael reveals his true identity and Tobit's hymn of thanksgiving turns into a prophecy of the future glory of Jerusalem (chapter 13). After the death of his parents, Tobias, with his wife and family, returned to Ecbatana to take care of his parents-in-law in their old age.

PLAN[14]

(Tb. 1-3)	*The Setting.*	Tobit and Sarah—their prayers heard simultaneously by God.
(Tb. 4-11)	*The Plot.*	The angel Raphael (the providence of God) brings about the marriage of Tobias and Sarah and the cure of Tobit.
(Tb. 12-14)	*Conclusion.*	The angel reveals his identity; Canticle of Tobit; all live happily ever after.

3) Literary Form and Date

The charming story of Tobit has been largely inspired by biblical models, especially by the patriarchal narratives of Genesis: Abraham and Sarah; Isaac and Rebekah; Jacob and Rachel. The portrayal of Raphael, for instance, is based on Gn. 24:40: "He [Abraham] said to me: 'The Lord, before whom I walk, will send his angel with you to prosper your way; and you shall take a wife for my son from my kindred.'" This example also shows with what freedom the author handles his sources in order to build up a new composition; it is obviously the *midrash* technique. Nor is he worried about precision in topography or chronology. Thus Tobit 5:6 (S) sets Rhages in the mountains and Ecbatana in the plain and has them

---

[14]See P. F. Ellis, *The Men and the Message of the Old Testament* (Collegeville, Minn.: The Liturgical Press, 1963), p. 460.

only two normal days' walk apart. In fact, Ecbatana is nearly 3,000 feet higher than Rhages and they are about 250 miles apart. Tobit could not have been a witness of the beginning of the schism in 931 B.C. (Tb. 1:4) and have been deported in 734 B.C. (Tb. 1:10). His son, born before the deportation (Tb. 1:9), can scarcely have heard of the destruction of Nineveh in 612 B.C. (Tb. 14:15). This is enough to indicate that Tobit is not historical; indeed it approximates more closely to the wisdom literature. We may well describe the book as a novelette; we do in fact find it surprisingly modern.

Its date is difficult to establish. There seems to be no reason why it might not have been written in the fifth century B.C., though a date even as late as the third century B.C. cannot be ruled out.

In Tobit 1:22; 2:10; 11:18; 14:10 a certain Ahikar is named, thus indicating a link between Tobit and *The Words* (or *Wisdom*) *of Ahikar*, a very ancient work extant in Syriac, Armenian, Arabic, and Slav versions. However, a substantial part of an Aramaic papyrus text was discovered in 1906-7 at Elephantine, Upper Egypt: it gives the story of Ahikar and a collection of his sayings.

> The action of the narrative centers about the court of the Assyrian kings Sennacherib (705-681 B.C.) and Esarhaddon (681-669 B.C.). Of other persons named therein, Nabusumiskun actually was a high official of Sennacherib, and Ahikar himself may be a reflex of Adadsumusur, a priest who officiated in the reigns of Sennacherib and Esarhaddon and exerted a certain amount of influence over them. All of the proper names fit well into an Assyrian milieu. For the sayings, too, a Mesopotamian origin is indicated by repeated references to Shamash as god of justice.[15]

Briefly, the story is that Ahikar, in high favor at the Assyrian court, was calumniated by his nephew (and adopted son) Nadan and his life was endangered. He was hidden by the officer sent to arrest him. Later, Ahikar was able to come to the aid of Esarhaddon and found himself reinstated, while Nadan died in prison. The author of Tobit refers to the moral of the story in Tobit 14:10 f. (Nadan has become Nadab), and he makes Ahikar the nephew of Tobit (Tb. 1:21 f.; 2:10; 11:18). The "words" of Ahikar are maxims addressed to Nadan (cf. Tb. 4). It is unlikely that there is direct

---

[15]ANET, p. 427.

literary dependence of Tobit on *The Words of Ahikar;* it seems that the author of Tobit echoes a well-known story.

4) *The Message*

The proverbial maxims of chapters 4, 12, 14 are little more than ornaments attached to the main narrative. That narrative is concerned with a double case of the just sufferer: Tobit, a model of observance and of charity, is the victim of an unfortunate accident; Sarah, an innocent girl, is grievously afflicted through no fault of her own. Both become the butt of bitter tongues (Tb. 2:14 [22]; 3:8) and, as a result, both seek to die (Tb. 3:7,15). Here we have the problems of the wisdom writers: Is virtue rewarded? Is life worth living? The key to the book is found in Tobit 3:16 f. [24 f.] and 12:12-15. The prayer of the two unhappy ones is presented to God by Raphael—and the angel receives the mission to help them; Azarias is indeed the instrument of God's providence. The author of Tobit has not only borrowed from Genesis the elements of his narrative, he has also read there the striking texts which show God's providence drawing forth good from evil (Gn. 45:4-8; 50:19-21). In the light of these he can show that suffering may be meaningful and he can present an optimistic view of life.[16]

Tobit obviously extols family virtues. The older couples, exemplary in their own lives, have brought up their children well; it is clear that the only son and only daughter motif suits the demands of the plot. Tobias and Sarah, in their turn, have a lofty ideal of marriage and show themselves keenly aware of their obligations to their parents. Great store is set by generous almsgiving; and an atmosphere of faith and trust in God—and joyful thanksgiving—is all-pervasive. This little romance needs no one to plead its cause; it has its honorable place in God's library and marks an important step in the direction of the fuller Christian ideal.

4. BARUCH

The manuscripts of the LXX have Baruch, Lamentations, and the Letter of Jeremiah after the Book of Jeremiah. In the Vulgate the Letter of Jeremiah becomes chapter 6 of Baruch; however, the long

---

[16]See R. Pautrel, *Tobie* (BJ), pp. 13 f.

title of the Letter clearly marks it off as a separate writing. St.
Jerome did not translate Baruch, hence the Vulgate text is really
Old Latin; indeed, many good manuscripts of the Vulgate do not
carry the book at all. It is undeniable that the writing is later than
Baruch (the disciple and secretary of Jeremiah), and that the attribution of it to him is in accordance with the practice of pseudepigraphy
—the deliberate attachment of a writing to a notable personage of
the past—much in vogue in the third century B.C. and after.

1) Analysis

PROLOGUE (BAR. 1:1-14)
A PENITENTIAL PRAYER (BAR. 1:15–3:8)
IN PRAISE OF WISDOM—IDENTIFIED WITH THE LAW (BAR. 3:9–4:4)
A DISCOURSE OF EXHORTATION AND OF CONSOLATION (BAR. 4:5–5:9)
APPENDIX: THE LETTER OF JEREMIAH (BAR. 6)

It is clear that Baruch (including the appendix) comprises four
literary forms: prayer; wisdom poem; prophetical discourse; and satire.
It is to be noted that the Greek of the prayer is full of Semitisms,
thus suggesting a Hebrew original. The Greek of the third section
is pure, and the discourse implies a speedy return to Jerusalem—
while the prologue refers to the beginning of the Exile. These factors
militate against the unity of composition and against the hypothesis
of a single author.

CONTENTS[17]   According to the prologue the book (or, more properly, the prayer of Bar. 1:15–3:8) was read during a religious assembly
in Babylon on the anniversary of the destruction of Jerusalem. Pilgrims
going to Jerusalem for the Feast of Tabernacles were to take the
prayer with them so that it might be recited in the house of the
Lord; and sacrifices were to be offered at the same time. This is
quite in conformity with the practice of Jews of the Diaspora from

---

[17]See A. Lefèvre, IB, pp. 734-37.

the time of Ezra; we have two similar prayers of Ezra, composed in analogous circumstances (Ez. 8; Neh. 9).

But the procedure indicated in the prologue would have been impossible five years after the beginning of the Exile (Bar. 1:2), that is to say, a pilgrimage to Jerusalem, the restoration of the sacred vessels, sacrifice in Jerusalem, and prayer for Nebuchadnezzar and his "son" Belshazzar.[18] We know that there was no regular cult, with the offering of holocausts, in Jerusalem after the destruction of the Temple until the arrival of the high priest Joshua (Ez. 3). The prologue is, therefore, an artificial composition or, if one prefers, an edifying story, one much later than the time of Baruch. The dates and proper names serve the purpose of inserting the regular event of an annual pilgrimage into the religious history of Israel; for that pilgrimage did recall the return from the Exile and did foreshadow the final restoration.

The penitential prayer of the exiles (Bar. 1:15—3:8) is an appeal to the divine mercy. The literary form, collective penitential psalm, is found throughout the Old Testament (for example, 1 Kgs. 8:46-53; Ps. 80 [79]; Sir. 36:1-17; Dn. 3:26-45). The prayer of Baruch is very much like those of Ez. 9:6-15, Neh. 9:6-37, and Dn. 9—to such an extent that some sort of mutual dependence seems assured. The undeveloped eschatology of Baruch would suggest that it is earlier than the others; we may date the prayer about the beginning of the second century B.C.

The wisdom section (Bar. 3:9—4:4) is exhortatory in tone, as indicated by the introduction and concluding formulas: Baruch 3:9-14; 4:2-4. The body of it is a hymn to wisdom (Bar. 3:14—4:1). The author has imitated the hymn of Jb. 28, but he was also largely inspired by Dt. 30 (cf. Dt. 4:1-8). We find a similar atmosphere in Sir. 1:1-20 and 24:1-32, and we may reasonably date the hymn about 200 B.C.

The discourse of Baruch 4:5—5:9 corresponds to the opening penitential prayer. In his address to the children of Israel (Bar. 4:5-9) the poet reminds them that the affliction of the Exile had come upon them because they had provoked the eternal God who had made them and because they had grieved Jerusalem their mother.

---

[18]See p. 377.

Then Sion speaks (Bar. 4:9-29): she reminds her children of the suffering they had caused her by their rebelliousness and of the exhortations she had addressed to the Everlasting on their behalf. Her cries have been heard and she foretells their speedy return. The Everlasting replies by the mouth of the Prophet and makes known to Sion that her sorrows are ended and that her children will be restored to her (Bar. 4:30–5:9). The connection of the discourse with the preceding parts would indicate that it too should be dated about the beginning of the second century.

The Letter of Jeremiah (Bar. 6), originally written in Hebrew but transmitted in a Greek version, is a satire against idols, one modeled on Is. 44:9-20 and even more closely on Jer. 10:1-16. The idolatry in question is that of Babylon under Alexander or the Seleucids who had restored the cult of the old Babylonian gods. The writing may be third century B.C. or later; its attribution to Jeremiah is patently pseudepigraphical.

2) *The Message*

Baruch helps us in some measure to grasp the reasons that explain the endurance of the communities of the Diaspora. These were, notably: the link with Jerusalem, maintained by means of letters, collections, and communion of prayers; the synagogue prayer nourished on the vivid memory of the past; the reading of the Sacred Books (especially Dt., Jer., and Second Isaiah); the cult of the Law; a profound sense of sin and a desire of conversion; finally, resistance to any form of idolatrous cult.[19]

The writing offers a deep analysis of sin. Sin is a perversion of a moral order based on God's justice (Bar. 2:12); it is a proud rejection of wisdom (Bar. 3:9 ff.), manifested in rebellion against the Law and in indifference to the warnings of the prophets (Bar. 1:18,21; 2:5,10,24). The antidote to sin is a humble return to God, the source of all good (Bar. 2:8; 30 ff.; 4:28) and the observance of the Law. In the Law Israel will find life (Bar. 4:1).

In the discourse God is named the Everlasting (Bar. 4:10,14,22,24) —a title found nowhere else in the Bible. He is the source of wisdom (Bar. 3:12,32); he is the Holy One *par excellence* (Bar. 4:22,37; 5:5).

---

[19]See A. Gelin, *Jérémie, Les Lamentations, Le Livre de Baruch* (BJ), pp. 283 f.

He is the only deliverer of the exiles (Bar. 4:18,23,29), for his characteristics are justice (Bar. 1:15; 2:6,9; 5:9) and mercy (Bar. 2:27; 3:1; 5:9). Salvation comes from the Everlasting God (Bar. 4:8) who has been offended but who manifests his glory, first by chastening and then by saving sinners. In short, Baruch is a drama of sin, of conversion, and of salvation.

5. DANIEL[20]

1) The Book

In the Hebrew Bible, Daniel is found among the Writings, between Esther and Ez.-Neh. The LXX and all other versions place it among the prophetical books, immediately after Ezekiel. In the LXX and the versions based on it the text of Daniel has certain additions not found in the Hebrew; these constitute the deuterocanonical[21] parts of the book. As they stand, they form a supplement to the original work and we shall leave them aside until the close of this section.

Daniel is written partly in Hebrew (Dn. 1:1–2:4a; 8-12), partly in Aramaic (Dn. 2:4b–7:28), and partly in Greek (Dn. 3:24-90; 13-14). (The passage Daniel 3:24-90 is inserted between 2:23 and 3:24 of the Hebrew.)

There is no particular difficulty in the use of Greek for the deuterocanonical parts: they are present in the LXX only. On the other hand the juxtaposition of Hebrew and Aramaic in the rest of the book is a riddle. Daniel starts in Hebrew and abruptly, at Daniel 2:4b, switches to Aramaic. Chapter 8 changes back to Hebrew and the book concludes in that language (chapters 13-14 form an appendix). None of the many proposed solutions of the problem is convincing, because the stubborn fact is that the distinction of language breaks across the natural twofold division of the book. To this must be added the other fact that the book is the work of a single author; we simply do not know why he decided to use two languages.

2) Division

The Book of Daniel falls naturally into two parts.

---

[20]See P.O Fiannachta-W.O h-Urdail (Harrington), *Leabhar Dhainéil* (Nenagh, 1965). The treatment of Dn. in the present chapter is a translation of my Introduction to this new Irish version of the book.

[21]See Harrington, *Record of Revelation: The Bible, op. cit.*, p. 64.

PART I: THE EPISODES (DN. 1-6)	
1) Daniel and his three companions in the service of Nebuchadnezzar	1
2) Dream of Nebuchadnezzar—the Composite Statue	2
3) The Image of Gold; the three companions in the furnace	3:1-23, 91-97
Addition: Prayer of Azariah; Canticle of the three youths	3:24-90
4) The madness of Nebuchadnezzar	4
5) The Feast of Belshazzar	5
6) Daniel in the Lions' Den	6

In each case Daniel and his companions come triumphantly through the trials on which their life, or at least their reputation, depends, and the pagans glorify God. The scene is at Babylon during the reign of Nebuchadnezzar, of his "son" Belshazzar, and of the latter's successor, "Darius the Mede."

PART II: THE VISIONS (DN. 7-12)	
1) The Four Beasts	7
2) The Ram and the Goat	8
3) The Seventy Weeks	9
4) The great Vision:	
a) The Time of Anger	10-11
b) The Time of the End	12

Daniel is the subject of these visions. They are dated in the reign of Belshazzar, of "Darius the Mede," and of Cyrus, king of Persia. Daniel is in Babylon.

APPENDICES	
1) Susanna and the Judgment of Daniel	13
2) Bel and the Serpent	14

3) Summary of Contents

The book opens by relating how Daniel and his friends were taken to Nebuchadnezzar's court in Babylon to be trained for royal service.

There, in a pagan environment and in spite of pressure to eat the king's rich fare, they remained faithful to the dietary prescriptions of the Jewish law. Though they lived on vegetables and water, they were sturdier than the other youths. God endowed them with wisdom beyond that of the wise men of Babylon (chapter 1).

Daniel proved the excellence of this wisdom when, without being told it, he was able to describe the king's dream and then went on to give its interpretation. The king acknowledged the greatness of Daniel's God; he appointed Daniel head of his wise men, with the three companions as his assistants (chapter 2).

When Nebuchadnezzar had commanded that all his subjects should worship a great golden idol—under pain of being cast into a fiery furnace—Daniel's three companions (he himself does not appear in this chapter) alone refuse to comply. The angry king ordered the furnace to be heated seven times more than usual, but once again he was moved to acknowledge the God of Israel when, to his astonishment, he saw the three youths, accompanied by an angel, walking unscathed in the midst of the flames. (The prayer and canticle [Dn. 3:24-90] are a later addition.) The three Jews were promoted to a higher rank (chapter 3).

Nebuchadnezzar revealed a dream in which he had seen a great tree cut down so that only its stump was left; Daniel interpreted the dream to mean that the king would become insane and would live like an animal for seven years. Sometime later, as the king was glorying over the greatness of Babylon, a voice from heaven reminded him that God alone held supreme authority; thereupon he became mad. After seven humiliating years his sanity was restored and in a hymn of praise he confessed that kingship, power, and glory belong to the God of Israel alone (chapter 4).

Nebuchadnezzar's supposed successor, Belshazzar, held a banquet for his nobles. During the feast they decided to drink wine from the sacred vessels which Nebuchadnezzar had taken from the Temple. Suddenly a hand appeared, writing on the wall. The king's sages failed to read the mysterious message and Daniel was called in. He explained that the message warned of the imminent fall of Belshazzar's kingdom. That night the king was killed and "Darius the Mede" won possession of the empire (chapter 5).

Daniel had now become one of the three presidents over the 120 satraps of the empire. The other presidents and the satraps were jealous of Daniel because they feared that Darius would appoint him over the whole realm. They accordingly prevailed on the king to issue an irrevocable decree forbidding, for a month, all petitions to any god or man. When Daniel was found praying to his God, the decree was invoked and the king was reluctantly obliged to command that he be cast into the den of lions. Next morning, to the king's great joy, Daniel was found unharmed—and his accusers were thrown to the lions. The king issued a decree that the God of Daniel was to be reverenced throughout the kingdom (chapter 6).

The second part of Daniel consists of visions which show the dramatic movement of historical events towards a determined goal, towards the time when God will break all earthly power and establish his kingdom on earth. Four successive empires are portrayed: the Babylonian, Median, Persian, and Greek—each surpassing its predecessor in evil. In this manner Antiochus IV Epiphanes is presented as the term of a flood of evil; thus the time was at hand when God would show his hand.

In the first vision (chapter 7) Daniel saw four beasts rising from the sea. An angel explained to him that these represented four empires: Babylonian, Median, Persian, and Greek (Seleucid); the "little horn" coming from the last of them was Antiochus IV. The Ancient of Days (God), in a judgment scene, condemned the four empires. Then appeared on the clouds of heaven one "like a Son of man," that is, a human figure. The angel explained that this heavenly figure, presented here as an individual, symbolized also the people of God, the "Saints of the Most High." This people will receive an everlasting kingdom which would be inaugurated after "a time, two times and half a time"—a reference to the approximate duration of the persecution of Antiochus (167-164 B.C.).

The second vision (chapter 8), explained by Gabriel, is closely related to the previous one. A two-horned ram (the Medo-Persian Empire) was opposed and destroyed by a he-goat (the Greek Empire) with a conspicuous horn (Alexander the Great). While the he-goat was at the height of its power the great horn was broken (death of Alexander) and four horns grew in its place (the fourfold division of Alexander's empire). Out of one of these horns sprouted "a little horn" (Antiochus IV from the Seleucid kingdom). In his pride this horn exalted himself to the host of heaven and challenged the Prince of the host (God) by defiling his Temple and prohibiting sacrifice; but the tyrant would be broken "by no human hand." The daily sacrifice will be offered again after 2,300 evenings and mornings—that is (roughly), after the three and one-half years of the persecution.

In the third vision (chapter 9) Daniel was puzzling over Jeremiah's prophecy that seventy years must pass before the desolation of Jerusalem would be ended (Jer. 25:11; 29:10) and he prayed to God for light on this mystery. While Daniel was praying, confessing his sin and the sin of his people Israel, the angel Gabriel came to interpret the seventy years: Jeremiah spoke of the captivity and the return from the Exile, but the full restoration, the advent of messianic times, would occur after *seventy weeks* of years.

The fourth vision (chapters 10-12) is a revelation of the final period preceding the messianic age. Although it is dated in the third year of Cyrus, the Persian period is sketched in a single verse (Dn. 11:2). The list of Persian kings is much abbreviated, for ten succeeded Cyrus. The fourth here is not the last of these kings (Darius III), but Xerxes the Great (486-465 B.C.) who undertook an expedition against Greece in 480 B.C. The rest of chapter 11 deals with the successors of Alexander the Great and gives a detailed account of the relations between Seleucids and Ptolemies down to the time of Antiochus IV (175-163 B.C.). Though this historical summary is cast in the form of a vision of events to come, very little of it is prediction in the proper sense. It is, rather, a résumé of past events and the only example of true prediction is the prophecy concerning the death of Antiochus (Dn. 11:44 f.).

Daniel's last vision (chapter 12) finally leaves the sphere of politics and moves to a higher plane. The goal of history is God's kingdom, which will come solely by God's own power and in his good time. In verses 2 f. we find the doctrine of the resurrection of the body and of retribution after death explicitly stated for the first time. Finally Daniel is ordered to "seal the book": its message is for the end time. Once again we are told that the persecution will last "a time, two times and a half a time."

4) Historical Background

An outline of the historical background is essential for an understanding of Daniel. Though the book ranges, in a general way, from the Neo-Babylonian Empire to Antiochus IV, it is mainly concerned with two periods: Nebuchadnezzar to Cyrus; and the first phase of the Maccabaean revolt. The necessary background is provided above in Chapter One.[22] It will be indicated later how the author has handled the history, especially the earlier part.

Daniel 11 is a veiled description of the history of the Ptolemies and Seleucids, culminating in the profanation of the Temple by Antiochus IV. Here we shall explain the historical references of the chapter.

ALEXANDER THE GREAT (336-323 B.C.)		
THE SELEUCID AND PTOLEMAIC EMPIRES		
THE SELEUCID EMPIRE	THE PTOLEMAIC EMPIRE	
Seleucus I Nicator 312-280	Ptolemy I Soter	323-285
Antiochus I Soter 280-261	Ptolemy II Philadelphos	285-246
Antiochus II Theos 261-246		
Seleucus II Kallinikos 246-226	Ptolemy III Euergetes	246-221
Seleucus III Keraunos 226-223		
Antiochus III (the Great) 223-187	Ptolemy IV Philopator	221-203
Seleucus IV Philopator 187-175	Ptolemy V Epiphanes	203-181
Antiochus IV Epiphanes 175-163	Ptolemy VI Philometor	181-146

1. Daniel 11:3 f. Alexander the Great died in 323 B.C. and his generals disputed possession of the empire. In 315 B.C., after seven years of struggle, four outstanding leaders stood out: Antigonus, the most prominent, who held all the territory from the Mediterranean to central Asia; Cassander, who ruled in Macedonia; Ptolemy Lagi (Dn. 11:5), who had possession of Egypt and southern Syria

---

[22]Pp. 46 f., 67-70, 86-90.

(in connection with him must be mentioned Seleucus his foremost general); and Lysimachus in Thrace. Antigonus aspired to be the sole successor of Alexander, with the understandable result that the others made common cause against him. In the ensuing struggle Seleucus came to the fore. Antigonus was defeated and slain in 302 B.C. at Ipsus in Phrygia. Seleucus won possession of Babylonia and Syria, and though assassinated in 280 B.C. was succeeded by his son Antiochus I. Ptolemy remained in possession of Egypt and his empire stretched as far as Damascus. By the year 281 B.C. we find the empire of Alexander divided into three great kingdoms: the kingdom of the Ptolemies (Egypt); the kingdom of the Seleucids (Asia); and Macedonia.

In 275 B.C. war broke out between Antiochus I and Ptolemy II; the latter invaded Syria but was repulsed. In 261 B.C. Antiochus I was succeeded by his son Antiochus II Theos and war broke out again; but this time it was the Syrian power which took the initiative.

2. Daniel 11:6. Peace was concluded in 252 B.C. and Ptolemy's daughter, Berenice, married Antiochus II—who repudiated his former wife, Laodice. Ptolemy II and Antiochus II died almost simultaneously. Laodice had Berenice and her infant son murdered.

3. Daniel 11:7. Seleucus II Kallinikos, son of Laodice, became king. Ptolemy III Euergetes succeeded in Egypt; he determined to avenge Berenice and her son; hence the third war between Egypt and Syria.

4. Daniel 11:8. Ptolemy III invaded Syria, won a victory, and retired with much booty. In 240 B.C. peace was concluded once more.

5. Daniel 11:9a. Seleucus II was succeeded by Seleucus III Keraunos (226-223 B.C.), and Antiochus III The Great (223-187 B.C.). With the latter a new era in the history of the Near East began. Antiochus III wished to get control of western Asia, but his first attempts were not wholly successful.

6. Daniel 11:10. In 217 B.C. he invaded Syria and pushed to the frontier of Egypt.

7. Daniel 11:11 f. He was disastrously defeated at Raphia by Ptolemy IV. For some years after this Antiochus was quite occupied in the eastern part of his empire.

8. Daniel 11:13. Then he turned to the West again. In 201 B.C. he reconquered Palestine.

9. Daniel 11:14 f. Gaza was taken after a long siege. The Egyptians launched a counteroffensive and the Syrians were driven back to the sources of the Jordan.

10. Daniel 11:16. But in 198 B.C. Antiochus won an overwhelming victory over the Egyptian general Scopas. In 197 B.C. the whole of Syria was incorporated into the empire of the Seleucids; and Palestine remained under the Seleucids until 142 B.C.

11. Daniel 11:17. Antiochus III made peace with Ptolemy V Epiphanes, and in 193 B.C. he gave his daughter Cleopatra in marriage to Ptolemy V.

12. Daniel 11:18. Then Antiochus turned against Asia Minor. He ignored the veto of the Romans; in 190 B.C. he was defeated at Magnesia by the Roman consul Scipio.

13. Daniel 11:19. He had to pay a very heavy indemnity. He attempted to pillage a temple of Bel at Elymais (Elam), but was killed.

14. Daniel 11:20. He was succeeded by Seleucus IV Philopator. This king was poisoned by his minister Heliodorus.

15. Daniel 11:21. Seleucus was succeeded by his brother Antiochus IV Epiphanes (175-163 B.C.) who had supplanted Demetrius and Antiochus, sons of Seleucus IV. It is the religious persecution of Antiochus IV that led to the Maccabaean revolt.

Antiochus IV Epiphanes determined to Hellenize his realm. Jason, brother of the high priest Onias III, had usurped the high priesthood. At Antioch he was confirmed by Antiochus. He promised to pay a large sum and to Hellenize Jerusalem. Jason's work of Hellenization was supported by many elements in Jerusalem and by the powerful Tobiad family of Ammanitis.

16. Daniel 11:22. Antiochus IV visited Jerusalem. On his return to Antioch Menelaus offered him a huge bribe in order to obtain the high priesthood. Menelaus entered Jerusalem and Jason fled to Ammanitis (172 B.C.). Onias III was killed by Andronicus, minister of the king.

17. Daniel 11:25-27. First campaign of Antiochus in Egypt (170 B.C.).

18. Daniel 11:28. On his return he despoiled the Temple.

19. Daniel 11:29-30a. Second campaign of Antiochus in Egypt (168 B.C.). He retired at the order of the Roman Legate who conveyed the veto of the Senate.

Meanwhile, at the rumor of the king's death, Jason attacked Jerusalem; Menelaus was able to hold out in the citadel north of the Temple. At the approach of Antiochus Jason fled. This revolt stirred up the anger of Antiochus against the Jews.

20. Daniel 11:30b-35. The great persecution (167-164 B.C.); massacre at Jerusalem (167 B.C.).

The Acra, a fortress dominating the Tyropean valley and the Temple, and manned by a strong Syrian garrison, was built (Dn. 11:39). The Temple was dedicated to Zeus Olympios and a pagan altar was erected over the altar of holocausts.

On the twenty-fifth of Chislev (December), 167 B.C., the first pagan sacrifice in the Temple was held; the pagan altar is the "abomination of desolation." Jerusalem received the status of a Greek polis. The Hellenized Jews were particularly active in persecuting the orthodox. The Samaritan temple on Gerizim was dedicated to Zeus Hospitalis.

21. Daniel 11:36-39. Antiochus IV had himself represented on his coins in the character of Zeus Olympios and with the title of Antiochus Theos Epiphanes.

22. Daniel 11:40-43. This seems to be a recapitulation of the campaigns of Antiochus. In 165 B.C. Antiochus went off to the East to undertake a campaign against the Parthians.

23. Daniel 11:44a. Rumors of the defeat of his troops in Palestine.

24. Daniel 11:44b-45. His plans for the destruction of Palestine were rendered ineffective by his death which occurred at Rabae in Persia (163 B.C.).

Meanwhile, the Maccabaean revolt had broken out in 167 B.C. The first phase of the holy war (167-164 B.C.) ended in an agreement on the fifteenth of Xanthikos (April), 164 B.C. There was a general amnesty and the ordinances that had caused the revolt were abolished. On the twenty-fifth of Chislev (December), 164 B.C., Judas Maccabaeus had the Temple purified and sacrifices offered; it was just three years after the pagan profanation.

THE VISIONS OF DANIEL		
COMPOSITE STATUE (DN. 2)		THE FOUR BEASTS (DN. 7)
Head of gold	The Babylonians	Lion with eagle's wings
Breast of silver	The Medes	The bear
Belly of bronze	The Persians	Leopard—4 wings, 4 heads
Legs, feet—iron, clay	The Greeks	Fourth beast—10 horns
	Antiochus IV	The little horn—persecution for three and one-half years (1260 days)
The great stone	Messianic kingdom	Kingdom of Saints of Most High
THE RAM AND GOAT (DN. 8)		THE 70 WEEKS (DN. 9:24-27)
	Babylonians	7 WEEKS—587-538 B.C.
Ram with 2 horns	Medo-Persians	
Goat with 1 horn	Alexander	
The four horns	Hellenistic dynasty	62 WEEKS—538-171 B.C.
	Persecution—1150 days	7th WEEK—171-164 B.C.
Broken by no human hand	Messianic kingdom	End of sin; everlasting justice.

5) *The Date of the Book of Daniel*

Traditionally, Dn. is a prophetical book: it was written by the Prophet Daniel towards the close of and immediately after the Babylonian exile. Jewish and Christian tradition is unanimous in this respect. But here again, as in the case of Second Isaiah, the traditional attribution of the book to Daniel and to the sixth century B.C. does not purport to settle a problem of literary and historical criticism. And the literary and historical criticism of Daniel make it quite clear that the book was written in the second century B.C. There are many arguments in support of this view.

THE LINGUISTIC   1. The Hebrew of Daniel is much later than the
ARGUMENT   sixth century B.C. It is that of an age subsequent to
Ezra and Nehemiah.

2. The Aramaic is certainly later than the fifth century B.C.

3. There are at least fifteen Persian loan-words, and three Greek words in Daniel; the latter (names of musical instruments) require a date after Alexander the Great.

THE HISTORICAL   The writer reveals an imperfect and inaccurate
ARGUMENT   knowledge of the political history of Babylon during the last years of the Neo-Babylonian Empire and the first years of Persian rule. It is inconceivable that he should have lived in that period.

1. A captivity in the third year of Jehoiakim (Dn. 1:1 f.) is unknown.

2. Belshazzar is represented as the last king of Babylon and as the son of Nebuchadnezzar. In fact, Belshazzar was not king and was the son of Nabonidus; the latter was the last king of Babylon.

3. Darius the Mede is said to have succeeded Belshazzar; in Daniel 9:1 he is called the son of Xerxes. History knows of no such person. (The author is apparently thinking of Darius III [338-330 B.C.], son of Xerxes I.) The writer has erroneously introduced a Median Empire, ruling over Babylon, between the Neo-Babylonian and the Persian empires.

4. On the other hand, the author is quite at home in the history of the Seleucid and Ptolemaic dynasties and he furnishes precise details from the Maccabaean period.

In short, we might say that, if the book were the work of a sixth-century B.C. prophet we would expect that the references to sixth-century events and personages would be historically accurate and that the history of later centuries would be couched in vague and general terms. Instead we find that the sixth-century B.C. background is inaccurately presented and that events of the second century B.C. are presented, though in veiled language, yet very exactly and in detail.

THE THEOLOGICAL   1. The interest of the Book of Daniel is chiefly
ARGUMENT   centered on the age of Antiochus IV; it has no message for men of the sixth century B.C. But, in the prophetical

writings, the message of a prophet is addressed to his contemporaries.

2. In Old Testament prophecy there is a lack of any determination of time and persons. In Daniel we find many details of time, names, and persons that are unusual in prophecy.

3. The doctrine concerning the angels, the resurrection, the last judgment, and eternal punishment are presented with a distinctness and in such a developed form that an age much later than the Exile is indicated.

A further argument is the position of Daniel in the Jewish canon. It is found among the *kethubim* (Writings) and not among the prophets; the collection of prophets must have been closed when the book appeared. In the Old Testament there is no reference to Daniel earlier than Mc.; it is particularly noteworthy that Sir. 49 does not mention it.

These arguments, taken cumulatively and added to the undoubted unity of authorship of the work, compel us to see in the Book of Daniel a writing of the Maccabaean age. The date of composition can be closely fixed from the consideration of chapter 11. There the struggle between the Ptolemies and the Seleucids is related with a wealth of detail. The climax is the reign of Antiochus IV and his religious persecution of the Jews. The culminating point of the dream of chapter 2 and of the visions is also the reign of this king: his downfall will herald the messianic age. The book was written during the persecution of Antiochus, before his death and before the successful result of the first phase of the Maccabaean war; but it appears to have been composed very shortly before these events. We must place it between 167 B.C. and 164 B.C. and, it seems, closer to the later date.

6) The Literary Forms of Daniel

We have established the fact that Daniel is not a sixth-century B.C. prophetical book, but a composition of the second century B.C. This immediately raises the question of the literary form of the book. We must consider separately the two parts of Daniel because, corresponding to these parts, the book is a combination of two literary forms:

1. Daniel 1-6: Haggadic *midrash* (though chapter 2 is largely apocalyptic).

2. Daniel 7-12: Apocalypse (though chapter 9 is *pesher midrash*).

MIDRASH[23] Daniel 1-6 is a haggadic *midrash* in the sense that on old traditions of the Exile a narrative is constructed which makes the traditions applicable to conditions during the persecution of Antiochus IV. The author of these chapters has written for the benefit of his readers of the early Maccabaean period. Building upon traditional material, he represents the young Jewish nobleman as playing in Babylon the same role that his descendants are called upon to play in Palestine. Nebuchadnezzar and Antiochus are very much alike: both are profaners of the Temple (2 Kgs. 25:9,13-15; 1 Mc. 22-24,57-62); and Babylon, like Antioch, is ranged against Jerusalem, the city of the true God. Daniel and his companions are scrupulously faithful to the food prescriptions of the Law (Dn. 1:8-16); the three companions refuse to adore the statue of the king (Dn. 3:12-18); the edict of Darius cannot prevent Daniel from praying to his God (Dn. 6:11)—all of these are apt lessons for Jews who are face-to-face with the persecution of Antiochus.

Furthermore, the resistance of Daniel and his companions, and their God-given wisdom, contribute to the acknowledgment of the power of Yahweh (Dn. 1:17; 2:46 f.; 4:34; 5:14-16). On his part, God worked prodigies to save them from the danger they incurred for his name (Dn. 3:49 f.; 6:22); the same will happen when the persecution of Antiochus will have exhausted the measure of God's patience.

The aim of these chapters is not merely, or principally, to describe who Daniel was or to narrate certain incidents in his life; it is, more especially, to magnify the God of Daniel by showing how he frustrates the purposes of the proudest monarchs while he defends his servants who trust in him. This is the author's message, of hope and confidence, to his suffering countrymen: If they are true and steadfast like Daniel the Lord will surely vindicate them. Given this purpose the historical inaccuracies are no problem. If Nebuchadnezzar is named instead of Nabonidus is it not because the former resembles Antiochus? The parallel is more striking and the message clearer when the villain of the piece is the great traditional enemy of Jerusalem. The author is interested in the trying and stirring times of Judas Mac-

---

[23]See pp. 323-26.

cabaeus and he has written to encourage his people in their struggle; his work is not, and was not meant to be, a history of Daniel and his times. He has exploited to the full the old traditions, but his only concern is to insure the fidelity and steadfastness of his persecuted brethren.

Daniel 9 offers a typical example of *pesher midrash*.[24] The seventy years of Jeremiah's prophecy regarding the end of the Exile and the restoration (Jer. 25:11; 29:10) are interpreted in a manner that makes them applicable to the Maccabaean period. The method is ingenious: the seventy years become *seventy weeks* of years and the period thus obtained is divided into three parts in order to work in the application. Despite the artificiality of the technique, the argument is theologically valid: this is another crisis in the history of God's people and the oracle of the Lord has lost nothing of its force. The God who brought back his people from Exile will deliver them from Antiochus; and this deliverance, too, is a presage and a guarantee of the final deliverance of messianic times. When Jeremiah (Jer. 25:11; 29:10) sets seventy years as the duration of the Exile he probably referred to the space of a man's life; his figure is not to be taken mathematically. The same must be kept in mind in Daniel 9:24-27.

Daniel 9:24 describes the blessings of the messianic age. In three expressions the writer tells how mankind will be reconciled with God: evil will come to an end; sin will be a thing of the past; guilt will be expiated and forgiven. Then, in place of infidelity, the people of God will practice justice; and whatever has been seen in "vision and prophecy" concerning the day of salvation will come to pass. Lastly a "holy of holies" will be consecrated—either the Temple or the high priest (cf. 1 Chr. 23:13).

The period until the advent of messianic glory covers seventy weeks of years; these are divided into three unequal periods: seven weeks; sixty-two weeks; and one week. The starting-point is the "going forth of the word," that is, the moment of the prophecy of Jeremiah (587 B.C.). At the close of the first seven weeks (of years) an anointed prince arises: this was Cyrus the Great (cf. Is. 45:1), who permitted the exiles to return home. Between 587 B.C. (the date of

---

[24]See p. 326.

the prophecy of Jeremiah) and 538 B.C. (the date of the edict of Cyrus), 49 years elapse (= seven weeks of years). During the second period of sixty-two weeks the rebuilding of the city is undertaken. In fact this was slow work, subject to many difficulties and much opposition; but sixty-two weeks is simply the number left over from the significant first seven weeks and the last week—it has no special relevance.

At the beginning of the seventieth week an "anointed one" was put to death (Dn. 9:26); he is obviously not the same as the anointed one (Cyrus) in verse 25. The high priest Onias III was assassinated in 171 B.C.; he would appear to be indicated. After this a prince appears who destroys city and sanctuary; he is Antiochus IV, as the next verse makes abundantly clear.

This prince will enter into an agreement with many, that is, with the Hellenistic Jews who supported him (Dn. 9:27). He will abolish sacrifice for "half of the week" and will defile the Temple with the "abomination of desolation" (that is, the dedication of the Temple to Olympian Zeus [cf. 2 Mc. 6:2]). The half week (that is, three and one-half years) during which sacrifices will cease is the equivalent of the "time, two times and half a time" of Daniel 12:7; 7:25 (cf. 8:14). In every case it is the approximate duration of the persecution of Antiochus IV which lasted just over three years. The persecution will cease when the "decreed end is poured out on the desolator."

This interpretation of verses 24-27 relates the literal message of verse 24 to the blessings of the messianic age, but finds the historical events of the Maccabaean period described in verses 25-27, events which the writer has himself experienced. The perspective is the same as in the visions of chapters 2, 7, and 8, the only difference being that, whereas these visions end with the messianic kingdom, the vision of the seventy weeks describes it first.

APOCALYPSE   The term "apocalypse" is from the Greek *apokalypsis* meaning "revelation" and indicates something revealed or disclosed to a select few. The name was given by Jews to a type of literature which was supposed to reveal the future and which was especially concerned with the last things. As a literary form the apocalyptic is closely related to the prophetical; it is, in fact, the child of prophecy.

Many passages in the prophetic books deal with the far horizons of time; they have the eschatological interest that is a feature of the apocalyptic.

> The apocalyptists believed that the end was near in their own days, and indicated the course of events that they thought would lead to the great dénouement of history, and the signs of the end. No more than the prophets did they think this climax would arise out of history by any natural evolution. They were persuaded that it could only come about by the direct intervention of God in history. This was not a new concept to the Jew. He believed that God had intervened in history before, in the Exodus and in other critical moments of the history of his own people. God was believed to be always in control of history, and an actor on the stage of history. He was never thought to be the sole actor, and all that happened was not ascribed to him. But in the divine intervention that was looked for to inaugurate the end of history, he was conceived of as the sole significant actor.[25]

While pseudonymity is not an essential feature of apocalypse, an apocalyptic work is almost always attributed to a venerated figure of the past. The reputed author is supposed to receive, in a series of visions, a revelation of God's plan working out in world events— and this revelation is represented as having been hidden for many years, laid up in a "sealed book." History is unfolded in symbols and finds its term in the epoch of the true author. The language is sometimes precise, but more frequently it is designedly vague—this in accordance with the literary fiction, since it is supposed to be prophecy. The apocalypse closes with a prediction of the imminent eschatological judgment and the advent of unending happiness, in other words, with the advent of the messianic age. A notable feature is the frequent intervention of angels; it is they who usually explain the mysterious symbols.

It should be observed that the apocalyptic form does not exclude true prediction of the future, and Daniel is prophetic to a certain extent. The apocalypse looks beyond the age of the writer to the messianic age. The visions of Daniel close, not with the downfall of Antiochus IV, but with the "kingdom that shall never be destroyed" (Dn. 2:44). Reference to the death of the tyrant (Dn. 7:26; 8:25; 9:26 f.) and to the restoration of the Temple worship is also true prediction.

---

[25]H. H. Rowley, PCB, n. 418 d.

The object of apocalypse is to show the providence of God at work in history and thus to inspire the readers with hope and confidence. Apocalypse was born in times of crisis. As a literary form it flourished from the second century B.C. to the second century A.D. The popularity of the form should be taken into account when interpreting apocalypse: features that appear very strange to us were part of a widespread and familiar literary convention. This fact alone would, for people of these centuries, dispel much of the mystery that attaches to the form.

On the other hand, the fact that these chapters of Daniel would have been recognized as apocalyptic by their first readers may cause us to wonder what effect they could have had. After all, these people knew that this was not prophecy but history. Or, to put it another way, since they were aware of the literary convention and would have realized that the writing was pseudoprophecy, how could they have taken it seriously? The truth of the matter is that these chapters set out a comforting and an entirely valid lesson from history. The author invited his readers to look to the past; then he sketched before their eyes a succession of empires—each had appeared, had dominated the contemporary scene, and had gone, leaving no trace behind. They would note, in contrast to the ephemeral powers, one constant element: the people of God. They could also see that time and again this people was at the mercy of a great power and on the point of extinction, but each time God had intervened; the great power had disappeared but Israel remained. The reminder of these facts gave absolute grounds for hope in the present crisis. Besides, the readers of Daniel believed that in just such a crisis the intervention of God, the establishment of his kingdom, would come; they could hope that it would follow the end of this persecution.

The narrative section of Daniel is a prelude to the visions. The story of Daniel assures us that, in the providence of God, persecution cannot achieve its purpose. The visions of the four animals and of the ram and the goat clarify this message. Indeed the burden of these visions is already present in the interpretation of the dream of Nebuchadnezzar. The history of the East is unfolded, centered around the kings symbolized by animals; symbols disappear in chapters 10-11. In every case the series closes with and concentrates on a personage who is the persecutor *par excellence*, Antiochus IV

Epiphanes. Both parts of the book are dominated by one outlook and are welded into a close unit. Daniel and his companions, deported to Babylon, were supported by God and overcame all trials. The same divine providence, through changing empires, continues to work for the coming of the kingdom of God; it continues to protect the people of God and insures its survival. The work of God is accomplished in the midst of trials, but its final realization is certain. The final vision of chapter 12 fittingly concludes the book by pointing to the messianic age that lies just beyond the time of trial.

When we understand Daniel as a combination of *midrash* and apocalypse the late date we are compelled to accept raises no difficulty. More than that, the book, apparently so mysterious, becomes readily understandable, and the historical inaccuracies in no way imperil inerrancy. If, on the other hand, in a spirit of ultraconservatism we tend to regard Daniel as the work of a sixth-century B.C. prophet, then the book is seen to be full of contradictions and inerrancy cannot be safeguarded. It is fitting that our study of the Old Testament should close with a spectacular vindication of the solid worth and positive achievement of modern biblical scholarship.

7) The Sources

Though Daniel is partly *midrash* and partly apocalyptic, it does not necessarily follow that the work is throughout original and altogether a product of its author's imagination. The episodes may have existed separately but were cast by the author in a special literary form with a view to the circumstances of his own time. In other words, in the episode section he seems to have taken old traditions of the Exile and has adapted them to the circumstances of the Maccabaean period. Similarly, some of the features of chapters 7-12 may be traditional, but the visions themselves were written by the author of the book. The existence of traditional material is borne out by the evidence of Qumran. The fragment of an Aramaic writing, "The Prayer of Nabonidus," discovered in Cave 4 seems to provide the basis for the story of Nebuchadnezzar's madness.[26]

Daniel may well be a historical figure; there must be some basis for the many stories linked to his name, here in the episodes, and

---

[26]See Harrington, *Record of Revelation: The Bible, op. cit.,* pp. 76 f.

in the supplement (chapters 13-14). Of course his role in the events recorded has been embellished, either in the traditions or by the author of Daniel. As proof of the historicity of Daniel we may not appeal to Ezek. 14:14,20; 28:3. The name Danel (Daniel) occurs in the Ras Shamra texts;[27] the Daniel mentioned by Ezekiel is this Phoenician wise man. This is obvious from the fact that, side-by-side with Noah, common father of humanity since the Flood, and with Job who was an Edomite, Ezekiel mentions Daniel the Phoenician, and precisely in a context that is concerned with virtuous men who are not Israelites.

8) The Author

In the period just before the Maccabaean revolt we can place the origin of a Jewish party called the *Hasidim* (the "Pious Ones"). Their characteristic attitude was loyalty to the Law at all costs and they vehemently opposed the spreading pagan influence. They wholeheartedly supported the Maccabaean rising (cf. 2 Mc. 14:6, where they are called Hasidaeans). However, they maintained their own viewpoint and standards and cut themselves adrift from the Maccabaean movement in its later stages when they judged it to have become a political movement and no longer a religious one. The Pharisees are the linear descendants of the Hasidim, with the Essenes (like those of Qumran) forming another branch.

The author of Daniel is clearly one of the Hasidim: he has the same deep-rooted aversion to Hellenistic ways and hatred of the tyranny which strove to impose these ways on faithful Jews, and the same unswerving loyalty to the Torah. His purpose was to bolster up the faith that was in danger of being stamped out by Seleucid aggression. He wanted to hearten his people and urge them to unyielding loyalty in the face of persecution. He based his summons to courageous faith on the affirmation that God ruled the course of history. "For when men believe that the issues are in the hands of God, rather than in human hands, they can act without fear of the consequences."[28] It is noteworthy that the prayers which reflect the

---

[27]Canaanite literary texts, mostly religious in character, of the fifteenth and fourteenth centuries B.C., discovered in 1929-1933 at Ugarit (Ras Shamra) on the coast of northern Syria.

[28]B. W. Anderson, *Understanding the Old Testament* (Englewood Cliffs, N.J.: Prentice-Hall, 1957), p. 515.

Hasidim outlook candidly admit the failures of Israel and appeal solely to the gracious goodness of Yahweh (Dn. 9:4-19; cf. 3:26-45). In short, Daniel sets forth the theology of the Maccabaean rising and it has been well named "the manifesto of the Hasidim." Though we are unable to name its author, he is one of the great writers of the Old Testament. It is fitting that he should mark an important stage in the progress of revelation; for in Daniel 12:2 f. the doctrines of the resurrection of the body and of retribution after death are explicitly formulated for the first time.

9) *The Supplements*

The Book of Daniel has been supplemented by way of insertion and by additions. The Prayer of Azariah and the Canticle of the Three Youths (Dn. 3:24-90) have been inserted in chapter 3; the narratives of the Judgment of Daniel and of Bel and the Serpent have been added to the book.

THE SUPPLEMENTS OF CHAPTER 3   Both passages, though now extant only in Greek, were originally written in Hebrew. The lovely prayer (Dn. 3:26-45) is a splendid testimony to Hasidim piety. It is a confession of the sins of the people with a view to obtaining God's mercy and is closely akin to the prayer of Daniel 9:4-19. Verse 38 indicates the situation under Antiochus IV. The Canticle of the Three Youths has three parts: (1) Daniel 3:52-56—a blessing; (2) Daniel 3:57-87—a hymn in praise of creation; (3) Daniel 3:88-90 —a thanksgiving hymn of the three delivered from danger. The introductory verses 25 and 51 serve as titles.

CHAPTERS 13-14   Though these chapters are now extant in Greek only, it is agreed that they were originally written in Hebrew or Aramaic. The Babylonian background of the narrative of Susanna is artificial. The teaching is that of the late wisdom literature: Calumniated innocence is divinely vindicated in answer to prayer, and wisdom is a privilege not of age but of virtue.[29] The episodes of Bel and of the Serpent are manifestly satirical; they are nothing else than a rather unkind "skit" on idolatry by a Judaism that is very sure of itself. The passage Daniel 14:31-42 (Daniel in the den of lions) is surely a doublet of Daniel 6:17-25. The two chapters,

---

[29]See A. Lefèvre, IB, p. 780.

so markedly different in style and content, give evidence of a rich fund of traditional stories about Daniel.

10) A Theology of History

Daniel deals not with single empires but with a succession of empires; it points out how their sequence is determined by God and declares that, when the appointed limit has been reached, they are destined to be overthrown by the kingdom of God. In the author's view history follows a timetable whose stages have been fixed by divine decree.[30] History is purposeful and moves towards a goal, and all of it is under divine control. We had occasion to point out in *Record of Revelation: The Bible*[31] that the sense of God's activity in the events of history is often lost; here we have, in a striking way, the typically Hebrew awareness of that truth. The author of Daniel is convinced that Antiochus is a puppet in God's hand; he has accepted the persecution as God's punishment of a sinful people and he is certain that the time is near when God will end Israel's years of desolation. And, all the while, he looks forward to the final stage, the establishment of God's kingdom.

He tells the story of the past in such a way that the persecuted Jews may understand that their sufferings had a place in God's purpose and may see that the tyranny of Antiochus fell within God's plan. The situation has not developed by chance or in defiance of the divine decree. Though the king may seem to succeed in his proud revolt against the Prince of princes, and may with impunity trample upon the people of the Prince, his triumph is illusory: "He shall prosper till the indignation is accomplished; for what is determined shall be done" (Dn. 11:36). And though it might seem that such emphasis on God's absolute control of human affairs must encourage a laissez-faire attitude, a directly opposite effect was intended and achieved. This confident assurance that history, divinely guided, moved towards a goal fixed by God, fired the tiny band of faithful Jews with indomitable hope when any hope seemed vain, and urged them to supreme effort where resistance seemed doomed to failure. Indeed, their plain duty was put before them in explicit terms: "The people who know their God shall stand firm and take action" (Dn.

---

[30]See Anderson, *op. cit.*, p. 526.
[31]P. 50.

11:32). This faith in God and firm confidence in his ways account
for the exalted spirit and amazing success of the Maccabaean rising,
especially in its first phase, the "three glorious years." Belief in
the justice of their cause has sustained little nations and has, more
than once, moved them to challenge empires. Even in our own
century we have seen this happen and, whether we are personally
involved or not, we must thrill that such things can be. And when
we recall that over and above the deep-rooted instinct of a spirited
people the Jews were conscious of their unique place in history and
of their special role in God's plan for mankind, we can appreciate
the effect of this powerful summons to fearless and resolute action.
"If God was for them, what did it matter how many battalions were
against them? And who cared how many battles were lost, as long
as the saints were fighting on the winning side?"[32]

The book looks always to the final victory, to the time of the
end, to the coming of the kingdom; the author sees the messianic
age about to dawn, just beyond the "time, two times and half a
time" of the persecution. Apocalypse is a child of prophecy and here
the link with the prophetical writings is clear. The prophets before
and during the Exile believed that the deliverance from Babylonian
bondage would herald the Messiah's appearance, and the author of
this book expected the great change to come with the death of
Antiochus; in both cases we have the characteristic foreshortening
of prophecy. The prophets have seen a vision and are overwhelmed
by the majesty of it; and if the kingdom will not come as speedily
as they had imagined, they are certain that it will come. God's victory
over the world is assured, and those who serve him faithfully will
have a glorious part in his triumph.

6. ESTHER

1) The Book

There is a notable difference between the Hebrew text and the LXX
text of Esther: the latter had additions which makes it one-third
longer. The Vulgate gives these additional passages in an appendix
(Est. 10:4—16:24). In the LXX the supplements occur throughout
the narrative. In Rahlfs' critical edition of the LXX (followed by

---

[32]Anderson, *op. cit.*, p. 528.

the *Bible de Jérusalem*) they are numbered as follows (the Vg. numbering is given in parentheses): Esther 1:1a-1 (11:2-12); 1:1m-r (12:1-6), 3:13a-g (13:1-7), 4:17a-i (13:8-18), 4:17h-z (14:1-19), 4:8 (15:1-3), 5:1a-2b (14:4-19), 8:12a-x (16:1-24), 10:3a-k (10:4-13), 10:31 (11:1).

We really have two editions of Esther, one considerably longer than the other. The question is further complicated by the fact that the Greek text has come to us in different forms: that of the great uncials; that of the Latin versions; that of the late revision of Lucian; and that which formed the basis of the Old Latin; in this respect, the Old Latin text is of first importance. It is nowadays generally accepted that the longer Greek text is later than the Hebrew. The editor wished to offer the Jews of the Diaspora "a work that would be more acceptable in a Hellenized milieu, more humane thanks to the suppression of traits too hostile to pagans (for example, Est. 9:5-19 [Heb.]), more religious also and showing more closely the action of Providence and the efficacy of prayer."[33] The supplements, taken together, form the deuterocanonical parts of Esther.

2) *Analysis*

CONTENTS   In the course of a great feast the Persian King Ahasuerus (Xerxes) summoned his Queen Vashti into the presence of his assembled nobles; she refused and was deposed. The Jewess Esther, niece of Mordecai, was chosen to succeed her. She revealed to the king a plot against his life which Mordecai had uncovered. The king's prime minister, Haman, furious because Mordecai refused to honor him as all others did, prevailed on the king to issue an edict of extermination against the Jews. Mordecai prevailed on Esther to plead for her people. Meanwhile Haman had decided to get rid of Mordecai and had built a special gallows for the purpose. However, the king recalled the service of Mordecai in uncovering the assassination plot and, ironically, it was Haman who suggested a fitting recompense. It came to pass also that Esther's plea was successful; Haman was denounced and executed and Mordecai succeeded him in office. A new decree permitted the Jews to massacre their enemies: they disposed of 75,000 Persians on the thirteenth of Adar

---

[33]Lefèvre, *op. cit.*, p. 779.

(the day originally fixed for the extermination of Jews) and Esther obtained authorization to extend the slaughter to the following day. The Feast of Purim was instituted to commemorate these events.

PLAN[34]

PROLOGUE (EST. 11:2-12 [1:1a-1])
XERXES AND VASHTI (EST. 1)
MORDECAI AND ESTHER (EST. 2:1–3:6)
THE JEWS THREATENED (EST. 3:7–5:14)
REVENGE OF THE JEWS (EST. 6:1–9:19)
THE FEAST OF PURIM (EST. 9:20–10:3)
APPENDIX (EST. 10:4–16:24 [11:2-12])

3) Date

According to the last verse of the Greek version of Esther (11:3) the book was introduced into Egypt in 114 B.C. The Hebrew original must be earlier than that date but, it seems, not much earlier. The Persian background has a romantic coloring which suggests that the Persian Empire had long ceased to exist. According to 2 Mc. 15:36 the Palestinian Jews celebrated in 160 B.C. a "day of Mordecai"; this presupposes the story of Esther, but not necessarily the book. However, the Maccabaean period—after the persecution of Antiochus IV (167-164 B.C.)—seems indicated; perhaps about the year 150 B.C. The Greek edition (containing the "supplements") is somewhat later, but again certainly before 114 B.C.

4) Literary Form

The Book of Esther was written to justify the Feast of Purim, a feast that was not of Israelite origin and had no religious significance. "It was not held (at least directly) in honor of the God of Israel

---

[34]According to the Vg. order.

(whose name is not even mentioned in the Hebrew Book of Esther); it was not connected with the ancient history of the Chosen People; and it contained no cultic element at all. It was a foreign feast, but its origins are obscure."[35] If we are to understand the purpose of the book and if we are to appreciate its true literary form we must know something of that feast.[36] The name of the feast, "Purim," comes from the Akkadian *pûru* meaning "lot" or "destiny," but apart from Esther 3:7 and 9:20-32, there is no reference to the casting of lots and it appears that this was not a feature of the feast. It seems certain that the feast originated in the communities of the Eastern Diaspora, perhaps at Susa. It probably commemorates a pogrom (some time in the fourth century B.C.) from which Jews escaped in a seemingly miraculous manner. On the other hand, the feast preserves certain characteristics that appear to have been modeled on a Persian New Year feast. Babylonian influence is indicated by the names: Mordecai = Marduk; Esther = Ishtar—that is, the names of the god and goddess of Babylon. The feast gradually made its way into Palestine and to Egypt.

The author is familiar with the administration of the Persian Empire, the situation of Jews in the empire, the character of Xerxes, and even the topography of Susa and the royal palace. But all this is only the background, the atmosphere of his story; many details are incredible or patently unhistorical. The real queen of Xerxes was Amestris and not Vashti or Esther. The decree of extermination runs counter to Persian policy as illustrated by Ezra-Nehemiah, and the long delay of eleven months (Est. 3:12-15) or nine months (Est. 8:5,13) between the edict and its execution is unlikely. It is simply not credible that Xerxes would have authorized the massacre of 75,000 of his own subjects—or that the Persians would have offered no resistance. We might add that Mordecai, deported in the time of Nebuchadnezzar (Est. 2:6), would have been about 150 years old at this time.

It is evident that we are not being served with anything approaching straightforward history; we must seek the literary form of Esther in another direction.

---

[35]De Vaux, *op. cit.*, pp. 515 f.
[36]See *ibid.*, pp. 515-17.

The book is a "legend of a feast." Everything in the story—Esther's elevation and the intervention of her uncle Mordecai, the hatred of Haman for the Jews, his punishment and the revenge of the Jews thanks to the esteem in which Esther and Mordecai were held by the king—converges on the feast which took place on the day after the massacre, and the final verses are an attempt to explain why the feast lasted two days (the fourteenth and fifteenth of Adar), "amid joy and banquets, amid festivities and the exchange of presents" (Est. 9:16-19). It is quite possible that the story has a historical foundation in some unexpected deliverance of the Jews of Susa from the threat of extermination, but we know nothing of the circumstances, and this historical basis would have been freely adapted until it became the "legend" of a feast.[37]

5) *The Message*

The Book of Esther is disconcerting. It is obvious that the additions of the Greek text have in view the softening of the general impression; the Old Latin (an excellent witness to the Greek text) omits Esther 9:5-19. Similarly, whereas the Hebrew does not mention the name of God, the additions (especially Est. 13:8—14:9) stress the power of God and his readiness to help his people. Yet the sentiments of the book are an understandable reaction to the hostility encountered by the Jews in the ancient world because of their aloofness; this harsh nationalism is one answer. The spirit of the book is not, and could not have been, the Christian ideal.

We should not forget, however, that the author is not describing historical events; the bloody massacre of enemies never did take place, and Jews living in ghettoes throughout the Greek world were aware that it was not so. Besides, the massacre is depicted as an act of self-defense (Est. 8:10), since a decree of the Persian king was unalterable (Est. 1:19; 8:5)—an idea suggested by Dn. 6:9,13. If God is not mentioned, it is nonetheless true that the events of the story are guided by Providence (cf. Est. 4:13-17; 3:1; 4:16), and the actors of this drama are aware that God does guide all the action. Ultimately the message of Esther is that God does not abandon his people but always comes to help them in distress.

7. JUDITH

Judith was written in Hebrew, but the original text is not extant and all later versions are based on a Greek text. The Vulgate is a

---

[37]*Ibid.*, p. 515.

revision by St. Jerome of the Old Latin with reference to an Aramaic version known to him.

1) Analysis

CONTENTS   Nebuchadnezzar, who was king of Assyria with his capital at Nineveh, called on his subjects of the West to support him in suppressing a rebellion of his Eastern vassals. The summons was ignored and he determined to avenge the outrage; he placed his general, Holofernes, in charge of a punitive expedition. The Assyrian army ravaged the Western provinces, and from Cilicia went down into Egypt. The Palestinian peoples submitted, with one exception: the Jews held out. Holofernes found his way to Jerusalem blocked by the fortified town of Bethulia, to which he promptly laid siege. The town was on the point of surrendering when it was saved by Judith, a pious and beautiful young widow. Relying on her charm and beauty (and trusting in divine help) she was able to get into the enemy camp and succeeded in beheading the drunken general. With its leader dead, the besieging army was routed. The inhabitants of Bethulia made offerings in Jerusalem from the immense booty, and the book closes with a thanksgiving hymn to the Lord.

PLAN

THE CAMPAIGN OF HOLOFERNES (JDT. 1-6)
THE SIEGE OF BETHULIA (JDT. 7)
JUDITH (JDT. 8-9)
JUDITH AND HOLOFERNES (JDT. 10-13)
THE VICTORY (JDT. 14:1—16:20)
EPILOGUE (JDT. 16:21-25)

2) Literary Form and Date

At first sight Judith seems to be the factual account of a striking deliverance of God's people. On closer study we find that the book shows "a superb indifference to history and geography."[38] The story

---

[38]BJ, p. 493.

is set in the reign of Nebuchadnezzar "who ruled over the Assyrians in the great city of Nineveh" (Jdt. 1:1), sometime after the return from the Exile and the rebuilding of the Temple (Jdt. 4:3). In reality, Nebuchadnezzar was king of the Babylonians and reigned in Babylon, while Nineveh had been utterly destroyed by his father, Nabopolassar. Furthermore, Nebuchadnezzar had taken Jerusalem and carried the Jewish people into exile; the return took place long after his death, under Cyrus the Great. Arphaxad, "king of the Medes," is a fictitious character; the name undoubtedly comes from Gn. 10:22. Holofernes and Bagoas were Persian officers of Artaxerxes III (358-337 B.C.)—two hundred years after the death of Nebuchadnezzar. The author's "presentation of Nebuchadnezzar, the Babylonian, as king of the Assyrians, waging war against Arphaxad, an unknown Median king, with an army commanded by the Persians Holofernes and Bagoas, is the equivalent of saying that Peter the Great, king of England, waged war against Arphaxad, the king of France, with an army led by Generals Eisenhower and MacArthur."[39] Judith is not mentioned in biblical history; significantly, her name means "Jewess." We find clear allusions to certain Greek customs (Jdt. 3:7 f.; 15:13) and to late Jewish customs (Jdt. 8:6). There is no trace of the monarchy, which was brought to an end by Nebuchadnezzar, and Judaea is ruled by a high priest as in postexilic times.

The geographical situation is no less confused. The route followed by Holofernes and his army (Jdt. 2:21-28) is "in defiance of geography."[40] Even when the Assyrians arrive in Samaria we are on no surer ground. Bethulia itself, the center of the drama, cannot be indicated on a map. The implication that it commanded the only route to Jerusalem (Jdt. 4:6 f.; 7:1-3) is, geographically speaking, nonsense. Instead of wasting time besieging a single fortress with his whole immense army (Jdt. 7:2), Holofernes could have left a contingent there and moved with the rest of his force along the coast, coming upon Jerusalem from the west, as Sennacherib had done (2 Kgs. 18:17).

We must presume that the geography of Palestine, at least, would have been familiar to the author and to those for whom he wrote.

---

[39] Ellis, *op. cit.*, p. 523.
[40] BJ, p. 494.

We cannot imagine that many Jews could have been ignorant of the respective roles of Assyria, Nebuchadnezzar, and the Persians in the destiny of Jerusalem. The only valid conclusion is that the author has deliberately multiplied the historical and geographical inaccuracies; and his object must have been to turn the attention of his readers from any precise historical context and bring it to bear only on the religious drama and its climax. He does not mean to teach a particular fact of Israel's history, but to present in a striking way the general sense of this history. In achieving this effect he has certainly been influenced by the apocalyptic form. We might even go so far as to regard his work as an apocalypse.[41]

At any rate it does appear that Holofernes is a synthesis of the powers of evil, and Judith (the "Jewess"), over against him, is an ideal representative of Judaism. The scene is set in the plain of Esdraelon (Jdt. 3:6), near the plain of Armageddon where John will place the eschatological battle (Ap. 16:16). Though the nation had seemed doomed God had brought about its triumph and the victory wrought through Judith was the reward of her prayer and of her scrupulous observance of the laws of ritual purity. Finally, the holy people went up in joyful procession to Jerusalem (Jdt. 15:12–16:20). The whole presentation is markedly apocalyptic.[42]

Judith was written in Hebrew, a fact that strongly suggests Palestinian origin. From the apocalyptic tone we might deduce that it was written to encourage Jews undergoing persecution. A likely background may be the persecution of Jews in Egypt by Ptolemy VII in the years following 145 B.C. Though we cannot be sure that this was its setting, it does seem reasonable to date the book to the end of the second or the beginning of the first century B.C.

3) *The Message*

Like Est. the Book of Judith describes a deliverance of the Jews by the intermediary of a woman. Judith, with her fidelity to the Law and her unshaken trust in God, becomes an instrument of God's justice. The prayer of Judith (chapter 9) is the key to the book: she calls on the God of her father Simeon who avenged the

---

[41]Cf. Ellis, *op. cit.*, pp. 526-29.
[42]See BJ, p. 494.

rape of Dinah (Gn. 34) to humble the Assyrians for their medi-
tated rape of God's sanctuary. God will hear, the "God of the lowly,
helper of the oppressed, upholder of the weak, protector of the
forlorn, savior of those without hope" (Jdt. 9:11). He will act to
save his people, for "there is no other who protects the people of
Israel but him alone" (Jdt. 9:14). Judith, the ideal representative
of her people, is another Daniel: a model of observance and an
inspiration to boundless trust in God.

Though Est. and Judith meet in the common theme of deliverance
by a woman, and though both illustrate the truth that God does
not abandon his people, the two books are really very different in
outlook. The former is candidly nationalistic and expresses something
of the exasperation of the ghetto mentality. Judith, on the other
hand, is universalist in perspective. Significantly, the salvation of
Jerusalem is wrought not in Judaea but at Bethulia, in the land of
the hated Samaritans. Even more striking, the religious issue of the
conflict is brought out by Achior, an Ammonite (Jdt. 5:5-21), who
is drawn to confess the true God (Jdt. 14:5-10). We have here an
echo of Ru. and Jon., and already something of the atmosphere of
that new age in which Jesus would hold up a Samaritan as a figure
of Christian love (Lk. 10:30-37) and would, raised from the earth,
draw all men to himself (Jn. 12:32).

Bibliography

This bibliography is not meant to be exhaustive and has been restricted, as far as possible, to works in English. An asterisk (*) indicates that a work carries an *Imprimatur*.

GENERAL

Albright, W. F., *From the Stone Age to Christianity*. New York: Doubleday, 1957².

Anderson, B. W., *Understanding the Old Testament*. Englewood Cliffs, N.J.: Prentice-Hall, 1957.

*Auzou, G., *The Word of God*. Trans. J. Thornton; St. Louis: B. Herder, 1960.

*Bauer, J. B., *Bibeltheologisches Wörterbuch*. Graz: Verlag Styria, 1962². I, II.

Black, M., and Rowley, H. H., editors, *Peake's Commentary on the Bible*. London: Nelson, 1962.

*Castelot, J., *Meet the Bible*. Baltimore: Helicon, 1960. I, II.

Dodd, C. H., *The Bible Today*. New York: Cambridge University Press, 1960².

Driver, S. R., *Introduction to the Literature of the Old Testament*. Cleveland: Meridian.

Eichrodt, W., *Theology of the Old Testament*. Trans. J. A. Baker; Philadelphia: Westminster Press, 1961.

*Ellis, P. F., *The Men and the Message of the Old Testament*. Collegeville, Minn.: Liturgical Press, 1963.

*Heinisch, P., *Theology of the Old Testament*. Trans. W. Heidt; Collegeville, Minn.: Liturgical Press, 1950.

*Jones, A., *God's Living Word*. New York: Sheed & Ward, 1961.

La Sainte Bible. Trans. into French under the direction of l'Ecole Biblique de Jérusalem. Paris: Cerf, 1957. (Second revised edition in fascicle form.)

397

*Leon-Dufour, X., editor, *Vocabulaire de Theologie Biblique*. Paris: Cerf, 1961.

*McEleney, N.J., editor, *Pamphlet Bible Series*. New York: Paulist Press.

*McKenzie, J. L., *The Two-Edged Sword*. Milwaukee: Bruce, 1956.

*Moriarty, F. L., *Introducing the Old Testament*. Milwaukee: Bruce, 1959.

*Orchard, B., *A Catholic Commentary on Holy Scripture*. London: Nelson, 1953.

*Robert, A., and Feuillet, A., editors, *Introduction à la Bible*. Tournai: Desclée, 1957. I.

*Robert, A., and Tricot, A., editors, *Guide to the Bible*. Trans. E. P. Arbez, and M. R. P. McGuire; New York: Desclee, 1960². I.

Rowley, H. H., editor, *The Old Testament and Modern Study*. New York: Oxford University Press, 1952.

———, *The Re-Discovery of the Old Testament*. London: Clarke, 1945.

———, *The Unity of the Bible*. Philadelphia: Westminster Press, 1955.

*Sullivan, K., *God's Word and Work*. Collegeville, Minn.: Liturgical Press, 1958.

*Vaux, R. de, *Ancient Israel, Its Life and Institutions*. Trans. John McHugh; New York: McGraw-Hill, 1961.

Wright, G. E., *God Who Acts*. Naperville, Ill.: Allenson, 1958.

———, *The Old Testament against Its Environment*. Naperville, Ill.: Allenson, 1958.

CHAPTER ONE

Beek, M. A., *Atlas of Mesopotamia*. H. H. Rowley, editor; London: Nelson, 1962.

Bright, J., *A History of Israel*. Philadelphia: Westminster Press, 1959.

Childe, V. Gordon, *What Happened in History*. Baltimore: Pelican, 1954².

*Daniel-Rops, H., *Sacred History*. Trans. K. Madge; New York: Longmans, Green, 1949.

Finegan, J., *Light from the Ancient Past*. Princeton University Press, 1952².

*Grollenberg, L. H., *Atlas of the Bible*. Trans. Joyce M. H. Reid and H. H. Rowley; Camden, N.J.: Nelson, 1959.

Gurney, O. R., *The Hittites*. Baltimore: Pelican, 1954².

*Heinisch, P., *History of the Old Testament*. Trans. W. Heidt; Collegeville, Minn.: Liturgical Press, 1952.

*Johnston, L., *A History of Israel*. London: Nelson, 1964.

*Lemaire, P., and Baldi, D., *Atlante Storico della Bibbia*. Rome: Marietti, 1955.

Pritchard, J. B., *Ancient Near Eastern Texts*. Princeton University Press, 1952².

———, *The Ancient Near East in Pictures*. Princeton University Press, 1954.

*Ricciotti, G., *The History of Israel*. Trans. C. della Penta and R. Murphy; Milwaukee: Bruce, 1955.

Wright, G. E., and Filson, F. V., *The Westminster Historical Atlas to the Bible*. Philadelphia: Westminster Press, 1956².

CHAPTER TWO

°Cazelles, H., *Levitique, Nombres* (BJ). Paris: Cerf, 1958.
Chapman, A. T., *An Introduction to the Pentateuch.* New York: Cambridge University Press, 1911.
°Harrington, W. J., *Genesis and Evolution.* Dublin: Dominican Publications, 1963.
°Hauret, C., *Beginnings: Genesis and Modern Science.* Trans. J. F. McDonnell; Dubuque, Iowa: The Priory Press, 1964².
°Jones, A., *Unless Some Man Show Me.* New York: Sheed & Ward, 1960.
°McKenzie, J. L., *Myths and Realities.* Milwaukee: Bruce, 1963.
Rad, G. von, *Genesis.* Trans. J. Marks; Philadelphia: Westminster Press, 1961.
°Vaux, R. de, *La Genèse* (BJ). Paris: Cerf, 1953.
°Vawter, B., *A Path Through Genesis.* New York: Sheed & Ward, 1955.

CHAPTER THREE

Bright, J., "Joshua," *Interpreter's Bible.* G. A. Buttrick, editor; Nashville, Tenn.: Abingdon, 1963.
Burney, C. F., *The Book of Judges.* London: Rivingtons, 1918.
°Cazelles, H., *Le Deutéronome* (BJ). Paris: Cerf, 1958.
Driver, S. R., *Deuteronomy.* Naperville, Ill.: Allenson, 1951.
Montgomery, J. A., *Critical and Exegetical Commentary on the Book of Kings.* H. S. Gehman, editor; New York: Scribner's, 1952.
Rad, G. von, *Studies in Deuteronomy.* Naperville, Ill.: Allenson, 1950.
Rowley, H. H., *From Joseph to Joshua.* New York: Oxford University Press, 1950.
°Vaux, R. de, *Les Livres de Samuel, Les Livres de Rois* (BJ). Paris: Cerf, 1958.

CHAPTER FOUR

°Chaine, J., *God's Heralds.* Trans. B. McGrath; New York: Wagner, 1955.
°Dheilly, J., "The Prophets," *Faith and Fact.* London: Burns and Oates, 1960.
Heaton, E. W., *The Old Testament Prophets.* Baltimore: Pelican, 1958.
°Kissane, E., *The Book of Isaiah.* Dublin: Browne and Nolan, 1960². I, II.
Mowinckel, S., *He That Cometh.* Trans. G. W. Anderson; Nashville, Tenn.: Abingdon, 1956.
Robinson, H. W., *The Cross in the Old Testament.* London: S.C.M. Press, 1960².
Robinson, T. H., *Prophecy and the Prophets in Ancient Israel.* Naperville, Ill.: Allenson, 1953.
Rowley, H. H., *The Servant of the Lord and Other Essays on the Old Testament.* London: Lutterworth Press, 1952.
————, editor, *Studies in Old Testament Prophecy.* Naperville, Ill.: Allenson, 1957.
°Vawter, B., *The Conscience of Israel.* New York: Sheed & Ward, 1961.
Zimmerli, W., and Jeremias, J., *The Servant of God.* Naperville, Ill.: Allenson, 1957.

CHAPTERS FIVE AND SIX

°Castellino, G., *Libro dei Salmi*. Turin: Marietti, 1955.
°Drijvers, P., *Les Psaumes*. Paris: Cerf, 1958.
°Dubarle, A. M., *Les Sages d'Israel*. Paris: Cerf, 1946.
Henshaw, T., *The Writings*. New York: Humanities Press, 1963.
°Kissane, E. J., *The Book of Psalms*. Dublin: Browne and Nolan, 1953. I, II.
Mowinckel, S., *The Psalms in Israel's Worship*. Trans. D. R. Ap-Thomas; Nashville, Tenn.: Abingdon, 1962. I, II.
°Murphy, R., *Seven Books of Wisdom*. Milwaukee: Bruce, 1960.
Oesterly, W. O., *The Psalms*. New York: Seabury, 1953.
Paterson, J., *The Wisdom of Israel*. Nashville, Tenn.: Abingdon, 1961.
Robinson, T. H., *The Poetry of the Old Testament*. Naperville, Ill.: Allenson, 1951.
Rowley, H. H., *Wisdom in Israel and in the Ancient Near East*. M. Noth and D. W. Thomas, editors; New York: Humanities Press, 1960.

CHAPTERS SEVEN AND EIGHT

°Abel, F. M., *Les Livres des Maccabees*. Paris: Gabalda, 1949.
Batten, L. W., *Ezra and Nehemiah*. Naperville, Ill.: Allenson, 1949.
°Bloch, R., "Midrash," *Dictionnaire de la Bible* (Supplement). Paris: Letouzey et Ané, 1957. V. Cols. 1263-1281.
Curtis, E. L., and Madsen, A. A., *The Books of Chronicles*. Naperville, Ill.: Allenson, 1952.
Dancy, J. C., *A Commentary on I Maccabees*. New York: Oxford University Press, 1954.
Fishel, H. A., *The First Book of Maccabees*. New York, 1948.
Welch, A. C., *The Work of the Chronicler, Its Purpose and Date*. New York: Oxford University Press, 1939.

CHAPTER NINE

Charles, R. H., *A Critical and Exegetical Commentary on the Book of Daniel*. New York: Oxford University Press, 1929.
————, *The Apocrypha and Pseudepigrapha of the Old Testament*. New York: Oxford University Press, 1913. I.
°Feuillet, A., "Jonas," *Dictionnaire de la Bible* (Supplement). Paris: Letouzey et Ané, 1948. IV. Cols. 1104-1131.
°————, *Le Livre de Jonas* (BJ). Paris: Cerf, 1957².
Gaster, T., *Purim and Hanukkah in Custom and Tradition*. New York: Schuman, 1950.
°Lattey, C., *The Book of Ruth* (Westminster Version). London: Longman's, Green, 1935.
Oesterly, W. O., *An Introduction to the Books of the Apocrypha*. New York: Macmillan, 1935.
Paton, L. B., *The Book of Esther*. Naperville, Ill.: Allenson, 1951.
Pfeiffer, R. H., *History of New Testament Times: With an Introduction*

to the Apocrypha. London: L. and C. Black, 1963[2].

Rowley, H. H., *Darius the Mede and the Four World Empires in the Book of Daniel.* Naperville, Ill.: Allenson, 1959[2].

––––––, *The Relevance of Apocalyptic.* New York: Association Press, 1964[3].

*Steinmann, J., *Lecture de Judith.* Paris: Gabalda, 1953.

al hag-gittith (H)—psalm direction; reference to Gath

al hash-sheminith (H)—psalm direction: "for bass voices"

al alamoth (H)—psalm direction: "for soprano"

Allelu-Yah (H)—praise Yahweh

'almāh (H)—young woman

ānî (H)—humble

'anawim (H)—the poor

apokalypsis (G)—revelation

Aram (H)—Mesopotamia

archisynagōgos (G)—an official who presides over a cult

archōn (G)—collective office

bar enash (H)—son of man

beneginoth (H)—psalm direction: "with stringed instrument"

berith (H)—covenant

biblos psalmōn (G)—book of psalms

darash (H)—to examine

deuteros nomos (G)—second law

diathēkē (G)—covenant

Diaspora (G)—the Dispersion

dibre hayyamim (H)—events of the past (i.e., the Chronicles)

'edah (H)—a worshiping community

el han-nehiloth (H)—psalm direction: "to the flutes"

gahal (H)—church

gebirah (H)—"Grand Lady"

go'el (H)—champion

haggadah (H)—form of midrash

halakah (H)—form of midrash (legal)

Hasidim (H)—the "Pious Ones"

hesed (H)—steadfast love

hōzéh (H)—a visionary

karath berith (H)—to cut (make) a treaty (covenant)

kethubhim (H)—the Writings

khamseen (H)—sirocco

kōh 'āmar Yahweh (H)—"Thus says Yahweh"

lamnasseah (H)—psalm direction: "to the choirmaster"

le/al Jeduthum (H)—name of chief musician (Psalms)

maqqabah (H)—hammer

mashiah (H)—one who anoints

402

maskil (H)—type of psalm (sapiential)

massa (H)—burden

megilloth (H)—"rolls"

melek (H)—king

meridarchēs (G)—governor

mizmor (H)—accompanied song or hymn

midrash (H)—to research

miktam (H)—type of psalm (atonement)

nābâ' (H)—to pour forth

nābî' (H)—prophet

nābû (H)—to call

nāsî' (H)—prince

nb' (H)—to seek

ne'ûm Yahweh (H)—oracle of Yahweh

nomos (G)—law

Paraleipomena (G)—"the things omitted" (i.e., Chronicles)

pekah (H)—governor

pesher midrash (H)—type of midrash (research-prophetical)

phēmi (G)—to say, speak

prophētēs (G)—prophet

psalmoi (G)—psalms

psalterion (G)—a collection of sacred songs

pûru (H)—destiny

ro'eh (H)—seer

rosh (H)—prince

Selah (H)—psalm direction: "pause"

semereth (H)—top

sepher tehillim (H)—a book of hymns of praise

shiggaion (H)—type of psalm (lament)

shir (H)—type of psalm

shophetim (H)—judges

stratēgos (G)—military general

tehillal (H)—type of psalm (praise)

tehillim (H)—hymns of praise

tephillah (H)—type of psalm (prayer)

tôrah (H)—teaching given by God

wasfs (H)—wedding songs

Index of Biblical References

404

General Index

Abel, F. M., 400
Abijam, 55
Abraham, 13
  as father of country, 6
  covenant with, 137
Ahab, 49-50
Ahaziah, 50, 57
Akkadians, 4-5
Albright, W. F., 150, 173, 203, 208, 278, 327, 397
Alcimus, War of, 91-92
Alexander Jannaeus, 95
Alexander the Great, 82, 372
  successors of, 82
Alexandra, 95
Allegory, 179
Amaziah, 58
Amon, 63
Amorites, 11-12
Amos, Book of, 180
  author, 180-81
  division of, 182
  message of, 182-83
Amphictyony, The, 22, 224-25
Anderson, B. W., 122, 151, 181, 184, 254, 328, 333, 385, 387-88, 397
Antigonus, 98
Apocalypse (literary form of), 381-84

Aristobulus I, 94-95
Aristobulus II, 95-96
Asa, 56
Assyria, 39-44
Astruc, Jean, 106
Athaliah, 57
Audet, J.-P., 274, 279
Autobiography, 179
Auvray, P., 202, 303
Auzou, G., 397
Azariah; see Uzziah

Baasha, 48
Babylon, 6-9, 46-47, 67-69
  exiles in, 71-72
Baldi, D., 19, 398
Baruch, Book of, 363-64
  analysis of, 364-66
  message of, 366-67
Barucq, A., 269
Batten, L. W., 400
Bauer, J. B., 218, 397
Beek, M. A., 398
Begrich, J., 289
Benoit, P., 239
Birkeland, 108
Black, M., 136-37
Bloch, S., 323, 400
Boismard, M.-E., 136
Bonnard, 218, 222-23

424

(CARPATHIANS)
CULTURE
EARLY BRONZE AGE
TRIPOLYE B
CULTURE
(BLACK
MACEDONIA
THES-
SALY
Troy
City VI
MIDDLE
HELLADIC
II
(Halys River)
Tarsus
Mersin
CYCLADES
Cnossus
CAPHTOR
CRETE
ALASHIYA
CYPRUS
N
SEA)